Liberalizing Foreign Trade

Volume 6

Liberalizing Foreign Trade

Edited by
Demetris Papageorgiou, Michael Michaely, and
Armeane M. Choksi

Volume 6

The Experience of New Zealand, Spain, and Turkey

NEW ZEALAND	*Anthony C. Rayner and Ralph Lattimore*
SPAIN	*Guillermo de la Dehesa, José Juan Ruiz, and Angel Torres*
TURKEY	*Tercan Baysan and Charles Blitzer*

Basil Blackwell

Copyright © The International Bank for Reconstruction and Development/The World Bank 1991

HF1411
L497
1989
Vol. 6

First published 1991

Basil Blackwell, Inc.
3 Cambridge Center
Cambridge, Massachusetts 02142, USA

Basil Blackwell Ltd
108 Cowley Road, Oxford, OX4 1JF, UK

Library of Congress Cataloging in Publication Data

Liberalizing foreign trade/edited Demetris Papageorgiou, Michael Michaely, and Armeane M. Choksi.
p. cm.
Includes index.
Contents: v. 1. Liberalizing Foreign Trade. The Experience of Argentina, Chile, and Uruguay — v. 2. Liberalizing Foreign Trade. The Experience of Korea, the Philippines, and Singapore — v. 3. Liberalizing Foreign Trade. The Experience of Israel and Yugoslavia — v. 4. Liberalizing Foreign Trade. The Experience of Brazil, Colombia, and Perú — v. 5. Liberalizing Foreign Trade. The Experience of Indonesia, Pakistan, and Sri Lanka — v. 6. Liberalizing Foreign Trade. The Experience of New Zealand, Spain, and Turkey — v. 7. Liberalizing Foreign Trade. Lessons of Experience in the Developing World
ISBN 0–631–16666–1 (v. 1). – ISBN 0–631–16672–6 (v. 6). – ISBN 0–631–17595–4 (7-vol. set)
1. Commercial policy. 2. Free trade. 3. International trade.
I. Papageorgiou, Demetris. II Michaely, Michael. III. Choksi, Armeane M., 1944–.
HF 1411.L497 1989
382'.3–dc19   88–37455
                                                                              CIP

British Library Cataloguing in Publication Data

A CIP catalogue record for this book is available from the British Library.

Typeset in 10 on 12pt Times
by TecSet Ltd
Printed in Great Britain by T. J. Press Ltd., Padstow

Contents

About the Editors

Demetris Papageorgiou is the Chief of the Country Operations Division in the Brazil Department of the World Bank. He has served as a senior economist in the Country Policy Department and as an economist at the Industry Division of the Development Economics Department.

Michael Michaely is the Lead Economist in the Brazil Department of the World Bank. Previously he was the Aron and Michael Chilewich Professor of International Trade and Dean of the Faculty of Social Sciences at the Hebrew University of Jerusalem. He has published numerous books and articles on international economics.

Armeane M. Choksi is Director of the Brazil Department in the Latin American and Caribbean region of the World Bank. He is co-editor with Demetris Papageorgiou of *Economic Liberalization in Developing Countries*, and has written on industrial and trade policy.

Editors' Preface

The General Objective

"Protection," said the British statesman Benjamin Disraeli in 1845, "is not a principle, but an expedient," and this pronouncement can serve very well as the text for our study of *trade liberalization*. The benefits of open trading have by now been sufficiently demonstrated and described by economic historians and analysts. In this study, we take them for granted and turn our minds from the "whether" to the "how."

The Delectable Mountains of open trading confront the pilgrim with formidable obstacles and there are many paths to the top. The direct route seldom turns out to be the best in practice. It may bring on rapid exhaustion and early collapse, while a more devious approach, skirting areas of excessive transition costs, may offer the best prospects of long-term survival.

Given the sharp diversity of economic background and experience between different countries, and indeed, between different periods in the same country, we should not expect the most favorable route to turn out the same for each country, except perhaps by accident. There are, however, fundamental principles underlying the diversities and it is our thesis that a survey and analysis of a sufficiently broad spectrum of countries over sufficiently long development periods may serve to uncover them.

With this object in view, we set out to study as many liberalization experiences as possible and aimed at including all liberalizations in developing countries in the post-world war period. However, the actual scope of this study had three limitations. First, we restricted the study to market-based economies. Second, experiences with highly inadequate data had to be excluded. Third, to be an appropriate object of study, an experience had to be of some minimum duration. Applying these criteria, we were left with the study of liberalization experiences in the 19 countries listed at the end of this preface. This volume deals with three of these countries (New Zealand, Spain, and Turkey). Five other volumes contain the rest of the country studies, and the seventh volume presents the synthesis of the country analyses.

Definitions

"Trade liberalization" implies any change which leads a country's trade system toward neutrality in the sense of bringing its economy closer to the situation which would prevail if there were no governmental interference in the trade system. Put in words, the new trade system confers no discernible incentives to either the importable or the exportable activities of the economy.

By "episode" we mean a period long enough to accommodate a significant run of liberalization acts terminating either in a swing away from liberalization or in a period where policy changes one way or another cease to be apparent.

The "episode of liberalization" thus defined is the unit of observation and analysis employed in each of our country studies.

Identification of Liberalization Episodes

There are three main indicators of a move in the direction of neutrality: (a) a change in the price system; (b) a change in the form of intervention; (c) changes in the foreign exchange rate.

Price system

The prices in question are nominal protection rates determining consumption patterns and, more importantly, effective protection rates affecting production activities. Any change which lowered the average level and distribution of rates of protection would count as a move toward neutrality. Typically, such a change would arise from a general reduction in tariffs, but it might also be indicated by the introduction, rather than the removal, of instruments of government intervention, or even, indeed, by the raising rather than the lowering of the incidence of government intervention. An instance of this might be the introduction of export subsidies in a protective regime previously biased against exports and favoring import substitution. Another instance might be the introduction or increase of tariffs on imported raw materials and capital goods in a regime where tariffs have previously escalated over the whole field, with the zero and lower rates applying on these imports.

Form of Intervention

The form of intervention may be affected by a change in the quantitative restriction (QR) system itself or by replacing QRs with tariffs. Although the actual changes might be assigned price *equivalents*, it is not feasible to assign price equivalents to their comprehensive effects. Moreover, the reactions they induce are so different from responses to price signals that they are better treated as a separate category.

The Exchange Rate

A change in the level of a *uniform* rate of exchange, since it does not discriminate between one tradeable activity and a other, is not of itself an instrument of intervention. A move from a *multiple* to a uniform rate would, however, be equivalent to a change in intervention through commercial policy instruments; changes in the rate would modify the effect of commercial policy instruments already in being, for example, where QR systems are operated through the exchange control mechanism itself or where tariffs effective at an existing rate become redundant at a higher rate. Failing detailed studies of the impact of exchange rate changes on QRs or tariffs we take as a general rule that a formal and real *devaluation* constitutes a step towards liberalization.

Policies and Results

We do not take the actual degree of openness of the economy as an indicator in itself of a liberalization episode. Liberalization policies may commonly be expected to lead to an increase in the share of external trade but this is not an inevitable result. For instance, if, starting from a state of disequilibrium, liberalization is associated with a formal devaluation imports may actually fall. Therefore attempts to detect liberalization by reference to trade ratios rather than to policy *intentions* would be misleading. Exceptionally, however, the authors of the country studies have used trade performance as an indication of liberalization, particularly where actual changes in imports can be used to measure the degree of relaxation, or otherwise, of QRs.

Measurement of Degrees of Liberalization

In each country study we have attempted to indicate the degree of liberalization progressively attained by assigning to each year a mark for performance on a scale ranging from 1 to 20. A mark of 20 would indicate virtually free trade, or perfect neutrality, a mark of 1 would indicate the highest possible degree of intervention. These indices are subjective and peculiar to each country studied and in no way comparable between countries. They are a rough and ready measure of the progress, or otherwise, of liberalization as perceived by the authors of the country study in question. They reflect, for instance, assessments of nominal and effective rates of protection, the restrictiveness of QRs, and the gap between the formal exchange rate and its equilibrium level.

Analysis of Successful Liberalization Exercises

To arrive at criteria of what makes for success in applying liberalization policies, the following questions might be asked in our studies.

1   What is the appropriate speed and intensity of liberalization?
2   Is it desirable to have a separate policy stage of replacement of nonprice forms of trade restrictions by price measures?
3   Is it desirable to treat productive activities during the process of trade liberalization uniformly or differentially?
4   If uniform treatment is indicated, how should it be formulated?
5   On what pattern of performance of the economy is the fate of liberalization likely to hinge?
6   Is it desirable to have a stage of export promotion? If so, what should its timing be in relationship to import liberalization?
7   What are the appropriate circumstances for the introduction of a liberalization policy?
8   How important are exogenous developments in deciding the sustainability of liberalization?
9   Finally, what *other* policy measures are important, either in their existence or absence, for a successful policy of trade liberalization?

Lurking behind many of these issues are the (potential) probable costs of adjustment of a liberalization policy and, in particular, its possible impact on the employment of labor.

Scope and Intention of our Study

The general purpose of our analysis is to throw up some practical guidance for policymakers and, in particular, for policymakers in developing countries where the economic (and political) climate tends to present the greatest obstacles to successful reform. It is for this reason that (as already explained) we have based our studies on the experience of a wide spread of countries throughout the developing world. All country studies have followed a common pattern of inquiry, with the particular analytical techniques left to the discretion of the individual authors. This approach should yield inferences on the questions raised above in two different ways; via the conclusions reached in the country studies themselves, and via the synthesis of the comparative experience of trade liberalization in these countries.

The presence of a common pattern of inquiry in no way implies that all country studies cover the same questions in a uniform manner. Not all questions are of equal importance in each country and the same quantity and quality of data were not available in all countries. Naturally, the country studies differ on the issues they cover, in the form of the analysis, and in the structure of their presentation.

The country studies are self-contained. Beyond addressing the questions of the project, each study contains sufficient background material on the country's attributes and history of trade policy to be of interest to the general reader.

The 19 countries studied classified within three major regions, are as follows.

Latin America

Argentina	by Domingo Cavallo and Joaquín Cottani
Brazil	by Donald V. Coes
Chile	by Sergio de la Cuadra and Dominique Hachette
Colombia	by Jorge García García
Perú	by Julio J. Nogués
Uruguay	by Edgardo Favaro and Pablo T. Spiller

Asia and the Pacific

Indonesia	by Mark M. Pitt
Korea	by Kwang Suk Kim
New Zealand	by Anthony C. Rayner and Ralph Lattimore
Pakistan	by Stephen Guisinger and Gerald Scully
Philippines	by Florian Alburo and Geoffrey Shepherd
Singapore	by Bee-Yan Aw
Sri Lanka	by Andrew G. Cuthbertson and Premachandra Athukorala

The Mediterranean

Greece	by George C. Kottis
Israel	by Nadav Halevi and Joseph Baruh

Portugal	by Jorge B. de Macedo, Cristina Corado, and Manuel L. Porto
Spain	by Guillermo de la Dehesa, José Juan Ruiz, and Angel Torres
Turkey	by Tercan Baysan and Charles Blitzer
Yugoslavia	by Oli Havrylyshyn

Coordination of the Project

Armeane M. Choksi, Michael Michaely, and Demetris Papageorgiou, of the World Bank's Latin American and Caribbean Region, are the directors of this research project. Participants in the project met frequently to exchange views. Before the country studies were launched, the common framework of the study was discussed extensively at a plenary conference. Another plenary conference was held to discuss early versions of the completed country studies, as well as some emerging general inferences. In between, three regional meetings were held to review phases of the work under way. An external Review Board consisting of Robert Baldwin (University of Wisconsin), Mario Blejer (International Monetary Fund), Jacob Frenkel (University of Chicago and Director of Research, International Monetary Fund), Arnold Harberger (University of Chicago and University of California – Los Angeles), Richard Snape (Monash University), and Martin Wolf (Chief Economic Leader writer, Financial Times) contributed to the reviewing process of the country studies and of the synthesis volume.

New Zealand, Spain, and Turkey are presented in this volume. The series' other publications are the following:

Volume 1: Liberalizing Foreign Trade. The Experience of Argentina, Chile, and Uruguay;
Volume 2: Liberalizing Foreign Trade. The Experience of Korea, the Philippines, and Singapore;
Volume 3: Liberalizing Foreign Trade. The Experience of Israel and Yugoslavia;
Volume 4: Liberalizing Foreign Trade. The Experience of Brazil, Colombia, and Perú;
Volume 5: Liberalizing Foreign Trade. The Experience of Indonesia, Pakistan, and Sri Lanka;
Volume 7: Liberalizing Foreign Trade. Lessons of Experience in the Developing World.

Part I

New Zealand

The late Anthony C. Rayner
Department of Economics and Marketing
Lincoln College
Canterbury, New Zealand

Ralph Lattimore
Department of Economics and Marketing
Lincoln College
Canterbury, New Zealand

Contents

List of Figures

List of Tables

1

Introduction

New Zealand in the early 1950s was a rich country with a real income per head surpassed by only two or three other countries in the world. In this respect, New Zealand differs from the other countries whose experiences with trade liberalization have been studied in this research project (see the preface to the volume). But, despite this initial advantage, the economy had – and still has – many of the characteristics of a developing country, based as it is on agriculture with a small and highly protected manufacturing sector. The attempts to liberalize trade in New Zealand were therefore as encumbered as those of many of the other countries in the World Bank study.

The Economic Climate: Prosperity, Protection, and Decline

The relative wealth of New Zealand in the 1950s in fact probably impeded the first attempts to liberalize trade: the high standard of living masked the losses that the economy was suffering as a result of high protection. Inevitably, therefore, the early movements toward liberalization failed to include the one essential ingredient of a true trade liberalization: that of improving efficiency in resource use by intentionally allowing domestic import-competing industries to be damaged by cheaper imports. This objective formed no part of policy until the early 1980s, when the condition of the domestic economy had so seriously deteriorated that the need for radical policy changes could no longer be ignored. By this time, relative economic stagnation had brought down per capita income from third place in the world ranking to around twenty-fifth. Inflation, balance-of-trade deficits, and rising unemployment continued year after year.

The dominating policy of protecting the New Zealand economy from the world was undoubtedly an expensive failure, whose legacy was an import-competing industry flawed by gross inefficiencies. In tracing New Zealand's attempts at trade liberalization since World War II it is interesting to observe how the political will hardened and the willingness to bear adjustment costs increased as the costs of protection began to make themselves felt.

In this respect, analysis of the New Zealand experience has a topical as well as a purely academic interest. Trade protection has long been entrenched in New Zealand, and the current moves toward liberalization may consequently founder. In highlighting the costs of protection, the gains to be derived from liberalization, and the relatively low adjustment costs entailed, the evidence gathered in this study may be of help in avoiding a policy reversal.

Liberalization Episodes, 1945–1987

The history of trade liberalization in New Zealand does not fit neatly into the coherent packages implied by the term episodes. Further, there is the problem, touched on above, of distinguishing what constitutes a "true" trade liberalization from measures whose liberalizing character may be incidental or even accidental. In one sense, therefore, it could be contended that liberalization, in some form and to some degree, has been part of the agenda since 1951, with a five-year interruption between 1958 and 1962. In another sense it could be argued that there was no "true" trade liberalization until 1984, when the deteriorating economic situation led to a major political swing, followed by a pronounced shift toward economic liberalism.

New Zealand's post-war experience with trade liberalization, however, does fall fairly logically into two periods, distinct in nature and divided by some years which saw no liberalizing initiatives at all. To cut a path through the definitional thicket, and in the interests of comparability with the other country studies, this analysis therefore addresses the New Zealand experience under the heading of two separate episodes: 1951–6 and 1962 to the present.

1951–1956: Limited Liberalization and Rapid Reversal

In 1950, New Zealand's imports were subject to tight quantitative controls through import licensing, tariff levels were high, and exchange controls were restrictive. From this illiberal base the country had its first flirtation with trade liberalization. The fortunate coincidence of a recently devalued currency with a boom in world commodity prices, in part engendered by the Korean War, had brought a balance-of-payments surplus in 1950. The government reacted by making major exemptions to import licensing from the start of 1951.

The intention of this liberalization, however, appears to have been strictly limited to permitting increased import consumption – a kind of removal of rationing. Indeed, safeguards were built into the derestriction to allow the reimposition of licensing whenever domestic industry was able to demonstrate damage resulting from the imports. Clearly, the rationalization of domestic import-competing industries was not part of the agenda.

Inevitably, when the causes of the trade surplus disappeared and the newly freed imports accelerated the movement into deficit, import licensing was reintroduced to resume its former role as a rationing device. The percentage of imports requiring licenses, which had fallen from 100 percent in 1948 to 40 percent in 1956, was returned to 100 percent in 1958. The first episode of apparent trade liberalization had concluded.

The Second Episode: Liberalizing Initiatives after 1962

While it may be debatable how far the policies of 1951–6 should properly be described as a true trade liberalization, they were sufficiently coherent and complete to qualify at any rate for the term episode. By contrast, the liberalizing measures adopted over the 25 years following 1962 certainly cannot be characterized as a single continuous initiative; however, the policies are connected, if rather loosely, in their shared goal of economic rationalization. The study thus treats the series of liberalizing moves of the past 25 years as a long single episode, dividing it for ease of exposition into three phases which, rather than marking changes in the full spectrum of trade policies, reflect significiant new initiatives in some aspects of the policy mix.

The First Phase (1962–1979)

The first phase started around 1962, quite soon after the conclusion of the first episode, and can be characterized as an attempt to move closer to neutrality in trade intervention by the provision of compensation to exporters for the effects of import protection. The forms of compensation varied widely from direct export subsidies to subsidization of inputs and tax concessions. Beginning with a few minor interventions, over the years the policy built up an accelerating momentum, aided by a chronically over-valued exchange rate.

The Second Phase (1979–1984)

The oil shocks of the middle and late 1970s aggravated the country's trade problems and brought home the high real costs of protecting import-competing industries. The policymakers responded by intensifying the export promotion effort, increasingly subsidizing agriculture, and launching a series of government-sponsored capital projects known as the "think big" scheme. At the same time, two important trade policy initiatives were introduced.

The first of these identified those industries considered least able to face international competition, which were then investigated in turn. A unique industry plan was developed for each, designed to make deliberate progress toward increasing international competitiveness. The full set of plans was complete by 1985.

The second trade policy initiative was perhaps even more significant. Stimulated once more by recognition of the costs of protection, its intention was to phase out the entire import-licensing system for the non-industry-plan industries. Any continued protection, if it was seen as necessary, was to be through tariffs alone. The method of removing licensing was through tendering ever increasing amounts until the license premia fell close enough to zero that the system could be abolished. Tendering began in 1981.

Both these trade policy initiatives had a real intention of forcing domestic industry to face greater international competition. It is also clear that there was an expectation that some rationalization would result. Thus, for the first time, a trade liberalization policy was put in place with a motivation of obtaining some of the real gains that result from adjustment.

Ultimately, however, the subsidization aspects of the policy mix – ever increasing export incentives, large-scale subsidies to agriculture, and the "think big" investments – became unsustainable. Overseas reaction to the export subsidies began to build up and, more importantly, the fiscal costs of the policies helped to lead the country into an economic crisis. The attempted remedy of tight central controls on prices failed to eradicate the root cause – the high internal deficit. The crisis led to a collapse of confidence in the government and the election of the opposition Labour Party with a substantial majority in July 1984. There then followed a radical change in domestic and trade policies that were unprecedented in New Zealand. The third phase of the second trade liberalization episode had commenced.

The Third Phase: (1984 onwards)
In fact, the impact of the crisis was less dramatic for trade liberalization than for domestic economic policies. While the main thrust of the new government's policy was to decrease government intervention in the economy and rely more on market forces, the reduction of protection proceeded along the lines already determined in the early 1980s, with perhaps some acceleration in phasing out licensing and implementing the industry plans. There were moves toward reducing tariffs on an announced schedule, but even this policy initiative had been planned before the 1984 election.

The changes in the other aspects of policy that influence trade have been more substantial. An initial devaluation of 20 percent was followed by a floating of the New Zealand dollar six months later. Exchange controls were removed over a short period of time. Interest rate controls were removed and the ensuing rise in rates strongly influenced the exchange rate. Almost the entire policy of export promotion and subsidization was removed. The cumulative effect of these changes on the export industries was considerable, particularly since the exchange rate did not move to levels that led to even the approximate balancing of trade through import stimulation.

The root of the problem lay in the government's inability to obtain a sufficient reduction in the size of the internal deficit. While the removal of the costly tariff compensation policy did induce a very significant fall in the deficit during the year after the election, the government was unable to sustain this reduction in expenditure. The effect of the internal deficit on interest rates and the real exchange rate was to make the costs of adjustment to trade liberalization greater than would otherwise have been the case. The political repercussions of these adjustment costs increase the likelihood that the third phase of trade liberalization, and perhaps the whole episode, will come to a premature conclusion before its economic benefits become apparent.

Plan of Study

As a background to the main analysis, the next chapter outlines the significant attributes of the New Zealand economy and its development since World War II. In chapter 3 the antecedents, implementation, and effects of the shorter aborted first episode are discussed. The long first phase (1962–79) of the second episode is covered in chapter 4, which describes the liberalization policy itself together with the other accompanying policies, and in chapter 5, in which the performance of the economy during the phase is examined. The policies introduced in the second and third phases are discussed in the next two chapters; because of the short time involved, the description of the performance of the economy during these final two phases is contained in a single chapter (chapter 8). Finally, in chapter 9 an overview of New Zealand's attempts at trade liberalization is given and the general inferences that can be drawn from this country's experiences are examined. An index of trade liberalization for New Zealand is presented in appendix 1, and a chronology of the main economic events in appendix 2. Additional tables of data are given in a background document (Rayner and Lattimore, 1988).

2
The New Zealand Economy

This chapter's brief sketch of the attributes of the New Zealand economy begins with the physical characteristics of the country and then goes on to examine its demography and labor force. General macroeconomic variables are next considered, and then investment, trade, and finally the government sector.

Land and Population

The total land area of this island nation is approximately 270,000 km², which is similar to the size of the British Isles or Japan. The country is quite narrow: two main islands total more than 1600 km in length, whereas the greatest width is 450 km. Therefore in relation to its area, the coastline is very extensive.

Growth and Distribution

By international standards, New Zealand is sparsely populated. At the 1981 census (the last available) there were 3.176 million people, a population density of 11.8 persons per square kilometer (the United Kingdom has 229 persons per square kilometer). Population distribution, however, is very uneven. Population densities exceed ten persons per hectare only in Central Auckland (18.9) and Wellington (12.5); for the 23 main urban areas the average density is 5.7 persons per hectare, while for the 14 secondary urban areas it is 2.0 persons per hectare. At the 1981 census, 83.59 percent of the population were resident in urban areas and 16.41 percent were rural. There has been significant growth in the urban proportion of the population (see Rayner and Lattimore, 1988, appendix table C.1), which rose from 67.93 percent in 1926 to 83.59 percent in 1981.

The extent of urbanization of the New Zealand population has obviously been related to the growth of the population (see Rayner and Lattimore, 1988, appendix table C.2) and the development of job opportunities in urban areas. Population growth declined continuously from an annual average rate of 2.12 percent for the five-year period ending April 1961 to 0.3 percent for the five-year period ending March 1981.

A large component of the projected population growth (see Rayner and Lattimore, appendix table C.3) is the rate of net annual migration. The range of projections, based on different assumptions about fertility and mortality rates and net migration, yields populations in 2016 of between 3.755 million and 4.008 million. The average annual population growth rates are between 0.50 and 0.70 percent.

The rate of natural population increase has fallen substantially in recent years, while the level of net migration has fluctuated from one year to the next (table 2.1). Net migration gains until 1968 were succeeded by losses in 1968, 1969, and 1970, followed by substantial gains until 1976, and then a reversion to large losses for the next six years (to 1982). Subsequently, net migration was positive until the outflow recorded in 1986.

The population movement into the urban areas has been paralleled by a continued drift from south to north (see Rayner and Lattimore, 1988, appendix tables C.4 and C.5). A large proportion of the New Zealand population is mobile. Between the censuses of 1976 and 1981, 43.3 percent of the population changed their place of residence.

Table 2.1 Total population and external migration

Year	Population (at March 31)	Natural increase (year ending March 31)	Net migration (year ending March 31)
1931	1,511,700	15,805	5,109
1941	1,636,230	22,123	714
1951	1,938,032	30,970	7,522
1961	2,414,296	43,608	1,620
1971	2,861,000	40,151	7,845
1973	2,973,200	35,415	25,475
1974	3,040,600	34,075	33,167
1975	3,012,500	31,525	29,141
1976	3,140,300	29,648	5,192
1977	3,155,400	28,218	− 16,270
1978	3,160,200	26,360	− 22,156
1979	3,158,200	26,939	− 26,544
1980	3,161,300	23,866	− 21,314
1981	3,170,900	25,644	− 16,209
1982	3,190,100	24,406	− 4,743
1983	3,230,000	24,483	15,442
1984	3,265,500	26,258	10,425
1985	3,291,300	24,318	217
1986	3,289,300	25,781	− 18,518

Source: Department of Statistics, *New Zealand Yearbook* and *Monthly Abstract of Statistics*, various years

Economic Activities

As New Zealand has an elongated shape, communication between the population centers has absorbed considerable resources. A long rail and road network and a coastal shipping service have been developed. The principal centers of population are mainly coastal and located on or near natural harbors; their economic activities are generally not based upon any particular industry. For rural centers, however, the industries present are likely to be based on the agricultural activity of that particular district. This is reflected in the predominance of the transport, food, wood, and nonmetallic industry groups in the provincial centers, industry groups which are markedly underrepresented in the metropolitan economies. While the number of single-industry towns is very small, a significant number of towns have industries based on the agricultural sector whose success depends on the viability of that sector.

Location quotients have been calculated for New Zealand (figure 2.1). A location quotient greater than unity represents an employment district where the industry group is more than proportionately represented. It should be noted that 57 percent of total employment is in industry groups with a location quotient greater than unity. These results indicate that industry is not evenly spread in New Zealand and that there could be significant regional variations in the response to changes in New Zealand's trade protection regime.

Characteristics of the Labor Force

Growth

Trends in the growth of the labor force (table 2.2) have differed from those in the population as a whole. As would be expected, increases in the labor force lag some 15 years behind the increase in total population. The labor force growth pattern has also been affected by the rates of net migration, since migrants are more likely to be members of the labor force. As of February 1984, the total labor force was 1.371 million, 42.0 percent of the population. In 1960, the labor force was 0.876 million, or approximately 36 percent of the population.

Immigration policy has been designed to encourage the entry of skilled labor while protecting domestic employment opportunities for New Zealand residents. For the year ending March 31, 1983, net migration gains were recorded for professional, technical, and related workers, and for persons "not actively engaged;" net migration losses were recorded for all other occupation categories (see Rayner and Lattimore, 1988, appendix table C.6).

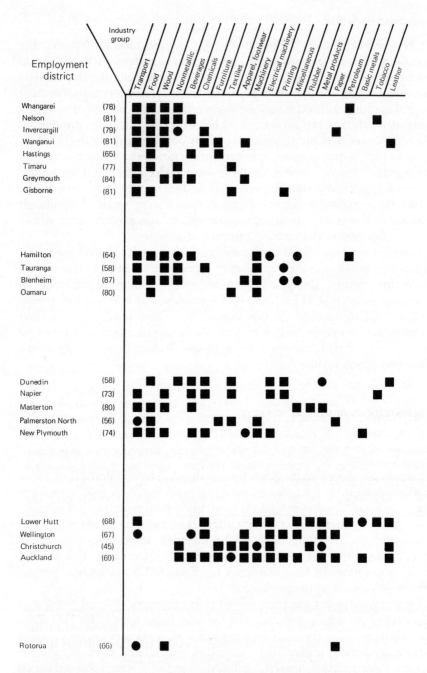

Figure 2.1 Locations quotients,1969–1970. The numbers in parentheses are the percentages of total employment in industry groups with location quotient LQ>1:■, LQ>1; ●, 0.90–0.99; 57 percent of total employment is in industry groups with LQ>1

Table 2.2 Labor force (thousands)

Year	Males	Females	Total
1950	559.2	176.7	735.9
1960	660.6	215.0	875.6
1970	779.2	311.5	1,090.7
1971	777.5	326.9	1,104.4
1973	807.8	348.0	1,155.8
1974	830.6	373.7	1,204.3
1975	843.2	385.2	1,228.4
1976	844.1	393.8	1,237.9
1977	847.6	404.5	1,252.1
1978	856.6	409.6	1,266.2
1979	855.6	427.2	1,282.8
1980	864.2	439.1	1,303.3
1981	870.9	450.7	1,321.6
1982	879.6	460.5	1,340.1
1983	883.5	471.3	1,354.7
1984	888.6	482.5	1,371.1

Source: Department of Statistics, New Zealand
Yearbook, various years

Age

The age structure of the New Zealand labor force reflects a population growing at a slow but steady rate. Thus, while there are more male workers in the younger age groups, they by no means dominate male workers in older age groups, as Rayner and Lattimore (1988, appendix table C.7) show. In contrast, for females, the under 25 year olds predominate because these workers typically withdraw from the labor force to raise families after a few years of paid employment. In 1981 females formed slightly over a third of the total, a proportion that has been growing steadily over the years.

Distribution

The distribution of the labor force industry classes is given in table 2.3 for 1984. The service sector employs 56.7 percent of the whole, with the remainder split between primary production and secondary industry in the proportions 1 : 2.7. Agriculture employs almost all those in the primary sector, while the further processing of agricultural products comprises the largest single employment class in manufacturing industry.

Table 2.3 Distribution of labor force by industry group, 1984 (thousands)

Industrial group	Males	Females	Total
Primary			
Agriculture, hunting, and fishing	98.0	34.9	133.0
Forestry and logging	9.8	6.6	10.4
Mining and quarrying	4.7	0.4	5.1
Total, primary	112.5	35.9	148.4
Manufacturing			
Food, beverages, and tobacco, including seasonal	57.9	16.4	74.3
Textiles, clothing, and leather	15.6	28.4	44.0
Wood and wood products	19.4	3.2	22.6
Paper and paper products, printing, and publishing	24.3	9.9	34.2
Chemicals, petroleum, rubber, and plastics	18.4	7.8	26.1
Nonmetallic mineral products	8.8	1.9	10.7
Metal products and engineering	27.4	4.6	32.0
Machinery, excluding electrical	15.1	2.3	17.5
Electrical equipment	10.2	5.9	16.0
Transport equipment	16.5	2.3	18.8
Other manufacturing	3.6	2.6	6.2
Total, manufacturing	217.1	85.2	302.3
Electricity, gas, and water	14.3	1.4	15.7
Construction	82.4	5.3	87.7
Wholesale and retail trade etc.			
Wholesale trade	46.4	18.1	64.6
Retail trade	59.6	58.0	117.5
Restaurants, hotels, etc.	15.1	23.7	38.8
Total, wholesale, retail, etc.	121.1	99.8	220.9
Transport and communication			
Transport and storage	57.4	10.8	68.2
Communications	19.8	15.2	35.0
Total, transport, etc.	77.1	26.0	103.1
Finance, insurance, etc.			
Finance	14.1	18.2	32.2
Insurance	8.0	5.8	13.8
Real estate and business services	30.4	22.9	53.3
Total, finance etc.	52.4	46.8	99.3
Community and personal services			
Public administration etc.	47.3	23.8	71.1
Sanitary services etc.	4.1	3.8	7.8
Education services	28.7	34.9	63.6

Table 2.3 (continued)

Research and scientific institutes	6.9	2.5	9.3
Health services	18.3	53.6	71.9
Other community services	10.1	12.5	22.6
Recreational services	12.7	7.1	19.7
Personal and household services	24.5	11.7	36.2
Total, community and personal services	152.6	149.9	302.2
International and extra-territorial bodies	0.4	0.3	0.7
Total in industry	830.0	450.6	1,280.6
Armed forces	11.9	1.1	13.0
Registered unemployed	46.7	30.8	77.5
Estimated total labor force	888.6	482.5	1,371.1

Source: Department of Statistics, New Zealand Yearbook, 1986

Education

The educational experience of the population are given by Rayner and Lattimore (1988, appendix table C.8) for the 1981 census and they can be assumed to be similar to those of the workforce.

Compulsory education in New Zealand is currently until age 15 (or approximately the fifth form year). For those whose specified their highest level of school attendance, 27 percent of those aged 15 and over had continued beyond the compulsory period. This proportion is higher for those passing through the education system now and is rising each year.

The number who had attended university was only 9.1 percent of the total. In interpreting this figure it is worth noting that attendance at university is not the same as obtaining a degree. Indeed there is a tradition in New Zealand of considering passes in subjects at university to be a qualification worth reporting to potential employers, even if the full degree is never completed. Once again, the proportion of those currently in the education system who are proceeding to university is higher than the population average given above. In summary, the educational attainment of the labor force is relatively high by general world standards, as one would expect given the wealth of the country. At the same time it is perhaps lower than might have been expected in comparison with other countries with similar income levels.

Unions

The proportion of unionists among total wage earners is shown in table 2.4 for five-yearly intervals. These figures underestimate the full degree of unionization since they do not include associations of employees that are not formally registered. However, associations tend to be less active in that they include such groups as state servants and agricultural workers.

One explanation for the relatively high union membership is that there has been provision for compulsory membership during most of the period, provided that a majority of members vote in favor of it. The issue of compulsory union membership has frequently been a bone of political contention.

Table 2.4 Proportion of wage earners who belong to registered unions

Census	Total wage earners	End of year nearest to census data	No. of workers on rolls of registered unions	Wage earners on rolls of registered unions (%)
1961	750,882	1960	332,362	44
1966	870,813	1965	353,093	41
1971	958,563	1970	378,465	39
1976	1,063,170	1975	454,991	43
1981	1,089,129	1980	516,297	48

Source: Department of Statistics, *New Zealand Yearbook*, various years

The loss of working days due to industrial action varies considerably from year to year, but tends to be high by international standards (see Rayner and Lattimore, 1988, appendix table C.9). While there are countries with a worse record, it is clear nevertheless that the degree of unionization does significantly affect the labor market and the flexibility of worker response to economic forces.

Wage Structure

Government involvement in wage determination is a further cause of rigidities. General wage orders (which give all employees a fixed absolute or percentage wage increase), wage freezes, wage rounds with guidelines, and negotiations based on traditional relativities have been widely used during the entire period. The result has been a reduced reaction to movements in the economy.

An indication of this is given by Rayner and Lattimore (1988, appendix table C.10) who show for a seven-year period from 1977 to 1984 the changes in nominal wages and in prevailing wages paid to all wage and salary workers, both by industry and by occupation group.

The highest and lowest variations of the nominal rates about the mean changes are + 12 and − 7 percent for industry and + 4 and − 5 percent for occupation groups. The equivalent figures for the prevailing rates are + 8 and − 7 percent and + 4 and − 5 percent. The coefficient of variation for the nominal rates is 4.2 percent for industry groups and 3.6 percent for occupation groups, and for prevailing rates 3.7 percent and 3.8 percent respectively. The total impression given is of a rigid wage structure rather than one responding to changes in the economy.

Unemployment and Labor Mobility

Unemployment in New Zealand has been very low during most of the post-World War II period, as shown in table 2.5. The situation has changed markedly in the past few years, however, returning to a situation rather more characteristic of the 1930s. The data shown are for the registered unemployed. Registration is a necessary prerequisite for obtaining an unemployment benefit, but since not all people are eligible for the benefit there are always more people seeking work than are registered as unemployed.

Table 2.5 Registered unemployed as a percentage of the labor force

Year	Registered unemployed (%)
1950	0.0
1960	0.1
1970	0.1
1971	0.3
1972	0.2
1973	0.1
1974	0.3
1975	0.3
1976	0.4
1977	0.6
1978	1.8
1979	2.0
1980	2.8
1981	3.7
1982	3.9
1983	5.6
1984	4.9
1985	3.3
1986	6.3

Sources: Department of Statistics, *Monthly Abstract of Statistics*, various years

Labor mobility over recent years has probably been fostered more by unemployment than by wage differentials, although the availability of the unemployment benefits has reduced this impact. The benefits are funded directly by the government and so are not an insurance scheme in a formal sense. Restrictions on receipt of the benefits are insignificant with two exceptions: the spouse of a worker cannot receive the unemployment benefit, and a married unemployed couple may not both receive the benefit at the single rate; only one partner needs to be registered and he or she then obtains the benefit at the married rate. As a result, there is less incentive for the other partner to register as unemployed. The registered unemployed data are therefore a downward-biased estimate of true unemployment.

A more accurate indication of the true unemployed figure is obtained from the five-year censuses, which indicated unemployment rates among wage and salary workers of 1.7 percent, 2.5 percent, and 5.5 percent for 1971, 1976, and 1981 respectively. While these figures are higher than those for the registered unemployed, they are still low by world standards.

The conclusion is inescapable that these institutional arrangements must to some extent impede the optimal deployment of New Zealand's highly skilled labor force. Nevertheless, despite these undoubted influences on flexibility, the actual mobility remains surprisingly high.

Gross National Product: Growth and Composition

The combination of a temperate climate with reasonably accessible land, and the agricultural background of the English colonists led New Zealand to develop an agriculture-based economy, originally geared to providing wool and later meat and dairy products to the United Kingdom.

With the exception of gold deposits (largely exploited during the nineteenth century), coal, and more recently, off-shore natural gas reserves, New Zealand is not rich in mineral resources. Economic activity has therefore continued to center on the production and export of agricultural products.

The effect of the Korean War on the price of wool was sufficient to push New Zealand's already high level of real gross national product (GNP) per capita to second or third place in the world ranking at the outset of the period covered by this study. Since then, however, the growth rates of GNP in New Zealand compared with those in the other countries of the Organization for Economic Cooperation and Development (OECD) have steadily eroded this ranking to somewhere in the middle twenties by the early 1980s.

The distinctive feature of the pattern of growth since 1959 (table 2.6) is the number of stagnant patches, particularly since the oil shocks of the

Table 2.6 Real and per capita gross national product for New Zealand, 1950–1984 (1977–1978 constant prices, March years)

Year	GNP (million NZ$)	GNP per capita (NZ$)	Annual growth rate of GNP (%)	Average growth rate of GNP (%)
1950	5,643	2,927	—	
1951	6,426	3,260	+ 13.9	
1952	6,181	3,052	− 3.8	
1953	6,215	2,995	+ 0.6	+ 4.7
1954	6,591	3,112	+ 6.0	(1950–4)
1955	7,099	3,279	+ 7.7	
1956	7,252	3,283	+ 2.2	
1957	7,440	3,288	+ 2.6	
1958	7,557	3,263	+ 1.6	+ 2.6
1959	7,567	3,206	+ 0.1	(1955–9)
1960	8,060	3,353	+ 6.5	
1961	8,516	3,453	+ 5.7	
1962	8,614	3.417	+ 1.2	
1963	9,071	3,523	+ 5.3	+ 4.9
1964	9,601	3,669	+ 5.8	(1960–4)
1965	10,232	3,841	+ 6.6	
1966	10,799	3,983	+ 5.5	
1967	10,566	3,849	− 2.2	
1968	10,531	3,798	− 0.3	+ 1.4
1969	10,596	3,779	+ 0.6	(1965–9)
1970	10,979	3,850	+ 3.6	
1971	11,410	3,939	+ 3.9	
1972	12,480	4,235	+ 9.4	
1973	13,922	4,616	+ 11.6	+ 4.9
1974	14,528	4,718	+ 4.4	(1970–4)
1975	13,938	4,456	− 4.1	
1976	13,630	4,330	− 2.2	
1977	14,327	4,545	+ 5.1	
1978	14,062	4,463	− 1.8	+ 0.6
1979	13,836	4,391	− 1.6	(1975–9)
1980	14,348	4,539	+ 3.7	
1981	14,428	4,550	+ 0.6	
1982	14,830	4,649	+ 2.8	
1983	15,445	4,782	+ 4.1	+ 1.6
1984	15,486	4,742	+ 0.3	(1980–4)
1985	15,560	4,728	+ 0.5	
1986	16,027	4,872	+ 3.0	

—, not applicable.

Source: Department of Statistics, Monthly Abstract of Statistics, various years

mid-1970s. Thus real GNP per capita in 1985 was at the same level as in 1974. The average annual rate of growth of this variable between 1951 and 1984 was only 1.1 percent.

The continued importance of the primary production sector, particularly pastoral agriculture, is the reason for New Zealand's ability to profit so greatly from the Korean War commodity boom and probably also explains its poor performance since then. Table 2.7 shows the size of the primary sector in 1955 and also its relative decline in the following 30 years as the service sector was growing. Manufacturing production grew slowly during the same period in relative, and therefore also in absolute terms.

Table 2.7 Share of gross domestic product by sector (percent)

Year	Primary	Manufacturing	Electric power and gas	Building and construction	Transport and communications	Community and social	Other services
1955	22.8	21.6	1.6	8.2		45.8	
1966	16.5	21.7	2.6	7.3	8.2	12.9	30.8
1977	12.6	23.1	2.1	6.2	8.5		47.5
1985	12.2	23.7	2.8	5.3	8.5		47.5

Source: Department of Statistics, Monthly Abstract of Statistics, various years

It should be noted, however, that much of the manufacturing sector has been devoted to processing agricultural products, while a further large part produces highly protected import substitutes. As a result, the structure of the manufacturing sector has remained relatively static over the whole period (table 2.8); in particular, the country has not developed a growing (or technologically advanced) metal products and engineering category, while the food, drink, and tobacco category remains large.

Table 2.8 Structure of manufacturing by value added (percent)

Manufacturing group	Percentage of value added in manufacturing		
	1938	1961	1984
Food, beverages, tobacco	27.9	23.6	30.0
Textiles, apparel, and leather	12.3	15.9	9.8
Wood and wood products	13.8	9.6	6.5
Paper, printing, and publishing	9.8	12.5	11.7
Chemicals, petroleum, and plastics	4.9	4.9	8.2
Nonmetallic mineral products	5.2	5.5	4.1
Basic metal industries	1.1	0.6	3.7
Machinery and metal products	20.6	25.2	24.9
Other manufacturing	4.4	2.2	1.1
Total	100.0	100.0	100.0

Source: Department of Statistics, Monthly Abstract of Statistics, various years

The more detailed classification of gross domestic product (GDP) for 1984 given in table 2.9 shows that exploitation of natural resources forms the basis of the primary sector, with agriculture continuing to dominate the

Table 2.9 Shares of gross domestic product and import content by production group (percent)

Production groups	Share of GDP (1984)	Cumulated primary input coefficient for imports (1982)
Agriculture	7.4	15
Fishing and hunting	0.4	14
Forestry and logging	1.2	9
Mining and quarrying	1.0	9
Food, beverages, and tobacco	6.8	16
Textiles, apparel, and leather	2.2	22
Manufacture of wood products	1.5	15
Manufacture of paper products and printing	2.6	19
Manufacture of chemicals, petroleum, rubber, and plastic	1.8	52
Manufacture of nonmetallic mineral products	0.9	14
Basic metal industries	0.8	52
Manufacture of fabricated metal products	5.6	28
Other manufacturing industries	0.2	16
Electricity, gas, and water	2.9	4
Construction	5.2	20
Trade, restaurants, and hotels	20.9	10
Transport and storage	5.7	23
Communication	2.9	6
Financing, insurance, real estate, and business services	11.3	7
Ownership of owner-occupied dwellings	3.6	12
Community, social, and personal services	3.4	19
Central government services	10.7	8
Local government services	1.2	13
private nonprofit services	0.7	9
Domestic services of households	0.1	0
Not allocated	− 1.4	—

—, not applicable.

Sources: Department of Statistics, *New Zealand Yearbook*, 1986; and *Input–Output Tables*

sector, while the alternative land use of forestry and logging remains small in comparison. More surprising, in view of the fact that the country has one of the largest fishing zones in the world, is the smallness of the fishing industry.

In contrast, the insignificance of mineral resources is clearly shown by the small size of the mining and quarrying production group. Hence, although use of natural resources is crucial to the New Zealand economy, it remains largely restricted to the growing properties of the soil.

A significant outcome of the concentration of the primary sector on agricultural commodities and of the manufacturing sector on processing these commodities is a considerable reliance of all sectors in the economy on imports, both of industrial raw materials and of machinery. This is indicated in the last column of table 2.9, which shows the cumulated value of imports as a percentage of total primary inputs for the various product groups. Manufacturing industries not based on agriculture rely particularly heavily on imports, with values of cumulated import inputs of up to 50 percent. The trading sector is therefore central to the economy and so its liberalization is of particular importance.

Capital Structure

A possible explanation for the poor performance of the New Zealand economy could be the rate of growth of the capital stock. In fact, from derived measures, it appears that the increase from 1960 to 1983 was only 90 percent, or an average annual increase of 2.8 percent. This is consistent with a measured increase in real output during the same time interval of 92 percent and indicates a fairly constant capital-to-output ratio over time, as is confirmed by sectoral studies.

The slow growth of capital and output is likely to be explained by a low investment ratio. Yet the ratio of measured gross investment to GNP has remained consistently around 22 percent throughout the period, suggesting that real depreciation rates are relatively high and that measured gross investment is in general not an accurate indication of real net investment. This may well be particularly true in periods of high inflation, when standard accounting measures of investment and depreciation are used.

Capital-to-labor ratios by industrial sector are given in table 2.10. Although the labor data used to calculate these relations are only based on the measured number of workers and take no account of their wages, the variability in the ratio is still surprisingly large. Of particular interest are the outliers. Electricity has a large capital-to-labor ratio owing to the effect of the capital intensive hydroelectric generation technology. The value for mining is probably not significant because the sector is so small.

Critical in understanding the New Zealand economy is the situation of the agricultural products group. The high value of its capital-to-labor ratio depends not so much on the technology involved as on the valuation placed on agricultural land, which forms by far the greatest part of the real capital stock of this sector. Although the ratio was very high in 1982 compared with most other sectors, this was at the end of a period when both the capital stock value and labor employed had remained relatively unchanged. Since 1982 the disequilibrium implicit in the relative size of the agriculture capital-to-output ratio has been corrected, with a very considerable fall in the value of land.

Table 2.10 Capital-to-labor ratios by industry group

Industry group	Capital stock (million 1966 NZ$)		Numbers employed 1982 (thousands)	K/L 1982 (thousand 1966 NZ$ per person)
	1962	1982		
Agricultural products	2,711	3,095	120.2	25.7
Fishing	8	38	5.2	7.3
Forestry	65	102	10.5	9.7
Mining	42	291	4.9	59.4
Food and beverages	262	651	63.8	10.2
Textiles and apparel	103	147	46.7	3.1
Wood and wood products	87	120	23.3	5.2
Paper products	135	292	33.0	8.8
Chemicals etc.	78	239	26.6	9.0
Nonmetallic mineral products	59	93	11.8	7.9
Basic and fabricated metal products and machinery	185	480	89.3	5.4
Other manufactures	18	28	6.4	4.4
Electricity	818	1,726	15.7	109.9
Construction	222	275	87.4	3.1
Trade and restaurants	671	1,230	214.3	5.7
Transport	875	1,189	70.7	16.8
Communication	169	329	35.7	9.2
Finance and insurance	380	1,288	93.4	13.8

Source: Nana and Philpott, 1984

The structure of New Zealand's industry can best be described as based on small units. Because the economy has not been centered on manufacturing, where economies of scale are likely to be very important, there has been little tendency for large-scale enterprises to develop. In addition, import protection has reduced the competitive pressures on local firms in manufacturing itself. In particular the use of import licensing has tended to split manufacturing based on imported components into fixed-size units. Thus the motor car assembly industry in New Zealand produces an inappropriately large number of makes and models, given the size of the country.

In 1982 there were 7,478 enterprise groups in the manufacturing sector, owning 11,064 location units and employing 296,751 workers, or 27 workers per location unit and 40 per enterprise group (see Rayner and Lattimore, 1988, appendix table C.11).

It is symptomatic that signs of large-scale enterprise can be seen in only one subclassification, the export meat works and abattoirs. At the time of the 1982 census there were 18 enterprise groups using 59 location units and employing 33,952 persons or 11.4 percent of total manufacturing employees. In these meat works there were 575 employees per location unit and 1,886 per enterprise group. Since the census there has been further concentration in this industry.

The total picture of industrial concentration in New Zealand therefore remains a picture of many small-scale enterprises not obtaining economies of scale, with the exception of the one major manufacturing industry engaged in the export trade where these scale economies have to some extent been achieved.

Foreign investors have always been an important source of finance; there has been continuing disquiet, at least during the post-World War II period, about the prospect of foreign companies' controlling the country. Restrictions on foreign investment in New Zealand have therefore been in place during the entire period.

In the following description the expression "overseas investment" is confined to situations where overseas interests have control over the local company, with control defined as ownership of 25 percent or more of the appropriate share capital. Using this terminology, table 2.11 shows the importance of overseas investment. This has represented around 10 percent of private investment during the whole period and around 1.25 percent of GDP. The share of overseas investment has tended to increase slightly over the years, with the result that the proportion of GDP accruing to foreign investors has also been rising, though it is still relatively small in total.

Overseas investment has been concentrated in manufacturing although the dominance of this group has declined in recent years as investment in banking and insurance has grown. The very small investment in the important primary sector can largely be ascribed to a combination of legal restrictions and the smallness of the typical units involved.

Table 2.11 Direct overseas investment and income earned: comparison with national accounts aggregates

Five-year periods	Net overseas investment (million NZ$)	Net overseas investment expressed as a percentage of national accounts aggregates			Income earned (million NZ$)	Income earned expressed as a percentage of GDP
		Private investment	Total investment	GDP		
1951–5	83.0	8.1	5.0	1.05	88.0	1.10
1956–60	105.1	7.6	4.4	0.97	118.3	1.07
1961–5	207.3	10.1	6.2	1.36	227.0	1.47
1966–70	234.9	7.8	4.8	1.09	317.7	1.47
1971–5	666.3	11.8	7.8	1.76	546.3	1.41
1976–80	1,159.4	10.6	6.6	1.24	1,052.1	1.37

Source: Department of Statistics, New Zealand Yearbook, various years

Foreign-owned manufacturing firms tend to be larger, to be more capital intensive, to be significantly more profitable, and to retain a greater proportion of their earnings than do their New Zealand-owned counterparts.

The Foreign Trade Sector

Balance of Payments

New Zealand has had a chronic deficit in its balance of payments on current account since World War II. The main component has been the continuous deficit on invisible transactions, which include overseas payments for other services such as insurance. Over recent years, an increasing proportion of these transactions has been interest on the substantial borrowings undertaken to insulate New Zealand from the more serious effects of the oil price shocks in the 1970s.

The balance-of-payments constraint has considerably influenced New Zealand's economic policy. Although in most years export receipts exceed import payments, the resulting positive visible trade balance has seldom been sufficient to offset the negative invisibles balance. One objective of the import-restricting and export-promoting policies of successive governments has therefore been to create greater visible trade surpluses. The balance of payments on current account, showing both the balance on trade transactions and the invisibles balance, is given in table 2.12.

Terms of Trade

It should be noted that balance-of-payments problems have been further aggravated by a long-term deterioration in the external terms of trade. By 1985, the terms-of-trade index (see table 2.13) was only 61 percent of its value in 1950.

Capital Flows

The chronic current account deficit has led to an external debt that has been rising in absolute terms during almost the entire period. Net capital outflows took place in only three years in the period 1956–85, and these were all of small amounts relative to GNP. The average capital inflow was 1.6 percent of GNP a year over the period 1956–84 and around 6 percent for the final three years.

The relatively tight exchange controls during almost the entire period are reflected in the fact that most of the borrowing was undertaken by the

Table 2.12 Balance of payments on current account (million New Zealand dollars)

Year	Current account	Trade transactions	Invisibles
1950	+29.0	+51.8	−22.8
1952	−46.8	+22.2	−57.9
1954	−80.1	−33.4	−46.7
1956	+2.7	+49.0	−47.7
1958	−67.0	−1.0	−66.0
1960	−47.6	+41.4	−89.0
1962	+5.2	+115.4	−110.2
1964	+1.8	+133.0	−131.2
1966	−86.6	+83.3	−169.9
1968	+72.9	+237.5	−164.6
1970	−25.8	+177.2	−203.0
1972	+208.4	+405.5	−197.1
1974	−815.7	−530.1	−285.6
1976	−623.1	−9.5	−613.6
1978	−392.4	+606.6	−998.9
1980	−549.3	+884.6	−1,433.9
1982	−1,845.0	+262.7	−2,107.7
1984	−991.5	+1,260.1	−2,251.6
1986	−1,892.1	+507.4	−2,399.5

Source: Department of Statistics, *Monthly Abstract of Statistics*, various years; Reserve Bank, *Reserve Bank Bulletin*, various years

Table 2.13 New Zealand terms of trade (1957 = 100)

Year	Export price index	Import price index	Terms-of-trade index
1950	92	80	119
1952	78	102	88
1954	93	95	108
1956	94	97	105
1958	81	100	85
1960	94	99	96
1962	91	97	94
1964	108	97	111
1966	105	99	107
1968	97	108	89
1970	109	126	87
1972	130	140	93
1974	185	165	112
1976	208	288	72
1978	270	347	78
1980	379	462	82
1982	482	629	77
1984	542	727	75
1985	664	907	73

Source: Department of Statistics, *New Zealand Yearbook*, various years, and *Monthly Abstract of Statistics*, various years

public sector; the reaction to the loosening of controls late in 1984 is similarly manifest in the large private capital inflow in the following year.

The chronic debtor status of the country is also indicated by the substantial decline in official overseas reserves relative to the current account payments (see Rayner and Lattimore, 1988, appendix table C.14). In 1960 the ratio of reserves to annual payments was 0.411. By 1984 it had declined to 0.117, but it then rose following the exchange rate float.

Table 2.14 New Zealand Exchange Rate

Year	US$ per NZ$ (Dec)	Exchange rate index (1979 = 100)
1950	1.4000	n.a.
1952	1.3945	n.a.
1954	1.3827	n.a.
1956	1.3831	n.a.
1958	1.3908	n.a.
1960	1.3918	n.a.
1962	1.3912	n.a.
1964	1.3848	n.a.
1966	1.3850	n.a.
1968	1.1121	n.a.
1970	1.1161	1,127
1972	1.1952	1,160
1974	1.3154	1,248
1976	0.9500	1,053
1978	1.0666	1,053
1980	0.9623	915
1982	0.7325	834
1984	0.4776	627
1986	0.5245	634

n.a., not available.

Source: Department of Statistics, Reserve Bank Bulletin, various years

Exchange Rate

The combination of a current account deficit and a stagnant economy suggests that New Zealand has not experienced an equilibrium exchange rate during this period. Over most of the country's history it has had a fixed, but occasionally adjusted, nominal exchange rate (see table 2.14). Adjustments were generally made in response to acute balance-of-payments current account problems and reflected internal issues such as inadequate profitability in the agricultural sector and occasional speculative pressures against the exchange rate.

During the 1970s the need for more movement in the exchange rate began to be recognized, largely as a result of differing rates of inflation between countries and fluctuations in the terms of trade. Large sudden movements were considered a disadvantage, but an exchange rate determined by a free market was also rejected on the grounds that it would not result in an appropriate long-term equilibrium rate.

In mid-1979 New Zealand therefore adopted a crawling peg exchange rate system. The rate was set, as in the past, in relation to a basket of currencies, and frequent small changes were made based on the difference between the rate of inflation in New Zealand and the rate of inflation in its major trading partners and on long-term changes in the terms of trade and other structural factors. Limits, which turned out to be too small, were set on the permitted changes. This system remained in use until mid-1982, when a fixed exchange rate was once more established.

A devaluation of 20 percent followed the July 1984 election, and the government reassessed (and removed) the considerable range of price and income controls in place. A variety of moves were taken to strengthen and extend the foreign exchange market and exchange controls were effectively abolished. The exchange rate was floated in March 1985. High domestic interest rates, however, have thus far prevented the exchange rate from falling closer to a current account balancing value.

Exports

Despite the continuing current account deficit over the period, exports have been growing faster than GDP, in volume at least. From 1950 to 1986 the export volume index (table 2.15) rose from 343 to 1,198, representing a rise of 249 percent or an average annual increase of 3.5 percent over the 36-year period.

New Zealand's major exports are dairy products, meat, wool, and manufactured items. Dairy product exports grew over the 36-year period by 97 percent (1.9 percent annual average), meat exports by 133 percent (2.4 percent annual average), and wool exports by 87 percent (1.8 percent annual average).

The greatest growth, though from a small base, was in manufactured exports. Volume indices are not available for the earlier years, but since 1972 exports of manufactured goods other than food have risen by 313 percent, or by an annual average of 12.5 percent.

In terms of value the composition of New Zealand exports has changed substantially (table 2.16). In 1950, wool, dairy products, and meat made up 86.4 percent of exports. By 1986 this proportion had fallen to 41.2 percent. Both wool and dairy products had fallen substantially in their contribution, while meat had risen from the 1950 level but had fallen from a peak contribution in 1970. The growth of other product exports from 13.6 per-

Table 2.15 Export–import volumes index (1982 = 1,000)

Year	All exports	Dairy produce	Meat	Wool	All imports
1950	343	588	417	547	365
1952	399	729	501	606	456
1954	359	570	498	545	455
1956	400	676	525	586	477
1958	433	712	504	667	512
1960	471	752	550	766	439
1962	498	750	577	843	484
1964	535	776	653	825	600
1966	552	844	599	895	678
1968	624	900	721	874	523
1970	724	937	835	1,000	673
1972	761	936	870	1,056	740
1974	692	942	769	722	1,032
1976	794	863	933	938	860
1978	849	901	915	849	787
1980	967	1,039	911	1,013	926
1982	1,000	1,000	1,000	1,000	1,000
1984	1,129	1,035	1,023	1,092	1,027
1986	1,198	1,156	970	1,024	1,093

Source: Department of Statistics, Monthly Abstract of Statistics, various years

cent in 1950 to 58.7 percent in 1986 reflects the diversification that has taken place in the economy. Along with manufactured goods, horticultural products and timber have grown significantly.

On a per capita basis (see Rayner and Lattimore, 1988, appendix table C.15), the free on board (f.o.b.) value of exports rose from NZ$191.12 in 1950 to NZ$2,659.22 in 1984. In real terms (deflated by the consumer price index), the annual rise over the 34-year period was only 2.8 percent.

The destinations of New Zealand's exports have changed considerably over the period from 1950 to 1985. In 1950, 66 percent of exports by value went to the United Kingdom, 10 percent to the United States, 3 percent to Australia, 4 percent to France, 3 percent to West Germany, 2 percent to Canada, and the remaining 12 percent to a range of other countries. In 1985, only 9 percent of exports by value went to the United Kingdom, 14 percent to the United States, 15 percent to Australia, 13 percent to Japan, 2 percent each to France, the People's Republic of China, Korea, Italy, West Germany and Canada, 1 percent to the USSR, 4 percent to Iran, and the remaining 30 percent to a wide range of destinations.

New Zealand exports have tended to grow more slowly over the whole period than the exports of other industrial or developing countries

Table 2.16 Composition of New Zealand exports by value (percent)

Year	Wool	Meat	Dairy products[a]	Other
1950	40.9	15.7	29.8	13.6
1952	34.2	16.4	33.2	16.2
1954	36.6	20.6	27.3	15.8
1956	33.0	23.0	29.5	14.5
1958	32.0	29.4	23.3	17.6
1960	33.9	25.2	26.0	14.9
1962	n.a.	n.a.	n.a.	n.a.
1964	36.8	24.4	22.7	16.1
1966	30.2	25.2	25.2	19.4
1968	19.3	31.2	25.4	24.1
1970	18.8	33.5	19.4	28.3
1972	16.6	28.6	25.6	29.2
1974	20.2	29.6	18.5	31.7
1976	19.1	24.6	16.5	39.8
1978	17.5	22.8	15.3	44.4
1980	18.1	23.0	15.4	43.5
1982	13.6	23.0	18.9	44.5
1984	12.9	20.0	16.3	50.8
1986	12.1	16.2	13.0	58.7

n.a., not available.
[a] Dairy products include butter, cheese, milk (dried and condensed), and casein.

Source: Department of Statistics, New Zealand Yearbook, various years, and Monthly Abstract of Statistics, various years

(Lattimore, 1987b). This is especially true for primary exports which grew at less than half the rate of other countries over the period 1960–81.

Imports

Because of its small population and limited mineral resources, New Zealand has to import goods that it does not have or cannot manufacture efficiently itself. The chronically overvalued real exchange rate has led to a demand for imports that has continually exceeded export receipts. Regulations on foreign exchange transactions, tariffs, and import licensing have been the significant techniques used to reduce the excess demand for imported products, especially of finished goods. Local industries have developed behind the protection barriers and use many imported intermediate goods to produce the final goods within New Zealand.

As a result, imports of manufactured goods have remained the principal component of total imports. They comprised over 65 percent by value of New Zealand's imports in 1986 and had been at even higher levels earlier (see Rayner and Lattimore, 1988, appendix table C.16). The other major imports have been fuels and chemicals (10.9 percent and 11.3 percent respectively by value of 1986 imports), which are items for which New Zealand does not have sufficient domestic production capacity.

A combination of overvalued exchange rates, rising import prices (especially oil), and declining real prices for exports (especially agricultural exports) has meant that the real per capita value of imports has grown significantly faster than that of exports – 2.3 times faster between 1950 and 1982 (see Rayner and Lattimore, 1988, appendix table C.15).

The change in the source of imports has been a significant factor in the country's import structure. In 1950, 60 percent of imports by value came from the United Kingdom, 12 percent from Australia, 7 percent from the United States, and the remaining 21 percent from a wide range of countries. In 1985, the import source pattern was 8 percent from the United Kingdom, 17 percent from Australia, 15 percent from the United States, and 18 percent from Japan, with the remaining 42 percent coming from a wide range of sources.

Trade Agreements

The changing patterns of export destinations and import origins reflect major changes in trade agreements.

During World War II and up to 1954, bulk purchase arrangements for meat and dairy products were in effect between New Zealand and the United Kingdom. These arrangements guaranteed the availability of all meat and dairy products to the United Kingdom at negotiated prices. At the same time, British preferential (BP) tariffs provided a low tariff rate on imports to New Zealand from the United Kingdom. The latter arrangement ceased on July 1, 1977.

For these two reasons, Britain was by far the most important trading partner for New Zealand in the early part of the period, despite their great distance apart. The dismantling of the various preferential arrangements following the entry of the United Kingdom into the European Community in 1973 represented an acceptance of political changes and economic realities but has exacted considerable adjustment costs. At the same time it needs to be noted that from 1973 New Zealand received special treatment from the European Community through Protocol 18. These arrangements continue to date but have been continuously scaled down since 1973.

The British trade relationship has been replaced by agreements with New Zealand's more natural trading partners, in particular Australia and

Japan and other countries of the "Pacific rim." With respect to Australia the agreements are the Closer Economic Relations Trade Agreement (CER) and its predecessor the New Zealand–Australia Free Trade Agreement (NAFTA).

Under NAFTA, which was agreed in August 1965, goods were listed under schedules and protocols that allowed various levels of "free trade." The central element was Schedule A to which goods were added, following negotiations, and which allowed for the elimination of import duties on those goods by both countries. Trade between Australia and New Zealand grew substantially, particularly in manufactured goods: between 1964–5 and 1981–2 New Zealand exports to Australia increased from NZ$99 million to NZ$532 million in constant 1977 values, while imports from Australia rose from NZ$371 million to NZ$705 million.

From January 1, 1983, NAFTA was replaced by CER. In general this agreement provided for the phased removal of duty rates by January 1, 1988, and the progressive liberalization of all remaining quantitative restrictions on trans-Tasman trade, with all such restrictions being eliminated by 1995. All performance-based export incentives were to be removed by 1987. Although the agreement applies to all goods, some products and industry groups have been granted modified programs in recognition of special adjustment needs. All aspects of government trade policy and company trading practices are included within the agreement, with the intention of enabling trans-Tasman trade to be conducted on the basis of equality of opportunity and fair competition.

There are other regional trade agreements involving New Zealand which are probably more significant to its partners than to itself. Until late 1985, trade arrangements for South Pacific Island bananas and oranges were supervised by a New Zealand organization called United Fruit Distributors Ltd. This company was granted a monopoly on imports of oranges and bananas (and some other fruits) and was obliged to import a significant proportion of these products from South Pacific Island countries. This monopoly and the trading arrangement have recently been terminated.

Obligations exist for New Zealand to accept imports from the Cook Islands, Niue, and Tokelau, which are New Zealand protectorates.

In 1971, New Zealand and Australia with the Cook Islands, Fiji, Nauru, Tonga, and Western Samoa formed the South Pacific Forum. Since then Papua New Guinea, Kiribati, Niue, the Solomon Islands, Tuvalu, and Vanuatu have become full members. The Forum has initiated a regional shipping service and studies into market expansion for island products. On January 1, 1981, the South Pacific Regional Trade and Economic Co-operation Agreement (SPARTECA), formed by the Forum countries, came into effect. This agreement provides for Australia and New Zealand to grant nonreciprocal duty-free and unrestricted access for most of the products exported by the Forum island countries. Closer economic cooperation and development assistance for the island countries is also covered by the agreement.

New Zealand's trade relations with the member countries of the Association of Southeast Asian Nations (ASEAN) (Indonesia, Malaysia, the Philippines, Singapore, Thailand, and, since January 1, 1984, Brunei) are governed by the ASEAN–New Zealand Joint Trade Study Group (established in 1976) which meets periodically to review trade developments. New Zealand also has bilateral trade agreements with each ASEAN member (except Singapore and Brunei, with which New Zealand has a scientific, industrial, and technological agreement).

Relations between New Zealand and China were normalized in 1972 and trade has expanded considerably. A joint trade commission meets annually to review developments in bilateral trade.

A New Zealand–Mexico scientific and technological agreement was signed in Mexico in August 1983.

A developing countries liaison unit was established in 1977 within the Trade Policy Division of the New Zealand Department of Trade and Industry. It is intended to help developing country exporters to find markets for their products in New Zealand. Assistance is available to 161 countries. The unit provides information on the New Zealand market, assists visiting businessmen and trade missions, and helps organize trade exhibitions in New Zealand.

Also with respect to developing countries New Zealand introduced special duty rates in the customs tariff as from January 1, 1972. On July 1, 1976, New Zealand introduced a revised generalized system of preference (GSP) which significantly increased the GSP coverage. The intention was to maintain specified margins of tariff preference for developing countries up to a level of 20 percent.

Fiscal Policy and the Government Sector

From the beginning of the period under review, the New Zealand economy has deteriorated at an accelerating rate. As has already been seen, unemployment, balance-of-payments deficits, and real per capita growth of GNP have all worsened from the middle 1950s. Since the mid-1970s the rate of deterioration has been particularly alarming. The fourth main objective of economic policy, price stability, has also suffered (table 2.17), with average inflation rates increasing from below 3 percent to almost 15 percent.

New Zealand had long held a commitment to state intervention through the social security system, state-owned enterprises, marketing boards, and a host of other devices. In the post-World War II period these were particularly aimed at giving security of employment by insulating the

Table 2.17 Inflation in New Zealand

Year ending Mar	Consumer price index	Annual inflation (%)	Average inflation over five years (%)
1950	195	—	
1951	217	11.1	
1952	234	7.8	
1953	244	4.3	6.1
1954	255	4.5	(1950–4)
1955	262	2.7	
1956	271	3.4	
1957	277	2.2	
1958	289	4.3	2.4
1959	300	3.8	(1955–9)
1960	302	0.7	
1961	308	2.0	
1962	316	2.6	
1963	322	1.9	2.7
1964	333	3.4	(1960–4)
1965	345	3.6	
1966	354	3.6	
1967	376	6.2	
1968	392	4.3	4.9
1969	411	4.8	(1965–9)
1970	438	6.6	
1971	485	10.7	
1972	517	6.6	
1973	563	8.9	10.5
1974	627	11.4	(1970–4)
1975	720	14.8	
1976	844	17.2	
1977	866	14.5	
1978	1,073	11.1	14.8
1979	1,236	15.2	(1975–9)
1980	1,438	16.3	
1981	1,660	15.4	
1982	1,936	16.6	
1983	2,040	5.4	12.0
1984	2,183	7.0	(1980–4)
1985	2,539	16.3	
1986	2,819	11.0	

—, not applicable.

Source: Department of Statistics, *Monthly Abstract of Statistics*, various years

domestic economy from external shocks. With this background it is not surprising that when faced with the various pieces of bad economic news as the period progressed, successive governments continued to react in true Keynesian spirit by intervening in the economy to an extent that increased in parallel with the seriousness of the problems. These interventions took the shape of increasing interferences with the microeconomic workings of the system, while the size of the government sector tended to increase, as therefore did its macroimpact on the economy.

Table 2.18 shows total taxation as a percentage of GNP at five-yearly intervals from 1950. The figures demonstrate clearly the relative growth of government income after the early 1970s. In fact, the growth of government influence on the economy was greater than these figures indicate, since the budget deficit has increased faster than taxation. Thus in 1984 total government expenditure was 42.2 percent of GNP, with the deficit after allowing for some nontaxation income being 8.8 percent of GNP. While it is difficult to obtain directly comparable measures for the early 1950s, similar figures were of the order of 30 percent and 2–3 percent respectively.

Table 2.18 Fiscal policy measures

Year	Total taxation as a percentage of GNP	Income taxation as a percentage of total taxation
1950	24.6	59.0
1955	25.3	61.5
1960	24.4	59.3
1965	23.9	64.9
1970	24.6	66.0
1975	29.2	74.6
1980	28.6	70.0
1985	30.2	70.1

Source: Department of Statistics, Monthly Abstract of Statistics, various years

New Zealand is unusual among OECD countries in the proportion of its tax revenue raised by income taxes. Table 2.18 includes data on this proportion and demonstrates how it expanded from around 60 percent in the early part of the period to almost 75 percent in the later years.

The periods that each major political party has served in office since World War II are given in table 2.19. The National Party has governed for 29 years and the Labour Party for 11 years.

Table 2.19 Periods in power for the political
parties

Periods in office	Party in power
1949–57	National
1957–60	Labour
1960–72	National
1972–5	Labour
1975–84	National
1984–present	Labour

Conclusion

The story that emerges is of a country that started the period wealthy and
with few economic problems but ended the period in a far less comfortable
position, with substantial deterioration in all the standard measures of
economic performance.

The initial government response to the deterioration in the economy was
to increase the size of the government sector. With no discernible signs that
this policy was achieving its ends, it is not surprising that there has recently
been a policy rebound, coupling trade liberalization with considerably
greater reliance on the market system through the economy.

3

The First Episode, 1951–1956

Liberalization and Accompanying Policies

Trade Policy Background

The trade policies operating in 1950, immediately before the first liberalization episode, were essentially those put in place in the 1930s – in the latter stage of the Great Depression – cemented by ancillary wartime restrictions from 1939 onwards. New Zealand in the 1930s was still a quasi-colony. In 1932, a conference of British Commonwealth countries was convened in Ottawa, Canada, to design a cooperative trade policy arrangement to address the threats of protectionism and competitive devaluations around the world.

The agreement arising from this conference affirmed BP tariffs at low rates for New Zealand shipments from the United Kingdom and raised most favored nation (MFN) tariffs at least 20 percentage points higher than the BP rates. New Zealand also agreed to encourage only the development of New Zealand manufacturing industries that were "economic or efficient" so as to minimize the effect of industrial development on traditional British exporters. In return, Britain agreed to maintain access for New Zealand pastoral exports. These new tariff rates were put into effect in 1934.

The immediate effect of the import restrictions was not large, since nearly 50 percent of New Zealand's imports then came from the United Kingdom and over 80 percent of exports were destined for the United Kingdom (table 3.1).

The first Labour government, which came to power in 1935, followed a strong import substitution policy using high MFN tariffs and quantitative restrictions on imports. The latter instrument, termed import selection, was introduced in 1938 and administered by an expanded Department of Industries and Commerce. The program was coupled with foreign exchange and financial controls administered through the new central bank, the Reserve Bank of New Zealand. This further move to control

Table 3.1 Destination and origin of external trade (percent)

	Exports					Imports				
	Britain	Australia	Japan	United States	Other countries	Britain	Australia	Japan	United States	Other countries
Year ending Dec										
1920	74	5	n.a.	16	5	48	17	n.a.	18	17
1930	80	3	n.a.	5	12	47	8	n.a.	18	27
1940	88	3	n.a.	4	5	47	16	n.a.	12	25
1950	66	3	n.a.	10	21	60	12	n.a.	7	21
1960	53	4	n.a.	13	30	43	18	n.a.	10	29
Year ending Jun										
1970	36	8	10	16	30	30	21	8	13	28
1975	22	12	12	42	12	19	20	14	13	34
1980	14	12	13	14	47	15	19	13	14	39
1982	14	15	13	14	44	9	20	17	16	37
1983	13	12	14	15	54	9	20	17	17	37
1984	10	14	16	13	47	9	20	21	15	35
1985	9	15	15	14	47	8	17	18	15	42

n.a., not available.

Source: Department of Statistics, *New Zealand Yearbook*, various years

imports met with fierce opposition from the British because import selection effectively broke the strengthened bilateral ties resulting from the Ottawa Conference. Nevertheless, the outbreak of World War II resulted in an immediate offer by Britain to buy the full New Zealand exportable surplus of agricultural products at guaranteed prices. During the war, this closeknit relationship was solidified by the creation of a Commonwealth pool of US dollar export earnings.

The guaranteed export price and market arrangements were not in New Zealand's favor, and the terms of trade deteriorated over this period, eliciting at least partial compensation from Britain in the form of foreign exchange grants.

The dollar pool and guaranteed market arrangements lasted well after the end of the war. They were not completely dismantled until 1954, seven years after the Statute of Westminster had been passed (1947) establishing New Zealand as a fully independent nation within the British Commonwealth. This was partly because New Zealand feared a slump in post-war agricultural prices similar to that of the early 1920s after World War I.

By 1945–6 New Zealand had locked itself into the new external policy stance. It had three components: a strong import substitution orientation of the domestic tradeable goods sectors; strong bilateral export links with Britain; and, overlaying these policies, a pervasive framework of regulations and controls to guide industrial development, local investment, savings, and the allocation of foreign exchange reserves.

In 1947, many Western countries began to develop multilateral approaches to trade and international finance, moves which New Zealand had rejected when they began in the 1930s. New Zealand was prominent in the discussions that led to agreements such as the General Agreement on Tariffs and Trade (GATT) and Bretton Woods but, with the Labour government still in power, used its influence to argue for sufficient caveats to allow New Zealand to continue import selection and exchange controls on the grounds that these policies were necessary to maintain balance-of-payments equilibrium. This stance was justified on the basis that other countries such as the United States were granted exemptions for new agricultural import quotas. The strongest stimulus, however, was probably mistrust of world markets for goods and finance, which reinforced a strong bilateral stance internationally. It is notable that, despite major participation at Bretton Woods, New Zealand joined the International Monetary Fund (IMF) and the World Bank only after many years of discussion.

In the new multilateral era, world trading conditions began to improve rapidly. The pace of economic growth quickened both in Asia and in Europe, stimulated by and in turn fostering the freer trading environment, particularly in manufactured products. The New Zealand manufacturing sector was almost completely insulated from these opportunities in trade terms and in technical exchange. Import dependence on Britain had increased markedly (table 3.1), partly as a result of US dollar rationing and partly as a result of the differential import protection offered to Commonwealth suppliers. While most industrialized nations were beginning to look outwards, New Zealand maintained a strong import substitution bias.

In 1949, the first National government was elected to office. This government was somewhat more in favor of private enterprise and began to remove some pricing control and rationing elements. During that year, the New Zealand pound was devalued 40 percent relative to the US dollar, in line with the devaluation of the British pound. In 1950, New Zealand export prices began to rise dramatically. A large balance-of-payments surplus (before official loan repayments) was expected and, at this time of high world food and fiber prices, New Zealand's GDP per capita had reached third place in the world ranking after Canada and the United States (Gould, 1982). Meanwhile the terms of trade improved to levels that would not be experienced again until the commodity boom of 1973–4: the index rose nearly 30 percent from 1949–50 (table 3.2) (and remained at this level into 1951). The stage was set for the government to begin the relaxation of policy intervention in imports.

Introduction and Implementation of the Liberalization Policy

The general aims of the policy of import liberalization appear to have been to put an end to wartime controls on consumers. This might also be interpreted as increasing the supply of goods to meet pent-up demand at the fixed (and recently devalued) exchange rate, given the increase in terms of trade. It is not clear that the import liberalization policy was designed to reduce protection for the import substitute sector.

In May 1950 an import advisory committee was established to advise the Minister of Customs on all matters relating to import licensing. This was an interim body pending the full establishment of the Board of Trade later that year. The Department of Industries and Commerce made submissions to the government arguing that responsibility for advising Customs on certain key commodities should not be devolved to the Board of Trade but should be retained by the precursor of the Department of Trade and Industry. The key commodities included important raw materials and capital equipment for the manufacturing sector as well as "finished and semi-finished goods that would directly or indirectly affect existing industry" (Department of Industry and Commerce, 1951). The government agreed to this split responsibility, giving the Department of Trade and Industry the mandate to foster growth in New Zealand industry.

The trade liberalization episode began in 1951 with major exemptions to the import-licensing schedule and the partial relaxation of foreign exchange controls for sterling transactions. The rate of import protection

Table 3.2 General economic indicators – episode 1

Year[a]	Terms of trade index (1957 = 100)	Current account deficit (−) (million NZ$)	Real wage index[b] (1955 = 1,000)	Real interest rate[c] (percent)	Nominal exchange rate (US$ per NZ$)	Wholesale price index (1955 = 100)	Export price index (1955 = 100)	Import price index (1955 = 100)
1949	92		933	n.a.	2.00	715	64.4	77
1950	119	+ 29.0	945	− 2.4	1.40	779	91.0	84
1951	119		967	− 7.0	1.39	907	106.8	99
1952	88	− 46.8	944	− 3.7	1.39	1,008	85.9	108
1953	104		961	0.0	1.39	998	95.5	102
1954	107	− 80.1	990	0.0	1.38	989	98.5	100
1955	111		1,000	2.0	1.38	1,000	100.0	100
1956	105	+ 2.3	985	1.4	1.38	1,038	97.5	102
1957	100		1,009	2.9	1.39	1,050	95.8	106
1958	85	− 67.0	976	0.9	1.39	1,080	81.8	106
1959	100		958	1.4	1.39	1,092	93.5	103

n.a., not available.
[a] The time periods are both calendar years and years ending March, so the phasing of changes is not exact.
[b] The average nominal wage for an adult male worker deflated by the consumer price index.
[c] The long-term yield on government stock, less the rate of increase in the consumer price index.

Source: Department of Statistics, *Monthly Abstract of Statistics*, various years

fell to around 34 percent. (Before 1951, the import protection rate would have been at least as high as it was in 1959, when a similar import-licensing program was in operation. For this reason the import protection rate in 1949–50 is assumed to have been 60 percent.) In the 1951 schedule, 326 items (50 percent of the total) were freed from import license provided the goods were sourced outside the hard (US) currency area. Some indication of the effects of these changes is seen in tables 3.3 and 3.4.

Table 3.3 Trade protection and real effective exchange rates – episode 1, 1949–1959

	Nominal protection rate[a] (%)		Real effective exchange rate index[b] (1949 = 100)		Real growth output (%)	
Year	Exports	Imports	Exports	Imports	Farming	Total primary and manufactured
1949	0.1	60.0	100	100.	+ 4	+ 5
1950	0.1	60.0	53	69	+ 3	+ 3
1951	0.1	34.0	53	82	− 1	+ 2
1952	0.1	34.0	73	83	+ 5	+ 2
1953	0.1	34.0	65	87	0	+ 4
1954	0.1	34.0	63	88	+ 2	+ 8
1955	0.1	34.0	63	89	+ 2	+ 4
1956	0.1	34.0	67	90	+ 1	+ 2
1957	0.1	34.0	68	88	+ 6	+ 5
1958	0.1	53.6	83	79	+ 5	+ 3
1959	0.1	53.6	73	82	+ 1	+ 4

[a] See text.
[b] The nominal exchange rate (in New Zealand dollars) inflated by the export (or import) price index and the nominal rate of export (or import) protection, deflated by the wholesale price index, expressed in US dollars.

In 1952, the Board of Trade removed import licensing from a further 98 items from nonscheduled (hard currency) areas, so that by this point 60 percent of import items were free from control. However, in March 1952 the liberalization process received a setback, at least with respect to some key commodities such as cars. The terms of trade fell from 119 in 1951 to 88 in 1952, and this New Zealand situation contributed to a US dollar reserves emergency in the sterling area. All current import licenses were canceled and motor vehicles were reinstated under the provisions of the Import Licensing Regulations. The effect of this change on motor vehicle imports can be seen in table 3.5, especially for assembled motor vehicles (competing imports for the domestic car assembly industry). A cosmetic change in import policy was included in the National government program. The original import selection regime was renamed "import licensing."

Table 3.4 Quantitative restrictions on imports,
1938–1986

Year	Percentage of imports requiring licenses
1938	100
1939	100
1940	100
1941	100
1942	100
1943	100
1944	100
1945	100
1946	100
1947	100
1948	100
1949	92
1950	84
1951	76
1952	69
1953	62
1954	55
1955	48
1956	40
1957	40
1958	100
1959	95
1960	90
1961	85
1962	80
1963	75
1964	74
1965	72
1966	57
1967	55
1968	52
1969	44
1970	42
1971	34
1972	31
1973	30
1974	30
1975	38
1976	25
1977	24
1978	24
1979	24
1980	21
1981	18
1982	22
1983	22
1984	24
1985	20
1986	18

Sources: Hawke, 1985; D. Galt, Department of Trade and
Industry, personal communication

Table 3.5 New Zealand car imports, 1944–1962

	Imports of motor vehicles (numbers)	
Year	Assembled	Knocked down packs
1944	3	–
1945	51	–
1946	2,311	4,902
1947	5,342	14,030
1948	4,223	6,770
1949	775	11,204
1950	2,736	13,837
1951	14,101	12,797
1952	21,364	17,809
1953	3,151	17,738
1954	11,377	28,807
1955	14,622	31,810
1956	7,166	29,071
1957	5,262	36,190
1958	4,001	25,057
1959	1,067	25,240
1960	2,592	29,819
1961	2,576	32,804
1962	3,286	34,573

–, negligible.

Source: Department of Statistics, Monthly Abstract of Statistics, various years

From 1950, the Board of Trade and the Department of Trade and Industry carried out numerous studies to monitor the effects of delicensing and to ensure that competing imports did not unduly affect New Zealand firms. The Department had retained its Customs advisory role for this purpose. In its 1956 annual report the Department stated that, while licensing in the dollar area was expanding, imports from Japan should be subject to the overriding consideration that "there be no likelihood of competition with New Zealand production."

Minor relaxations to import licensing continued in 1956 and 1957, but the liberalization process was beginning to falter. In 1957 import-licensing control was returned to the Department of Trade and Industry while the Board of Trade carried out a review of tariffs. In reviewing the licensing system the Department concluded that

1   most industries then protected by licensing would probably find it difficult to meet competition from imports under prevailing rates of import duty, and

2   controls of items still subject to import licensing had been relaxed as far as was consistent with giving a measure of protection to New Zealand manufacturing; for example, limited exports of many classes of clothing had been permitted.

In 1957 dairy export receipts fell 19 percent and the terms of trade dropped 15 percent to a level of 85 in 1957–8. Given the fixed exchange rate, foreign exchange reserves also fell to their lowest level in five years.

On January 1, 1958, the liberalization program was ended. The system of (foreign) exchange allocation and import licensing was reintroduced; import priorities were reset for essential foodstuffs, raw materials, machinery, and medical supplies. The remaining available funds were to be allocated in the most reasonable way: "A fixed amount of overseas funds would be allocated to each tariff item, except those few for which no allocation was *possible*" (Department of Trade and Industry, 1958). Import levels were set basically at their 1956 levels except that licenses would be made available on demand for essential industrial and farming inputs. In 1964, Elkan (1972) estimated that import protection was probably higher during the period 1958–63 but no firm estimates are available.

Accompanying Policies

The trade policy changes that initiated and terminated this episode coincided with major political change: the liberalization episode began with the election of the first National government and ended two months after the second Labour government was elected to office. Plainly, ideological differences were at least partly responsible for these policy shifts.

Apart from the trade policy shifts, the major break with traditional policy made by the new National government was its willingness to take strong action – tested in the wharf strike of 1951 – against union wage demands. This attitude probably had a significant influence on the labor market throughout the 1950s.

In many respects, however, policies other than those specifically geared to liberalizing trade remained very much in line with those that preceded the episode. The National government continued state housing and other public investment projects begun by Labour. The fixed exchange rate policy was maintained throughout the period (the exchange rate, as shown in table 3.2, remained unchanged throughout), and the monetary policy tended to accommodate fiscal policy.

Trade agreements continued to follow the pattern begun during wartime. There was a fear that depressed world-market conditions would follow World War II. Bulk purchase arrangements for export meat continued until 1954, as did New Zealand's participation in the US dollar pool. These arrangements reinforced a foreign policy based almost exclusively on bilateral relations with a slow growth economy, Britain. Major export items were directed to Britain, and foreign and trade policy measures ensured a continuing preference for British imports. In this environment, the necessary adjustments to world-market changes were made slowly and with difficulty. Almost inevitably, an outside shock, such as occurred in 1957, would result in policy retrenchment.

Economic Performance

Foreign Trade

New Zealand's heavy dependence on agricultural exports, which had actually increased from 1946 to 1951, remained high throughout the episode (table 3.6). There was little incentive to expand nontraditional exports in the prevailing climate of high consumer demand, since the liberalization was designed to prevent competition with domestic production, and import protection for local manufacturing remained high.

One example of imports competing with domestic industry is the car assembly industry. New Zealand has never had a car manufacturing industry but has assembled foreign-made cars with varying proportions of local components. In 1951 and 1952 imports of assembled cars were increased from 2,000 units to 14,000 units and 21,000 units respectively (table 3.5). The table shows that while the assembly of cars in New Zealand from "knocked down" packs was reduced by about 7 percent in 1951, it increased by 40 percent in 1952 in spite of the increase in competing imports. In 1953, car assembly remained static in spite of the large reduction in competing imports. The same occurred in 1956 (with a reduction in assembly) and again in 1958. This is evidence of the degree of demand management at the micro level, and of nonprice rationing. Car sales were regulated by foreign exchange deposit requirements, queuing, and financial regulations governing hire purchase arrangements.

Table 3.5 also provides evidence of the limited extent of the market accessible to import-competing firms when import protection effectively excludes the possibility of exporting. The total supply (and revealed demand) for cars grew after 1944 from a very small amount to a maximum of only 46,000 vehicles in 1955. Over the period 1959–62 the supply of cars had fallen to an average of 32,000 cars per year.

Table 3.2 shows that import prices fell slightly over the period 1952–8, reflecting the growth in world output during the reconstruction period and

Table 3.6 Relative importance of pastoral exports, 1941–1969

Year	Pastoral exports as percentage of total visible exports
1941	95.6
1946	90.4
1951	97.4
1956	94.5
1961	94.0
1966	91.0
1967	90.0
1968	86.8
1969	84.1

Source: Department of Statistics, New Zealand Yearbook, various years

the stability in world product and financial attitudes adopted by the major industrial countries.

Export prices were volatile, reflecting the usual adjustment patterns of commodity markets and New Zealand's dependence on agricultural commodity exports. The deficit in the balance of payments before borrowing alternated from negative to positive as a result of the fixed exchange rate policy and fluctuating export prices.

The liberalization episode did not lead to an increase in the importance of trade. This may be gauged by the data on trade per capita presented by Rayner and Lattimore (1988, appendix table C.15). Over the period 1950–60, the volume of exports and imports per capita fell. Clearly the relaxation in import protection was highly selective and maintained protection for the import substitution sector.

Over the early part of the liberalization episode, foreign public debt declined even in current New Zealand dollar terms (table 3.7), in spite of the 26 percent decline in the terms of trade in 1952. Foreign debt rose 15 percent in real terms over the whole episode (1951–7).

This income performance did not match growth in other industrialized countries. It has been estimated that New Zealand's real income level had fallen to seventh position by 1960 from third in 1953 (Gould, 1982).

Over the decade 1949–59, agricultural output (which was mainly destined for export) grew at an annual average rate of 2.5 percent (table 3.3), despite an increasingly unfavorable real effective rate of exchange. There are two reasons for this. First, a wide range of new farming technologies became available at this time, building on earlier advances in farm management, fertilizers, and grass variety selection. Second, New

Table 3.7 New Zealand public debt, 1948–1958 (million New Zealand dollars)

Year	Overseas	Domestic	Change in government borrowing as percentage of GNP
1948	210	988	n.a.
1949	162	1,068	n.a.
1950	158	1,130	5.3
1951	156	1,178	3.3
1952	156	1,152	0.0
1953	156	1,180	1.8
1954	176	1,234	4.4
1955	196	1,262	2.6
1956	192	1,278	0.6
1957	208	1,304	2.0
1958	208	1,358	2.5

n.a., not available.

Source: Department of Statistics, *New Zealand Yearbook*, various years

Zealand was able to expand the agricultural land base and farm numbers through a variety of programs to settle new farmers. In some respects this period was New Zealand's "green revolution."

Of course, the rate of farming output growth needs to be seen within the context of the real effective exchange rates (REERs) for exports and imports. The trade policy setting constituted a significant tax on exports.

Prices

The modest monetary expansion to accommodate fluctuating fiscal deficits contributed to inflation rates averaging 4 percent over the decade of the 1950s (table 2.17). This inflation in the presence of financial controls meant that real interest rates on government bonds were negative until 1955 and less than 3 percent throughout the remainder of the episode.

REERs for both the export- and import-competing sectors (see table 3.3) were high at the beginning of the episode, reflecting the devaluation, high export prices, and trade policy liberalization. The REER for exports fell markedly with the terms of trade, the import rate less so owing to the fixed exchange rate. The export rate then tended to rise over the period to 1955 and the import rate tended to fall as a result of liberalization. This trend was reversed in 1957 when import controls were reintroduced and export prices fell.

Overview of the Episode

There is considerable doubt whether this episode, despite its marked reduction in the coverage of import licensing, should strictly be termed a liberalization program at all.

Economic management by the first National government continued most of the interventions of the previous government. It did this in an economic climate highly favorable to traditional New Zealand exports, which added to the pent-up domestic demand that remained after World War II. Real output in manufacturing grew at a modest pace to satisfy this demand, but such growth was eventually to be limited by the size of the market, given high remaining levels of import protection. The critical questions are how much more it would have grown in a less protectionist environment and to what extent the manufacturing sector would have developed in competitive areas without protection.

Since the underlying philosophy of market regulation and import substitution remained, export dependence on agriculture was reinforced. Thus it was perhaps only a matter of time before a drop in the terms of trade would provide an excuse for extensive reimposition of import licensing.

4

The Second Episode, Phase One, 1962–1979: Liberalization and Accompanying Policies

Introduction of the Policy

Antecedents

The second Labour government came into power in late 1957 and immediately reintroduced blanket import-licensing controls in an attempt to protect the fixed exchange rate and the foreign exchange reserve position. This action brought the first liberalization episode to a close. Import licensing remained in place throughout the three-year term of this government.

In 1960, a new National government came into office which would remain in power throughout the episode with one break from 1972 to 1975. During its first term in office (1960–3), the National government slowly began to alter the degree of import substitution bias in various ways. This process continues to the present day. For this reason the period from 1962 to date is taken to be one long liberalization episode.

Within this episode it is possible to distinguish three phases. In the first phase of this second episode (1962–79) there does not appear to have been a significant reduction in protection for the import-competing sector and indeed there were some increases in assistance. The reduction in import substitution bias came about through increasing "tariff compensation" to the export sector. The second phase of the second episode (1979–84) is characterized by an actual reduction in import protection accompanied by even greater tariff compensation. When the policy mix of phase two proved unsustainable in 1984, the third phase began (1984 to date); this involved reducing both import protection and tariff compensation.

Objectives

The first phase of this liberalization episode encompasses seven governments of both major parties. The period 1962–79 saw major commodity
market (figure 4.1) and policy changes abroad, including the two oil
shocks, the commodity boom of 1972–5, and accelerating world inflation
beginning in the Vietnam War era. Consequently, there were many
changes in policy direction. Initially, however, the episode began with
three principal objectives:

1   to continue to encourage import-competing industries with selective
    import protection;
2   to promote increased export earnings from the agricultural sector
    through production assistance in achieving target rates of growth
    in investment, output, and exports (sheep numbers and farmers'
    incomes became leading indicators of policy balance);
3   to diversify the export base through export incentives to the nonagri-
    cultural manufacturing sector.

Policy Implementation

Import Protection

The first objective involved refining the import-licensing system to remove
restrictions (other than tariffs) on goods that did not compete with the
output of New Zealand industry. As can be seen in table 3.4, import
licensing covered 74 percent of all imports at the beginning of the episode.
This coverage declined almost monotonically over the episode to 24
percent by 1979.

   In 1962 the government introduced a change in the import-licensing
policy, affirming selective supplementary import licenses for materials that
were subsequently used to produce export items. This was perhaps the first
explicit recognition that the import protection system was affecting the
pattern of export development; the only previous tariff compensation
provided to the export sector had been in the form of government-
sponsored research, quality control and extension services, subsidized (at 1
percent) overdraft facilities for the agricultural marketing boards, and
international market development services provided by the Department of
Trade and Industry.

   Tariff levels changed little throughout the period. From time to time,
however, the wholesale sales tax system (with differential rates ranging
from 10 to 60 percent) was modified to dampen demand for so-called

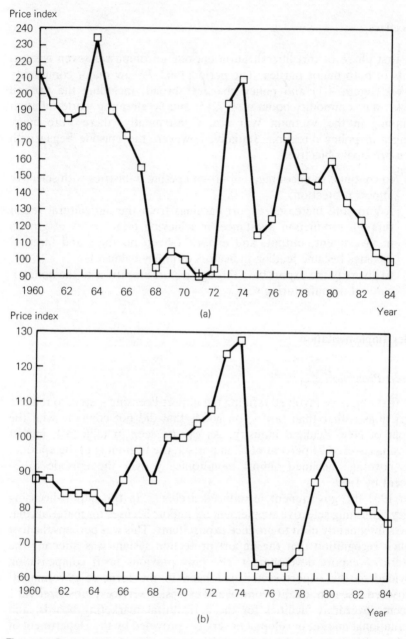

Figure 4.1 Real export prices for agricultural products. The New Zealand export price for each commodity was converted to US dollars and deflated by an index of gross domestic product for OECD countries expressed in US dollars (1970=100): (a) wool (greasy, slipe, and scoured); (b) beef (fresh, chilled, or frozen); (c) sheep meat (fresh, chilled, or frozen); (d) butter

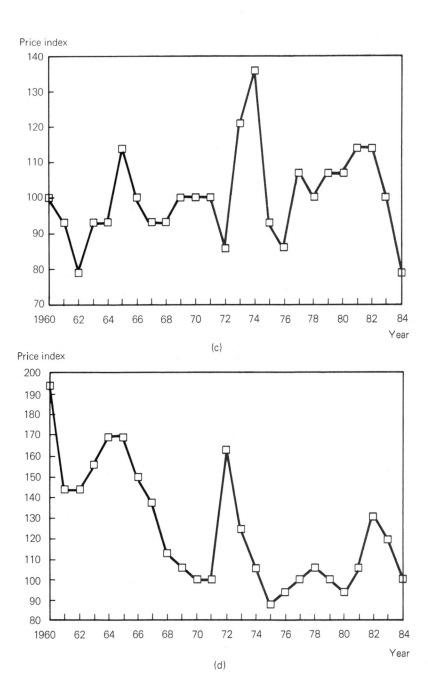

Figure 4.1 (continued)

"luxury" products, many of which were imported goods. In 1967, for example, the sales tax was raised from 33.3 to 40 percent for cars and from 20 to 40 percent for motorcycles. Both products have a high import content. Similarly high sales taxes were applied to other import products, including computers, electronic equipment, cameras, and perfume, which added to the domestic price of imports.

Export Growth

Production grants and subsidies to the traditional export sector, agriculture, were also increased throughout this phase. Farmer development expenditures had been tax deductible (up to specified limits) since before 1964. These limits were changed regularly to stimulate investment in primary agriculture.

In 1966, the "nil standard value" scheme was introduced, enabling farmers to postpone indefinitely the tax liability on increased livestock numbers. In 1968 the fertilizer subsidy was raised and special depreciation allowances were introduced for the meat processing industry. Pesticide subsidies were introduced in 1969. In 1970, farm incomes fell and fertilizers subsidies were raised again, and then further raised in 1971. Government finance was made available to the meat processing industry in 1971 to help it meet the higher hygiene standards imposed by importing countries. In 1973 farm incomes rose significantly with overseas prices, and farm subsidies were reduced.

The approach to farm subsidies was based on income adequacy. This approach reinforced traditional thinking that farming was the only basis for economic growth. Clearly a political concept so solidly entrenched would be difficult to dislodge when it was eventually decided in 1984 to begin dismantling the policy.

The first oil shock coincided with large reductions in overseas prices for agricultural goods (figure 4.1). From 1976 onwards, agricultural subsidies rose significantly, firstly to buffer farmers against declining prices and secondly to stimulate export growth in order to finance a major new emphasis on government-sponsored capital projects, many of which were designed to replace imported energy. These projects formed part of the "think big" strategy of government.

In 1976 the livestock incentive scheme was introduced, which amounted to a 200 percent tax write-off for increased stock numbers when taken in conjunction with the "nil standard value" scheme. Then, in 1978, in the face of continuing low export prices, the supplementary minimum price scheme was introduced.

The export promotion package during this episode also included some elements of the state capital development projects sponsored by the government. The "think big" approach actually began in 1965 when the government approved the development of the New Zealand Steel Company which was intended to generate export earnings as well as to replace imports. In 1968 the government reached agreement with a private consortium to build an aluminum smelter at Bluff with a long-term electricity supply at low prices. The output of aluminum ingots was to be exported. Later in this phase, the ammonia–urea plant and the Motunui synthetic fuel plant (two "think big" projects of the late 1970s) were developed with long-term export earning potential based on developing natural gas reserves. In at least two instances the "think big" approach involved projects cascading from other projects. Governmental concern that the supply of electricity generated by large-scale state hydroelectric development in the South Island might outstrip demand fueled the decision to undertaken the long-term agreement for the Bluff smelter. Similarly, the ammonia and synthetic fuel plants are linked to earlier state investment in natural gas exploration which found major reservoirs of the Taranaki coast. Again, finding gas raised public concerns as to how it might be used.

Export Diversification

In 1967 an export development conference was held which resulted in the introduction of a 150 percent tax write-off for tourist development expenses. The following year a general export incentive scheme was introduced based upon the value of increased export sales over a base year. This was the first in a series of export incentive programs that continued until 1985. Measures were also introduced to assist the fishing industry, which became increasingly export oriented.

The export incentive schemes were mainly designed to stimulate exports of nontraditional products (though, perhaps because they were subject to control by government departments, these schemes have always included some traditional products such as hides). Traditional products such as carcasses and primal meat cuts, bulk wool, apples, and bulk dairy products were not included; these products were marketed through special credit arrangements involving the large agricultural marketing boards. Three of these boards (the Meat, Dairy, and Apple and Pear Boards) had monopoly export control.

The different treatment accorded to the products controlled by these boards has two explanations. Firstly, the public and policymakers tended to view the export and marketing organizations, and the credit subsidies embodied in them, as net export subsidies. While this perception is undoubtedly correct for the credit facilities, the evidence suggests that the regulatory control available to the marketing boards in the form of export licensing tended to tax exports rather than subsidize them. The second reason is that the export incentive schemes were an attempt to diversify exports away from the traditional products.

In 1968 an export incentive scheme was introduced in the form of a tax deduction of 15 percent of specified increases in export income. In 1972 the deduction was increased to 20 percent. In 1977 the scheme was changed to a net export incentive based on total rather than incremental exports. The estimated nominal value of the export incentive program is given in table 4.1.

Monetary and Fiscal Policy

Throughout most of the phase – from 1964 until after the first oil shock – the government followed a traditional fixed exchange rate policy with foreign exchange control regulations. Until 1971 the New Zealand dollar

Table 4.1 Nominal percentage rates of assistance for exports and imports, 1958–1986

| Year | Nominal export subsidies | | | | Other manufacturing | Nominal import protection |
	Sheep meat	Wool	Beef	Dairy		
1958	0.1	0.0	0.1	0.2	0.0	55
1959	0.1	0.0	0.1	0.2	0.0	55
1960	0.1	0.0	0.1	0.2	0.0	55
1961	0.2	0.0	0.1	0.2	0.0	55
1962	0.2	0.0	0.2	0.2	0.0	55
1963	0.3	0.0	0.2	0.2	0.0	55
1964	0.3	0.0	0.2	0.2	9.0	55
1965	0.4	0.0	0.3	0.2	9.0	55
1966	0.4	0.0	0.3	0.2	9.0	55
1967	0.4	0.0	0.3	0.2	10.0	55
1968	0.4	0.0	0.2	0.2	14.0	55
1969	0.3	0.0	0.2	0.2	12.0	55
1970	0.3	0.0	0.1	0.2	12.0	55
1971	0.3	0.0	0.1	0.2	12.0	55
1972	0.5	0.0	0.1	0.2	11.0	55
1973	0.7	0.0	0.2	0.1	16.0	55
1974	0.9	0.0	0.3	0.1	15.0	55
1975	1.1	0.0	0.4	0.0	14.0	55
1976	1.3	0.0	0.5	0.0	13.9	55
1977	1.6	0.0	0.5	0.7	13.9	55
1978	1.9	0.0	0.6	1.4	13.9	55
1979	2.2	0.0	0.7	2.1	17.4	55
1980	2.2	0.0	0.9	0.4	17.4	55
1981	9.3	13.9	5.2	0.4	17.4	55
1982	24.6	20.4	5.2	0.4	17.4	49
1983	34.0	7.0	1.1	0.4	17.4	43
1984	34.0	7.0	1.1	0.4	17.4	37
1985	1.0	0.0	0.5	0.2	8.7	34
1986	1.0	0.0	0.5	0.2	4.4	30

Source: Lattimore, 1987

was fixed against sterling, with a major devaluation in late 1967. From 1971–3 a fixed rate was maintained against the US dollar. From 1973–9 the exchange rate was fixed in relation to a trade-weighted basket of currencies.

The targets of both monetary and fiscal policy throughout the episode were employment, real output, and business viability. Indeed, commentators from the Reserve Bank of New Zealand have often maintained that monetary policy was purely accommodating over the phase, with no explicit inflation goals or monetary growth targets. This Keynesian approach to fiscal policy is illustrated by the volatility of money supply growth shown in table 4.2.

The result was a gradual acceleration in domestic inflation rates after 1967, caused by the fixed exchange rate policy, the 17.5 percent devaluation in 1967, and increasing inflation rates worldwide at the time. In New Zealand as elsewhere, inflation rates moved to double digit levels in the early 1970s, but the New Zealand rates were generally higher than those of other OECD countries throughout the phase to 1979 (table 2.17).

The money supply was influenced directly throughout the phase by frequent changes in the reserve ratios of financial institutions and indirectly by varying controls over interest rates. These controls resulted in nonprice rationing of the available credit and enabled government to direct the usage of funds to some extent. An exception was the period 1976–81 when a relatively flexible interest rate policy was in place.

Table 4.2 M1, M2, and M3: annual percentage rate of growth, 1967–1982

Year ending Mar	Money supply M1	Other demand deposits	Money supply and other demand deposits M2	Time deposits	Money supply and selected liquid assets M3
1967	0.4	1.2	0.9	21.8	5.1
1968	− 2.9	4.3	1.5	11.2	3.7
1969	4.0	5.3	4.8	14.5	7.2
1970	7.2	1.8	3.8	23.8	9.1
1971	5.0	4.0	4.4	14.9	7.5
1972	13.1	6.0	8.7	13.6	10.3
1973	25.0	18.2	20.9	28.0	23.3
1974	14.4	12.4	13.2	20.1	15.6
1975	2.6	2.1	2.3	3.5	2.8
1976	19.8	8.3	13.2	23.9	17.0
1977	5.9	5.7	5.7	31.5	15.6
1978	1.8	2.3	2.1	27.9	13.3
1979	18.3	14.9	16.4	28.9	22.5
1980	5.5	1.3	32.2	27.4	15.7
1981	14.2	6.3	9.9	17.5	14.2
1982	17.5	7.8	12.5	19.8	16.7

Source: Reserve Bank of New Zealand, Reserve Bank Bulletin, various years

Before 1976, controls on interest rates and other forms of credit were pervasive. The government directly set interest rates on national and local government securities and overdrafts and set deposit rates at trading and savings banks.

As mentioned earlier, fiscal policy complemented monetary policy in the effort to maintain output and employment. The government ran a high persistent budget deficit throughout this phase, particularly after 1973 (table 4.3). The rising deficit at this time was associated with expanding social and welfare programs to provide a national superannuation scheme, increasing benefits for the rising number of unemployment beneficiaries, expanding export assistance measures, and the proliferating government capital projects.

From 1938 to 1984, New Zealand operated a system of foreign exchange control regulations. From 1958 all export receipts were required to be returned to New Zealand via the banking system. In addition, controls were in place on all foreign exchange payments from New Zealand and on private holdings of foreign currencies and securities by New Zealanders. In 1962, profit repatriation to foreign parent companies was considerably relaxed and extended to enable foreigners to repatriate capital gains.

In 1966 a limited market in overseas securities was permitted under the close supervision of the Reserve Bank. Capital controls were thus one sided. New Zealand residents were under strict supervision of capital outflows; foreign companies were not. Even in joint venture operations New Zealand firms required Reserve Bank approval that varied depending on the balance-of-payments situation (Economic Monitoring Group (EMG), 1984).

Table 4.3 Government budget data, 1970–1980

Year ending Mar	Total government expenditure (million NZ$)	Total government revenue (million NZ$)	Fiscal deficit before borrowing (million NZ$)	Fiscal deficit (percentage of GDP)	Annual percentage change	
					Expenditure	Revenue
1970	1,354	1,278	76	1.5	8.6	14.9
1971	1,636	1,556	81	1.4	20.8	21.8
1972	1,903	1,830	72	1.1	16.3	17.7
1973	2,262	1,056	206	2.6	18.9	12.3
1974	2,679	2,438	242	2.6	18.5	18.6
1975	3,462	3,072	390	3.9	29.2	26.0
1976	4,444	3,443	1,002	8.7	28.4	12.1
1977	4,578	4,072	506	4.4	3.0	18.3
1978	5,669	4,974	694	4.6	23.8	22.2
1979	6,848	5,402	1,446	8.3	20.8	8.6
1980	7,587	6,560	1,027	5.2	10.8	21.4

Source: Reserve Bank of New Zealand, Reserve Bank Bulletin, various years

Political Considerations

The National Party came to power in 1960 in the aftermath of the so-called "black budget" introduced by Labour to control expenditure. This budget contained a number of unpopular measures, including sales taxes on alcohol, tobacco, and other items to control spending. The leader of the new National government, Sir Keith Holyoake, was able to capitalize on the situation.

The National government did not reverse Labour's objectives but their approach to achieving them was perhaps less ideological. They promised a policy of industrial development through selective import protection in both the public and private sectors. However, they also attempted to stimulate the traditional and nontraditional export sectors.

In 1960 an industrial development conference was held which generally accepted the infant industry argument for industrial growth. This conference was the first of what was to be a long series of similar conferences – the most recent was in 1985 – to test public acceptance of industrial and economic policy and to explore potential changes. A review of the customs tariff was also begun in 1960.

The National government established an agricultural production conference (APC) in 1964 to explore the growth potential of the sector. The APC was to be an important turning point, because the criteria it established for judging the adequacy of export sector policies would be used for 20 years.

The industrial development conference had reaffirmed the desirability of the import substitution policy. Without making the connection explicit, the APC defined growth targets for agricultural livestock and farmers' incomes as necessary adjuncts to ensure a reasonable rate of economic growth. The APC made a series of policy recommendations which were reaffirmed by the national development conference (NDC) established in 1967.

The conferences had established a pattern of economic development strategy based on intersectoral consensus. The NDC finally achieved a measure of consensus and recommended the phasing out of the import-licensing system and its replacement with tariffs in 1969. However, after much lobbying, the government in its 1972 budget announced its decision to postpone implementation of these recommendations: significant increases in export incentives were introduced instead. This consensus approach to the politics of economic policymaking assisted in maintaining the National Party in power for four consecutive terms from 1960 to 1972.

This first phase was thus one of attempting to find a politically acceptable adjustment path away from the constraints of high import protection. The export sector was increasingly bought off with tariff compensation until the end of the 1970s. It appeared to be simply not possible to negotiate structural reform publicly. Presumably the political conditions were also insufficiently favorable to attempt it privately.

5

The Second Episode, Phase One, 1962–1979: Economic Performance

Introduction

Taken in isolation New Zealand's economic performance in the early 1960s looks respectable enough. Over the period 1960–5 real GNP grew at a rate of 4.9 percent per year, the terms of trade were at high levels by historic standards, and unemployment was very low. Employment was growing at 2 percent per year.

The structural problems are more apparent in the trade performance. The 3 percent annual growth rate of exports from 1960 to 1964 imposed a real restraint on growth. The proportion of exports remained at over 80 percent in agricultural products. Not surprisingly, the relative volume of nonagricultural exports actually declined from the 1950s to the period 1960–4 (table 2.16).

Real export prices for the principal agricultural products were high in the early 1960s, especially for wool and dairy products (as shown in figure 4.1). Thus one of the important preconditions for growth was being met.

Foreign Trade and Protection

Estimates of Trade Protection

No consistent time series of import protection and export subsidization is available for New Zealand for the post-World War II period. This section describes the estimates that are available in an attempt to paint a picture of changes throughout this liberalization phase. Some important evidence on import protection toward the end of the first phase relates to policy changes in phase two; for this reason protection levels over both phase one and phase two are considered together in this section.

Elkan (1972) has estimated nominal and effective rates of import protection for selected industries for the period 1955–8 and 1964–7. Elley (1976) estimated protection for 1972–3. O'Dea and Horsfield (1981) have done the same for 1978–9. Candler and Hampton (1966) and Hampton (1965) provided other protection estimates over the period 1955–79. The scope and methodologies adopted in these studies varied, but an attempt has been made (EMG, 1984) to bring the estimates together. The EMG results for selected industries are presented in the first four columns of tables 5.1 and 5.2.

The weighted average nominal import protection reported at the bottom of table 5.1 has been computed using domestic use weights taken from Lattimore (1986) for the periods from 1955–8 and 1978–9. For later periods, industry figures were not available in detail at the time of writing but average estimates for the periods 1981–4 and 1984–5 were available; these are also presented in table 5.1.

Table 5.1 Nominal rates of import protection, 1955–1985 (million New Zealand dollars)

Industry group	1955–8	1964–7	1972–3	1978–9	1981–4	1984–5
Food[a]	30	30	30	30	n.a.	n.a.
Beverages	120	134	64	13	n.a.	n.a.
Tobacco	120	134	64	13	n.a.	n.a.
Textiles	29	62	29	21	n.a.	n.a.
Footwear and clothing[b]	44	88	56	48	n.a.	n.a.
Furniture	44	68	28	21	n.a.	n.a.
Printing	21	30	0	0	n.a.	n.a.
Leather products	21	53	36	29	n.a.	n.a.
Rubber products	22	56	44	37	n.a.	n.a.
Chemical products	29	45	33	26	n.a.	n.a.
Petroleum products	17	3	− 10	0	n.a.	n.a.
Nonmetallic minerals	4	23	19	13	n.a.	n.a.
Basic metal products	5	61	12	6	n.a.	n.a.
Metal products	39	81	39	32	n.a.	n.a.
Machinery	46	59	33	36	n.a.	n.a.
Electrical products	42	92	63	36	n.a.	n.a.
Transport equipment	61	48	52	23	n.a.	n.a.
Miscellaneous products	34	74	45	37	n.a.	n.a.
Weighted average excluding food	43	61	36	25	[c]	[d]
All industries	34	54	35	26	50	37

n.a., not available.
[a] Author's estimates, customs tariff range 0–45 percent.
[b] Weighted average clothing 66 percent, footwear 34 percent.
[c] Estimated on the basis of the weighted average tariff of 30 percent (Manufacturers' Federation, 1985) plus the average import-licensing premium reported by Lattimore (1987a).
[d] The average tariff (footnote c), plus the average import-licensing premium over the period 1981–5 (rounds 1–30) based on data from the Department of Trade and Industry.

Table 5.2 Effective rates of protection due to import protection in manufacturing industries, 1955–1979 (percent)

Industries	1955–8	1964–7	1972–3	1978–9
Beverages and tobacco	−31.3	−9.6	61.0	20.8
Wool textiles	78.3	101.7	89.0	44.8
Other textiles	41.1	195.5	67.1	a
Footwear	57.1	98.7	68.7	51.1
Clothing	124.4	1,105.4	169.4	139.7
Furniture	91.9	200.0	41.3	−28.7
Printed products	16.3	29.4	−19.2	−12.1
Leather goods	37.4	192.9	112.1	84.0
Rubber goods	21.8	90.6	111.1	67.5
Chemical fertilizers	−23.8	−29.7	−1.5	8.9
Petroleum products	42.8	−39.7	−65.9	−47.5
Other chemicals	45.7	75.6	104.6	77.0
Nonmetallic minerals	−15.1	13.9	22.8	16.6
Basic metal products	−5.8	161.8	10.3	3.0
Metal products	83.2	616.5	99.5	74.2
Machinery	135.9	99.2	57.0	81.1
Electrical products	116.6	406.1	365.3	b
Vehicles assembly	2,428.3	101.5	−165.4	40.8
Other transport goods	38.5	32.8	49.8	c
Miscellaneous	69.0	186.4	92.8	77.1

[a] Included in wool textiles.
[b] Included in machinery.
[c] Included in vehicle assembly.

Source: EMG, 1984

It must be recognized that the quality of protection estimates varies between time periods. Elkan (1972) made direct estimates of the extent to which the New Zealand prices of manufactured products exceeded the landed cost of competing products for the periods 1955–8 and 1964–7. Since these are direct estimates some confidence can be placed in their accuracy. In the mid-1950s the import-licensing policy was being dismantled but it was reinstated in 1958 and carried on in this form into the 1960s. The average nominal protection estimate reflects this movement, rising on average from 34 percent in the period 1955–8 to 54 percent for the period 1964–7. The protective effect of the tariff itself is thought to have remained virtually the same over the whole phase, with tariff reviews merely changing definitions. This distribution of the tariffs after the end of the first phase, when the average tariff was 30 percent is shown in table 5.3.

At the end of the first phase, tariffs remained essentially the same as they had been at its inception, and the introduction of an import license tendering system (to be discussed in chapter 6) provided an opportunity to measure directly the extent of import protection for the first time since the

Table 5.3 Tariff rates, 1981–1982: goods outside industry plans

Tariff (%)	Manufacturing output (except industry plans) (million NZ$)
Free	85
1–10	318
11–20	527
21–5	365
26–30	322
31–40	2,213
41–50	604
Over 50	12
Specific tariffs	283

The weighted average of the tariffs is 30 percent.

Source: Department of Trade and Industry, *Import Licensing Worksheets*, various years

Elkan study for 1964–7. In 1981–2 the average import license premium was 20 percent (table 6.1), giving an average nominal import protection rate of 50 percent (table 5.1). While the 1981–2 estimate could be low, given the narrow coverage of goods entering the early tender rounds, it is very similar to that estimated for the period 1964–7. This calls into question the lower intervening estimates for 1972–3 and 1978–9 shown in table 5.1, since import protection policy for import-competing industries was not changed in the 1970s and the tariff alone offered 30 percent protection.

The estimates for 1972–3 and 1978–9 were not made directly but were projected from Elkan's 1964–7 estimate based on movements in price indices, a technique that is prone to error given the broadness of the indices and the effects of technological change.

For these reasons, the nominal rates of import protection are assumed to remain at around 54 percent throughout this first phase.

Effective rates of protection (table 5.2) were considerably higher and more variable than nominal rates throughout the phase. This reflects the interrelationships between firms in the various industries and the *ad hoc* way in which the government and the Department of Trade and Industry controlled and administered the import-licensing system. Import-licensing protection was available virtually on demand, as the Department attempted to develop new and existing import-competing firms. Protection rates were limited mainly by the willingness of consumers to pay for domestically purchased goods.

The reductions in import-licensing coverage, referred to earlier, involved delicensing goods not produced in New Zealand and raw materials required by industry. The tight licensing restrictions that remained on levied goods, however, maintained the high level of effective import protection.

Foreign Trade

During the 1960s the volume of imports grew at an average annual rate of 5.3 percent, matched by an equivalent rate of export growth (Rayner and Lattimore, 1988, appendix table C.15). In the 1970s the trade gap widened.

The changes in import composition reflect the pattern of border protection. Imports of finished goods declined as a share of imports from 41 percent in 1960 to 28 percent in 1980. In absolute terms, real imports of finished or manufactured goods increased by only 8 percent over this period (Rayner and Lattimore, 1988, appendix table C.16).

The share of oil and chemical imports increased to compensate for this declining share. In short, imports became increasingly concentrated in raw materials and capital equipment, with little increase in import penetration of the final goods markets. This is consistent with the estimated constant high import protection rate throughout the phase.

The composition of exports changed quite markedly. Exports of manufactures and other nontraditional products, mainly from primary New Zealand commodities such as fish, horticultural products, grain, and seeds, increased from 16 to 44 percent of total exports over the period 1964–80. Growth was particularly rapid over the decade 1966–76. Most of the products were eligible for the export tax incentives.

During the 1950s the ratio of imports and exports to GNP was above 25 percent (33 percent in 1950, 26 percent in 1956). By 1960 the ratio had fallen to 20 percent. In 1970 the ratio was 16 percent and it remained at that level in 1980.

Foreign borrowing changed markedly from the beginning to the end of the phase (Rayner and Lattimore, 1988, appendix table C.13). Over the 1960s total foreign capital inflows averaged 1 percent of GNP, but in the 1970s government and private overseas borrowing increased rapidly, except during 1973–4 when the terms of trade were at very high levels. This pattern of high external borrowing continued beyond the end of this phase.

Macroeconomic Performance

Production Growth

At the outset of this episode there were concerns with the relative rate of growth of the economy. New Zealand was beginning to fall seriously behind other industrialized countries in terms of GDP per capita,

Table 5.4 Per capita gross domestic product of
New Zealand among the highest income
countries, 1953–1978

Year	New Zealand's position
1953	Third
1960	Seventh
1965	Eighth
1970	Seventeenth
1975	Nineteenth
1978	Twenty-second

Source: Gould, 1982

especially over the decade of the 1960s (table 5.4). This reflects both relatively high rates of population growth in New Zealand and the high rates of economic growth in other industrialized economies.

The average rate of growth in total real GNP was slow in the mid-1960s (table 2.6). It rose to average 4.9 percent from 1970 to 1975 when export prices were at record levels, and then fell again to 0.6 percent in the late 1970s. The real output of selected industries is given in table 5.5 (and Rayner and Lattimore, 1988, appendix tables C.20 and C.21). From 1964 to 1969 farm output continued to grow at over 3 percent a year, slowed rapidly during the 1970s, and then accelerated again to over 3 percent from 1979 onwards.

Fluctuations in beef and sheep production both contributed to the higher 1960s growth and the negative growth at times during the 1970s, but after 1979 sheep production was the major contributor to the accelerating growth of agriculture.

In the manufacturing sector, the largest industry was associated with the processing and marketing of food and fiber products. The food manufacturing sector almost doubled in size over the period 1964–80. The electrical and metal products industries also grew rapidly. In the latter part of this phase the picture changed. The highly protected clothing and car assembly industries declined in size from the period 1974–7, as did the carpet industry which was less protected. In fact all industries shown in table 5.5 declined in real net output from the mid-1970s with the exception of the food manufacturing sector.

The first three industries listed in table 5.5 are highly export oriented, the remainder much less so. The reasons underlying their changing fortunes in the late 1970s are thus somewhat different. The increasingly overvalued exchange rate affected them all. Industry assistance was quite different for each, as the export and import protection rates show.

Table 5.5 Real value added,[a] selected industries, 1961–1982 (million 1978 New Zealand dollars)

Year	Food manufacturing	Wood products	Carpets	Car assembly	Clothing	Metal products	Electrical products
1960	383	180	13	32	92	92	42
1961	345	193	16	41	99	105	52
1962[b]	411	195	21	45	102	113	58
1963	297	142	22	48	100	93	52
1964	328	152	22	54	91	108	67
1965	293	172	19	52	91	126	82
1966	355	184	20	56	96	143	75
1967	322	172	21	55	93	140	76
1968	373	157	25	41	90	127	64
1969	389	164	27	37	85	128	63
1970	375	166	29	56	93	145	69
1971	388	173	31	50	95	169	77
1972	458	177	30	58	101	183	81
1973	516	192	31	68	100	191	81
1974	408	221	33	79	111	220	94
1975	539	241	30	79	119	245	150
1976	589	218	24	57	109	222	164
1977	686	253	27	70	131	279	150
1978	n.a.	n.a.	n.a.	n.a.	n.a.	n.a.	n.a.
1979	605	187	17	55	110	231	143
1980	n.a.	n.a.	n.a.	n.a.	n.a.	n.a.	n.a.
1981	n.a.	n.a.	n.a.	n.a.	n.a.	n.a.	n.a.
1982	710	204	22	69	109	230	152
Percentage increase 1964–82	116	34	16	28	20	83	127

n.a., not available.
[a] Value added deflated by the consumer price index.
[b] The definition of value added was changed in 1962–3 making it difficult to compare performance before and after that period.
Source: Department of Statistics, Census of Manufacturing, various years

Employment

Total employment increased by around 50 percent from 1960 to 1980, mainly in the service sector of the economy, while employment in the agricultural sector (farming and food manufacturing) increased by 26 percent, from 145,000 to 183,000. Perhaps surprisingly, the farm workforce remained stable over the period (table 5.6).

The changes in employment from the mid-1970s are interesting. From this time the exchange rate was increasingly overvalued as a result of monetary, fiscal, and exchange rate policies. The agricultural sector was at least partially compensated for these effects of overvaluation by production and export subsidies. The import-competing industries – car assembly, metal fabrication, clothing, and electrical products – did not receive such compensation, however. In spite of the high levels of import protection, employment levels began to fall in all these industries.

Table 5.6 Employment, selected industries, 1960–1983 (thousand full-time persons)

Year	Farming	Food manufacturing	Car assembly	Wood products	Clothing	Carpets	Metal products	Electrical products
1960	114	31	2.4	18.1	18.7	1.2	8.9	4.7
1961	112	32	2.8	19.0	19.3	1.5	9.7	5.5
1962	112	33	3.0	19.1	19.4	1.8	10.0	5.9
1963	112	34	3.2	18.6	19.0	1.8	11.1	6.6
1964	114	34	3.9	18.8	19.6	1.9	11.8	7.4
1965	114	35	4.1	19.9	20.3	2.0	13.1	8.7
1966	115	36	4.3	20.6	20.7	2.4	14.3	9.3
1967	115	37	4.1	20.7	21.0	2.6	14.7	9.5
1968	113	39	3.7	19.4	20.0	2.5	14.1	8.7
1969	111	40	3.5	19.7	19.2	2.8	14.4	8.7
1970	105	42	4.0	20.2	20.2	2.9	15.2	9.2
1971	106	43	5.0	20.2	21.4	3.1	17.8	10.0
1972	104	44	5.5	19.9	21.2	3.2	18.4	10.0
1973	103	45	5.8	20.6	20.5	3.2	19.3	10.3
1974	108	46	6.4	21.9	20.5	3.0	20.5	11.4
1975	103	63	7.0	22.9	21.1	2.5	23.0	14.2
1976	108	66	7.3	23.7	20.3	2.8	23.0	18.5
1977	112	67	6.6	24.1	21.5	2.9	24.3	14.4
1978	117	n.a.	n.a.	n.a.	n.a.	n.a.	n.a.	n.a.
1979	114	66	8.6	22.6	20.5	2.1	24.1	15.9
1980	117	n.a.	n.a.	n.a.	n.a.	n.a.	n.a.	n.a.
1981	112	n.a.	n.a.	n.a.	n.a.	n.a.	n.a.	n.a.
1982	117	70	6.8	22.3	18.1	2.3	23.1	15.6
1983	118	n.a.	n.a.	n.a.	n.a.	n.a.	n.a.	n.a.

n.a., not available.

Sources: Department of Statistics, Census of Manufacturing, various years; Wallace and Philpott, 1984

Investment

Net investment in the major farm types is given by Rayner and Lattimore (1988, appendix table C.22). Net investment in dairy farms remained high at the beginning of the episode but fell along with investment in sheep farms until 1972. The rise in export prices in 1973–4 resulted in a temporary increase in investment in all types of farms. Investment remained low throughout most of the 1970s but began to increase thereafter until the end of the phase. The impetus for this rise was a brief increase in the terms of trade in 1979, followed by increasing production and export subsidies after the export price fell again in 1980–1.

Price Variables

From 1964 to 1970 the consumer price index rose on average by around 4 percent a year with a larger rise in 1967 following devaluation. These rates were modest in OECD terms at the time.

From the commodity price boom onwards, the inflation rate accelerated to an average of around 13 percent from 1974 to 1980. This was significantly higher than for other OECD countries.

The real and nominal exchange rates and the terms of trade are given in table 5.7. At the beginning of this phase the real exchange rate was maintained while the terms of trade remained higher; however, both declined after 1967. Following the 1967 devaluation, the real exchange rate fell almost continuously with export prices until 1975 when, following the first oil shock, it began to rise, but much more slowly than the decline in the terms of trade. With a brief fall in 1979 coinciding with a short rise in the terms of trade, the real exchange rate continued to rise until 1980.

Table 5.7 Terms of trade and real exchange rate, 1958–1985

Year	Exchange rate		Terms of trade index (1957 = 100)	Price nontradeables index (1982 = 1,000)	Price tradeables (primary and manufactured) index[c] (1982 = 1,000)	Real exchange rate index[d] (1982 = 1,000)
	Nominal (US$ per NZ$)	Index[a] (foreign exchange per NZ$; 1976–7 = 1,000)				
1958	1.40	1133	85	178	171	1041
1959	1.40	1205	100	185	172	1075
1960	1.40	1214	96	184	176	1045
1961	1.40	1214	90	186	172	1081
1962	1.39	1215	94	190	172	1105
1963	1.39	1220	99	192	177	1085
1964	1.39	1218	111	195	187	1043
1965	1.39	1221	108	197	190	1037
1966	1.37	1225	107	199	192	1036
1967	1.37	1074	101	210	189	1111
1968	1.12	1067	89	230	201	1144
1969	1.11	1070	88	231	214	1080
1970	1.12	1066	87	233	224	1041
1971	1.14	1062	83	235	241	975
1972	1.19	1096	93	247	271	912
1973	1.36	1259	113	254	317	801
1974	1.40	1181	112	261	319	818
1975	1.22	1004	78	274	350	783
1976	1.00	996	72	362	437	829
1977	0.97	996	79	495	503	984
1978	1.04	996	78	550	575	957
1979	1.02	924	86	640	698	917
1980	0.97	866	82	755	799	945
1981	0.87	814	76	879	919	956
1982	0.75	788	77	1000	1000	1000
1983	0.67	742	74	1031	1044	987
1984	0.58	659	75	1082	1108	977
1985	0.50	605	73	1231	1265	973

[a] Trade-weighted basket of major bilateral rates, in terms of foreign currency units.
[b] 1958–76: wholesale price index of service industry (14–21) output; after 1976, producer price index (outputs).
[c] Weighted average output prices of the primary and manufacturing industries (1–13); see footnote b.
[d] The price of nontradeable goods deflated by the price of tradeable goods.

Sources: exchange rate index, Reserve Bank of New Zealand, Wellington, and IMF, *International Financial Statistics*, various years; terms of trade index, Department of Statistics, *Monthly Abstract of Statistics*, various years; price tradeables index, Lattimore, 1987a.

Table 5.8 Real effective exchange rates[a] relative to nontradeables indices (1970 = 100)

| | Exports | | | | | Import-competing manufacturing |
Year	Sheep meat	Wool	Beef	Dairy	Other manufacturing	
1958	119	66	149	97	n.a.	n.a.
1959	144	71	140	77	n.a.	n.a.
1960	136	61	153	69	153	133
1961	149	67	151	94	149	133
1962	163	69	161	93	147	131
1963	144	67	156	82	147	129
1964	138	53	151	76	131	128
1965	111	65	153	74	128	125
1966	125	68	136	81	125	121
1967	133	79	129	90	126	123
1968	117	112	123	98	105	107
1969	108	97	105	97	104	104
1970	100	100	100	100	100	100
1971	100	106	92	95	96	96
1972	113	98	90	59	96	96
1973	81	49	80	77	95	98
1974	69	44	75	91	86	94
1975	80	65	120	87	75	77
1976	90	62	126	85	79	80
1977	94	55	153	98	97	98
1978	102	66	147	95	99	101
1979	100	69	119	103	100	105
1980	100	67	113	114	102	107
1981	90	72	123	106	108	113
1982	78	73	133	84	107	116
1983	77	88	126	84	96	108
1984	82	80	117	86	83	99

n.a., not available.

[a] The reciprocal of the New Zealand dollar price of goods inflated by the nominal rate of assistance and deflated by the price of nontradeables. The export and import price of other manufactured goods is taken as the average GDP deflator for OECD countries in US dollars.

Indices of REERs for major sectors are given in table 5.8. The REERs for agricultural exports are highly variable, mainly because of volatile world-market conditions. From the beginning of the episode, the REER for meat and manufactured products improved (fell) until 1970, while for wool and dairy products it deteriorated. The REERs for all sectors improved from 1970 to the time of the first oil shock and commodity boom. At the end of this phase, the REERs for all sectors except beef and import-competing production were 20 percent lower than they had been in

Table 5.9 Real wages and interest rates, 1951–1985

Year	Average real wage index[a] (1977 = 1,000)	Annual change in average real wages index (%)	Real interest rate[b] (%)
1951	792		− 7.0
1952	776	0.1	− 3.7
1953	790	(1951–4)	0.0
1954	811		0.0
1955	823		2.0
1956	810		1.4
1957	829	− 0.1	2.9
1958	801	(1955–9)	0.9
1959	785		1.4
1960	820		4.3
1961	817		3.0
1962	822	0.1	2.7
1963	822	(1960–4)	3.6
1964	819		3.8
1965	840		2.2
1966	841		2.5
1967	834	0.1	0.1
1968	830	(1965–9)	2.3
1969	836		1.9
1970	887		0.2
1971	985		− 3.8
1972	1,006	5.4	0.8
1973	1,040	(1970–4)	− 1.3
1974	1,063		− 3.5
1975	1,040		− 6.6
1976	1,008		− 8.6
1977	1,002	− 0.1	− 4.9
1978	1,016	(1975–9)	− 0.8
1979	1,034		− 4.3
1980	1,044		− 4.9
1981	1,080		− 2.5
1982	1,041	− 1.9	− 2.3
1983	972	(1980–5)	9.8
1984	937		7.2
1985	886		− 3.1

[a] The average wage deflated by the consumer price index.
[b] The average interest rate on registered new mortgages less the rate of increase in the consumer price index.

Source: Department of Statistics, Monthly Abstract of Statistics, various years

1970. It is important to note that from 1970 to 1980 the REER for export manufacturing remained unchanged while that for the import-competing sector improved.

The real wage grew very slowly during the period 1964–9, as it had done since 1951 (table 5.9). However, as inflation increased and the terms of trade improved in the early 1970s, real wages rose rapidly. After 1975 the terms of trade deteriorated sharply but real wages did not follow. Instead they were roughly maintained at 1972–4 levels until 1980.

The same table provides a measure of the real interest rate. During the 1960s the real interest rate remained positive and averaged 2.6 percent. It would have been higher except for the inflation generated following the 1967 devaluation. As discussed earlier, interest rate controls were widely used throughout this episode and the interest on deposit regulations at least exerted moral suasion on the finance markets. As inflation increased from 1970, the real interest rate fell and remained negative throughout the decade, frequently by more than 4 percentage points.

6

The Second Episode, Phase Two, 1979–1984: Liberalization and Accompanying Policies

With the passage of time it became increasingly apparent that the policy of tariff compensation was not addressing some critical problems of the domestic economy. In particular, it was clear that some at least of the protected "infant industries" were becoming less internationally competitive rather than more. With this realization, moves were started to increase the competition faced by these industries. The changes were not intended to be dramatic, however: a gradual evolution rather than a revolution would be an appropriate description. Yet the cumulative significance of the policies put in place was to be profound and lasting.

Introduction of the Policy

Economic Circumstances

Using any standard economic measure, the economy's performance during the 1970s had been lackluster. Real income was hardly growing, unemployment was rising fast, inflation was high, and the current account trade deficit was growing ever larger. As a symptom of this depressed state of the economy, net migration was negative for the six years 1977–82.

These unsatisfactory circumstances cannot be wholly attributed to the oil shocks of the middle and late 1970s, for other countries (which were at least as dependent on imported oil) recovered more quickly. The real problem lay deeper, in the static nature of manufacturing industry in New Zealand. The very substantial import protection had permitted the import substitute industries to shirk the reorganization and restructuring that would have been forced on them by overseas competition. They were therefore very inefficient by world standards. In addition, the tariff compensation policy of the first phase had tended to direct its subsidies and tax concessions toward the more traditional export industries. Finally, the combination of import restrictions, tariff compensation, and other government policies had caused the nominal exchange rate to be set at values far above any free-trade equilibrating level. It was therefore very difficult for new export industries to develop and prosper.

The manufacturing sector, as a result, had remained inefficient, and static in the general mix of commodities it produced. For example, the proportion of total value added in manufactures provided by the food processing industry was 30 percent in 1984, only marginally larger than the 1938 figure.

The growing realization of the necessity to revitalize manufacturing and break out of the stagflation of the economy led to moves to liberalize trade. It had become increasingly clear that some of the "infant industries" simply developed into chronic invalids tied to ever more costly life support systems.

Political Circumstances

A brief sketch of New Zealand's political system may be helpful in understanding the changes in political climate that colored the second and third phases of liberalization.

New Zealand has a very stable political system based on a single house, with elections three years apart at most. Each electorate returns as a single member the candidate obtaining the greatest number of votes at the election. While such a "first past the post" system as a whole is stable, this particular form of democracy appears to favor a two-party outcome, with large swings in party representation from one election to the next resulting from relatively small shifts in public opinion. As a result, although the system itself is stable, the policy of the government in power may nevertheless be quite unstable. This potential instability, which is always present in the system, became very much a reality in New Zealand during the 1980s.

Partly for this reason, the political climate during the second phase of the liberalization differed from that of the first, and even more radically from that of the third. The second and third phases of the episode coincided with a downturn in the fortunes of the National Party, which had been in power with a comfortable majority virtually throughout the long first phase.

During the second phase the National Party continued in power but with a majority that fell with each election. This had the effect of coloring their policymaking with a certain pragmatism which, reinforced by their known predilection for intervention, was unlikely to generate confidence that the new trade policies would survive if the government ran into economic difficulties.

The low profile of the second phase was reflected in the lack of public discussion about the significance of trade liberalization, in contrast with the considerable public debate about the continuing bad performance of the economy in general and the various interventionist controls imposed by the government.

The pressure and motivation for the whole ideological movement toward reliance on the market, which was to become the hallmark of policy in the third phase, originated in the Treasury, which was largely staffed with economics graduates from the universities, in conjunction with leading figures in the financial sector. In the second phase of liberalization their powers of persuasion were by and large insufficient to shift the pragmatism of the government. Notable exceptions were the moves toward import liberalization and some deregulation of the transport industry, but many of the other domestic policies became increasingly interventionist.

Finally, some mention should be made of the pressures exerted by the IMF and the OECD. The former organization in particular was very critical of the intervention-ridden import-protected nature of the economy in its experts' report released at the end of 1980 (*Reserve Bank Bulletin*, December 1980). It is doubtful whether this report had more than a marginal influence on the pragmatic mind of the government at that time. It may have advanced the easing of import licensing but had no obvious impact on other aspects of policy – which in fact were to become more restrictive after the IMF report, rather than less.

The General Nature and Aims of the Policy

Conflicting elements in the policy itself, engendered by differing motivations among those responsible for it, preclude a general statement of the objectives of the trade policies undertaken during this second phase of the episode.

Restricting the discussion to the import-licensing system, there can be no doubt that the aim was to reduce the import substitution industry's reliance on this means of protection. Nevertheless it is not clear that the intention was to remove protection in its entirety. The desirable level of the tariffs that were to replace licensing remained undetermined. There was certainly an intention to increase the degree of competition faced by these industries, but the extent of this intention differed between the government and its policy advisors.

The government itself, which was led during this period by Prime Minister Robert Muldoon, can be described as ambivalent about the issue: it had some appreciation of the costs imposed by the inefficiencies of the protected industries, yet at the same time its stock-in-trade was the ability to cure all economic ills by intervention. Given this ideological persuasion, it seems doubtful that the government would have failed to counter any large-scale employment costs of restructuring with some restoration of protection.

The younger members of the Treasury, the Department of Trade and Industry, and the Reserve Bank were more single-minded on the issue. Their economic training had strongly impressed on them that protectionism was a costly policy whose removal was overdue. Adjustment costs were for them a necessary evil.

While, for the latter group at least, the replacement of the import-licensing scheme was clearly part of a grander strategy of trade liberalization, the government's vision was much more restricted. In fact, while slowly increasing the quantity of import licenses and putting these out to tender, it was continuing the policies of the first phase of this episode. Subsidization of exports and of import-competing industries reached a climax, while at the same time the government tried to preserve the real exchange rate at a level considerably above long-term equilibrium. There was no convincing evidence that the government intended to move out of its traditional role of intervening in trade matters.

Detailed Policy Implementation

In the following detailed description, the trade liberalization policy during this second phase is divided into four sections. Of these, the first three can be considered to be new initiatives, whilst the fourth is a continuation of the policies of the preceding phase.

The Industry Plan Industries

Certain of the import-competing industries were singled out as having special problems. For each of these industries, plans were developed to phase in increased competition over a period of time. They are therefore referred to as the industry plan industries.

The specific plans were developed by the Industries Development Commission, which started this exercise in 1979, or by government departments. The plans were subject to public hearings and discussions with the industries, but for each the decision was reached to gradually phase out the protection afforded by licensing. However, in most cases the final level of tariff protection was left to be determined by a review toward the end of the planning horizon.

A schematic description of the various plans is given in figures 6.1 and 6.2. From this it can be seen that the planning toward import liberalization had started in 1979 but that the first tender round of the first industry plan (which was, not surprisingly, textiles) did not take place until 1981.

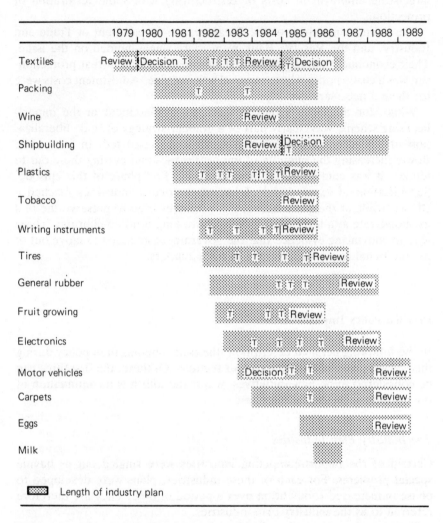

Figure 6.1 Industry plans (the Industries Development Commission's industry study program): T, import-licensing tender round

Not all New Zealand's problem industries had plans developed during this period to allow them to move to a more competitive environment. For some, the lack of international competitiveness was so severe that no moves were made to reduce their protection. This was particularly true of the industries that were being developed or expanded during the period under the "think big" strategy intended to develop import-competing industries such as steel, oil refining, and alternative fuel production.

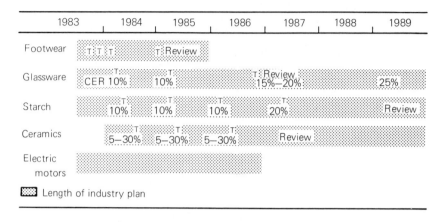

Figure 6.2 Industry plans (interdepartmental studies). The CER came into force on January 1, 1983, and provided for the allocation of import licenses for specified products from Australia. Licenses of varying values within the range 5–30 percent were allocated to various groups within the ceramics industry. The electric motors industry was exempt from September 30, 1986. T, import-licensing tender round

Import Licensing

Import licensing had long been the main trade intervention used to protect industries. Table 3.4 shows how the use of this device had changed over the years. Its coverage had fallen from 75 percent of imports to only 18 percent in the years from 1963 to 1981. However, this shift was not the liberalization that it might appear to be, since it reflected a concentration of licensing in those areas where there was a significant import-competing sector. Empirical estimates (see chapter 3) tend to indicate that average nominal import protection was maintained at over 50 percent throughout the first phase.

The new policy on licensing announced tentatively in the 1979 budget put increasing values of licenses out to tender from March 1981 onwards. When the premiums paid were reduced as a result, the decision was made whether to allow licenses on demand. When the premiums remained low for more than one round, or where the full value of licenses available was not tendered for, it was assumed that they could be made freely available.

The development of this policy from its inception to 1985 can be seen in table 6.1, which illustrates both the considerable increase in the value of licenses put out to tender and the fall in average premium paid after the first round.

Another indication of the success of the tendering policy in reducing the influence of licensing is illustrated in figures 6.3 and 6.4, which give the

Table 6.1 Import licensing premiums (exclusive of tariffs), 1981–1985

Round	Date	License allocation (million NZ$)	Successful premium (million NZ$)	Average premium rate (%)
1	Mar 1981	10.7	1.75	16
2	Mar 1981	5.9	1.08	18
	1981	16.6		17
3	May 1982	13.2	4.61	35
3a	Aug 1982	18.8	3.09	16
4	Nov 1982	8.4	1.60	19
	1982	40.4		23
5a	Jan 1983	14.3	1.36	10
5b	Mar 1983	0.2	0.01	5
6	May 1983	138.0	2.20	2
7	May 1983	18.8	1.20	6
8	Jun 1983	24.2	4.86	20
9	Jul 1983	3.5	1.16	33
10	Aug 1983	1.5	1.25	83
11	Nov 1983	4.6	1.00	22
	1983	205.1		6
12	Mar 1984	15.5	1.08	7
13	May 1984	122.2	1.44	1
14	May 1984	18.3	7.31	40
15	May 1984	40.4	2.40	6
16	Aug 1984	18.4	1.40	8
17	Oct 1984	19.4	0.40	2
18	Oct 1984	13.4	6.86	51
19	Dec 1984	453.7	15.00	3
	1984	701.3		5
20	Feb 1985	56.7	14.49	26
21	Mar 1985	10.4	0.57	5
22	Apr 1985	21.7	10.06	46
23	May 1985	183.4	0.92	1
24	May 1985	24.5	7.63	31
25	Jun 1985	49.0	2.46	5
26	Jul 1985	49.2	11.48	23
27	Aug 1985	6.2	0.25	4
28	Oct 1985	47.2	4.35	9
29	Oct 1985	69.6	0.75	1
30	Nov 1985	720.3	10.92	2
31	Nov 1985	92.8	2.96	3
	1985	1,331.0		8
Weighted average 1981–5				7

Source: data supplied by Department of Trade and Industry, Economics Division

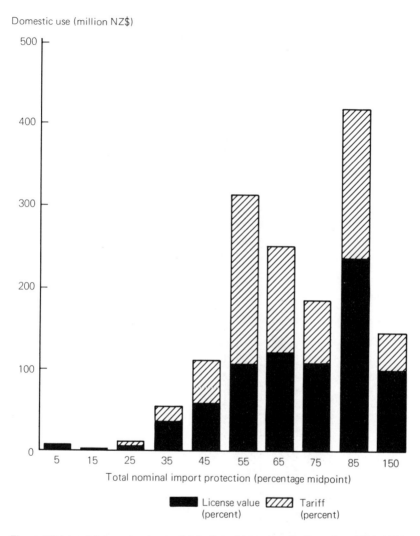

Domestic use (million NZ$)

Total nominal import protection (percentage midpoint)

■ License value (percent)   ▨ Tariff (percent)

Figure 6.3 Import license tenders – distribution of import protection rates, 1981–1984 (tender rounds 1–12)

distributions of nominal protection for the periods 1981–4 and 1984–5. They show the proportion of protection attributable to tariffs and to import licensing. It is very clear that by the latter period the protection afforded by the quota restrictions themselves had become insignificant compared with tariffs.

Domestic use (million NZ$)

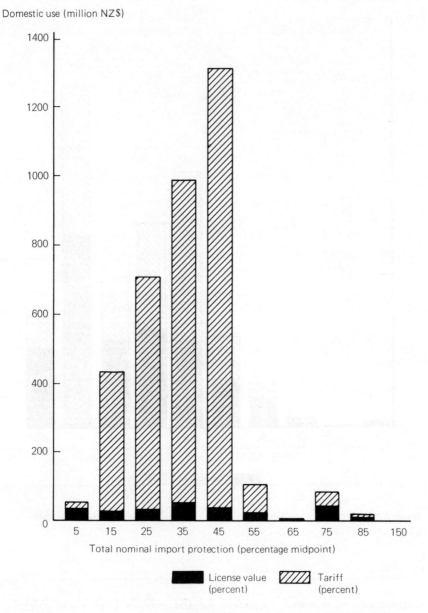

Total nominal import protection (percentage midpoint)

████ License value   ▨▨▨ Tariff
     (percent)   (percent)

Figure 6.4 Import license tenders – distribution of import protection rates, 1984–1985 (tender rounds 13–26)

Tariff Reform

In contrast with the considerable progress made on the removal of quotas, no progress was made in tariff reform apart from the setting up of preliminary discussions with a view to subsequent reductions. The resulting policy was not implemented until the third phase.

Continuation of Tariff Compensation

The policy of tariff compensation characteristic of the first phase continued unabated alongside these moves toward real liberalization of imports. Indeed, the rates of assistance rose substantially during this second phase. Table 4.1 shows the particularly significant increases in the sheep and beef industries, where price supplements were extensive to protect farmers from falling world prices and the overvalued New Zealand dollar. This sudden unplanned increase in the size of these forms of assistance ultimately helped overturn the policy in 1984. In fact, before the end of the second phase it had already become clear, even to the government, that the policy of tariff compensation could not continue at its current levels.

Accompanying Policies

The years to 1984 saw the climax of the Muldoon style of government. They also saw the, perhaps inevitable, crisis that it led to, with a major policy reversal following the general election of July 1984.

The prime minister had given the impression to the electorate that he was able, by government fiat, to cure all economic ills. The problem with delivering this promise was that, in a "small" trading country with a domestic economic environment largely based on a market system, the freedom of the government to control the economic fate of its people was far more limited than it suspected.

The government's interventionist approach combined Keynesian control of macrodemand with attempts at the micro level to override market forces by setting price and quantity controls at disequilibrium levels. The conspicuous failure of this approach left the electorate and both the main political parties temporarily suspicious of any policy that too blatantly espoused interventionism.

The failure of the approach also led to the end of Muldoon's premiership and his leadership of the National Party. However, memories are short and, given the policy swings inherent in New Zealand's three-year electoral cycle, if the noninterventionism of the third phase is also perceived to be a failure, then interventionism may once more prove electorally popular.

Fiscal Policy

The budgets from 1981 to 1984 were described as "fine tuning" exercises. As such they were prepared more than once a year. Apparently minor adjustments were made to taxation and expenditure policies without any longer-run targets than managing aggregate demand.

Fiscal drag caused revenues from personal income tax to increase and permitted the government to give ostensible reductions in tax rates which did not in fact compensate for the effects of inflation. Average income tax rates thus continued to increase and the top marginal rate of 66 percent applied to lower and lower levels of real income.

At the same time export incentives and other tax concessions were having a significant impact on revenue from company income tax. It was becoming progressively easier for accountants to reduce, or eliminate, the tax bills for corporations, particularly if they were involved in the export trade.

State wage indexation to private sector rates ensured rapid growth in the expenditure on government employees. Added to this was the increased cost of subsidies given to the agricultural sector. There were half-hearted efforts to reduce expenditure between elections but, given the Keynesian approach of the government, this was not easy to accomplish while unemployment was rising to unprecedentedly high levels.

The net effect of the forces acting on taxation and expenditure was to raise the average level of the budget deficit higher than had been experienced before. As table 6.2 shows, even the nonelection years of 1982 and 1983 still had deficits of 6.5 percent and 6.9 percent of GDP, while the traditional election bribes in 1984 acted to raise the budget deficit even higher, to 9.1 percent. It was clear to all economic observers that a crisis was at hand.

Table 6.2 The budget deficit, 1980–1984

Year	GNP (million NZ$)	Fiscal deficit before borrowing (million NZ$)	Fiscal deficit (percentage of GDP)
1980	20,632	1,027	5.2
1981	23,950	1,525	6.6
1982	28,710	1,818	6.5
1983	31,508	1,767	6.8
1984	33,807	3,101	9.1

Source Department of Statistics, *Monthly Abstract of Statistics*, various years; *Budget Statement*

Monetary Policy

In broad terms, the years before July 1984 saw the final acts of a Canute-like strategy of attempting to control the whole financial system. As fast as a restriction was put in place in one of the finance markets, the market would respond by growing in a new way. This led to new restrictions and innovations. As a result the monetary history of the period became quite complex.

The period began with a system of controls over the reserve asset ratios of trading banks, which were regularly raised and lowered, together with variations in the official Reserve Bank lending rate. In addition, other financial institutions had to hold varying proportions of their assets in government stock. Finance companies and life insurance companies were also obliged to hold government stock, each in different proportions.

The following is a chronology of the main events in monetary policy during the period.

Apr 1981   Reserve Bank instructed to participate in the short-term money market to bring down interest rates

July 1981   1 percent reduction in the official bank rate

Nov 1981   Increases in lending rates by financial institutions restricted

Mar 1982   Suppliers of finance proposing to institute new services instructed to give the Reserve Bank notice of the price they are proposing to charge

Apr 1982   Move to close some of the loopholes in the March policy

Jun 1982   12-month freeze on wages, prices, interest rates, etc.

Jul 1982   Move to close some of the loopholes with respect to interest rate controls in the June freeze

Aug 1982   Further attempts to tighten up the March 1982 restrictions

Mar 1983   Government stock security ratios for finance companies tightened from 18 to 20 percent

Apr 1983   Credit guidelines imposed on trading banks to limit the growth in lending. One week later these guidelines were extended to finance companies, savings banks, building societies, etc.

Jun 1983   Interest rate controls extended

Jul 1983   Reductions in government interest rates announced; private sector told it was expected to follow suit

Nov 1983   Maximum limits placed on mortgage interest rates

Dec 1983   Government security ratios for finance companies and building societies increased because they had been exceeding the permitted growth in credit

Jan 1984   Government security ratios further increased and trading bank growth controlled

Feb 1984   Interest rate controls extended again
           Further tightening of trading bank reserve asset ratio
Apr 1984   Some easing of trading bank reserve asset ratio
May 1984   Any exceeding of the guidelines on credit growth by finance
           companies to lead to exactly equal increase in government
           stock holding required
           New general interest rate controls imposed on all members of
           the finance sector
           Tightening of trading bank reserve control
Jun 1984   Further tightening of trading bank reserve control

In some ways, it is not very valuable to examine the monetary data for the period. Indeed, the very scale of the interventions, and the reorganization of the financial instruments involved, means that the figures themselves are not very informative.

Table 6.3 shows the annual movements in various measures of the money supply and the credit base between 1980 and 1986. The notable features of the movements in monetary aggregates during the period are firstly the effects of the monetary squeeze in 1983 when the government attempted to reduce the rate of inflation and secondly the relatively rapid growth of the credit base throughout the period.

The other aspect of monetary policy can be seen in the interest rate changes during the period (see table 6.4). A feature of the interest rate changes worth noting is the impact of the tight monetary policy of 1983.

Table 6.3 Aggregate measures of money and credit: end-March yearly increases, 1980–1985 (percent)

Year	Consumer price index	M1	M2	M3	Private sector credit	Domestic credit
1980	16.3	6	3	16	21	14
1981	15.4	14	10	14	20	15
1982	16.6	17	13	17	30	23
1983	5.4	4	−1	12	4	10
1984	7.0	8	4	12	15	14
1985	16.3	3	−5	15	22	12
1986[a]	15.3	13	9	20	21	21

End-Mar nominal values (million NZ$)

1985		3,338	5,657	20,646	15,111	22,317

[a] The 1986 increases are for January 1985 to January 1986, except for the consumer price index which is for December 1984 to December 1985.

Sources: Reserve Bank of New Zealand, Reserve Bank Bulletin, various years; Department of Statistics, Monthly Abstract of Statistics, various years

Table 6.4 Nominal interest rates, 1980–1985

Period	Average yield on government securities[a]		Average rate of interest on new registered mortgages[b]
	Short term	Long term	
Yearly figures			
1980	11.89	13.28	11.38
1981	11.74	13.07	12.89
1982	11.75	12.89	14.30
1983	11.10	11.32	15.16
1984	12.54	12.22	14.21
Monthly figures			
Dec 1984	17.31	16.85	14.53
Mar 1985	20.00	17.52	15.11
Jun 1985	20.00	17.33	15.92
Sep 1985	23.00	18.50	17.19
Dec 1985	18.00	17.00	17.46

[a] Yearly figures for years ending in December.
[b] Yearly figures for years ending in March.

Source: Department of Statistics, *Monthly Abstract of Statistics*, various years

This was accompanied by all manner of control so that interest rates did not rise in the more controllable section of the finance markets. The effects of the controls themselves can be seen in the negative real interest rates at the beginning of this period. These may in fact have continued beyond 1982 since inflationary expectations must have exceeded the 5 percent price increase, which was held down by rigid controls.

Exchange Rate Policy

The period started when the New Zealand dollar was put on a crawling peg system in mid-1979. The maximum change of 0.5 percent per month was manifestly too small and the currency became progressively more and more overvalued. Despite this, in June 1982 there was a return to a fixed rate against a basket of currencies, as part of a general wage and price freeze. The intention was to prevent the price of imports rising with a weakening of the domestic currency.

The rate was devalued by 6 percent against the basket in March 1983 in reaction to an Australian devaluation. This fixed rate was then held for the next 16 months, but as time passed it became increasingly clear that the overvalued fixed rate was not tenable in the long term. With the lead up to the July 1984 election there was no doubt in the minds of the finance sector that the winners in the election would have to devalue by a substantial amount. The result was speculation against the dollar on an unprecedented scale. Phase two exchange rate policy thus ended on a clearly unstable note.

Controls and Other Direct Interventions

New Zealanders have long tended to give electoral support to governments that show their willingness to impose controls on the economy. While this might seem at odds with the picture of the country as a frontier society, it fits better with the idea of a society that has relied on the United Kingdom to look after its interests over many years rather than rebelling against the parental influence. Be that as it may, the second phase of this liberalization episode saw the climax of willing acceptance of tight central control.

At the beginning of the period, price controls only operated on a small range of commodities, including such goods as milk, eggs, butter, bread, petrol, electricity, and public transport charges. However, in June 1982 the government imposed a comprehensive wage, price, rent, interest, dividend, and fee freeze, initially for 12 months.

The price freeze could not, of course, be applied to all commodities. In particular, market-determined prices and secondhand goods remained uncontrolled. In addition, by August 1982 the controls were eased to the extent that certain unavoidable cost increases were allowed to be incorporated into price changes. These included the effects of permitted wage increases and alterations in import component costs. Even in these cases, however, the price increases required authorization, so that the system remained tightly controlled.

In May 1983 the freeze was extended to the end of February 1984 and widened to include such items as employees' reimbursement allowances. The price freeze was followed, in March 1984, by a price surveillance regime. This limited the frequency of price changes and, for large organizations, required prior notice of increases, which could then be refused. In addition, smaller firms were required to show, from sales and profits returns, that they had not been making excessive profits.

The price restrictions were not severe or long-lasting enough to cause substantial market disequilibria. As a result little in the way of black markets developed. There was the inevitable renegotiating of arrangements, however, to permit some bending of price controls, particuarly for larger items such as rental accommodation.

In addition to the wage freeze itself, other state interventions in wage determination continued throughout the period. These are more relevant to phase three of this episode and will therefore be discussed in chapter 7.

The main intervention in the area of investment during this phase came from the government's own projects. These were undertaken either by the government itself (in the case of the hydroelectric and irrigation schemes) or by the government in partnership with private enterprise. Typically, contracts for the partnership project were arranged in such a way that the price and cost risks were largely borne by the government.

The aim of these "think big" projects was to produce either import substitutes or exports. They were large enough to have a very significant impact on total investment during the period of their construction and on the balance of trade. Unfortunately the *ex ante* decision to undertake these projects does not appear to have been based on commercial grounds and *ex post* they have proved to have very low – negative, in the case of the synthetic fuel plant – rates of return.

At the time that the decision was being made to undertake these projects, the Treasury was moving towards setting a uniform requirement of a 10 percent real rate of return on government projects. This rule was clearly not applied in planning the "think big" projects.

Other interventions in investment activities, except through the general interest rate controls discussed above, were generally mild. There were various tax incentives for investment, in the form of accelerated write-off allowances, but these were relatively uniform across sectors and time. The government had set priorities of access to investment finance in earlier periods, giving the export industries the most advantageous position, but these arrangements had already largely disappeared before the second episode began.

The one investment intervention that became very significant during this period was the traditional agricultural sector's access to freely available loans at subsidized rates of interest. The interest differential had become very large with the increase in general interest rate levels in the late 1970s. As a result, several distortions became apparent in agriculture. Land tended to be overdeveloped, overcapitalized, and certainly overpriced. In addition there was less diversification than was desirable. The problems arising from this intervention exacerbated the already very serious economic difficulties of pastoral agriculture during the following years.

One final aspect of government control worth noting concerns restrictions on international capital movements. No significant change was made during this period to the traditionally tight rules concerning the ownership and shifting of overseas funds, though their application was eased somewhat.

The advent of international credit cards had made things much easier for the traveler, since no restrictions were imposed on their use overseas. More significantly, major users of international currencies were becoming more sophisticated in their manipulation of the rules. This became very apparent in the foreign exchange crisis in July 1984 when very substantial sums were moved from country to country to take advantage of the speculation against the New Zealand dollar and its subsequent devaluation.

Trade Agreements

Quite as significant as the moves toward liberalizing imports during the second phase of the episode were the changes taking place in the country's trading relationship with Australia.

NAFTA had accomplished much since its formation in 1965, but had begun to lose momentum. It was therefore replaced by CER from January 1, 1983. In general, this agreement provided for the phased removal of duty rates by January 1, 1988, and the progressive liberalization of all remaining quantitative restrictions on trans-Tasman trade, with all such restrictions being eliminated by 1995. All export incentives based on the performance of exporting companies were to be removed by 1987.

Although the agreement applied to all goods, some products and some industry groups were granted modified programs in recognition of their special needs. All aspects of government trade policy and companies' trading activities were included within the agreement, with the long-run aim of enabling trans-Tasman trade to be conducted without government influence and without the dumping of commodities by companies. The goal was true free trade, based on equality of opportunity and fair competition.

The intention of CER is quite clearly to move to a common market linking the two countries. Such an agreement may prove to be less vulnerable to political fluctuations than trade policy in general. Thus it could well be that the introduction of CER in 1983 has a more durable influence on the country's trade relations than any of the other policy developments during the second episode. It should be observed, however, that CER is very much a second-best trade solution compared with overall free trade, since Australia is a somewhat similar economy to New Zealand and itself maintains significant tariff barriers.

7

The Second Episode, Phase Three, 1984 and Onwards: Liberalization and Accompanying Policies

While there is a certain imprecision about when the middle phase of the second liberalization episode began, there can be no doubt as to the date it ended. The general election of July 1984 saw the National government replaced by a Labour government and a shift in general economic policy that, without fear of exaggeration, can be called dramatic. Yet the movement in trade policy within this radical change in the general policy stance was much more an acceleration than a revolution in existing policies. Thus the period from July 1984 is more accurately characterized as a third phase in a long-running liberalization episode than as a new episode in its own right.

As explained in the last chapter, the policies of the Muldoon era had become increasingly unstable. The size of the budget and trade deficits, the attempts to suppress pressures in the economy artificially through a vast range of controls, and the continuing inflation, unemployment, and economic stagnation all made a substantial policy shift inevitable. In the last months of the government its attempts to avoid its fate had some of the characteristics of a Greek tragedy in which the years of policy mismanagement eventually reaped the harvest of electoral revenge.

The ensuing flight from interventionism was unsurprising in view of the bad reputation it had earned under the previous government. What was surprising was the extent of the economic policy reversal that took place over the next three years; that the traditionally interventionist Labour Party should have espoused such a free market, so untrammeled by governmental control, could not have been predicted. Why, for instance, should a party normally interested in nationalizing industry move into large-scale corporatization of major government departments, particularly at a time in the electoral cycle when the costs were more likely to be seen than the benefits?

On trade matters, as mentioned, policies continued largely unchanged, except perhaps with a more convincing expectation that they would be carried through. Industry plans and import-licensing liberalization both progressed as previously scheduled. Tariff reductions were initiated, but not dramatically, at least as far as the import-competing industries were concerned. Even the rapid phasing out of the various tariff compensation policies was largely a continuation of changes already set in train.

The one exception to this idea of an evolution rather than a revolution in trade policy concerns the international currency market. Exchange rate policy and the rules on foreign exchange transactions were both affected by major changes arising from the new government's substantially altered approach to the domestic economy.

The difficulty in evaluating this phase is that it is too close in time to be able to observe anything other than the short-term economic consequences of the new policies. However, this will mainly pose problems in chapter 8.

Introduction of the Policy

Economic Circumstances

The severe economic crisis that New Zealand was suffering when the government called a general election for July 1984 had not manifested itself in an immediate and dramatic downturn in the level of economic activity. Indeed, as table 7.1 shows, 1984 in fact demonstrated an unusually high level of growth, by the low standards of the preceding two decades, apparently caused by the combined short-term effects of expenditures on the "think big" projects and the large fiscal deficit of an election year.

The immediate evidence of the economic crisis was the run on the New Zealand dollar, which resulted from the sure knowledge that it would have to be devalued following the election. However, there were more deep-seated problems that could not be resolved by a mere devaluation. The fiscal deficit, which was 9.2 percent of GNP, was starting to cause severe structural difficulties – in particular, overvaluation of the real exchange rate, which in turn was aggravating the chronic balance-of-payments deficit.

More importantly still, the roots of the stagflation of the preceding decade had not been removed; if anything, the government's fiscal policy and general interventionism had exacerbated the problems. The wage and price freeze of June 1982 had temporarily suppressed the symptoms of these ills without, of course, bringing about an effective cure. The freeze would inevitably have to end if there was not to be a shift towards a centrally planned economy, but once this happened all the symptoms of economic disorder would equally inevitably reappear.

Table 7.1 Gross domestic product in the 1980s (index at
1977–1978 prices)

Year ending Mar	GDP	Percentage change
1980	102.8	—
1981	103.8	+ 1.0
1982	108.7	+ 4.7
1983	109.3	+ 0.6
1984	112.1	+ 2.6
1985	119.5	+ 6.6
1986	121.4	+ 1.6

—, not applicable.

Source: Department of Statistics, Monthly Abstract of Statistics,
various years

The final months before the election evoked an extraordinary flurry of attempts to use controls to counter market pressures, particularly in the finance sector. Fortunately the economy showed enough resilience and "animal spirit" to doom each successive attempt to failure. Attempts to control the foreign exchange market were equally ineffective, and the months leading up to the election saw a succession of speculations against a fixed exchange rate that had become increasingly expensive to defend.

The state of the economy made a change in both domestic and trade policy imperative; moreover, the problems were sufficiently deep-rooted that the policy changes needed to tackle them would have to be correspondingly radical.

Political Circumstances

The economic events leading up to the election ensured considerable freedom for the incoming Labour leaders to undertake radical reforms. Perhaps equally significant were the precise circumstances of the transfer of power. The foreign exchange crisis into which the country was catapulted by the election was worsened by a wrangle between Muldoon and the incoming Lange administration about who should perform the inevitable devaluation. While the official transfer of power was not supposed to take place for several days after the election, the currency crisis could not wait for such legal niceties.

As a result, the new administration spent its first days in office attempting to cope with a situation that would have daunted even experienced governments. However, there were three individuals in the new government who knew what they wanted to do and had the personal standing to make it happen. The group was led by Roger Douglas, the

Finance Minister and a successful businessman, and included the government's two other finance spokesmen. By the end of the few days of crisis, the three had established a power base in the Cabinet that was to hold for the rest of the Party's term of office. The triumvirate was thus in a good position to push through their desired economic policies, foreshadowed by Roger Douglas some years before in his book *There's Got to Be a Better Way*. In other situations the policies would be described as Thatcherite or as Reaganomic – instead, the noninterventionist policy encapsulated in the budgets and legislation that were to follow was dubbed "Rogernomics." It was certainly not traditional Labour Party policy.

It was not that Prime Minister David Lange was a weak individual who allowed the finance trio to ride roughshod over everyone. On the contrary, if he had not put his substantial support behind the policies they would have eventually been reversed by the more traditional members of the Cabinet and Caucus. But the influence of those first few days of crisis in persuading the prime minister of the viability of Douglas's policies was to be very important once the adjustment costs of the economic change, with their attendant political pressures, began to make themselves felt.

The Treasury Ministers were strongly supported by the senior members of their ministries who had for some years been convinced of the folly of the previous government's economic policies. Indeed there had reportedly been several forceful confrontations between Muldoon and his advisors. The contrasting harmony with the new administration made the officials' work more satisfying, even if more exhausting. There was, of course, some disagreement with the new policies inside the State Services, as there was within the government itself, but this was relatively minor.

Nature and Aims of the Policy

The general objective of economic policy during phase three is not hard to describe: it was simply to reduce the influence of government in the economy and rely more on market signals. The aim was to move away from a regulated environment where the government attempted to "pick winners" through its many interventions, a task seen to belong more properly to entrepreneurs, who could be expected to perform it more efficiently than planners and politicians. The new government certainly saw a place for social policy, but believed in achieving it through well-targeted income redistribution.

The trade component of the general economic policy package was less transparent, however. The determination to move toward a greater reliance on internal market forces was clearly much more forceful than the commitment to free trade. Certainly there was lip service to free trade as a laudable long-run aim, but the necessary legislation to achieve this aim was not immediately forthcoming. Removal of protection was accelerated, particularly for import licensing, and a start was made toward reducing tariffs on imports of commodities which were also made in New Zealand. Tariffs were entirely removed in cases where there was no domestic industry to protect. The industry plan industries continued along their respective paths toward having to face external competition.

While the continued movement toward free trade is not in question, some economists were disappointed that the steps taken were not more radical: complete removal of tariffs and import licensing, or at least an announced short timetable for their removal, would have been quite in keeping with the speed of some of the other policies. Had this been done soon after the 1984 election the short-term adjustment costs, if any, would have been countered before the 1987 election by export-led growth resulting from the weaker New Zealand dollar. The fact that the Lange government did not take advantage of its electoral position to act firmly and fast to achieve free trade may prove very costly to the economy if another electoral swing follows the Lange administration.

Detailed Policy Implementation

The moves to liberalize import licensing in general, and the industry plan industries in particular, continued unabated in phase three. Licensing became a matter of little consequence for importers as the phase progressed. The data on the size of the tender rounds and the premiums paid (see table 6.1) illustrate the continued acceleration of the program through this period, and have been described in the earlier chapter. The new developments in tariff reform and in the tariff compensation policy are discussed under separate headings below.

Tariff Reform

Plans for an orderly, but slow, reduction in tariffs discussed before the 1984 election envisaged two general reductions followed by a major review. The change in government, together with successful pressure by manufacturers and unions, resulted in the plans' being postponed for a year. There may also have been some conflict on this issue between the Treasury and the Department of Trade and Industry.

Reform consequently proceeded so slowly that the first general reduction of tariffs, on commodities that were also produced in New Zealand, was by 5 percent on July 1, 1986. A further 10 percent reduction was to follow on July 1, 1987, with a major review in 1988. Opinions on the 1988 review varied from the suggestion of some politicians and officials that reductions should be speeded up, with a final common level below the

20 percent originally proposed, to an expressed desire by manufacturers that no review take place at all.

In addition to these general tariff measures, which were planned well in advance, two reductions occurred as a result of rapid governmental decision making. The first was aimed at helping farmers by reducing tariffs on the imported commodities used by them as inputs. The second was much more sweeping and involved the removal of all tariffs on goods not produced in the country. Any industry that could demonstrate damage from the cheaper imports could get the offending commodity taken off the free list. This particular policy change obviously had several important gains for the economy but did not contain the essential ingredient of a real liberalization, where the aim must be to force changes on domestic industry.

Tariff reform was rapid for noncompeting imports, but at a snail's pace for competing imports. The lack of progress for this latter group of commodities casts doubt on the genuineness of the Labour administration's commitment to full trade liberalization. Yet the tentative steps that did occur toward a reduction should be put in context. While the tariff levels that remained were still very high by OECD standards, the reductions that did take place were the first in the country's European history! Perhaps the first steps will prove to have been the most difficult and further reductions will proceed more quickly.

Removal of Tariff Compensation

The one aspect of trade policy where change was very rapid was in the removal of the edifice of tariff compensation that had been building up since the inception of the second liberalization episode. Taxation incentives for exporters and product price supplementation for farmers had both been planned for removal by the previous government because of their cost and the overseas reactions they caused. This plan was implemented by the new administration, but was taken much further. Douglas's first budget, in November 1984, saw the removal of most of the many-faceted means of industrial subsidization, particularly in the traditional agricultural sector. Fertilizer subsidies, irrigation subsidies, interest rate subsidies, development subsidies, and research and advisory subsidies, together with many more, were either immediately axed or phased out over a short period.

The net effect for the agricultural sector was very severe. Agricultural deregulation and desubsidization came at a time when there were already problems caused by weak overseas markets and more importantly by the consequences of land prices in the early 1980s that were perhaps twice their true value (Taylor, 1987). This particular difficulty was considerably exacerbated by the rise in market interest rates following the freeing of the finance sector. The size of the July 1984 devaluation saved agriculture from an immediate crisis, but the gain proved to be short lived once the New Zealand dollar was floated the following year.

There can be little doubt that there was a need to remove subsidies, both because of their immediate fiscal cost and because of the various inefficiencies in factor use and product choice that they engendered. Nevertheless, the rapidity of their removal, in contrast with the far more deliberate pace of liberalization, meant that for a time the net impact of trade policy moved against exporters. There can be no doubt that this made the costs to the economy of adjusting to liberalization significantly greater than need have been the case.

Accompanying Policies

Muldoon had spent the three years preceding the change of government moving from intervention to intervention at a pace that was sometimes almost frenetic. Douglas moved with equal rapidity, but his economic policies almost always involved major new initiatives aiming for neutrality and better targeting.

It must be relatively rare in the economic history of any country for so many new policies containing so much internal consistency to be initiated. Most of the Finance Minister's moves followed the precepts of neoclassical economic theory. Certainly, the policy package contained flaws, the lack of controls to remove noncompetitive behavior in labor and product markets being the most significant. The timing of the trade liberalization was also open to question.

Despite these minor criticisms, the magnitude of the economic reform received extensive note and commendation by overseas commentators. Ironically this publicly stated approval proved costly to the effort to restructure, by helping to increase the value of the New Zealand dollar and thereby harming the export sector. It was growth in this sector that was required to lead the conomy through the costs of restructuring following the introduction of the economic reform package.

The majority opinion on economic policy suggests that the initiatives of the Lange administration should succeed. Yet the deep-seated chronic problems of the New Zealand economy in the early 1980s meant that there could be no easy and rapid solutions. The short electoral cycle, in contrast, predicates that solutions be seen to be working rapidly. Finally, problems with the timing of reform have made some of the adjustment costs higher than necessary. The net effect of these three drawbacks is that the electorate might prove unwilling to allow this experiment in economic policy sufficient time to prove itself.

Fiscal Policy

More new initiatives were launched in fiscal policy than in any other area. The size of the fiscal deficit inherited from the previous government required the most urgent attention: it had been 9.2 percent of GNP for the 1983–4 financial year (table 6.2). Reduction of expenditures, particularly in the tariff compensation area, and fiscal drag allowed this to be reduced to 7.2 percent and then 4.3 percent in the following two years. The latter figure, the lowest for ten years, was a considerable achievement.

As well as reducing the fiscal deficit, the government initiated major reforms in the tax structure.

1   A value-added tax was introduced at a 10 percent level to help reduce the heavy reliance on personal income tax for raising revenue. Even with the new tax, the proportion of revenue raised by personal income tax only fell from 63.3 percent to 50 percent.
2   The top marginal rate of personal income tax was dropped from 66 percent to 48 percent.
3   Various welfare benefit schemes were reformulated into a negative income tax.
4   The top marginal tax rates were made uniform on personal income tax, company income tax (following the removal of the double taxation of dividends), and nonsalary benefits paid to employees. The final step to uniformity, that of taxing capital gains, was not taken, however.
5   Attempts were made to reduce the use of tax loopholes.

These changes in fiscal policy all clearly fell within the coherent policy package of greater reliance on the market and neutralizing the impact of government interventions. The policy was extended to fully fund the budget deficit by internal borrowing, so as to avoid influencing the monetary base. Given that the removal of the Reserve Bank from the foreign exchange market demonetized these transactions as well, control over the monetary base became less disturbed by extraneous factors.

Government investment expenditures are included in total government expenditure and so form part of the fiscal deficit. There should thus be no intention to reduce the fiscal deficit to zero. However, during this period the government also reduced its direct involvement in investment projects and corporatized the major investment departments, as discussed below. The outcome of these changes will be to reduce the fiscal deficit, and its influence on the money supply, still further. They will not affect total borrowing in the capital market, however.

Monetary Policy

The shift in monetary policy, in July 1984, was more dramatic than any of the other policy changes. Before the election the finance sector had been one of the most tightly regulated in the world, with large numbers of price and quantity controls in place. These were specific to the various parts of the market and were changed frequently in the last years of the National administration. Douglas's policies transformed the sector to among the least regulated. It responded to this new liberty by becoming the most conspicuous growth industry in the economy.

The pathway to the liberalization of monetary policy can be seen in the following chronology of the main events (the first part of this chronology was given in chapter 6).

Jul 1984   General election and immediate removal of almost all interest rate controls. A tight general monetary stance then followed with continued credit restrictions on trading banks

Aug 1984   Moves to improve the efficacy of Reserve Bank open-market operations
Further interest decontrol, including the restriction that ordinary savings banks could only pay 3 percent
Relaxation of the reserve asset ratio for trading banks
Credit guidelines removed

Sep 1984   As part of the policy of reliance on active and effective public debt policy, the reserve asset ratio for trading banks further relaxed

Jan 1985   Public debt policy shifted from a tap system to a tender system

Feb 1985   Abolition of entire asset ratio system for financial institutions

Nov 1985   More banks permitted

Almost the entire liberalization had been accomplished in seven months. The frenetic imposition of regulations leading up to July 1984 was replaced by a system where the only significant monetary policy instrument became the manipulation of the public debt, operating largely through a tendering system but also through open-market operations.

The sudden removal of controls allowed new varieties of financial institution to develop and generally improved the service provided by the sector. With the further opening up of banking itself, the system became highly competitive throughout the diverse organizations that make up the financial sector.

The data on the money supply shown in table 6.3 give some indication of the tightness of monetary policy under the new regime. The standard measures of the money supply exhibited slower rates of growth than the inflation rate. This is not an accurate measure of the full situation with respect to money and credit, however, since during this period the whole financial sector was undergoing considerable structural change.

A more meaningful measure of the tightness of the policy is shown by the changes in interest rates during the period. Table 6.4 illustrates the increases that followed the deregulation of the market and the tightening of credit. The one feature of these data that signifies the move to a new era in monetary policy is the shift to positive real interest rates that took place. This shift should have an important impact on the economy's savings and investment behavior. Given the past tendency to overconsumption, relative to production, the corrective influence of positive real interest rates was long overdue.

Exchange Rate Policy

The currency crisis inherited by the government in July 1984 was immediately countered by a 20 percent devaluation. There was no option but to devalue, given the pressure on the New Zealand dollar and the lack of time to develop any longer-run strategy. The extent of the devaluation was generally considered appropriate and was a measure of the degree that the dollar had been allowed to become overvalued. In any case, the inflow of capital from abroad following the devaluation made it clear that there was no expectation of a further devaluation in the short run.

The only other alteration in exchange rate policy came when the currency was floated in March 1985. Since that time, as far as is known, there has been virtually no interference by the authorities in the free-floating regime. The float is supposed to be one of the cleanest in the world.

The policy changes were clearly supposed to be part of a trade liberalization package. The initial devaluation was intended to help exporters and do away with the need for continuing tariff compensation. The float was then meant to remove the dangers of direct governmental influence in setting an appropriate nominal rate.

Of course the indirect governmental influence on the real exchange rate, and on the nominal rate in a free-float environment, remains large. High interest rates in particular exert a powerful influence. It was therefore not surprising that the nominal and real exchange rates both tended to rise following the float, as is shown in table 7.2. The deleterious implications of these rates for the tradeables sector, as discussed earlier, seriously threaten the continuation of the entire liberalization episode.

Table 7.2 Exchange rates following July 1984

End of period	US mid-rate (US$ per NZ$)	Exchange rate index[a] (1978 = 1,000)	Real exchange rate[b] (1982 = 1,000)
1984			
Jun	0.6339	784	992
Jul	0.4947	627	
Aug	0.4995	627	
Sep	0.4889	627	998
Oct	0.4883	627	
Nov	0.4875	627	
Dec	0.4773	627	951
1985			
Jan	0.4707	627	
Feb	0.4487	627	
Mar	0.4623	621	941
Apr	0.4538	625	
May	0.4484	611	
Jun	0.4783	647	964
Jul	0.5245	670	
Aug	0.5387	696	
Sep	0.5455	693	979
Oct	0.5785	730	
Nov	0.5668	709	
Dec	0.4995	627	1,007
1986			
Jan	0.5363	660	
Feb	0.5193	632	
Mar	0.5340	647	1,028
Apr	0.5821	683	
May	0.5665	680	
Jun	0.5480	660	1,073
Jul	0.5188	644	
Aug	0.4865	604	
Sep	0.4885	602	1,096
Oct	0.5080	629	
Nov	0.5116	629	
Dec	0.5245	634	1,111
1987			
Jan	0.5413	645	
Feb	0.5594	662	

[a] The exchange rate index is a measure of the value of the New Zealand dollar in relation to a trade-weighted basket of overseas currencies. It was set at 627 before the March 1985 float.

[b] The real exchange rate series was calculated quarterly as the ratio of the price of nontradeables to the price of tradeables.

Sources: Reserve Bank of New Zealand, Reserve Bank Bulletin, various years; Lattimore, 1986b

Controls and Other Direct Interventions

Price Controls

The price controls that had been in operation during the Muldoon administration were reinforced immediately after the 1984 election as a temporary expedient until the November 1984 budget, when they were largely removed. The last remaining general price control, the rent freeze, was removed in February 1985. Restrictions remained on a few commodities such as eggs, bread, and butter, which had traditionally been controlled, but this list too was reduced over the government's term of office.

There was a clear intention to link the deregulation of prices to trade liberalization. The Finance Minister frequently stated that competition from imports would help restrain the freed prices. On occasion, direct threats were made to liberalize imports if domestic price increases were not kept under control. However, the threats were never carried out. The extent to which domestic prices increased under their newly delivered freedom will be examined in chapter 8.

Wages

For wages the pattern of deregulation was essentially identical, with the difference that state interventions in wage determination continued even when no wage freeze was in place. Two types of intervention had traditionally been used: general wage orders, which gave all wage and salary earners increases that were fixed in percentage or absolute terms; and controls on such things as the frequency and scope of wage rounds and the use of compulsory arbitration procedures where agreement between the bargaining sides was not possible. The aim of the first policy was to reduce union pressure for wage increases. There is little evidence that it achieved this end, while the failure to relate the size of the orders to productivity change meant that their net effect tended to be inflationary. Not surprisingly, the Labour administration turned its back on this particular form of intervention.

The new administration continued to use the second form of intervention, but too often guidelines as to the order of magnitude considered acceptable to the government simply became the bottom line for the various determinations that followed.

One final and important aspect of the continuing government involvement in wage determination is in state sector salaries. The significance of these salaries is not just that the number of state employees is large, but also that state increases tend to be copied by the private sector. This becomes particularly serious since the state salaries are determined by previous private sector increases, so that there is potential for an unstable dynamic adjustment process. A further complication is that salaries for higher state servants are determined separately and attempt to allow for the effects of nonsalary remuneration for private sector executives. The large increases that have been justified in this way have then tended to flow through the rest of the state sector and so on out to the rest of the private sector.

While the Labour government approved the principle of "free wage bargaining" as part of its pro-market stance, these various imperfections in the labor market made it an unattainable ideal. Unfortunately the government has not been able to determine a satisfactory alternative to the current system where wage determination is dominated by monopolistic unions and monopsonistic employers.

Industry
The National government's various interventions in industry, either through direct investment, subsidies, or investment tax incentives, were also all rapidly phased out by Labour, with the exception of some continuing investment incentives. The latter, however, were made neutral in their application to all branches of industry.

International Capital
Controls on international capital movements, which had been very restrictive for decades, were rapidly dismantled after the 1984 election. Since the end of that year there have been essentially no limits on private individuals either investing in any other part of the world or borrowing from any source available. The latter had become particularly important, given the high nominal interest rates in New Zealand. While the use of forward cover to avoid the exchange rate risk has canceled out the interest rate advantage of borrowing from overseas, some farmers, in particular, have used overseas finance. How far they have covered their exchange position is not yet known.

In the same way New Zealand companies borrowing from overseas, who had been subject to restrictions (although these were not as severe as those for private individuals), were essentially granted complete freedom to make any international financial contracts.

Finally, overseas investment in New Zealand, already relatively relaxed, had its remaining restrictions removed after the end of 1984.

The swiftness of the shift to a complete removal of restrictions on international currency movements is important for understanding the current situation of the economy. The movement away from a fixed exchange rate regime very considerably decreased the amount of official borrowing from overseas. However, the deregulation of international capital movements meant that increases in private borrowing more than compensated for the official decline. Thus in 1984 private borrowing was NZ$312 million and official borrowing was NZ$2,047 million. In 1985 the figures were NZ$2,482 million and NZ$905 million respectively (Rayner and Lattimore, 1988, appendix table C.13).

It is the size of private borrowing (and hence of overseas investment in New Zealand) that has kept the floating dollar so high. However, the relaxation of controls on international capital movements has made it impossible to return to a fixed exchange rate or to deal directly with any overshoot of the rate.

Trade Agreements

No significant new trade agreements were made during this final phase of the second liberalization episode. Indeed, it is arguably preferable for a small country to take part in free trade with all countries rather than to bind itself within the trade walls of a major partner. Nevertheless, the moves toward economic union with Australia that continued during this period should be looked on as advantageous because of their immediate impact in reducing protection on imports from that country. For this common market to realize its advantages in the long run, however, Australia should also liberalize her trade or the common external tariff should be eliminated.

Other Important Policy Changes

Among the other policy initiatives of the government in the years 1984–7 were two more of note. The first was the corporatization of state trading enterprises such as the Post Office, the forestry, electricity generation, and coal industries, and land management. While ultimately accountable to Parliament the new corporations were expected to operate on standard commercial lines, both making a profit that would be taxed and by repaying capital borrowed from the state with commercial loans on which interest would be due.

The reorganization entailed some considerable reductions in employment – around 50 percent in the coal industry. As important as the efficiency gained by these changes was their impact on the fiscal deficit, since it led to both increased revenue in the long run and a capital payment in the short run, while reducing the probability of the government's having to fund losses arising from what had been its trading arms.

The second policy initiative was a move toward what was termed the "user pays" principle. This particular philosophy had many applications, extending in a minor way even to health and education. Most important were the requirements for some branches of the state services to raise a considerable proportion of their own funding. Thus the Department of Scientific and Industrial Research and the Ministry of Agriculture and

Fisheries were both expected to move toward a goal of 50 percent funding over a period of three years.

The aim was to ensure a closer relationship between the work done by these organizations and the needs of the economy. Yet the policy was potentially flawed to the extent that it did not take adequate notice of the "public good" aspect of research. Not surprisingly the kind of research undertaken by these two departments changed markedly toward an emphasis on projects of short duration that met the needs of specific firms. Long-term research therefore suffered.

Other government departments were also expected to raise part of their revenue by doing contract work for the private sector. Thus the Ministry of Works was able to tender for commercial jobs. The net effect of both these movements into the private sector was to crowd out existing contractors or research groups, an outcome hardly compatible with the general policy emphasis on the virtues of a market economy. The intention was to reduce net expenditure on these departments without actually reducing the number of employees in them. However laudable the aim, the serious implications for the economy were insufficiently taken into account.

8

The Second Episode, Phases Two and Three, 1979 and Onwards: Economic Performance

For several reasons it is very difficult to differentiate the impact of the policies instituted during the second and third phases of the second liberalization episode. In the first place, the time periods involved are both short: the second phase only lasted for five years and the third phase has had a shorter life to date. Secondly, New Zealand was experiencing its normal three-year macroeconomic cycles during this time. Thirdly, the changes in other aspects of economic policy between the two phases were more dramatic than were the changes in trade policy. Hence, the effects of the former on the domestic economy are likely to have swamped the effects of the latter. Lastly, the changes in trade policy itself did not clearly coincide with the boundary between phases two and three, but tended to overlap.

There is, moreover, little to be gained from showing the detailed performance of the New Zealand economy separately for the periods 1979–84 and 1984 onwards – presenting two snapshots, as it were, rather than a single longer-term view. The approach adopted here is therefore to describe the performance of the economy for the full period from 1979 onwards. Wherever appropriate during this description, the differential effects of the policies in the two phases will be highlighted.

Foreign Trade

Aggregate Performance

The aggregate performance of the foreign trade sector was affected by a number of factors and the specific influence of each cannot be separated from those of the others.

1   . Restrictions on imports were gradually reduced from 1981 onwards, firstly through increasing the size of import quotas and then, after 1984, through some relaxation of tariffs.
2   Export subsidies were at their height in the first part of the period, but were rapidly reduced after 1984.
3   The value of the nominal exchange rate was reduced considerably in the middle of 1984 and then, following the float in early 1985, tended to fluctuate.
4   The "think big" projects had a significant impact on imports during their construction phase and on net exports following their commission.
5   The cyclical variations in the macroeconomy continued to have an impact on trade performance.

At the aggregate level all that is observed is the net effect of the various factors. Despite a careful examination of the aggregate trade data, it has not proved possible to distinguish the separate effect of each item.

Composition of Imports and Exports

In view of the number of disparate influences at work, the impact of trade policies is easier to discern from an examination of changes in the composition of imports and exports than in their aggregate performance.
    The following discussion highlights those aspects of the trade statistics that illustrate the influences of trade policy. For exports, volume measures rather than value are discussed, to counteract the influence of price changes on the data.

Exports

The volume of traditional exports of meat, dairy products, and wool was largely unchanged over the period 1980–6; there was no clear evidence of a decline at the end of the period. However, exports of horticultural products grew considerably, particularly for the new export of kiwifruit, but also for apples. This evidence of diversification in land use reflects long-term influences rather than a short-term response to trade policy, given the production response delays involved. Fish exports grew by 59 percent during the period, again illustrating a long-term diversification. Manufactured exports also grew, but only in a few commodities. Particularly significant were the 21 percent growth in carpeting and the 73 percent growth in aluminum. The latter was attributable to one of the "think big" projects.

Imports

On the import side it is possible to see more evidence of the effects of the trade policies. For example, imports of fertilizers fell dramatically in the year ending June 1986 to about half the typical value for the period. Thus, although the response to the removal of export subsidies and the rising real exchange rate was not obvious from agricultural export figures, it is very clear in terms of production inputs. Outputs must fall in the longer run unless there is an equally major return to fertilizer user.

The effect of the "think big" projects can also be seen in the 81 percent rise in imported aluminum oxide for smelting and, at the very end of the period, in the fall in total imports of fuels and of refined fuels in particular. Both are effects of the domestic production of synthetic petrol, of other uses of natural gas as a fuel, and of the extension of the oil refinery.

There are some indications of the effects of liberalizing imports but they are still not very strong, probably because the residual tariff levels remain high. In particular it is worth noting that the proportion of fully assembled imported cars rose from 7 to 16 percent over the period as the local car assembly industry was made to face increasing overseas competition. More evidence can be found of the effects of liberalized imports on employment figures, where finer categories can be examined. These will be discussed below.

In general, the examination of more detailed trade data confirms the earlier suggestion that the "think big" projects had considerable influence on the changes in trade during this period. The reason for the relatively small effect of trade liberalization was that it was still limited in extent and that short-run elasticities are low. However, the pattern of trade observed was clearly greatly influenced by the restrictive trade policy that had been in operation for the whole post-World War II period.

The effect on foreign debt of liberalization is critical for its survival. The atypical deficits on merchandise trade seen during this period, combined with the perennial large deficit on services (which has been growing fast with the increasing size of the foreign debt), have brought a considerable current account deficit (table 8.1). The rapid growth in this deficit, shown by its high proportion to GDP, has brought a corresponding substantial growth in total foreign debt. In 1984 the removal of export incentives, the continued limited freeing of imports, and the rise in the rate of interest all combined to worsen the situation. The devaluation of that year did not compensate for the other trade policy changes in the short run, and the subsequent rise in the value of the currency exacerbated the situation.

Following the dollar float, concern about the foreign debt has eased, primarily because, with borrowing shifting from the government to the private sector, data on indebtedness are now less readily available while there is some sense of reassurance that the debt will be taken care of by

Table 8.1 Balance of trade on current account (million New Zealand dollars)

Year ending Mar	Merchandise trade	Invisibles[a]	Current account	Current account as a percentage of GDP
1980	+ 284	− 1,109	− 825	− 4,2
1981	+ 505	− 1,328	− 823	− 3.6
1982	− 14	− 1,614	− 1,628	− 5.8
1983	− 158	− 1,846	− 2,004	− 6.4
1984	+ 622	− 1,855	− 1,233	− 3.6
1985	− 396	− 2,422	− 2,818	− 7.3
1986	− 392	− 2,556	− 2,948	− 6.7

[a] Invisibles include some small net transfers.

Source: Department of Statistics, Monthly Abstract of Statistics, various years

commercial decisions based, presumably, on the ability to service and eventually repay the debts. Yet this relaxation of concern may be injudicious, since the real burden on the nation in terms of the positive merchandise trade balance required for repayment and servicing the debt will be just the same, whoever is nominally responsible.

The danger is that when the real burden of the debt becomes apparent the pressures to reduce imports and increase exports may cause a reversal of the current trade liberalization policy. In addition, the apparent exchange rate "overshooting" that has fostered the growing deficit may occur again but in the reverse direction once the international finance market becomes aware of the size of the foreign debt. Again, any dramatic fall in the value of the currency is likely to lead to pressures for government intervention.

Macroeconomic Variables

Gross Domestic Product

Real GDP increased every year from 1980 to 1986, but the total growth involved was small. The indices of GDP at constant prices for the years ending in March, from 1980 to 1986, were 102.8, 103.8, 108.7, 109.3, 112.1, 119.5, and 121.4 (Department of Statistics, *Monthly Abstract of Statistics*) – an average annual rate of 2.8 percent. This was concentrated in two bursts of 6.6 percent in 1982 and 1985, however, following pre-election stimulation of the economy in 1981 and 1984.

The amount and pattern of growth achieved during these years was much the same as it had been since the early 1970s. As such, it continued to be poor by international standards, but there is no indication of any unusual economic contraction arising from trade liberalization.

The combined effects of fiscal drag clawing back more and more income into government revenue, a redistribution of income away from wage and salary earners, and the growing population prevented employees from gaining from this growth in real output. The index of real disposable income for wage and salary earners, which was 1,000 for the year ending March 1980, had dropped to 943 by the year ending March 1986 (Department of Statistics, *Monthly Abstract of Statistics*). Thus the growth in GDP was of no direct benefit to those working, but it did prevent the greater rise in unemployment which would otherwise have followed from the increase in the size of the labor force. It also allowed a higher consumption of public goods and increased use of transfer payments for social welfare because of the increased size of the government sector.

Gross fixed capital formation grew as a percentage of GDP during the period (table 8.2). By 1986 it had reached a value of over 25 percent of GDP, which would appear to be large enough to permit long-term growth in the economy. Certainly its value exceeds, by more than three times, the reported consumption of capital. Yet doubts remain about the productivity of the investment undertaken, at least in the past, given the generally poor history of growth in the economy. There is some indication of an increase in the share of investment made by the private sector during this period, as seen in table 8.2. However, the variability of private sector investment over the business cycle makes it difficult to draw any strong inferences on this question.

Of interest is the steady growth in the proportion of investment devoted to plant, machinery, and other equipment. While 32 percent is not high by

Table 8.2 Gross fixed capital formation, 1980–1986

Year ending Mar	Gross fixed capital formation as a percentage of GDP	Private investment as a percentage of total gross fixed capital formation	Investment in plant, machinery, and other equipment as a percentage of gross fixed capital formation
1980	20.6	67.9	28.5
1981	20.7	69.1	30.3
1982	23.7	70.3	29.3
1983	24.8	65.9	32.5
1984	24.5	64.4	32.8
1985	24.1	70.0	32.1
1986	25.4	n.a.	n.a.

n.a., not available.

Source: Department of Statistics, *Monthly Abstract of Statistics*, various years

OECD standards, it is significantly higher than the values typical of earlier years. For example, in the 1970s the proportion ranged around 25–7 percent. The increase can be seen as an indication of the gradual restructuring of the economy over this period.

Employment

Aggregate Trends
The main trends in aggregate employment and unemployment (table 8.3) show a large rise in registered unemployment during the first years of the period, a fall from 1984 to 1986, and the beginning of an upturn in 1986. Assisted unemployment fell at the end of the period as part of the government's plan to phase out this kind of intervention. The total of registered unemployed and those on special schemes continued falling beyond the end of the time period under consideration. Aggregate employment rose during most of the period, although that too has faltered since 1986.

Table 8.3 Aggregate employment and unemployment, 1980–1986 (annual percentage change)

Year ending Mar 31	Registered unemployed	Assisted unemployed	Surveyed employed
1980	11.1	10.5	1.3
1981	54.1	− 21.8	− 0.3
1982	29.1	30.9	1.0
1983	15.6	23.6	0.5
1984	36.9	31.0	− 0.5
1985	− 19.7	12.8	3.5
1986	− 14.1	− 22.9	2.5

Source: Reserve Bank of New Zealand, Reserve Bank Bulletin, various years

It is difficult to attribute the aggregate changes in employment and unemployment to specific aspects of government policy. For example the trend to increasing unemployment during the earlier years could be blamed on trade liberalization or on the growth in the labor force. Alternatively, it could have been a supply-side response to the ever increasing impact of the government sector. Equally, the decrease in unemployment from early 1984 could have been a response to the more-market strategies of the new government or, following the Keynesian model, to the mammoth budget deficit of that year.

The most likely explanation for the observed changes in aggregate employment and unemployment is that they were simply the effects of the three-yearly cycle of the economy, built around a Keynesian-inspired system of budgetary election bribes. This cyclical effect was superimposed on an upward-trending level of unemployment, which may have been partly the result of the increasing government role in the economy. Clearly, the aggregate data on employment allow too many interpretations to be useful in assessing the effects of trade liberalization. As with the trade data, an examination at the sectoral level may be more fruitful.

Sectoral Trends

As a first approach to examining the sectoral changes, table 8.4 shows the employment growth by aggregate sector from 1980 to the year for which the latest data are available, 1985. What is immediately clear from the figures is that the growth in total employment, which was still insufficient to prevent unemployment doubling, occurred outside manufacturing industry. Apart from the very small electricity sector, the growth was concentrated in the finance and services industries.

Table 8.4 Differential employment changes by aggregate sector, 1980–1985 (percent)

Industry	Employment change	Change relative to total industry
Agriculture, hunting, forestry, and fishing	+7.2	+2.1
Mining and quarrying	0.0	−5.1
Manufacturing – total	−0.2	−5.3
Electricity, gas, and water	+14.3	+9.2
Construction	+1.1	−4.0
Transport, storage, and communication	−3.7	−8.8
Wholesale, retail trade, hotels, etc.	+ 6.9	+1.8
Finance, insurance, etc.	+18.2	+13.1
Community and personal services	+12.9	+7.8
Total industry	+5.1	0.0
Registered unemployed	+100.0	

Source: Department of Statistics, *New Zealand Yearbook*, various years

The lack of employment growth in manufacturing can be interpreted as part of a worldwide trend toward the service sector. It can also be interpreted as a response to the difficulties faced by the import-competing industries as a result of trade liberalization.

Within the various sectors of the manufacturing industries employment changed at differing rates (table 8.5). Here the impact of the relaxation of import quotas from 1981 onwards begins to show up more clearly.

The most highly protected industries show the biggest changes: the entire transport equipment industry in particular exhibited a marked decline in employment. The decrease in textiles, clothing, and leather,

Table 8.5 Differential employment changes by manufacturing categories, 1980–1985 (percent)

Industry	Employment change
Total manufacturing	− 0.2
Seasonal food processing	+ 1.7
Other food, beverages, and tobacco	+ 1.7
Textiles, clothing, and leather	− 7.8
Wood and wood products	+ 8.1
Paper, paper products, printing, and publishing	+ 3.9
Chemicals, petroleum, rubber, and plastics	− 1.0
Nonmetallic mineral products	− 3.5
Metal products and engineering	+ 7.3
Machinery except electrical	+ 1.1
Electrical machinery and equipment	+ 0.2
Transport equipment	− 14.7
Other manufacturing	+ 0.5

Source: Department of Statistics, *New Zealand Yearbook*, various years

however, is less uniform. For example, the strongly protected subcategory of wearing apparel had an employment drop of 11.4 percent, while the export-related leather and fur industries showed a growth of 16.3 percent. The growth in wood and paper products is again related to the export orientation of these commodities, while the growth in metal products and engineering tended to be concentrated in fabricated metal products, which could not appropriately be imported.

Even within categories that showed little overall change there were significant falls in employment in subsectors, caused by growth in imports. For example, employment in the radio and television industry fell by 9.4 percent despite a growth of 0.2 percent in the overall category. Again, employment in the tire and tube industry fell by 16.7 percent despite a fall of only 1.0 percent in the group as a whole.

Clearly the relaxation of import quotas led to employment losses in the import substitute industries. This was compensated by growth of employment in other parts of manufacturing – some of it export related and some in nontradeable commodities. But the lack of employment growth in manufacturing as a whole, despite some growth in the economy, suggests that the employment increases ascribable to export gains were insufficient to offset the losses due to imports. This situation will presumably right itself once the exchange rate falls low enough to reduce the balance-of-payments deficit significantly.

Another indication of the effect of import liberalization on domestic industry can be obtained from the manufacturing censuses. Table 8.6 shows employment change and import penetration for the so-called

Table 8.6 The employment effects of import liberalization within the development plan industries, 1979–1984 (percent)

Industry	Employment change 1979–84	Imports – industry turnover for 1984	Year of first tender
Woolen mills	−22.7	6.87	1981
Knitting mills	−4.5	22.27	1981
Clothing	−9.5	2.68	1981
Carpets	+16.1	7.45	1985
Tires	−6.2	25.40	1983
Plastics	+5.1	4.07	1982
Motor assembly	−13.0	10.76	1985

Source: Department of Statistics, *Monthly Abstract of Statistics*, various years

development plan industries (those industries considered so vulnerable to competing imports that specific plans have been made for trade liberalization in each, rather than applying the general liberalization policies).

The figures here show employment falling in most of these industries but rising in two of them. The rises can be explained, but the figures in general are less convincing that those for manufacturing categories. The problem is that the use of employment data from manufacturing census years rules out both 1980 and 1985, while merely considering the year in which tendering was first allowed does not give an accurate indication of the liberalization achieved. This depends on the size of the tender and the degree of protection beforehand.

Price Variables

The details of the changes to the consumer price index during this period are included in table 2.17. This shows that prices were increasing at over 15 percent a year for the years 1980–2 and were then held to around 6 percent for 1983 and 1984 by the price "freeze." Following decontrol in late 1984, prices rebounded to around 16 percent in 1985 and then started to fall in 1986 once the increase held back by the freeze had taken place. In late 1986 the 10 percent value-added tax gave a temporary boost to inflation once more, but the underlying trend continued downwards toward single figures. While this level of inflation would be the lowest achieved in 15 years, apart from during the period of the freeze itself, it would still be far higher than that of most of the country's major trading partners.

Interest rate movements during the period are given in table 6.4. This shows the negative real rates at the start of the period whilst interest rate controls were in force, followed by positive real rates during the wage and price freeze. Decontrol at the end of 1984 brought nominal rates to unprecedentedly high levels in order to maintain these positive real rates. Since then the nominal rate shifts have followed the changes in the inflation rate.

Values for the exchange rates and the terms of trade are given in tables 5.7 and 7.2. The movement in the real exchange rate is particularly significant in showing that the major devaluation of 1984 was only able to bring it down by a maximum of 5 percent and that this boost to the tradeables sector was quickly eroded. Thus, by mid-1986 the real exchange rate had returned to a level 8 percent above that of the quarter before the 1984 devaluation. When it is recalled that the level at that time was considered to be about 20 percent above what was required for trade to move closer to a long-term balance, the degree of exchange rate overvaluation at the end of this period becomes apparent.

Conclusion

Phases two and three of New Zealand's second episode saw the first real, although gradual, attempt to liberalize trade, followed by a Herculean attempt to liberalize the domestic economy. The concentration on the latter during the period from 1984 onwards tended to upstage the continuing slow changes in the former. Nevertheless, some real progress was made: import licensing reached a stage where it was confidently expected to be discarded for all but a few industries; tariffs were reduced significantly for the first time in the country's post-World War II history.

Both reforms were achieved without any politically obvious adjustment pain up to 1986. The economy continued to perform in its usual lackluster fashion except for the brief upsurge in 1985, largely caused by the "think big" projects. Prospects for the future looked brighter, however, with the gains from the liberalization yet to appear and investment rates increasing.

Yet there was one major problem in this scenario. The float of the exchange rate in 1985 had taken place alongside a fiscal deficit that continued to be high relative to GDP. This combination, together with the favorable international press coverage of the domestic economic reforms, had helped to cause an overshoot of the exchange rate policy by an amount that may have been as much as 20–30 percent.

The resultant depressive effect on the tradeables sector helped to cause the economic downturn that was being experienced by 1987. In particular, there was no indication of the export-led growth, stimulated by a lower real exchange rate, required to ensure the sustainability of the policies. Meanwhile the visible pressure on the import-competing industries lent support to their call for high tariff levels to replace the quotas that were being removed.

Thus a relatively high domestic inflation rate countering the gains made by the nominal devaluation, which was then not compensated for under the dollar float, put the liberalization policies, domestic and trade, at some risk. In particular, the political will to complete the trade liberalization that had been begun in 1979 was under siege.

9
Overview and Inferences

The 40 years covered by this study of trade liberalization in New Zealand saw many changes, some gradual and some extraordinarily swift and even drastic. But beneath these surface movements the structure of the economy has been remarkably resistant to change. The highly protected internationally inefficient manufacturing sector with which the period began is still essentially unchanged; exports in the late 1980s are still largely based on agricultural produce, as they were in the late 1940s.

At the outset, the country's wealth obscured the need for structural change. But over the years the costs of inaction became more and more obvious in the stagnation of the economy, the increasing expense of preserving the traditional exporting and import-competing industries, and the mushrooming budget and trade deficits involved in trying to maintain the standard of living of the golden years of the early 1950s.

Eventually, when these policies became economically and politically unsustainable, a slow reduction in import protection began in the early 1980s, followed by rapid and far more significant reforms of many other aspects of economic policy in 1984. It is too early for the results of these changes to have manifested themselves in a major restructuring of the economy, but it is quite clear that change is accelerating and, more important still, that attitudes to change are shifting. It appears to be much more widely accepted that the structural change is necessary and that a return to the old aim of simply preserving the status quo is no longer tenable.

Hence, while the structure of the economy has yet to exhibit the major changes required to break out of the stagnation of the past, it seems much more likely to do so than at any other time in the preceding 40 years. Yet there is no certainty of avoiding a policy reversal. Indeed, some features of the present situation make reversal a distinct possibility.

The Benefits and Costs of Trade Liberalization

True trade liberalization in New Zealand is too new, and has been too slowly implemented, to yield, as yet, any demonstrable benefits. The benefits are demonstrated not as positive improvements but rather as costs averted in ending the long tenure of import restriction. The latter has very clearly led to a manufacturing industry that, at least in part, is very inefficient, with resultant higher costs and lowered living standards. It is difficult to make categorical predictions using a counterfactual approach, yet it appears most unlikely that the stagnation of the past 30 years, and the more recent chronic unemployment, inflation, and trade deficits, would have occurred if the liberalization of imports in the early 1950s had been maintained. The potential benefits of freer trade can therefore be seen in the costs to the country of its addiction to protection.

The costs are also difficult to measure given the limited restructuring that has taken place so far. Such costs are likely to be seen in increases in unemployment in the industries where import restrictions have been relaxed. There is certainly a public presumption that such gross unemployment costs are occurring, although there has been little investigation of the validity of this assumption or of whether the net unemployment costs have in fact been lowered by the establishment of new enterprises.

To estimate the full gross value of increased unemployment would require detailed examination of each subsector of manufacturing industry to determine how much unemployment import liberalization had caused or how much employment export assistance had created. Even if this daunting analysis were undertaken, it would be flawed by the difficulty of identifying the causes of the employment changes.

An alternative approach is to attempt to draw conclusions from more aggregated figures. For example, the number of registered unemployed increased from 49,000 in February 1981, the year that the first tendering for import quotas occurred, to 58,000 in 1985. In some sense 9,000 – 0.6 percent of the 1986 estimated workforce in the nonprimary sector – thus represents an upper limit on the net increase in registered unemployment caused during this period by the liberalization. On top of this there would also have been an increase in nonregistered unemployed, to give an absolute maximum value for the net increase in unemployment of perhaps 14,000, or 1 percent of the nonprimary workforce.

Of course, this so-called "upper bound" estimate depends on several strong assumptions about the neutrality of the effects of government macropolicies, the cyclical state of the internal economy, and the influences of the rest of the world. None of these assumptions can be confirmed, so the figure must remain largely speculative.

Another approach is to examine the broad trends in the more detailed employment data underlying the relative changes shown in table 8.5. Thus the drop in employment from 1980 to 1985 of 3,500 in transport equipment, 3,800 in textiles and clothing, and 1,300 in footwear, tires, and radio and television manufacture combined can probably all be attributed to substitution of imports. These three total 8,700 and turn out to be quite consistent with the upper bound estimate discussed previously. This figure assumes that there would have been zero growth in employment in the absence of import competition. Once more, therefore, the accuracy of the figure depends on assumptions about the neutrality of other factors.

In one sense, 8,700 can be considered a lower bound estimate of the true effect of imports on employment, since it was obtained from only a limited number of sectors. Imports would have had a depressing, though smaller, influence in some other industries.

What can be concluded from this discussion? It appears that a fall in employment of somewhere in the range 5,000–10,000 would be a very approximate confidence interval for the gross effect of the import liberalization policy to February 1985.

In contrast, the tariff compensation policies of the period to 1984 presumably led to an increase in employment, or at least prevented a decrease, in the export industries. This would be very difficult to measure in practice, and indeed in principle it is not clear that such measurement would be appropriate if the subsidies were seen as simply neutralizing other aspects of trade policy.

Once the impacts of the manifold policy changes that occurred from 1984 onwards are taken in account, attributing further employment changes to specific aspects of these policies becomes an almost impossible task. With so many changes occurring essentially simultaneously, the resulting classic identification problem prevents separation of the individual policy effects. Aggregate unemployment started to rise from mid-1986, as explained in the previous chapter, but it is doubtful whether this was the result of trade liberalization *per se* so much as a cyclical phenomenon. Insofar as trade matters were involved, the rising value of the real exchange rate was probably more significant for unemployment than the gradual reduction in protection.

The most that can be gleaned from the New Zealand experience is that perhaps around 0.7 percent of the workforce was made unemployed by the import liberalization up to 1985. This is an estimate of the gross effect, since no attempt was made to measure the effects of other aspects of trade policy during this period.

Clearly, considerable structural adjustment will be required when some parts of the New Zealand economy finally face world prices. Hence there will be significant gross unemployment effects in due course. However, there is sufficient evidence of factor mobility and entrepreneurial skills to suggest that the net unemployment effects are likely to be small, at least assuming that the real exchange rate is not prevented from falling to appropriate levels by other aspects of economic policy.

The Importance of a Clear Liberalization Plan

New Zealand's experience suggests that a clear pre-announced plan for trade liberalization is desirable. The first episode had no such stated intent, so that firms had no incentive to make adjustments to production processes or plans. In contrast, the tendering system for the removal of import quotas that began in 1981 was clearly stated and well understood, and there was little attempt by interested parties to reverse the policy. Even within the industry plan industries this scheduled liberalization has proceeded without interruption, even if slowly.

However, the question of the tariff levels that will replace the quotas was not settled in advance. The industry plans allow for this determination to take place at a pre-arranged future date. For other industries the tariff reform package contained a first reduction of 5 percent, followed a year later by another of 10 percent, and thereafter by a major review. This imprecision has resulted in considerable pressure from rent seekers. Their aim is to replace quotas with higher tariffs than are currently in force or, at the very least, to resist any further reductions in tariffs.

These pressures have elicited some indications from politicians that they will be sympathetic to calls for protection where the industry concerned can show evidence of actual, or even potential, damage from imports. If this approach were adopted as the policy of the government it would, of course, spell the end of the whole liberalization episode.

At times the politicians appear almost schizophrenic about protection. The same politicians who deride the European Commission, Japan, and the United States for their protection of domestic agriculture, pointing out the costs to the local consumers of these policies, will talk of the problems facing domestic industry from cheaper imports and forget to mention the potential gains to New Zealand's consumers.

With no firmly designed policy for tariff reduction to fall back on, it is harder for ministers to resist appeals for help. The rent seekers, for their part, are encouraged by the absence of a specified schedule for tariff reform to devote resources to influencing the policy in directions that would suit themselves. So, even after six years of dismantling quotas and two years of tariff reductions, producers cannot be confident even about the direction in which tariffs may move after 1987.

In a situation where no one has any idea what the target levels for tariff policy will turn out to be, plans for appropriate restructuring of the import-competing industries in anticipation of liberalization become futile. A vicious circle is created in which this lack of a definitive plan in itself makes full liberalization less probable, while at the same time making it harder to minimize the costs of the structural adjustment so clearly required by the economy.

The Speed of Reform

Implementing a liberalization program in a democratic system poses particular problems. When the electoral cycle is only three years long and the political parties are evenly balanced and oppose each other on most issues, these problems are considerably exacerbated. In particular, the electorate has to be persuaded of the cost effectiveness of any substantial policy change within a very short time if the party pursuing reform is to remain in office. In such a system, reforming policies whose benefits and costs take time to emerge are at risk: the perceptions of the electorate, which by definition cannot be based on reliable assessment of impacts, become paramount and may be self-fulfilling.

Even with the impetus of reforming zeal, it was some months before the new policies initiated in 1984 began to be implemented on a large scale, and longer before some aspects were put into operation. This left only a short time for the net benefits to become apparent before the 1987 election. As a result, the efficacy of both trade and domestic liberalization policies inevitably remained a matter of electoral speculation.

An additional political problem with trade liberalization is that, whereas the gains for the voters are in any case not dramatic, particularly in the short run, losses are potentially substantial for the rent-protecting pressure groups, who are publicly very vocal and privately very effective in lobbying for their own interests. Given these problems, it is difficult to sustain the public will to support liberalization for a long enough time for it to be effective, particularly if there is increased gross unemployment that can rightly or wrongly be attributed to trade liberalization by its opponents.

None of the foregoing necessarily predicates an optimal speed for reform. The more rapid the reform, the greater the chance of benefits emerging within the three-year electoral cycle, but the greater also the potential for significant adjustment costs. Nevertheless, the slower the reform, the more opportunity there may be for the pressure groups to mount an effective campaign against it at the time of the next election.

In some ways, the main inference to be drawn from the New Zealand case is simply that the length of the electoral cycle could be a distinct obstacle to the success of a trade liberalization.

The Place of Export Promotion

A policy of tariff compensation for the export sector was central in the first phase of New Zealand's second liberalization episode. In retrospect, this appears to have been undesirable for several reasons.

Firstly, the second-best nature of tariff compensation tends to have been overlooked. A more competitive growing manufacturing sector was essential for the economy to achieve the growth observed in other OECD countries. Yet the protection afforded the import-competing sector enabled the continuation of efficiency levels which were extremely low by world standards. If government had peeled away this protection, while avoiding overvaluation of the exchange rate, a more effective import-competing sector would have been forced to develop. Exporters would then not have required the tariff compensation.

A problem associated with a mixture of protection and tariff compensation is that there is more potential for mistakes over policy instruments. Thus, for efficiency, both the protection and the compensation need to be uniform across all sectors. In fact, the chances are that these interventions will be made in response to lobbying and so are very likely to be selective and extremely variable in degree. This was indeed so in New Zealand, inducing far greater inefficiencies that would otherwise have been the case. The chronic inability of the economy to develop an efficient import-competing manufacturing sector, or to recover after the oil shocks, was most certainly the result of protracted allegiance to the infant industry argument and to multitudinous nonuniform attempts to compensate the rest of the economy for the costs of the infants.

The second problem with tariff compensation is its fiscal cost. This needs to be covered by extra taxation, by borrowing, or by the reduction of other government expenditures. The first leads to efficiency loss, the second to a channeling of savings away from productive investment, and the third to a weakening of other government objectives. There is the further risk that, as occurred in New Zealand, the total fiscal cost of compensation may get out of hand, with very serious effects on the budget deficit.

The final problem raised by a tariff compensation policy is the difficulty of shifting from such a policy to one of true trade liberalization. New Zealand rapidly reduced compensation in 1984, while at the same time only slowly continuing to reduce protection. For a time, therefore, the overall balance of intervention moved against the export industries: their costs remained high because of the direct and indirect effects of tariffs, while the compensation that they had received for these extra costs was largely removed. As a result these industries if anything tended to contract, rather than to expand as they should have done with liberalization. The final removal of import restrictions will ultimately solve this timing problem, but in the meantime real resource costs are involved in the temporary contraction of the export industries.

Appropriate Circumstances for Introducing a Liberalization Policy

The first liberalization episode in New Zealand is a clear example of inappropriate circumstances in which to introduce such a policy. The combination of the impermanence of the boost in export earnings, the fixing of the exchange rate, and the lack of commitment to reform made curtailment of the episode inevitable.

The circumstances surrounding the third phase of the second episode, in contrast, were auspicious. The financial problems caused by the tariff compensation policy meant that some kind of reform was inevitable, the long stagnation of the economy stiffened the political will for initiating reform, and attribution of the economic crisis to the preceding period of pervasive economic controls made decontrol an attractive alternative.

Three further circumstances favorable to reform were the under-utilization of resources, which allowed for a restructuring to take place; the initial opening of the labor market by a small reduction in trade union monopoly powers (later reversed); and, finally, the almost total financial freeing of markets to allow the movement of capital to meet demand, while the real interest rate became positive to stimulate savings.

Not all circumstances were favorable: the liberalization faced serious distortion in the economy arising from decades of ever increasing interventions. The size of the task was dauntingly large.

The Value of an External Trade Agreement

Virtually throughout the second episode New Zealand and Australia were moving closer to forming a free-trade zone. Starting under NAFTA in 1965 and accelerating with the implementation of CER in 1983, the trade agreements made free trade with Australia appear inevitable, even though there was continued disagreement about the extent to which tariffs toward the rest of the world should be reduced.

The lack of lobbying to prevent the implementation of the Australian common market can be interpreted in part as indicating that its advantages would be limited: in some ways the two economies are too similar for the potential trading gains to be very large. As a result, New Zealand producers were not so worried by the prospect of the removal of protection. At the same time, however, exporters had success in penetrating the Australian market, as evidenced by the considerable growth in trade between the two countries and the fact that the trade balance became much less biased in favor of Australia. Some limited export-led growth of manufacturing occurred as the barriers to trade with Australia were removed.

It is doubtful whether these industries would have expanded in a free-trade environment with the rest of the world. To this extent CER may arguably not be in the long-term interest of the country if trade liberalization is eventually fully implemented. Nevertheless, one of the most valuable byproducts of the agreements with Australia has been the realization that, far from spelling the end for New Zealand's manufacturing industry, they have in fact assisted it. This lesson may have somewhat reduced the resistance to a broader liberalization.

Exchange Rate Regimes

The various exchange rate regimes used during the post-World War II period have each had their own particular problems but chronic overvaluation of the real exchange rate has been constant throughout. Under the fixed and crawling peg systems, foreign exchange transactions were considerably restricted. In addition, governments pursued inflationary macroeconomic policies. The net result was that, although the nominal value of the dollar fell owing to the successive devaluations initially and to the monthly adjustments latterly, the real exchange rate did not move enough to overcome the continuing balance-of-payments deficits. Furthermore, the devaluations themselves were typically accompanied by speculation against the currency, which proved costly, particularly in 1984.

In contrast, the float of 1985 overcame these acute speculations though the resultant short-term variations in the nominal value of the currency caused difficulties for exporters. Moreover, continuing inflationary macropolicies together with overseas approval of the domestic liberalization kept the real exchange rate at levels that made exporting less and less profitable, as domestic costs continued to rise relative to those of the country's trading partners.

The high value of the real exchange rate reduced the prospects for continued trade liberalization in both episodes. Yet these values occurred under both the main exchange rate regimes. In principle a float system should facilitate adjustment to a level that will allow export-led growth. But, for this to occur in the short run, other policy measures need to be made compatible, as discussed below.

Sustainability of the Liberalization Policy under Other Policy Measures

The fiscal deficit was reduced from 9.2 percent of GNP in 1984 to around 4 percent of GNP in 1986. Furthermore, the deficit is now being fully funded by internal borrowing from a recently decontrolled financial sector to maintain a tight monetary policy and combat inflation. This attempt is indeed showing some success, but the cost is high nominal and real rates of interest.

These high rates of interest, combined with the now free foreign exchange markets and a good international press, have attracted considerable capital inflows. As a result, the free nominal exchange rate has appreciated and the real exchange rate has risen even further. Their values appear to be considerably above any long-term equilibrium level.

There is no doubt that the traditional pastoral export sector, still by far the most important source of New Zealand's exports, has had very serious economic difficulties. It was faced with the overshoot of the exchange rate, the fall in world agricultural commodity prices, and the faster reduction in tariff compensation than in import protection. The nontraditional export sector has faced similar but not quite so intense problems. The import substitute industries too have felt the pressure from the overvalued real exchange rate. As a result their fears of the implications of further trade liberalization have been intensified.

All parties are becoming increasingly aware of the importance of the size of the fiscal deficit for the economic health of the tradeables sector. However, this knowledge is not easy to translate into the appropriate – but unpopular – action to reduce the deficit, given the political imperatives of the three-year electoral cycle.

As a consequence, it is hard to predict how long the current liberalization episode is likely to survive. Its viability is becoming increasingly fragile as adjustment costs, partly caused by the value of the exchange rate, appear in domestic manufacturing. The exchange rate also prevents these costs from being compensated by export-led growth. Were the trade policy to have another three years in which to demonstrate success, its future might be more secure. However, the increasing pressure on both main political parties as the next election approaches makes the continuing movement toward full trade liberalization under the incoming government by no means a certainty.

Postscript (July 1988)

The election of August 1987 returned the reforming Labour Party to power and so might appear to have given the liberalization policies another three years of life to prove themselves. However, since then the stock market crash of October 1987, the appearance of adjustment costs and a general economic downturn, both leading to increased unemployment, and internal conflict within the Labour Party and within the National opposition have all combined to make the continuation of these policies seem more in doubt now than at any other time in this decade. As a result the doubts expressed above as to whether these policies would be given sufficient time to demonstrate success remain as true now as when the original statement was written in early 1986.

Appendix 1 Index of Trade Liberalization

The liberalization index shown in table A1.1 and figure A1.1 is based in the period of the late 1930s and 1940s, when virtually all imports were subject to an administrative selection process and exports were, likewise, often subject to long-term political arrangements with the United Kingdom. This introverted trade policy stance is judged to be quite illiberal, and the base index is shown accordingly at 5 on a scale of 20 to reflect what is thought to have been an average rate of nominal import protection in excess of 60 percent (domestic use weighted).

The index is raised for the period of the early 1950s to reflect the partial dismantling of the import-licensing program by the first National government in response to historically high terms of trade and a fixed exchange rate policy.

Import licensing was reintroduced across the board for the year 1958. The subsequent period is taken to have been very illiberal, with an index of the order of that for the period to 1950.

From the early 1960s tariff compensation measures began to be introduced. Increasingly these policies offset the effects of import protection, peaking in 1984 when the degree of export subsidization of a few export industries equaled the rate of nominal import protection.

From 1964 to 1984 there was very little change in the protective effect of the tariff, though there were clarification changes from time to time. Until 1981 there were changes in the system of import licensing (quotas). The coverage of quotas diminished as licensing was progressively removed from intermediate inputs. Licensing remained in place for final goods. Evidence on the effect of this switch together with other policy changes (wholesale sales taxes and government purchasing arrangements) is mixed. The switch itself tends to indicate that import protection was increasing, but some studies would rebut this. The index gives a comprehensive picture of little change in liberalization until 1981.

In 1981, import licensing began to be liberalized significantly. Industry plans were also introduced for sensitive industries, involving some planned increases in import penetration. In 1986, further small decreases in import

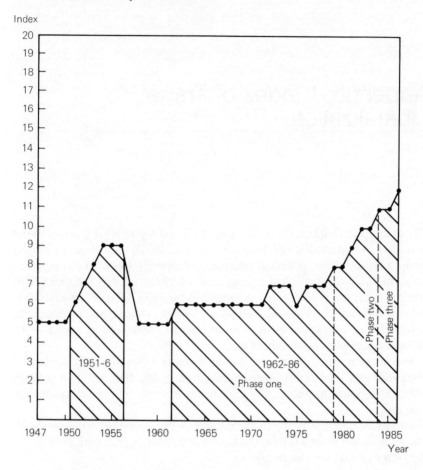

Figure A1.1 Index of trade liberalization, 1947–1986

protection occurred as a result of tariff removals on noncompeting imports and 5 and 10 percent reductions in tariff rates in 1986 and 1987. The increasing index from 1981 reflects these trends.

Table A1.1 Index of trade liberalization

Year	Value of index
1950	5
1951	6
1952	7
1953	8
1954	9
1955	9
1956	9
1957	7
1958	5
1959	5
1960	5
1961	5
1962	6
1963	6
1964	6
1965	6
1966	6
1967	6
1968	6
1969	6
1970	6
1971	6
1972	7
1973	7
1974	7
1975	6
1976	7
1977	7
1978	7
1979	8
1980	8
1981	9
1982	10
1983	10
1984	11
1985	11
1986	12

Appendix 2 A Chronology of Principal Economic Events

1949	Major devaluations
1950	Board of Trade established
1951	Commencement of first episode
1951	Removal of import licensing begun
1958	Reimposition of import licensing
1958	End of first episode
1960	The first industry development conference held
1961	Tariff development board established
1962	Commencement of second episode, phase one
1962	First export incentives – manufacturing
1962–3	Farmer tax incentives
1964	Agricultural production conference
1965	Introduction of NAFTA
1967	Major devaluation
1968	First of a series of general export incentive schemes introduced
1971	Government announces plan to replace import licenses with tariffs in five years
1972	Government supports proposals by manufacturers for orderly removal of import licensing
	Export incentives increased
1975	Tariff review
	Sales taxes increased on noncompeting imports and import licensing tightened
1976	Tourism and agriculture incentives expanded
1977	Export incentive scheme applied to total manufacturing and some processed products, on a value added basis.
1978	Government embarks on major import substitution projects (the "think big" projects)
	Supplementary minimum prices introduced for traditional agricultural products
1979	Commencement of second episode, phase two

1979	The first of a long sequence of industry development plans commenced, with special concessions for restructuring
1979, Jun	Adoption of a crawling peg exchange rate system
1981, Mar	Import licensing tendering scheme initiated
1982, Jun	Imposition of comprehensive freeze on wages, prices, and interest rates
	Return to a fixed exchange rate
1983	Introduction of CER
1984, Apr	Government agreement to extend removal of import licensing
1984, early	Phase out of supplementary minimum prices and export incentives announced
1984, Jul	Commencement of second episode, phase three
1984, Jul	Election of Lange Labour government
	Devaluation by 20 percent
1984, late	Removal of wage and price controls
	General deregulation of the economy, particularly of the finance sector
	Removal of export subsidies to agriculture
1985, Mar	Floating exchange rate policy adopted
1985, Dec	Tariff removal for noncompeting imports
1986, Jul	5 percent tariff reduction for many competing imports
1986, Sep	Variable wholesale sales taxes replaced by 10 percent GST (value-added tax) at retail
1987, Jul	10 percent tariff reduction for many competing imports

References

Budget Statement. Wellington: Government Printer.

Candler, Wilfred and Peter Hampton (1966) "The measurement of industrial protection in New Zealand." *Australian Economic Papers*, June.

Department of Industry and Commerce (1951) *Annual Report, Appendices to the Journals of the House of Representatives*. Wellington: Government Printer.

Department of Statistics, *Census of Manufacturing*, various years, Wellington: Government Printer.

Department of Statistics *Input–Output Tables*, various years. Wellington: Government Printer.

Department of Statistics, *Monthly Abstract of Statistics*, various years. Wellington: Government Printer.

Department of Statistics, *New Zealand Yearbook*, various years. Wellington: Government Printer.

Department of Trade and Industry (1958) *Annual Report, Department of Trade and Industry, Appendices to the Journals of House of Representatives*. Wellington: Government Printer.

Department of Trade and Industry, "Import licensing worksheets." Unpublished paper, Department of Trade and Industry, Wellington.

Elkan, P. G. (1972) "Industrial protection in New Zealand 1952–67." Wellington: New Zealand Institute of Economic Research, Technical Memo no. 15.

Elley, Valmai (1976) "Effective protection in selected New Zealand manufacturing industries in 1972/73." Wellington: Project on Economic Planning, Economics Department, Victoria University of Wellington, Occasional Paper no. 29.

EMG (Economic Monitoring Group) (1984) *Strategy for Growth*. Wellington: Economic Monitoring Group, New Zealand Planning Council.

Franklin, S. Harvey (1978) *Trade Growth and Anxiety: New Zealand Beyond the Welfare State*. Wellington: Methuen.

Gould, John (1982) *The Rake's Progress: The New Zealand Economy since 1945*. Auckland: Hodder and Stoughton.

Hampton, Peter (1965) "The degree of protection accorded by import licensing to New Zealand manufacturing industry." Canterbury: Lincoln College, Agribusiness and Economics Research Unit, Research Report no. 12.

Hawke, Gary (1985) *The Making of New Zealand*. Oxford: Oxford University Press.

IMF (International Monetary Fund) *International Financial Statistics*, various years. Washington, DC: IMF.

Lattimore, Ralph (1986) "Economic liberalization and its impact on agriculture." Paper presented to the Australian Agricultural Economic Society, New Zealand Branch Meeting, Blenheim, New Zealand.

Lattimore, Ralph (1987a) "Economic adjustment in New Zealand." In *Economic Adjustment: Policies and Problems*. Washington, DC: IMF.

Lattimore, Ralph (1987b) "Trade relations: coming of age." In *Rural New Zealand: What Next?* Canterbury, New Zealand: Lincoln College.

Manufacturers' Federation (1985) "Effective tariffs by industry." Mimeo. New Zealand Manufacturers' Federation, Wellington.

Nana, Ganash and Bryan Philpott (1984) "Output, labour and capital employed." Wellington: Project on Economic Planning, Economics Department, Victoria University of Wellington. Internal Paper no. 169.

O'Dea, Desmond and Ann Horsfield (1981) *Rate of Return on Capital Assets in Manufacturing and Agriculture, Adjusted for Protection*. Wellington: New Zealand Institute of Economic Research.

Rayner, Anthony and Ralph Lattimore (1988) "The timing and sequencing of trade liberalization policies: New Zealand, statistical appendix." Available from the Brazil Department, World Bank, Washington, DC.

Reserve Bank of New Zealand, *Reserve Bank Bulletin*, various years. Wellington: New Zealand.

Taylor, Neil W. (1987) "A review of farm incomes, and current financial trends in the New Zealand sheep and beef industry." Wellington: New Zealand Meat and Wool Boards' Economic Service, Paper no. 1961.

Wallace, Richard and Bryan P. Philpott (1984) "Project on economic planning." Wellington: Economics Department, Victoria University of Wellington, Working Paper.

Part II

Spain

Guillermo de la Dehesa
Chief Executive of Banco Pastor, Madrid

José Juan Ruiz
Director General, Ministry of Economy and Finance, Madrid

Angel Torres
Director of the Instituto de Credito Oficial, Madrid

Contents

List of Figures

List of Tables

Acknowledgments

Completion of this study would not have been possible without the useful comments of the many people who read the many earlier versions. Those people include the participants in the regional conferences in Athens, Madrid, Jerusalem, and Lisbon, the members of the panels, and especially Armeane Choksi, Mario Blejer, Jacob Frenkel, Deepak Lal, Michael Michaely, Demetris Papageorgiou, and Martin Wolf.

Extensive data collection efforts were made for this study. Manuel Beltrán and Miguel Santos prepared the computer programs that were used to obtain data on tariffs and quantitative restrictions, while Diego Ramos and his staff did crucial work on other data and computer tasks. Maria Trinidad Flores carried out most of the typing of this research project, often overcoming unforeseen difficulties.

Finally, we would like to thank the Spanish Ministry of Economy and Finance, and especially the Secretaria de Estado de Comercio and the Secretaria de Estado de Economía, for providing us with the facilities needed to complete this work.

Introduction

Spain's liberalization of trade can be characterized as a steady liberalizing trend that has been punctuated by three major upswings. Each of the upswings was followed by periods of very slow progress lasting three to four years. We have analyzed both the characteristics of the major liberalization episodes and Spain's macroeconomic policies from 1959 to 1982. Our main goal was to present statistical evidence on Spanish economic performance following each episode of greater liberalization.

We have focused on the main relationships between trade and domestic variables in order to draw inferences about the proper timing and sequencing of liberalization. Our methodology rested on a framework that enabled us to relate trade liberalization, economic background, and economic performance in a systematic way, and consequently to shed some light on the main factors underlying the liberalization episodes, their economic consequences, and why each episode was temporarily halted.

Some remarks on the quality of the data base are necessary. Unfortunately, the collecting of statistical information in Spain has not kept pace with the country's economic development over the past three decades. The lack of certain data prevented a more rigorous analysis of the relationships among important economic variables. For example, no suitable statistical time series on the 1960s was available, and we were forced to rely on cross-sectional data obtained from input–output tables and on national account statistics. Some homogeneous statistical time series on the 1970s were developed, but the limited number of observations precluded the possibility of reliable statistical inferences. Hence the empirical results are based mainly on bivariant analysis (Spearman's rank correlation), and therefore the inferences drawn must be carefully judged. Simultaneous causation and interdependence are not captured by this analytical tool.

In chapter 1 we describe Spain's economy and the major economic developments that took place between 1940 and 1986. We then describe the long-term pattern of growth of the economy in a more detailed way. In chapter 2 we describe the pattern of commercial policy and the methods used to construct our index of liberalization.

The three liberalization episodes identified by the index, namely those of 1959–66, 1970–5, and 1977–80, are described in chapter 3. We describe and analyze Spain's monetary, fiscal, exchange rate, and export promotion policies during each of the episodes, along with prices, wages, interest rates, and capital movements.

Chapter 4 is devoted to examining the performance of the economy following each liberalization episode. The evolution of prices, inflation, wage costs, external transactions, output, employment, and capital investment are detailed to show the real effects of the episodes. The impacts of liberalization on the various sectors of the economy are discussed in chapter 5.

In chapter 6 we summarize our findings and suggest inferences about the proper timing and sequencing of trade liberalization, based on Spain's experience.

1

The Spanish Economy

The modern economic history of Spain can be dated from the beginning of the nineteenth century. Following the Napoleonic wars, the once huge and powerful Spanish Empire lost its dominant place in the European political arena. What followed was a long political, economic, and cultural retreat from the rest of the continent.

Despite this retreat, the political climate in Spain remained extremely unstable. Colonial and civil wars and attempted coups d'état marked the country's history during the nineteenth century, and during the twentieth century Spain has experienced two periods of monarchy (1900–31, 1975–present), two dictatorships (1923–31 and 1939–75), a parliamentary republic (1931–6), and a bloody civil war (1936–9).

Until the late 1940s, Spain was an agrarian nation with most of the socioeconomic characteristics of an underdeveloped country. A lack of entrepreneurial spirit, combined with political and institutional factors, prevented the agricultural sector from becoming the engine of economic development that it became in several other European countries. The Industrial Revolution bypassed Spain, and for most of the nineteenth century industrialization was confined to Catalonia and the Basque country, and concentrated in only a few sectors such as textiles and metallurgy.

Spain's failure to build an industrial base stemmed from its decision in 1874, following the reestablishment of the monarchy, to adopt an inward-looking development strategy. Liberal tariff legislation and measures to encourage foreign investment that had been adopted in the mid-1850s were revoked because of pressure from textile, agricultural, and mining interests. Self-sufficiency and import substitution became the ideals of Spanish economic policy. Hence protectionism became the rule.

The repatriation of capital from Cuba and the Philippines in 1898 after those colonies were lost to Spain, as well as neutrality during World War I, helped to diversify Spanish industrialization, but the Civil War of 1936–9 left the Spanish economy in ruins. The new political regime under Franco found its economic and political home in the Falange, the Spanish Fascist party. Self-sufficiency, or autarky, again became the prime objective of economic policy, and was reinforced in 1948 when the United Nations excluded Franco's regime.

In a country poorly endowed with natural resources and lacking capital and a strong industrial base, self-sufficiency could not be a path to sustained economic growth. That became manifest in 1959, when a foreign exchange crisis compelled Spain to make a fundamental change in its economic policy. The economic stabilization and trade liberalization program adopted at that time produced a wave of prosperity in the Spanish economy during the 1960s in a context of strong rates of growth throughout Western Europe. At the same time, intensive structural changes took place that turned Spain from an agrarian into an industrialized country. In the mid-1970s, however, the world economic crisis, in combination with inherent limitations in Spain's domestic economic policies, led to a slowdown of economic growth. Nonetheless, the period between 1939 and 1986 was generally a period of economic progress, particularly after 1950. As figure 1.1 shows, real gross domestic product (GDP) declined only in 1945, 1948, 1959, and 1981.

The Import Substitution Period: 1939–1959

Most studies of the Spanish economy during the Franco regime have tended to ignore the period between the end of the Civil War and the 1960s. Nevertheless, some knowledge of what happened between 1939 and 1959 is crucial to understanding the developments that took place in the following decades. As figure 1.1 shows, and contrary to what is normally thought, Spain enjoyed a quite substantial rate of economic growth during the 1950s. In fact, the real rate of GDP growth during those years clearly makes it possible to distinguish two phases in Spain's economic development:

1   a phase of economic reconstruction after the Civil War, that is, 1939–50;
2   a period of self-sufficiency (1951–9) when the strategy of import substitution initially led to economic expansion and then, given the economic constraints of such a strategy, brought about the exchange rate crisis of 1959.

The differences between these two phases are important, even though the country's economic philosophy remained the same. The chief characteristics of that philosophy were strict regulation, public intervention, and protectionism.

A main characteristic of the reconstruction phase (1939–50) was the implementation of price controls. Suspicious of free-market forces, the Franco regime sought to control every aspect of economic activity: prices,

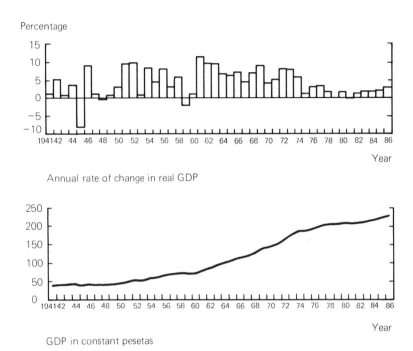

Percentage

Annual rate of change in real GDP

GDP in constant pesetas

Year

Figure 1.1 Long-term pattern of growth, 1941–1986

wages, factor and product markets, and trade. Imbalances in demand quickly appeared, leading to mounting pressures on prices. Given the existence of a price-control system, pressure on prices then caused the creation of black markets. A rationing system was established as early as 1939, and public agencies were created to control the distribution of foodstuffs and other agricultural products and to fix the prices of both agricultural and industrial commodities.

The result of such intervention was distortion of relative prices. Although agricultural prices were kept below market levels, industrial prices grew at a relatively fast pace, thereby creating incentives to reallocate resources to the industrial sector. Figure 1.2 shows that the ratio of industrial to agricultural prices grew from 109.7 in 1941 to 146.2 in 1950. These price signals were readily understood by economic agents, who increasingly devoted more resources to industrial investment in order to restore production capacity and to take advantage of the new economic climate. Private industrial investment was reinforced by public investment, making gross capital formation the driving force of economic growth.

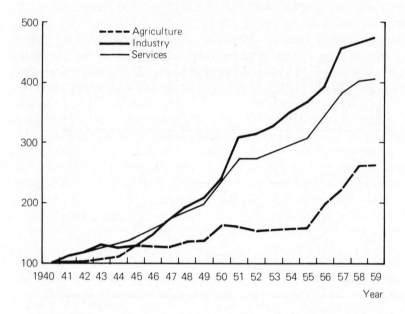

Figure 1.2 Sectoral gross domestic product deflators, 1940–1959 (1940=100): – – –, agriculture; ———, industry; ———, services

The agrarian sector, however, continued to be the most important sector in the economy, and natural disasters and poor harvest were quickly reflected in changes in GDP. Real GDP growth averaged around 0.4 percent annually during the period 1941–5 and then rose to 2.3 percent in the next five years owing to a particularly outstanding rate of growth in 1946, namely 10.4 percent. For the 1940s as a whole, average annual GDP growth in real terms was 1.2 percent.

Although the economic system continued to be plagued by controls and regulations in the 1950s, several events contributed to an improved political and economic situation. One was that the United States began to soften its attitude toward General Franco's dictatorship, as shown by disbursements of bilateral American aid. Furthermore, most of the foreign ambassadors who had left Madrid in the mid-1940s returned in 1950, ending the political isolation of the Franco regime (Viñas et al., 1979).

From an economic point of view the 1950s were notable for a strong and sustained real rate of GDP growth, which averaged 5 percent annually during the decade. Relative prices continued to be favorable to industrial development, as the ratio of industrial to agricultural prices rose from 193.2 in 1951 to 229.7 in 1955. Although the ratio then began to decline, private and public investment together with direct intervention in the public sector through the Instituto Nacional de Industria (INI) continued to shift resources to the industrial sector.

Although accurate data are not available, some studies indicate that at least a million people migrated from rural areas to urban and industrial areas of Spain during the 1950s (Banco de Bilbao, 1978). This demographic shift reduced the importance of the agricultural sector while enlarging the industrial workforce. Meanwhile, growth in the amount of foreign investment in Spain's industrial sector brought about substantial technological improvements, resulting in dramatic gains in industrial productivity.

But whatever its successes, the philosophy of economic self-sufficiency in Spain and its relative indifference to the advantages of international trade made it difficult for the country to maintain stable prices. During the 1940s, price controls and protection for domestic products had made it difficult to achieve a balance between supply and demand. Thus, by the time the 1950s arrived, Spain found that the only way to keep inflation under control was to allow a gradual increase in imports. But this growth in imports, coupled with sluggish growth in exports resulted in an appreciation of the real exchange rate that eventually produced a balance-of-payments crisis. It was at that point in 1959 that Spain began to abandon its philosophy of self-sufficiency and imports substitution.

Table 1.1, which shows Spain's balance of payments in selected years between 1940 and 1960, illustrates to some degree the development of the balance-of-payments crisis in the late 1950s that eventually caused Spain to relinquish its views about the desirability of self-sufficiency. As the table shows, Spain had a current account deficit of US$59 million in 1940. This deficit had disappeared by 1945, but reappeared again in 1946 and continued through 1949 (not shown in table 1.1).

Table 1.1 Balance of payments, selected years, 1940–1960 (million US dollars)

	1940	1945	1950	1955	1958	1959	1960
Imports	108.0	240.6	352.1	558.7	789.5	758.5	688.1
Exports	180.0	232.4	414.0	446.2	531.0	523.3	745.2
Trade balance	72.8	− 8.2	61.9	− 112.4	− 258.5	− 235.2	57.1
Net services	6.9	25.2	− 11.0	118.7	102.4	134.0	246.1
Transfers	6.8	11.7	2.1	73.3	87.6	72.9	90.1
Current account	− 59.0	28.7	53.0	79.6	− 68.5	− 28.2	393.3
Long-term capital	14.2	− 44.4	− 2.9	81.7	73.5	97.6	126.1
Overall balance	− 44.8	− 15.6	50.1	161.3	5.1	69.3	519.4
Short-term capital	0.7	− 7.6	39.2	− 14.1	65.0	n.a.	n.a.
Gross foreign reserves	n.a.	n.a.	n.a.	224.5	65.6	217.1	589.1

n.a., not available.
Sources: Chamorro et al., 1975; González, 1979; Ministerio de Comercio, various years

Some observers have argued that the reappearance of the current account deficit in the late 1940s marked the actual end of the period of self-sufficiency, but that its demise was masked until the latter part of the 1950s by the financial assistance provided by the United States. That assistance eventually could not hide the huge growth in Spain's trade balance deficit (table 1.2).

Table 1.2 Trade balance deficit

Year	Trade balance (million US$)
1952	− 52.0
1953	− 56.5
1954	− 91.3
1955	− 112.4
1956	− 250.9
1957	− 303.7
1958	− 258.5

This growth in the trade balance deficit was not caused by a decline in exports but rather by an ever increasing demand for imports. As table 1.3 indicates, Spain's exports in the 1940s and 1950s multiplied at a fairly good pace, rising threefold from US$96.2 million in 1940 to US$309.8 million in 1950 and then doubling between 1950 and 1960 from US$309.8 million to US$630.7 million. During these 20 years, Spain's exports were predominantly agricultural products, which accounted for somewhat more than 50 percent of exports each year.

Although imports (see table 1.3) more than doubled between 1940 (US$172.5 million) and 1950 (US$296.7 million), it was their continued rise in the mid-1950s which became a cause for concern. By 1955, as imports (especially of capital goods and intermediate inputs) boomed, exports failed to keep pace, leading to the swift rise in the trade balance deficit during the period 1953–8. (Imports of consumption goods, incidentally, were severely controlled during this period and never accounted for more than about 3 percent of annual imports.)

The growing gap between imports and exports in the mid-1950s stimulated an even tighter stance on trade policy. As shown in table 1.4, Spain's import-licensing system became increasingly restrictive up to 1957, when only 14.4 percent of all import requests were approved. The implicit premium on imports granted by this form of protectionism grew steadily between 1950 and 1959, together with the strategy of import substitution, regardless of their costs to the country. The import penetration ratios shown in the table clearly indicate the high degree of economic isolation and lack of international competitiveness resulting from the system. Estimates by Donges (1971) indicate that import substitution accounted for

Table 1.3 Structure of trade flows, selected years, 1940–1960 (percent)

	1940	1945	1950	1955	1960
Imports					
Food, beverages, and tobacco	32.50	20.30	18.90	18.10	12.10
Energy products	17.40	15.10	15.00	14.80	17.10
Nonelaborated products	22.10	35.60	24.20	24.70	21.80
Intermediate inputs	15.10	15.60	23.30	21.90	23.40
Capital goods	11.20	11.80	16.90	18.30	22.80
Agriculture	0.90	0.70	1.10	2.50	1.90
Industry and transport	8.80	8.00	14.40	24.50	18.40
Services	1.50	3.10	1.40	1.30	2.50
Consumption goods	1.70	1.60	1.70	2.20	2.90
Total (%)	100.00	100.00	100.00	100.00	100.00
Total (million US$)	172.50	246.80	296.70	546.10	589.30
Exports					
Food, beverages, and tobacco	61.40	70.70	50.10	56.10	50.00
Enery products	0.20	1.50	0.20	0.30	0.50
Nonelaborated products	11.50	22.50	10.20	16.70	10.40
Intermediate inputs	21.00	16.40	16.50	14.20	25.70
Capital goods	1.40	0.90	3.10	1.90	2.20
Agriculture	0.00	0.00	0.10	0.30	0.10
Industry and transport	1.30	0.70	2.80	1.40	1.20
Services	0.10	0.20	0.20	0.20	0.90
Consumption goods	4.50	8.00	19.90	10.80	11.20
Total (%)	100.00	100.00	100.00	100.00	100.00
Total (million US$)	96.20	216.60	309.80	361.80	630.70

Source: González, 1979

60 percent of growth in consumption goods, 24.4 percent of growth in intermediate inputs, and 106.4 percent of growth in capital goods during this period.

The Years of Prosperity: 1960–1975

The years between 1960 and 1975 produced the most important and sustained wave of economic prosperity in the recent history of Spain. As shown in figure 1.1, the growth of real GDP averaged 5.8 percent annually between 1960 and 1975. During the 1960s, per capita income grew each year by 6.4 percent, substantially above the 2.8 percent attained in the period 1939–59 and the 0.9 percent registered between 1906 and 1930. The impressive growth of the 1960s allowed Spain to close the gap between itself and the nations of northern Europe and thus become part of the

Table 1.4 Trade policy, selected indicators, 1940–1960

Degree of openness of the economy

	1951	1955	1959	
Import/GDP	10.5	9.8	10.2	
Export/GDP	12.2	7.1	6.4	

Performance of licensing system

	1952	1954	1956	1957
Import requests	149,325	91,712	131,633	129,621
Authorized licenses	30,060	23,978	27,552	18,735
Percent approved	20.1	26.1	20.9	14.4

Assessment of import premiums

	1950–1	1954–5	1958–9
Wholesale prices (1948–9 = 100)	141.1	194.8	234.6
Import unit value (1948–9 = 100)	83.0	86.6	92.8
Import premium	170.0	224.9	252.8

Imports as percentage of total consumption

	1941	1951	1958
Total industry	26.3	23.5	14.0
Consumption goods	22.4	22.4	5.6
Intermediate inputs	22.1	18.6	17.6
Capital goods	67.3	52.7	29.4

Contribution to growth of import substitution (%)

	1941–50	1951–8
Consumption goods	75.2	60.2
Intermediate inputs	69.9	24.4
Capital goods	49.0	106.4

Sources: González, 1979; Donges, 1971

industrialized world. There is a consensus that three factors were crucial to this outcome (González, 1979).

1   Spain took advantage of the possibilities of growth created by the economic transformation of the 1950s. The agrarian economy of the late 1940s had shrunk, giving way to a growing urban and monetary economy endowed with an intermediate level of technology and appropriate and flexible human capital.

2   The gradual opening of the economy after 1959 allowed Spain to share in the economic boom enjoyed by most of the European countries during the 1960s. European prosperity had an important

impact on foreign direct investment and tourism receipts in Spain, and simultaneously encouraged a large emigration of labor that reduced unemployment while increasing transfers of funds from abroad.

3   The evolution of relative prices and the higher mobility of the labor force throuh internal and external migration resulted in a sustained process of industrialization.

Nevertheless, there were other factors that prevented a more thorough transformation of the economy. Among them were a lack of structural reforms in the tax system, the financial system, and the labor markets. One explanation for these failures is that there were inherent conflicts between liberalization of the country's economy and the authoritarian nature of its political regime. To reform the labor market, it would have been necessary to allow the legalization of trade unions and to give them permission to strike, two actions which ran counter to the very nature of Franco's dictatorship. Any deep-seated reform of the financial system, where creation of new banks was forbidden, interest rates were controlled, and a huge part of financial resources were channeled through compulsory rules, would have challenged the country's private bankers, the most powerful group within Spain's political system. Only the most necessary market-oriented reforms were introduced during the economic crisis of 1959–60, and when that crisis ended market forces again took second place to discretionality. New "development plans" were introduced in 1964, and the liberalization lost momentum. Economic competition was again replaced by subsidies, tax exemptions, and the arbitrary granting of financial privileges, all of which create strong incentives for special interests while reinforcing the power of politicians. A new liberalization phase started in 1970, when Spain entered into a preferential agreement with the European Economic Community (EEC). However, another economic crisis in 1973, and Franco's physical decline, prevented any major change in domestic economic policies until 1977, after Franco had passed from the scene.

The pattern of Spanish economic growth between 1960 and 1975 can be seen in table 1.5. Rapid economic growth on an average annual basis (5.8 percent) was accompanied by a substantial inflation rate (7.8 percent), a high trade balance deficit (around − 5.2 percent of GDP), and a nearly balanced current account. The last two columns of table 1.5 show two very important features of this period. First fiscal policy was very orthodox; in fact, the public sector was a net lender to the system, mainly because of a surplus in the social security system. Second the unemployment rate was quite low, never exceeding more than 1.5 percent.

Table 1.6 summarizes the economic transformation of the Spanish economy between 1960 and 1975. Economic growth came about chiefly

Table 1.5 Principal economic indicators, 1960–1975

Year	Gross domestic product[a]	Rate of inflation[b]	Trade balance[c]	Current account balance[c]	Fiscal deficit[c]	Rate of unemployment
1960	0.9	1.3	0.5	3.7	1.3	1.4
1961	11.3	2.0	− 2.3	1.8	2.8	1.4
1962	9.6	5.9	− 4.6	0.4	1.9	1.2
1963	9.5	8.9	− 6.2	− 1.1	0.4	1.3
1964	6.8	6.8	− 5.3	0.2	0.6	1.1
1965	6.2	13.2	− 7.5	− 2.1	0.4	1.2
1966	7.1	6.3	− 7.4	− 0.2	0.3	1.0
1967	4.3	6.6	− 6.0	− 1.5	0.7	1.1
1968	6.9	4.8	− 5.4	− 0.8	0.3	1.5
1969	8.8	2.2	− 5.6	− 1.2	0.6	1.3
1970	4.1	5.7	− 5.1	0.2	0.7	1.1
1971	5.0	8.2	− 3.8	2.0	− 0.6	1.3
1972 .	8.1	8.2	− 4.3	1.1	0.3	2.2
1973	7.9	11.4	− 5.0	0.8	1.1	2.6
1974	5.7	15.7	− 8.0	− 3.7	0.2	3.0
1975	1.1	17.0	− 7.0	− 3.3	0.0	4.1
Average						
1960–70	7.1	5.8	− 5.0	− 0.2	0.9	1.2
1971–5	5.3	11.0	− 5.5	− 0.5	0.3	2.6
1960–75	5.8	7.8	− 5.2	− 0.3	0.7	1.7

[a] Real rate of growth.
[b] Consumer price index
[c] As a percentage of GDP.

Source: Instituto Nacional de Estadística, various years

because of an expansion in private consumption (5.8 percent on an average annual basis) and an expansion in capital formation (9.6 percent on an average annual basis). As a result the share of investment in GDP grew from 16.3 percent in 1960 to 25.5 percent in 1975. A large transformation also took place in the degree of openness of the Spanish economy. In 1964 the ratio of imports and exports to GDP was around 20 percent; in 1975 it exceeded 30 percent. Exports of goods and services grew at an annual average of 14.5 percent in real terms, and their share of GDP increased from 6.1 percent to 14.2 percent. Meanwhile the average annual real rate of growth of imports was 14.0 percent, and their share of GDP increased from 6.3 percent in 1960 to 17.2 percent in 1975.

These changes were accompanied by a dramatic transformation in the sectoral origin of GDP. Agriculture, which accounted for 22.3 percent of national output in 1960, grew on average well below growth in total GDP and consequently its share of national output declined to 11.5 percent.

Table 1.6 Spain's domestic economy, 1960–1975

	Average real rate of growth (%)	Share of economy (%)		
		1960	1965	1975
Demand				
Private consumption	5.8	70.7	68.3	68.7
Public consumption	5.8	13.2	10.1	8.7
Gross capital formation	9.6	16.3	21.3	25.5
Domestic demand		100.2	99.7	102.9
Export goods and services	14.5	6.1	10.3	14.2
Import goods and services	14.0	− 6.3	− 10.1	− 17.2
GDP market prices	5.6	100.0	100.0	100.0
Supply				
Agriculture	2.2	22.3	26.3	11.5
Industry	8.3	28.7	34.1	38.9
Construction	7.4	5.5	6.6	6.5
Services	6.3	43.5	43.0	43.1
GDP factor cost	6.4	100.0	100.0	100.0
Income distribution				
Labor	7.5	48.9	53.1	62.7
Capital	3.9	17.0	16.3	12.1
Public sector	5.2	3.6	3.6	3.2
Other	4.0	30.4	27.0	21.9
Disposable income	6.0	100.0	100.0	100.0
Labor market				
Agriculture	− 2.8	40.5	34.8	22.9
Industry	1.4	23.5	25.8	26.9
Construction	2.8	6.7	7.8	9.9
Services	2.7	29.2	31.7	40.3
Total employment	0.6	100.0	100.0	100.0

Source: Banco de Bilbao, 1978

Industrial output grew at an average annual rate of 8.3 percent in real terms, while construction and services had average growths of 7.4 percent and 6.3 percent respectively. Industry accounted for around 29 percent of GDP at the beginning of the expansion in 1960; by 1975 its share had risen to almost 40 percent. Construction's share of GDP remained steady at around 6 percent, while services also remained steady at about 43 percent.

These changes in the composition of output were accompanied by a transformation of the labor force. Employment in agriculture decreased on average by 3.3 percent each year, reducing its share of the total labor force from 34.0 percent in 1964 to 23.7 percent in 1975. Nonagricultural employment grew by 2.5 percent on average, while total employment growth averaged 0.8 percent a year. Industry's share remained stable, while construction's share increased by 2.2 percentage points. Most of those who lost their jobs in agriculture were absorbed by the services sector, whose share of total employment increased from 30.8 percent in 1964 to 38.3 percent in 1975.

The developments in the structure of employment and GDP suggest that increases in apparent productivity during the period 1960–75 were substantial. A rough estimate is that productivity gains for the economy as a whole were an annual average of 5.3 percent. In the nonagricultural sector the gain was 4.1 percent; in the agricultural sector it was about 5.8 percent.

To summarize, the 1960–75 period was a phase of sustained expansion and equilibrium in both Spain's external accounts and its public sector budget. Nevertheless, inflationary pressures were strong during this period, and the combination of inflation with a growing trade imbalance periodically forced the authorities to introduce stabilization measures that slowed down growth for a couple of quarters and then gave rise to a new expansion. In this stop–go cycle, the slowdowns occurred in 1967, 1970–1, and 1975.

During these 15 years the openness of the Spanish economy increased by 10 percentage points. Agriculture lost importance, both as a source of output and as an employer of labor, while the services sector share of both employment and output rose to around 40 percent. Near-equilibrium in the external sector was maintained mainly by a net saving in the public sector financial position. The dynamism of production contrasted strongly with a lack of structural reforms in production, factor, and product markets. The economy remained largely controlled and regulated, and when the first oil shock demonstrated the necessity of flexibility and quick adaptation, Spain's economic performance deteriorated.

Adjustment to the International Crisis: 1975–1985

A third phase in the evolution of the Spanish economy began around 1975–6 and ended around 1985. As can be seen in figure 1.1, real GDP growth fell to an average of 1.9 percent between 1975 and 1986. The inflation rate rapidly increased to an average of 14.8 percent, the unemployment rate climbed from 4.9 percent in 1976 to over 20 percent in 1985, the current account remained in deficit for most of the period, and a growing deficit appeared in the public sector. Table 1.7 depicts the evolution of the main economic variables during the period.

Spain, which at that time imported around 75 percent of its energy requirements, was unprepared to adjust quickly to the first oil price increase in 1973. Because of the unsettled situation in domestic politics, the Franco government decided not to translate the increase in imported oil prices into domestic prices. As a result, the huge transfer of funds abroad

Table 1.7 Principal economic indicators, 1976–1986

Year	GDP[a]	Rate of inflation[b]	Trade balance[c]	Current account balance[c]	Fiscal deficit[c]	Rate of unemployment
1976	3.0	17.6	− 6.8	− 4.0	− 0.3	4.9
1977	3.3	24.5	− 5.1	− 1.8	− 0.6	5.6
1978	1.8	19.8	− 2.7	1.1	− 1.8	7.5
1979	0.2	15.7	− 2.9	0.6	− 1.7	9.2
1980	1.5	15.6	− 5.5	− 2.4	− 2.0	11.5
1981	− 0.2	14.5	− 5.4	− 2.7	− 3.0	14.3
1982	1.2	14.4	− 5.1	− 2.3	− 5.6	16.2
1983	1.8	12.2	− 4.9	− 1.7	− 4.8	17.8
1984	1.9	11.3	− 2.5	1.4	− 5.3	20.6
1985	2.2	8.8	− 2.4	1.4	− 6.7	21.9
1986	3.0	8.8	− 2.6	1.8	− 5.7	21.5
Average						
1976–82	1.5	17.4	− 4.8	− 1.6	− 2.1	8.4
1983–6	2.2	10.3	− 3.1	0.7	− 5.6	19.9
1976–86	1.9	14.8	− 4.2	− 0.8	− 3.4	12.6

[a] Real rate of growth.
[b] Consumer price index
[c] As a percentage of GDP.
Source: Instituto Nacional de Estadística, various years

brought about by deterioration in Spain's terms of trade was not accompanied by a decrease in real wages (Martínez Méndez, 1982). On the contrary, wages boomed between 1973 and 1976 in both nominal and real terms. These wage increases enhanced the direct effects of the external shock and put the Spanish economy on a path of unsustainable growth. Nominal growth expenditures accelerated, and both inflation and the current account deficit intensified. This disequilibrium was made worse by macroeconomic policies to accommodate the path taken by Spain at that time.

As figure 1.3 shows, however, the situation changed after 1977. Between 1977 and 1981 (but excluding 1980) the rate of inflation and the rate of real growth both decelerated. The disinflation process continued between 1982 and 1986, although the rate of growth once more began to accelerate. Both domestic and external factors, including the second oil shock in 1979, the escalation in real interest rates throughout the world, and greater variability in exchange rates, were responsible for these developments. Important domestic factors included wage moderation, a decline in inflationary expectations, and a new financial policy. The decline in the inflation rate was accompanied by a major improvement in Spain's external position.

Inflation (%)

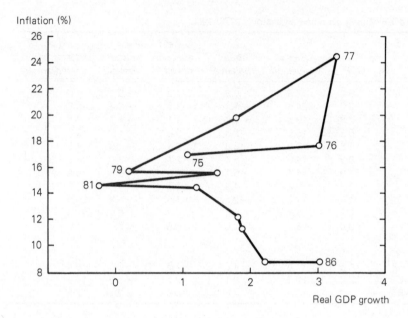

Figure 1.3 Inflation and economic growth, 1975–1986

From 1976 to 1982 (but excluding 1978 and 1979) the current account remained in deficit and outstanding external debt climbed from less then $9 billion to more than $30 billion. The period 1983–6, in contrast, was characterized by a permanent current account surplus, a reduction in outstanding debt to less than $24 billion, and an increase in foreign reserves, which at the end of June 1987 were almost equivalent to the entire external debt.

Despite this progress, two major problems remained during the whole period. The first was the unemployment rate of more than 20 percent, the highest among the countries of the Organization of Economic Cooperation and Development (OECD). The second was the public sector deficit, which hovered around 5 percent of GDP in the years from 1980 to 1985. Two factors accounted for the public sector deficit. One was the size of the transfers which had been made during the 1970s to individuals, families, and business enterprises to cushion the effects of the economic crisis. The other was the increasing burden of servicing public sector debt.

As far as structural changes are concerned, the period 1976–86 was characterized by continuity in some of the trade initiated during the 1960–75 period (table 1.8); that is, the Spanish economy continued to open up. Exports of goods and services climbed from around 14 percent of GDP in 1977 to over 24 percent in 1985, advancing at an average annual real rate of 7 percent. Imports, representing around 18 percent of GDP in 1985,

Table 1.8 Spain's domestic economy, 1976–1986

	Real rate of average growth (%)	Share of economy (%)	
		1980	1985
Demand			
Private consumption	1.5	69.5	65.2
Public consumption	4.3	10.0	11.2
Gross capital formation	− 0.9	21.1	17.0
Domestic demand		100.6	93.4
Exports of goods and services	7.0	18.2	24.5
Imports of goods and service	2.6	− 18.8	− 18.6
Supply			
Agriculture	0.9	10.5	9.3
Industry	1.4	33.5	32.1
Construction	− 0.9	5.8	5.6
Services	2.6	50.2	52.9
Total	1.9	100.0	100.0
Employment			
Agriculture	4.3	17.5	15.5
Nonagriculture	0.5	82.5	84.5
Industry	− 2.4	26.1	23.1
Construction	− 3.3	10.4	8.7
Services	1.2	42.0	44.1
Nonclassified	—	4.0	8.6
Total	− 1.2	100.0	100.0
Unemployment rate	—	11.5	21.9

—, not applicable.

Source: Instituto Nacional de Estadística, various issues

increased by an average annual real rate of 2.6 percent. Agriculture's share of GDP decreased from 10.1 percent in 1975 to 9.3 percent in 1985. Construction lost one point during the same period, while industry's share of GDP fell from 38.9 percent in 1975 to 32 percent in 1985.

On the demand side, economic growth was based mainly on an increase in private consumption. Contrary to what happened in the period 1960–75, gross capital formation declined in real terms by an annual average of 0.9 percent. From 1975 to 1986, in fact, investment did not grow in real terms except in 1980, 1985, and 1986. To replenish the stock of capital that had existed in 1975, Spanish investment would have had to grow more than 6 percent annually for seven years, without taking into account the technological obsolescence that affects most capital stock. Public consumption has been the most dynamic component of domestic absorption, although its share in GDP remained moderate.

2

The Index of Liberalization

In this chapter we describe the methodology used to construct the trade liberalization index for the period 1955–86 (figure 2.1). The index is based on quantitative and qualitative information that is used to identify the main episodes of trade liberalization between 1960 and 1986.

Three aspects of the Spanish economy were used to construct the index. First we carried out a detailed analysis of Spain's import policy, concentrating on both price devices and quantitative restriction devices that affected imports. Second Spain's export promotion policies were analyzed. Third we included estimates of real effective exchange rates for both imports and exports.

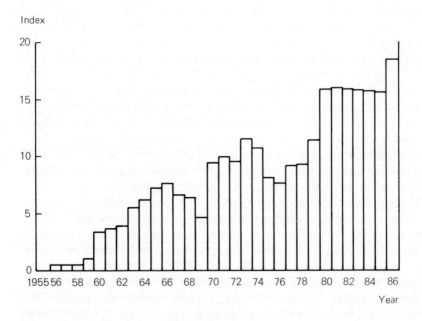

Figure 2.1 Trade liberalization index, 1955–1986

Tariffs on Imports

Spain's first trade liberalization measures were introduced in 1959, and in 1960 these were followed by a new tariff structure. Although the new tariff structure was intended to be very simple, it gradually became rather complex. Different tariffs were applied to identical or quite similar goods, depending on the country of origin or the final use of the good. To make things even more complicated, a large number of tariff exemptions and tariff reductions were put into place over the years.

A lack of data on nominal tariffs throughout the period under study compelled us to construct the Spanish tariff structure using computerized methods. Our main goal was to allocate total tariff revenues to each of the commodities covered by tariff legislation. To avoid misleading results, we concentrated on determining net tariff revenues. In this way we were able to assess discriminatory use of tariff exemptions and reductions. Only *ad valorem* nominal tariffs were taken into account.

Column 1 in table 2.1 shows the evolution of the average nominal tariff between 1960 and 1983. It was calculated as the ratio of total net custom revenues to the value of nonenergy imports. As can be seen in table 2.1, the average nominal tariff declined from 16.5 percent in 1960 to 11.2 percent in 1966, and then gradually declined further to 9.1 percent in 1971. After a small and temporary rise in 1972, the nominal tariff declined to 6.8 percent in 1974 before rising somewhat between 1974 and 1978, when a new decline began. In 1981 a record low rate of 5.0 percent was attained, followed by a moderate rise in 1982.

Table 2.2 depicts the evolution of nominal tariff rates between 1971 and 1980 according to the Brussels nomenclature. The highest tariff rates were imposed on section 6 (shoes), 7 (wood and furniture), 10 (chemical industries), 11 (rubber), 12 (other chemical products), 13 (iron and steel), 16 and 17 (machinery), 18 (transport equipment), and 20 (construction equipment).

Our analysis of the percentage of total imports subject to different tariff rates in 1971 showed that more than 30 percent of the products, accounting for 16 percent of total imports, were subject to tariff rates greater than 20 percent. By 1980 only 5 percent of the products, accounting for 3.3 percent of total imports, were subject to tariff rates higher than 20 percent.

The apportionment of customs figures among national accounts also points to a smooth process of tariff removal. Semimanufactures, with an average tariff of around 7.4 percent in 1971, were taxed at about 4.4 percent in 1980. The nominal tariff rate on capital goods declined from 14.4 to 11.3 percent, while the average tariff on light manufactures declined from 9.9 to 6.8 percent. (As we show later, however, domestic

Table 2.1 Components of the liberalization index, 1960–1983

	1	2	3	4	5	6	7	8	9
					Under		State		
Year	Tariff	ICGI(P)	DFX	Liberalized	quota	Bilateral	trading	Other	Bias
1960	16.5	0.0	2.0	40.0	20.0	20.0	19.0	1.0	112.8
1961	14.4	0.0	2.6	45.0	18.0	18.0	17.0	2.0	113.6
1962	13.3	0.0	3.4	55.0	15.0	15.0	15.0	3.0	114.7
1963	12.6	0.0	4.3	59.5	12.4	11.9	10.7	5.5	126.1
1964	13.2	0.9	5.3	63.5	12.5	6.6	12.1	5.2	101.9
1965	9.8	2.6	8.4	67.3	11.9	7.1	2.1	11.6	102.9
1966	11.2	2.7	10.0	71.2	8.3	7.6	2.0	10.9	108.4
1967	11.6	2.4	10.5	76.8	6.8	6.8	1.9	7.7	113.7
1968	10.5	1.9	10.4	75.9	5.7	8.1	1.2	9.0	110.2
1969	9.6	2.5	11.6	77.4	5.8	7.5	1.4	7.9	107.9
1970	9.5	1.6	11.2	76.2	5.5	6.7	1.1	10.5	106.0
1971	9.1	1.9	12.6	75.7	7.5	5.1	1.1	10.7	105.2
1972	9.2	2.1	13.6	74.2	7.8	5.4	1.1	11.5	109.4
1973	8.6	2.1	13.5	80.4	4.9	4.9	0.7	9.1	109.2
1974	6.8	2.5	12.8	85.2	2.9	3.9	1.1	6.8	91.5
1975	7.3	2.0	14.0	79.6	6.7	5.1	0.7	7.8	93.1
1976	8.2	2.2	13.0	78.6	7.1	5.0	0.8	8.5	95.2
1977	8.0	2.2	14.6	78.3	6.9	6.6	0.3	7.9	94.2
1978	8.1	2.6	14.3	80.0	7.1	5.1	0.4	7.4	103.4
1979	7.9	2.9	14.0	79.4	5.1	6.6	1.1	7.8	103.6
1980	6.1	2.6	13.5	91.0	1.4	3.4	0.3	3.9	89.8
1981	5.0	2.6	13.8	88.0	2.2	5.2	0.5	6.3	87.8
1982	5.4	2.6	14.3	87.0	1.0	5.0	0.7	8.3	90.0
1983	5.5	2.6	14.0	86.0	1.0	5.0	1.1	8.9	86.7

Column 1, nominal average tariff rate (authors' estimates based on net custom revenues.
Column 2, ICGI, border adjustment tax; (P) is the average protective component (authors' estimates).
Column 3, export tax rebate (authors' estimates).
Column 4, percentage of imports under liberalized status (authors' estimates).
Column 5, percentage of imports under quota status (authors' estimates).
Column 6, percentage of imports under bilateral trade (authors' estimates).
Column 7, percentage of imports under state trading (authors' estimates).
Column 8, percentage of imports under other trade regimes.
Column 9, ratio of real effective exchange rate for exports to that for imports.

light manufactures were protected by means of an import-licensing system.)

In sum, Spain's tariffs fell steadily after 1960, and simultaneously the structure of protection became more homogeneous. Although we do not have estimates of effective protection rates, except for the 1960s, we endorse the hypothesis that tariff protection declined during the period analyzed.

Table 2.2 Structure of nominal protection

Brussels nomenclature	1971		1975		1980	
	Average rate[a]	Standard deviation	Average rate	Standard deviation	Average rate	Standard deviation
1	4.9	15.9	6.1	14.5	4.1	5.2
2	0.9	9.2	1.0	8.2	1.5	3.5
3	4.1	8.5	3.5	7.3	2.7	6.3
4	5.5	20.4	3.5	13.9	3.5	2.8
5	0.1	5.4	0.0	23.1	0.0	0.5
6	9.6	12.4	7.6	9.3	5.0	9.8
7	10.8	10.5	10.1	8.7	4.1	10.6
8	2.8	7.2	1.7	6.0	1.6	5.2
9	1.9	8.0	2.6	7.1	1.7	6.0
10	9.4	12.8	5.3	8.6	5.4	9.2
11	11.5	12.2	12.3	9.3	8.0	10.1
12	21.7	7.5	19.2	6.6	10.0	9.7
13	17.3	10.9	15.6	9.7	8.7	8.9
14	1.1	8.7	0.7	7.3	0.5	2.0
15	7.3	8.0	4.9	6.9	4.8	11.0
16	14.8	9.6	12.1	8.4	11.4	10.7
17	16.8	17.9	10.7	15.9	8.8	10.7
18	15.1	14.6	12.6	10.7	8.1	8.7
19	17.1	7.3	15.7	6.5	7.9	12.5
20	28.0	9.6	25.2	8.6	11.9	10.1
21	0.0	0.0	0.0	0.0	0.0	1.8
Total A[b]	7.7	12.3	5.5	10.7	3.8	5.9
Total B[c]	9.1	12.3	7.3	10.7	6.1	5.9

[a] Customs revenues as a percentage of imports.
[b] Average total customs revenues as a percentage of total imports.
[c] Average total customs revenues as a percentage of nonenergy imports.

Border Adjustment Tax

An indirect tax, the *Impuesto del Tráfico de Empresas* (ITE), was levied on the total value of each commercial transaction in Spain. It was a cascade tax, which made it nearly impossible to know the real tax burden on any good. To the extent that the border adjustment tax on imports (ICGI) was higher than the ITE on similar domestic products, domestic products were favored by the tax structure and the ICGI functioned as an additional tariff. Estimates similar to those described in the case of tariffs were made to calculate ICGI nominal rates. Once this result was obtained, we made an estimate of the "protective component" of the ICGI that was then included in the index of liberalization.

Table 2.3 Structure of border adjustment tax

Brussels nomenclature	1971 Average rate[a]	Standard deviation	1975 Average rate	Standard deviation	1980 Average rate	Standard deviation
1	6.1	4.2	5.3	4.1	5.4	3.0
2	4.1	2.6	5.6	2.5	3.6	3.1
3	6.5	2.1	5.4	2.4	6.3	3.4
4	5.3	12.1	2.9	13.3	2.8	4.7
5	1.7	3.4	1.0	4.4	0.5	3.1
6	11.1	4.5	10.6	3.9	9.9	2.8
7	11.8	2.6	11.9	2.5	10.6	2.8
8	4.9	3.0	5.3	2.8	5.2	2.7
9	6.5	2.9	6.8	2.7	6.0	3.1
10	13.2	5.2	10.3	5.1	9.2	4.1
11	10.6	4.5	11.9	4.3	10.1	4.8
12	12.6	2.0	12.5	1.4	9.7	2.7
13	12.6	3.1	12.0	3.2	8.9	2.7
14	2.6	4.0	2.4	3.8	2.0	3.5
15	12.6	3.8	9.9	3.8	11.0	3.8
16	10.8	2.9	10.7	3.5	10.7	2.7
17	12.2	5.6	11.4	5.9	10.7	4.9
18	10.1	2.6	9.5	2.7	8.7	2.3
19	14.1	0.9	14.0	1.3	12.5	3.1
20	13.5	2.9	13.5	2.8	10.1	3.2
21	1.9	0.1	2.0	0.1	1.8	0.1
Total A[b]	8.1	5.2	6.7	5.2	5.3	4.2
Total B[c]	9.4	5.2	8.8	5.2	8.4	4.2

[a] Customs revenues as a percentage of imports.
[b] Average total customs revenues as a percentage of total imports.
[c] Average total customs revenues as a percentage of nonenergy imports.

Table 2.3 captures the main features in the evolution of the structure of the ICGI. The highest rates were found in section 6 (shoes), 7 (wood and furniture), 10 (chemical industries), 11 (rubber), 12 (other chemical products), 16 and 17 (machinery), 18 (transport equipment), 19 (shipbuilding), and 20 (construction equipment). The average ICGI rate declined from 9.4 percent in 1971 to 8.4 percent in 1980, and the standard deviation fell one point. The ICGI rates included in table 2.3 do not measure the protective component of the border adjustment tax. Instead, they measure the total indirect tax paid by importers. To determine the protective component of the ICGI we must estimate the indirect taxes paid on similar domestic goods. Lack of data prevented such an exercise at the disaggregation level shown in table 2.3, and we were forced to rely on aggregate figures. Column 2 in table 2.1 shows our estimate of the protective component of the ICGI on imports as a whole. As can be seen, we estimate the ICGI added around 2 percentage points to the aggregate nominal tariff.

Trade Regimes

Until 1986, Spanish law placed all imports under one of four different trade classifications.

1   Liberalized trade (QRL): this classification covered all commodities that needed only an import declaration for statistical purposes. These commodities did not need an import license, whereas all other imports needed licenses which were issued by the Ministry of Trade.
2   Global trade (QRG): this classification was an intermediate stage for commodities progressing toward complete liberalization. Each year the Ministry of Trade announced how much of each commodity (in terms of value) could be imported without restrictions.
3   Bilateral trade (QRB): this was a more restrictive classification that covered imports not included in the other classifications.
4   State trading (QRST): this classification covered imports of products whose sales were totally regulated by the government (i.e., petroleum and tobacco) and certain agricultural commodities.

All these trade classifications are included in our import liberalization index as follows:

$$MLI = m(t, ICGI, QRL, QRG, QRB, QRST)$$
$$m1 < 0, m2 < 0, m3 > 0, m4 > 0, m5 < 0, m6 < 0$$

where the import liberalization index (MLI) is a function m of nominal tariffs t, the border adjustment tax on imports ICGI, the percentage of liberalized trade QRL, and the shares in otal imports of global trade QRG, bilateral trade QRB, and state trading QRST. We assume that liberalization increases when tariffs and ICGI are reduced ($m1 < 0$, $m2 < 0$) and when the shares in total imports of liberalized and global trade increase ($m3 > 0$, $m4 > 0$). Also, liberalization increases when the shares in total imports of bilateral trade and state trading decrease ($m5 < 0$, $m6 < 0$).

Columns 4, 5, 6, and 7 in table 2.1 show the evolution of these trade classifications. The percentage of total imports under each trade classification for each year between 1960 and 1983 was estimated on the basis of license requests to the Ministry of Trade. The table shows a clear trend toward an easing of quantitative controls. Imports under the liberalized classification increased from 40 percent of total imports in 1960 to 86 percent in 1983, while imports coming into the country under quotas fell from 20 to 1 percent. Imports under the bilateral trade classification declined from 20 to 5 percent, while those under state trading fell from 19 to 1.1 percent. Column 8, denoted "Other," captures the remaining import flows. This is a residual and nonrestrictive classification which is not included in our index.

Promotion of Exports

Spain's export promotion system was based mainly on two mechanisms. One is an export rebate (DFX) (see table 2.1, column 3) that is symmetrical with the ICGI border tax. If the tax rebate granted to a commodity is greater than the actual amount of indirect taxes paid, there is an implicit export subsidy that must be taken into account in the liberalization index. Since Spain suffered recurrent hard currency constraints until at least the mid-1970s, it has been assumed here that any measure which fosters greater hard currency revenues should be considered to be a liberalization device. Although a mechanical interpretation of this assumption can lead to conceptual problems, the export rebate has been a major factor in reducing the anti-export bias introduced by protectionism. Hence an increase in the export rebate is viewed as a liberalization measure.

Column 3 in table 2.1 shows the evolution of the export tax rebate. The column shows export rebates as a percentage of total exports, as it is nearly impossible to determine the subsidy component of the rebate. In any case, the total percentage is also meaningful since it shows the relative incentive to sell domestically or abroad.

The second mechanism for promoting Spain's exports was an export credit system. Especially from 1971 onwards, Spain developed a sophisticated export credit system aimed at giving its exporters financial resources at rates cheap enough to allow Spanish exports to compete in international markets. Unfortunately, data shortcomings prevented us from including this system in developing our liberalization index.

The Effect of Real Effective Exchange Rates

The final building block of the liberalization index is the bias ratio – the ratio of the real effective exchange rate for exports to the real effective exchange rate for imports. Real effective exchange rates for imports and exports were estimated as follows.

$$\text{REEM} = \frac{e}{1 + t}(1 + \text{ICGI})$$

where REEM is the real effective exchange rate for imports, e is the trade-weighted exchange rate, t is the nominal tariff rate, and ICGI is the border adjustment tax for imports. If we assume that e remains unchanged, trade liberalization will mean an increase in REEM.

$$REEX = \frac{e}{1 + d}$$

where REEX is the real effective exchange rate for exports and d is the border adjustment rebate for exports. If we again assume that e remains unchanged, an increase in the export rebate d implies trade liberalization and consequently a decline in REEX.

If the ratio of bias is above 100, the economy has an anti-export bias due to a protectionist structure. Column 9 in table 2.1 shows the evolution of this variable. Although lack of data prevented inclusion of some important components (implicit tariff rate due to quantitative restrictions, export credits, etc.) in the estimates of REEM and REEX, the evolution shown in column 9 is more important than the ratio for each year. It clearly indicates that Spain gradually liberalized its trade between 1960 and 1983.

Each building block in table 2.1 has been weighted to create the liberalization index depicted in figure 2.1. As the figure demonstrates, Spain's long-term movement toward greater liberalization followed a rather smooth path marked by major liberalization episodes in 1959–66, 1970–5, and 1977–80.

3

Spain's Three Trade Liberalization Episodes

Spain's Trade Policies before Liberalization

For 20 years after the end of the Spanish Civil War in 1939 the trading system of Spain was characterized by extensive restrictions on imports and external payments, a heavy reliance on bilateral clearing agreements, and a complex exchange rate structure. Spain's policy of autarky during this period was partly the result of international distaste for the Franco dictatorship (broken only partially by a military agreement with the United States in September 1953) and partly a matter of ideological choice. The ideology of the regime was a combination of the traditional conservative values of the Church and the Army, and Spain's economic success was seen as a matter of secondary importance.

This policy, however, brought Spain to an economic dead-end whose characteristics included a highly overvalued exchange rate, a permanent balance-of-payments deficit, extremely low reserves of foreign currency, a rising rate of inflation, and a small and inefficient industrial sector.

As Spain's economic circumstances continued to deteriorate, Franco's advisers – and mainly his deputy, Admiral Carrero Blanco – persuaded him to bring "new blood" into the government. In 1957 Franco appointed a number of technocrats affiliated with the Catholic lay association Opus Dei to key posts in the economic ministries. In the same year an Office of Economic Coordination and Programming was entrusted with the task of applying economic criteria to political decisions. This office employed a group of economists who had received a modern education in economics at the recently created Department of Economics at the University of Madrid. A year later, Spain joined the Organization for European Economic Cooperation (OEEC), the World Bank, and the International Monetary Fund (IMF).

Despite these changes, Franco and some of his aides remained reluctant to alter Spain's internal economic policies. The event that finally led to a plan to try to stabilize the Spanish economy was a report issued by the Minister of Commerce in 1959 stating that the country was virtually bankrupt: Spain did not have enough foreign currency to pay for any imported products, even the most necessary of foodstuffs. The report noted that Spain's entrance fees for joining the World Bank and the IMF had been paid by means of a loan from the Manufacturers Hanover Trust Company of New York. It was the threat of Spanish insolvency that finally caused Franco to accept the necessity of changing Spain's economic policies.

Within the regime there was a clear division of views regarding the stabilization plan, with the Falangists and the Army being most opposed to it. Their continued opposition over the next several years made it impossible to complete the modernization program proposed in 1959. As the balance-of-payments crisis faded away and Spain's foreign reserves increased, trade liberalization and the reform of labor and financial markets were postponed and industrial intervention gained momentum. Once more, a traditional Spanish saying proved to be accurate: "It is impossible to make important economic reforms while the balance of payments is in surplus or near equilibrium."

The First Liberalization Episode: 1959–1966

Spain's initial liberalization and stabilization program was outlined in a memorandum sent by Spanish authorities to the IMF and OEEC in June 1959 (Viñas et al., 1979). The most important elements of the plan can be summarized as follows.

1   A uniform exchange rate system was to be introduced, thus putting an end to multiple exchange rates. In accordance with IMF guidelines, an initial par value of 60 pesetas per US dollar was established. That was a substantial devaluation of the value of the peseta.
2   Spain agreed to liberalize very rapidly at least 50 percent of its imports from convertible currency countries. Nonliberalized private trade would be undertaken under a system of nondiscriminatory quotas except for a margin no higher than 10 percent that would be reserved for imports subject to licensing. State trading was to be limited almost exclusively to agricultural products. Imports from nonconvertible currency countries would continue under bilateral trade agreements.

3   In order to avoid an unsustainable trade deficit, on July 27, 1959, the authorities instituted an advance deposit of 25 percent of the import free on board (f.o.b.) value for all private imports. It was suspended on January 23, 1960.

4   Spain's tariffs would be reformed. The general level of duties would be higher than before, but not so high as to jeopardize trade liberalization. The new tariff structure became effective on June 8, 1960.

5   A new law would be passed to provide more incentives to attract foreign capital.

Implementation of the First Liberalization Episode

In addition to tariff reform, the 1959 plan included progressive reductions in quantitative restrictions and reorganization of the import trade system. Imports were placed under one of four classifications: (a) the free list; (b) those subject to quotas; (c) those requiring individual licensing; (d) those imported through state trading. The largest difference among them was the degree of discretion allowed in approving an import request.

The government had in principle no power to restrict the value of imports on the free list. Importers submitted an import "declaration" to the Ministry of Trade which had to be approved automatically. Imports under the other three classifications shared the common freature of being subject to restrictions, although the administrative procedures for each classification were different.

Under the global quota system (initially thought of as a temporary classification for imports subject to quantitative restrictions before they were included in the free list) the Ministry of Trade announced the quota, generally for six-month periods. After the quota was announced, importers could then apply for import licenses. If total requests exceeded the quota, the authorities either reduced the amounts approved or totally denied certain requests. In many cases, however, the total amount of imports allowed proved to be higher than the original quota. Although the administrative procedures were complex, the broadly held opinion is that the system worked relatively well. Doubts exist, however, concerning the fairness of the criteria used to allocate licenses. As might have been suspected, certain importers fared better than others.

Under the state trading rules certain goods were imported directly by public agencies, while others, although under the control of the government, could be imported by private individuals. These rules covered goods subject to government monopoly, such as oil products, tobacco, and most agricultural products, including textile materials of agricultural origin.

Because of international commitments, the scope and the discriminatory rules for state-traded imports were substantially reduced after 1959.

Imports of goods not included on the free or global quota lists and not subject to state trading were authorized under a "bilateral import regime" which included unilateral licensing of imports not subject to the bilateral quotas, mainly consumer goods. This arrangement was applicable mainly to imports from nonconvertible currency countries. Spanish economic authorities were given complete discretion either to approve or to reject import applications under this system.

The first free list was published in July 1959, and it contained most foodstuffs and raw materials not controlled under state trading rules, many spare parts, and numerous kinds of equipment.

If the year 1950 is used as the reference point, goods on the free list accounted for 55 percent of private trade with the EEC countries. Global quotas covering certain raw materials and semimanufactured goods were established in August 1959. In 1960 the free list was enlarged to include chemicals, nonferrous metals, and several iron and steel goods, most of which had previously been included on the global quota list. The free list was broadened again in 1961, affecting mainly iron and steel and machinery goods. At the same time, certain textile products were added to it. In 1962, possibly the year of greatest liberalization, virtually all chemical, iron and steel, and machinery imports were added to the free list, as were most imports of shoes and leather, paper products, and textiles. From 1963 to 1966 a new enlargement of the free list was published every year, but in 1966 liberalization was halted for four years.

During the first years of liberalization, the free and global quota lists applied only to imports from OEEC members, the United States, and certain other countries. The geographic scope of the lists was steadily extended, and by 1964 it applied in practice to nearly all countries. One of the few exceptions was Japan.

The data in table 2.1 (see chapter 2) help in assessing the progress in trade liberalization attained over these years. Prior to 1959, only 6 or 7 percent of Spain's imports were wholly or partly free from restrictions of some kind.

Given the gradual elimination of quantitative restrictions Spain began to give greater attention to its tariff system. The existing tariff system, established in the 1920s, had become obsolete, and a new tariff structure was put into effect in 1960. Earlier, fearing an excessive surge of imports, Spain had provisionally increased certain duties and had established rules for advance deposits on all private imports. The new *ad valorem* tariff system covered 3,300 items instead of the approximately 1,000 on the earlier list. Its main quantitative features were as follows: 25 percent of items had tariff rates of less than 17 percent, 50 percent had tariff rates between 17 and 35 percent, and 25 percent had tariff rates of more than 35 percent. The average tariff was 24.9 percent.

Criticisms of the New Tariff Structure

The new tariff structure was criticized on several grounds.

1   The new tariffs were based on an exchange rate of 50 pesetas per US dollar. Since the par value that was adopted was 20 percent higher, the implicit average rate of nominal protection for domestic substitutes for imports increased to almost 50 percent.

2   Computation of the new tariffs was based on differentials between international and domestic prices. Established as the tariff equivalent of Spain's previous quantitative restrictions, the new rates tended to sustain protection for Spanish products. Between 1959 and 1966, apparently in response to this criticism, Spain gradually reduced its duties.

It has been estimated, in fact, that the average new tariff rate was 10 percent lower than that initially proposed. A few days after the publication of the new tariff law, "transitory" duties were levied on textiles, metal products, and machinery at rates about 20 or 30 percent lower than those initially proposed. This was also the case for certain noncompetitive equipment goods, whose legal duty was 30 percent but whose "transitory" duty was 5 percent. The use of "transitory" duties, continuously renewed, was a common way to modify tariff rates. The common view was that transitory duties made it easier to resist the usual domestic political costs of tariff reduction.

In addition to selective interventions like those discussed above, the government also carried out general tariff reductions in 1963, 1964, and 1965. Tariff policy was often used as an anti-inflationary tool, and this was the reason why all tariffs were reduced by 5 percent in 1963 and again in 1964. In addition, the introduction of a new border tax was offset by an equivalent decrease in tariff rates. The net effect was to reduce tariffs by almost 25 percent. Finally, in August 1965, a further 10 percent tariff reduction was introduced, this time mainly for textile imports.

The Spanish tariff structure was also made more complicated by the establishment in 1963 of a *prélèvement* on agricultural products. In Spain, this received the name *derecho regulador* and constituted a *de facto* liberalization of many imports previously subject to the global quota or the state trading system.

The use of these variations in the tariff schedule introduced an element of complexity into the tariff that ran counter to one of the initial goals of tariff reform, namely simplicity. The proliferation of exemptions and subsidies as tools of industrial policy, especially after 1964, hindered coordination of commercial trade policy. As a result of all these measures, however, both nominal and effective rates of protection decreased and inequality in the inter-industrial structure of protection became less. This is illustrated in table 3.1.

Table 3.1 Nominal and effective rates of protection (manufacturing), 1962 and 1966

		Nominal rate of protection			Effective rate of protection		
		Unweighted average	Weighted average	Standard deviation	Unweighted average	Weighted average	Standard deviation
Finished consumer goods	1962	30.0	44.7	21.0	70.0	79.9	51.7
	1966	20.7	21.7	9.8	55.4	47.8	57.5
Intermediate products	1962	28.8	30.2	14.5	64.7	80.3	69.3
	1966	15.7	16.5	8.3	54.0	61.3	39.8
Investment goods	1962	26.2	29.8	9.9	37.9	47.1	29.4
	1966	13.7	14.6	5.7	32.7	37.3	21.0
Total manufactures	1962	31.6	34.3	17.1	62.1	76.3	60.2
	1966	16.9	17.5	8.1	51.1	54.2	41.9

Source: Donges, 1971

The Second Liberalization Episode: 1970–1975

On June 29, 1970, Spain signed a preferential trade agreement with the EEC that became effective on October 1. Under the agreement many tariffs were reduced and numerous commodities were transferred from the global quota list to free-import status. Although limited, the preferential agreement with the EEC was important because it paved the way for new measures adopted by Spain between 1972 and 1974.

The chief characteristics of this second liberalization episode were a reduction in the levels of dispersion of nominal tariffs, reductions in the extent and restrictiveness of the quantitative restriction system, and improvements in Spain's export promotion measures.

Economic Circumstances Prior to 1970

The expansion of the economy that had started in 1960 began to lose its momentum in 1966. The inflation rate rose, and equilibrium in Spain's balance of payments began to erode despite a growing surplus in net services.

In November 1967 Spain's economic authorities approved a program that included a 16.7 percent devaluation of the peseta, tighter financial policies, and a freeze on prices, wages, and other incomes in 1968–9. The program was very successful. The inflation rate plummeted, and the external account improved. These changes were compatible with a rather high rate of GDP growth and, when the new period of liberalization began in 1970, Spain seemed to have recovered its macroeconomic stability. The economy was growing at a rate of more than 4 percent a year, the inflation rate was slightly over 5.7 percent, and the country had a current account surplus. This economic progress, however, hid several structural weaknesses and rigidities.

First it was evident that Spain's agricultural policy – an attempt to maintain the country's traditional agricultural system – was blocking the modernization of the agricultural sector. The policy had the effect of deteriorating Spain's agricultural trade balance while stimulating inflation through agricultural support prices that kept the prices of agricultural products higher than they would have been without subsidies.

Another structural weakness was Spain's fragmented industrial sector. Small- and medium-sized enterprises were unable to take advantage of economies of scale, which in turn prevented them from keeping pace with technological change.

Political Circumstances Prior to 1970

Political unrest had begun to become evident in Spain by the end of 1969. After 30 years in power, Franco's regime began to experience difficulties. In the view of most observers, the regime hindered the transformation of Spain into a modern country governed by democratic principles like those enjoyed by other European nations (Anderson, 1970). However, Franco, then 78 and in poor health, remained determined to maintain his authoritarian regime. Hence the years between 1970 and 1975 witnessed a pervasive struggle over the survival of "Francoism without Franco."

Franco took two major steps to try to quell unrest while at the same time guaranteeing the survival of Francoism. He named as his successor Prince Juan Carlos and appointed Admiral Carrero Blanco as prime minister while reserving for himself the title of Head of State.

The new government overlapped with the financial scandal derived from the Matesa affair. In August 1969 the government discovered that export credits valued at at least 10,000 million pesetas had been fraudulently used by the company Matesa. The Matesa staff, linked with Opus Dei, were arrested. The ministers of commerce and finance also appeared to be involved in the affair. The political implications of the Matesa scandal were very important, given that the right-wing elements of the regime tried to take advantage of the situation and to get rid of the Opus Dei technocrats. Franco decided to reorganize his cabinet in October, and named new minister to 13 of the 18 posts in the cabinet. Technocrats involved in the financial scandal and Falangists involved in the political struggle both disappeared from the Council of Ministers.

Meanwhile, political unrest increased steadily. In a country where strikes were forbidden, there were 1,547 strikes in 1970, 542 in 1971, and more than 850 in 1973. Violence was growing in the Basque country, and the terrorist group ETA found wide social support. The 1970 Burgos trial, where 16 members of ETA were tried, helped to tarnish the national and international image of Franco's regime. Already limited political rights were restricted further in December 1970, when a "state of exception" was declared in the country. Although Franco commuted the six death penalties pronounced by the Burgos tribunal, the political situation continued to be tense until a democratic regime was finally established in 1977.

Implementation during the Second Liberalization Period

Spain's preferential trade agreement with the EEC included a timetable for reducing nominal duties. The proposed timetable for tariff reductions is shown in table 3.2. Only coal, iron and steel products, and certain other commodities were excluded from the agreement, and at least 60 percent of Spain's imports from the EEC were affected by the schedule of tariff cuts. But the scheduled reductions, based on gross actual tariffs, did not take into account Spain's complex system of lower tariff rates for many industrial and regional purposes. The actual reductions in Spain's tariffs were therefore substantially less than the timetable suggests.

Table 3.2 Timetable of Spanish tariff reductions (percent)

Commodities	1970	1973	1974	1975	1976	1977
List A	10	20	30	40	50	60
List B	5	10	10	15	20	25
List C	5	10	10	15	20	25

Under the agreement, Spain's system of quantitative restrictions was also to be revised. By 1976, only 5 percent of Spain's imports from the EEC were to be included in Spain's global quotas. To achieve this target, Spain agreed to increase annually the average value of total quota imports from the EEC countries by 13 percent and the value under each of its 84 specific quotas by at least 7 percent. Quotas that were not binding during two consecutive years were automatically liberalized.

In turn, the EEC countries agreed to substantially reduce their tariffs on Spanish industrial exports. The average tariff reduction was 60 percent (30 percent in 1970, 50 percent in 1972, and 60 percent in 1973), although some exceptions were also included in the agreement. The EEC tariff reductions on Spanish agricultural products were smaller, and were less than those granted to some other Mediterranean countries.

In addition to the EEC agreement, other liberalization measures were implemented between 1972 and 1974. They were temporary, with their duration conditioned on "the continuation of present economic conditions." The legislation under which the tariff reductions were adopted was only in force for periods of three or six months and had to be renewed by a new decree when it expired. Given this approach, it is hard to believe that Spain had devised a systematic program to reduce protection. It seems more probable that the Spanish authorities intended to reduce trade restrictions when inflationary pressures mounted and to raise them when pressures by local manufacturers intensified or when inflation receded.

After a selective reduction in import duties in November 1972, a more extensive tariff cut for industrial products was introduced in June 1973. Goods were classified under three groups depending on their degree of effective protection. Those with average or higher than average protection experienced nominal tariff cuts of 10 and 20 percent respectively. Tariffs on goods with lower than average protection were not, in general, modified. Exceptionally, for a small group of items, reductions exceeded 20 percent.

The 1973 cut affected about 54 percent of all imported items subject to tariffs. About 19 percent of the imported industrial goods were items whose tariffs were only 5.5 percent or less, while 16 percent were agricultural goods for which import duties were not the main protective device.

In January 1974 Spain again reduced tariffs on all imported industrial goods by 5 percent except for those whose nominal tariffs were already less than 5 percent. This cut was increased to 10 percent in April 1974. But in June 1975, when Spain had a deficit in its current account, the 1973 and 1974 reductions were revoked.

The liberalization of quantitative restriction followed a similar pattern. In December 1972 the Ministry of Commerce replaced the traditional system of long lists of products not subject to quotas with a short list showing those goods that were subject to quotas. All goods not on the new short list were automatically considered liberalized. In October 1972, and in June 1973 and 1974, additional agricultural and industrial goods that had been subject to state trading rules or quotas were placed under the free-import regime.

However, this trend toward liberalization was reversed late in 1974 and early in 1975, when all these imported goods were again made subject to global quotas. As a result, the degree of trade liberalization in Spain by mid-1975 was no better than it had been in 1966, except for Spain's commitments within the EEC preferential agreement which remained unchanged.

The Third Liberalization Episode: 1977–1980

The third liberalization episode took place between 1977 and 1980. It was an attempt at rapid liberalization that slowed down when the second oil shock hit the Spanish economy.

As in the second episode, the main measures adopted were across-the-board and selective tariff cuts, further easing of the quantitative restriction system and modification of Spain's export promotion scheme, chiefly a major provision of funds to support export credits and the export tax rebate mechanism.

Several government declarations were issued stressing Spain's intention to foster external competition and the integration of the Spanish economy into world markets. No concrete goals were established, however, possibly because the Spanish government thought that Spain would soon become a full member of the EEC and decided to wait until full membership was achieved before outlining a detailed program. But Spanish membership of the EEC did not take place until 1985. Meanwhile, the 1979 oil shock, a disturbed political climate, and the difficulties of negotiating full EEC membership slowed the pace of liberalization.

Trade liberalization during the 1977–80 period was encouraged by two events, however. In June 1979 Spain signed a trade agreement with the seven members of the European Free Trade Agreement (EFTA) which was designed to gradually eliminate all barriers to trade between Spain and EFTA. One result of this agreement was that Spain extended to the EFTA countries the same benefits accorded to EEC members under the 1970 preferential trade agreement. Then, in July 1980, a royal decree approved the tariff reductions that resulted from the Tokyo Round of negotiations under the General Agreement on Tariffs and Trade (GATT) (Torres y Gamir, 1986 a, b).

Spain's Economic Circumstances in the 1970s

The period between 1973 and 1977 in Spain was marked by enormous political turmoil as the Franco regime came to an end with the death of the dictator in 1975. Dramatic economic disequilibria accumulated during those years and finally erupted in 1977, the year of the first general election in Spain in four decades. The new democratically elected government had to tackle a raging inflation rate (24.5 percent), a large balance-of-payments deficit, a rising unemployment rate (4.1 percent), and the emergence of a public budget deficit.

These problems were too difficult to be solved by the winning party in he 1977 election, the Democratic Center Union (UCD). Since the UCD did not have a majority in the Spanish Parliament, President Suárez worked with other political forces to produce the so-called *Pactos de la Moncloa* (Moncloa Pact). The main goal of the Moncloa Pact was to carry out a classic stabilization program in order to reduce domestic expenditures and put an end to the growing disequilibrium in Spain's external accounts (Ministerio de Economía, 1977). In mid-1977 the Spanish peseta was devalued by 20 percent against the US dollar, ceilings on wage increases and public sector expenditures were established, and tighter monetary targets were set.

This stabilization program achieved considerable success. In 1978 Spain's current account registered a small surplus (1.1 percent of GDP), and the inflation rate was reduced by nearly 5 percentage points. But the success of the program also produced high social costs. Domestic demand and GDP stagnated, and the unemployment rate rose to 6.3 percent in 1978. Furthermore, a deliberate decision to expand social benefits caused the public sector deficit as a percentage of GDP to triple in 1978.

Political Circumstances of the 1970s

During the period 1977–1982, Spain's political structure was not stable. Terrorism, and unrest among the armed forces resulting from the shift towards democracy, led to an attempted military coup in 1981. Except for segments of the armed forces, however, the Suárez government was supported by Spain's major political parties. This support of the majority allowed the government to carry out its economic program, since Spain's people soon realized that the only way to secure democracy was to adjust Spain's economic system to the new realities of international interdependence and thus to integrate Spain with the rest of the EEC. Commercial policy was seen as an active contributor to improvements in the flexibility of the economy, to enhancing the competitiveness of the tradeable sector, and to preparing the economy for full membership of the EEC.

Implementation of the Third Liberalization Episode

The third liberalization episode did not begin with a detailed program. General transfers of imported commodities from the restricted list to liberalized status occurred in January 1978, June 1978, and April 1979. Practically all imported goods that had been subject to global quotas at the end of 1974 were transferred to the free list, and other industrial and agricultural goods were also liberalized. From then on, except for certain items, there was no further liberalization and the import regime remained quite stable until March 1986.

The years 1975 and 1984 are good indicators of the situation before and after the third liberalization. Substantial progress was achieved in liberalizing industrial products. Unrestricted imports increased, while goods covered by global quotas or state trading procedures decreased. The pattern was similar for agricultural and energy imports, although the evidence is not quite as definitive. An increase in bilateral agricultural imports mainly reflected the privatization of liberalization of imports previously subject to state trading rules. However, an increase in the percentage of energy imports under "other regimes" was basically the result of a rise in the value of imports by the public sector after the second oil shock for monopoly reasons and not for restrictive purposes.

Tariffs during the Third Episode
A temporary increase in tariffs introduced in 1976 was abolished in February 1977, while a 20 percent transitory surcharge, also introduced in 1976, was eliminated in July 1977. Tariff reductions, which started in 1978, had the same transitory character as they did during the second episode. The first reduction, which was only good for three months, applied to industrial commodities and amounted to a 20 percent fall in rates greater than 10 percent but was only applicable to the portion exceeding 10 percent.

A new three-month across-the-board tariff reduction was then approved in April 1979. Specific duties were reduced by 15 percent, while *ad valorem* duties underwent a progressive reduction. Rates between zero and 10 percent were reduced by 10 percent, rates ranging from 10 to 20 percent were cut by 20 percent, tariffs between 20 and 30 percent were cut by 30 percent, and the reduction for duties exceeding 30 percent was 40 percent. This decree was renewed in July and October 1979 and January 1980. In April 1980 the across-the-board reduction was modified to 18 percent for commodities taxed at tariff rates between 10 and 20 percent, 27 percent for goods with tariffs between 20 and 30 percent, and 36 percent for goods whose rate exceeded 30 percent. These reductions were maintained until 1986, when a new liberalization episode started, this time associated with Spain's membership of the EEC. In addition, tariff reductions under the EFTA agreement and the Tokyo Round of GATT negotiations came into force in July 1980.

The results of Spain's tariff policy during this period can be seen in table 3.3. Nominal protection in industrial sectors decreased, while the fiscal adjustment tax on imports remained fairly stable, though its protective aspect decreased as domestic taxation of import-competing goods substantially increased.

By broad categories, nominal tariff protection fell by 26.5 percent in manufacturing industries, 6.6 percent in equipment goods, and 17.7 percent in extractive industries. The simple average of all nominal tariffs decreased by 17.9 percent. Plastics, transport materials, nonmetallic minerals, textiles, shoes, and cloth had higher than average tariff protection. The structure of fiscal adjustment taxes was quite similar, and there

Table 3.3 Nominal protection for industry, 1976 and 1983 (percent)

	1976			1983		
Sector	Tariffs	Border adjustment tax	Tariffs plus border adjustment tax	Tariffs	Border adjustment tax	Tariffs plus border adjustment tax
Metallic minerals	0.2	5.8	6.1	0.1	5.4	5.5
Metal products	3.3	7.7	11.1	3.7	8.9	12.6
Nonmetal products	16.3	12.2	28.6	12.4	10.4	22.9
Chemical	9.4	11.7	21.2	6.3	11.2	17.6
Subtotal	6.2	9.5	15.7	5.1	9.8	14.9
Machinery	12.7	10.4	23.1	9.6	12.2	19.9
Transport equipment	10.1	10.4	20.5	16.5	13.6	30.1
Subtotal	12.2	10.4	22.6	11.4	11.0	22.5
Food and beverages	5.2	6.5	11.8	3.6	7.2	10.9
Textiles	16.7	13.0	29.7	12.4	13.5	26.0
Shoes and apparel	13.0	11.1	14.2	11.3	11.7	23.0
Wood and furniture	5.6	8.1	13.7	5.7	8.4	14.2
Paper and printing	7.3	10.1	17.5	5.2	6.6	11.8
Plastics	22.3	13.3	35.6	16.9	13.5	30.4
Miscellaneous	13.4	8.5	22.0	7.5	7.0	14.5
Subtotal	9.8	8.8	18.7	7.2	8.3	15.6
Average	10.4	9.9	20.4	8.5	9.8	18.3
Standard deviation	5.5	2.3	8.0	4.9	2.7	7.4
Coefficient of variation	0.57	0.23	0.39	0.58	0.28	0.40

was a strong correlation between protection through tariffs and protection taxes. However, there was a concentration of imports in the lower tariff ranges. In 1983, about 81 percent of all imports, by value, and 44 percent of all tariff items were subject to tariffs between zero and 10 percent.

Spain's Macroeconomic Policies, 1959–1980

The evolution of the macroeconomic policies that shaped the economic environment in which the liberalization episodes took place is described in this section.

First, the Spanish economy continued to show distortions that hampered the functioning of factor markets. In the labor market, for example, labor mobility was limited by several regulations concerning the duration of labor contracts that made it difficult and costly to dismis redundant workers. Furthermore, the wage boom that preceded the transition for dictatorship to democracy paved the way for the implementation of several types of income policies that had substantial impacts on the wage structure and the subsequent unemployment suffered by some subgroups in the labor force.

Spain's capital market was also affected by economic intervention. Domestic interest rates were subject to ceilings aimed at keeping real interest rates negative, barriers to entry for additional lenders were very strong, and foreign banks were barred from Spain until the late 1970s. Credit rationing was a normal practice in the 1960s and early 1970s, and some sectors took advantage of funds channeled to them on special and privileged conditions. Exchange controls on capital outflows, although they declined, remained substantial and thus tended to isolate the Spanish capital market from world markets.

All three liberalization episodes were preceded by stabilization of the economy through tighter financial policies combined with devaluations in the nominal exchange rate. Fiscal conservatism helps to explain the success of the first liberalization episode, given that the monetary impacts of fiscal disequilibria would have been difficult to absorb in view of the few variables that were effectively controlled by the monetary authorities.

A final remark is related to exchange rate policy. The real exchange rate of the peseta appreciated during the three episodes because changes in the nominal exchange rate could not accommodate Spain's higher inflation rates *vis-à-vis* its major trading partners. This trend started in the period of fixed rates and continued when exchange rates were allowed to float, beginning in 1973. In the late 1970s, though, Spain's monetary authorities paid more attention to exchange rate management and tried to avoid real appreciation of the peseta *vis-à-vis* the currencies of the EEC countries.

Monetary Policy

Spain's monetary policy in the 1950s and 1960s was basically passive. The priority given to public sector financing by means of issuing government securities that could automatically be pledged or monetized at the Central Bank impeded monetary control. However, when Spain was confronted by accelerating inflation and balance-of-payments difficulties in 1957, an attempt was made to implement a restrictive policy. This effort had little immediate effect, although a decision was made to stop issuing automatically pledgeable securities at the end of 1958.

The stabilization plan of 1959 included effective measures of monetary restraint. The success of the program depended on sound monetary policy – in particular, avoiding excessive growth in liquidity. The effective measures were primarily credit ceilings and an increase in interest rates.

A ceiling on credit to the private sector reduced the rate of growth of such credit from 16 percent in 1958 to 7 percent in 1959. Lending from the Central Bank to the public sector was also restricted, and direct financing of public enterprises, except for agricultural marketing agencies, was halted. To deter imports and to reduce liquidity, a 25 percent advance deposit on imports was imposed until January 1960. Furthermore, rediscount rates increased by 1.5 percent.

By mid-1960 Spain's balance-of-payments situation had improved substantially. Monetary policy was then relaxed. The Bank of Spain reduced its basic rate of interest and removed the ceiling on lending to the private sector. At that time the financial requirements of the public sector did not constrain monetary policy, and Spain was able to provide cheap and abundant financing to the private sector to foster economic growth. This was accomplished chiefly through the development of preferential credits to priority sectors and by the granting of automatic credit in the form of "special rediscounts." These posed the same basic problems of monetary control that had occurred in the 1950s.

The policy of easy money in the 1960s is reflected in table 3.4. Money growth in 1959 reflected the restrictions of stabilization but was offset in 1960 by the behavior of quasi-money. From 1961 onward, monetary policy was expansive with respect to both money and quasi-money. The money supply grew at an annual average rate of 16.8 percent in the period 1959–66, more than accommodating the annual growth in nominal GDP over the same years (12.3 percent). Initially, the private sector was the major contributor to money creation. The public sector played a more important role after 1964, while the external sector injected liquidity into the system until 1965 when recurrent balance-of-payments deficits appeared.

A monetary policy designed to control monetary aggregates and interest rates on a continuous basis did not exist until 1973. Until then, the major monetary instrument used in Spain was direct rationing of credit on an *ad hoc* basis at times of crisis. The last shortage of credit took place at the end of 1969. Its restrictive effects were intense but short lived. Spain's Central Bank quickly raised the ceilings on ordinary and special rediscount lines of credit. Following this episode, the monetary authorities decided that the time had come to establish a gradualist approach to monetary control. They defined their policy objectives in terms of rate of money growth and sought to reach this target by controlling the monetary base. Legal controls on interest rates led to the adoption of a broad concept of money that included sight, saving, and term deposits (the so-called M3), to avoid the uncertainty caused by shifts in less inclusive concepts of money. Monetary expansion was high up to 1973. With a new government in office and increasing inflation, a gradual policy of monetary deceleration started by mid-1973. As a consequence, real balances decreased substantially in 1974 and 1975. Overall, M3 increased by 21 percent on average between 1970 and 1975, more than 3 percentage points above GDP growth, and real balances increased by 8.7 percent.

Table 3.4 Monetary policy indicators, 1959–1985

Year	M3	GDP deflator	Real balance	Real growth in GDP
First liberalization episode				
1959	6.9	5.8	1.0	− 2.2
1960	15.0	0.4	14.5	0.9
1961	17.6	1.8	15.5	11.3
1962	20.5	5.7	14.0	9.6
1963	17.2	8.5	8.0	9.5
1964	21.8	14.9	6.0	6.6
1965	19.6	9.4	9.3	6.2
1966	15.6	8.1	6.9	7.1
1967	15.4	7.7	7.1	4.3
1968	18.8	5.0	13.1	6.9
1969	18.8	4.4	13.8	8.3
Second liberalization episode				
1970	16.0	6.8	8.6	4.1
1971	20.5	8.0	11.6	5.0
1972	23.9	8.7	˙14.0	8.1
1973	25.2	11.8	12.0	7.9
1974	20.5	16.6	3.3	5.7
1975	18.6	16.7	1.6	1.1
1976	18.4	16.7	1.5	3.0
Third liberalization episode				
1977	19.6	22.8	− 2.6	3.3
1978	19.8	20.2	− 0.3	1.8
1979	19.5	16.7	2.4	0.2
1980	17.7	13.9	3.3	1.5
1981	15.4	13.7	1.5	− 0.2
1982	16.6	13.5	2.7	1.2
1983	12.1	11.9	0.2	1.8
1984	12.9	11.3	1.4	1.9
1985	9.6	6.0	3.4	2.2

Sources: Banco de España, various years; Instituto Nacional de Estadística, various years

Money restraint was one of the major components of the stabilization program implemented in the summer of 1977 to deal with internal and external imbalances. As a result, M3 in real terms showed a negative rate of growth in 1977 and 1978. Between the end of 1977 and mid-1979 an increase in net foreign assets and increasing borrowing requirements in the public sector accounted for roughly 80 percent and 60 percent respectively of growth of the monetary base. Given the Central Bank's strong commitment to M3 targets, credit to the private sector decelerated substantially from 23.5 percent in 1976 to 15.2 percent in 1978 and 1979. Meanwhile, credit to the public sector increased on average around 30 percent, thereby raising its share of total credit by nearly 3 percentage points. Monetary policy was more permissive in 1979–80. M3 grew slightly more than nominal GDP, and real balances slowly increased.

Fiscal Policy

A clear change in fiscal policy was announced in the memorandum on stabilization sent to the OEEC in 1959. There was an explicit promise to follow a balanced-budget policy and noninflationary financing of the deficit. In addition, the memorandum pledged to reduce the burden of the financial deficits of public firms and to design a general plan for public investment (Viñas et al., 1979).

For these purposes, two sets of measures were announced. The first, for the period July–December 1959, included an increase in some taxes (the petrol tax and tariffs) and a limit of 80 billion pesetas for total public expenditures. The second set, covering 1960, was only a list of targets. The objectives were to reach a balanced budget (again with a ceiling on expendiures of 80 billion pesetas) and to eliminate government borrowing from the Central Bank.

The initial commitments were legally implemented in July 1959 through several decrees which increased tax rates on certain goods and services and included a transitory rise in customs duties. Total budget expenditures of the government stayed within the limits, although extra-budget expenditures, primarily by public enterprises, grew at a faster pace. No important actions were taken in the public sector except for an increase in the price of certain public services. The same happened in relation to the rationalization of public investment projects.

As can be seen in table 3.5, the most outstanding feature of fiscal policy during the first liberalization episode was its restrictive nature. There was a small (1 percent of GDP) public sector budget surplus for each year. Total revenues and expenditures experienced a steady rate of growth until 1964 and then grew faster than GDP, thus moderately increasing the participation of the public sector. Similar growth rates in government revenues resulted in a substantial reduction in government borrowing requirements.

Fiscal policy during the second liberalization episode was quite similar to policy during the first episode. Current revenues grew on average by 20.2 percent annually between 1971 and 1975, while current expenditures increased by 20.5 percent and capital expenditures rose by 19 percent.

The public sector surplus was always larger than investment outlays, leaving sizable savings available for capital transfers. A large part of the public savings was generated by the social security system. It could be said that the public sector operated in the following way: the social security system was the ultimate lender, the central and local authorities were the

Table 3.5 Fiscal policy indicators, 1959–1984 (percent of gross domestic product)

	Current			Capital		
Year	Revenues	Expenditures	Savings	Revenues	Expenditures	Public sector borrowing
1959	15.8	11.5	4.2	0.5	3.8	1.1
1960	17.1	12.2	4.9	0.4	4.2	1.3
1961	17.3	11.7	5.6	0.4	3.7	2.8
1962	17.7	13.0	4.7	0.4	3.5	1.9
1963	17.0	13.2	3.8	0.4	3.8	0.4
1964	17.9	13.2	4.7	0.4	4.4	0.7
1965	19.0	14.2	4.8	0.4	4.6	0.5
1966	18.8	14.2	4.6	0.4	4.6	0.4
1970	22.9	18.8	4.2	0.3	3.7	0.7
1971	23.0	19.7	3.3	0.3	4.1	− 0.6
1972	23.4	19.7	3.7	0.3	3.8	0.3
1973	24.1	19.7	4.4	0.3	3.5	1.1
1974	23.3	19.8	3.5	0.2	3.5	0.2
1975	24.8	21.2	3.5	0.2	3.7	0.0
1977	26.9	23.7	3.1	0.2	3.9	0.6
1978	27.5	26.2	1.4	0.2	3.3	− 1.8
1979	28.8	27.7	1.1	0.2	3.0	− 1.7
1980	30.4	29.2	1.2	0.2	3.4	− 2.0
1981	31.1	30.3	0.8	0.2	4.0	− 3.0
1982	30.8	31.6	− 0.8	0.2	5.2	− 5.8
1983	32.7	32.7	0.0	0.2	4.9	− 4.8
1984	31.9	33.3	− 1.4	0.2	3.7	− 5.0

Sources: Banco de España, various years; Ministerio de Economía y Hacienda, various years; Comin, 1985

ultimate borrowers, and the official credit institutions acted as financial intermediaries, issuing securities and channeling funds to the private sector.

A main budgetary deficit was recorded in 1971 but did not reappear again until 1976, when it began to increase steeply. For the whole period, current savings remained positive (around 3.7 percent of GDP) and the public sector registered an annual surplus of about 0.3 percent of GDP. During this period the public sector did not cause monetary management problems, and the government contribution to growth in the monetary base was about 23 percentage points.

Income and other taxes (excluding social security taxes) accounted for 50 percent of revenues, while social security taxes accounted for 40 percent. Revenues raised by indirect taxes were about twice the amount of funds collected by direct taxes. But the fiscal system suffered from generalized tax evasion as well as substantial tax exemptions granted to specific types of taxpayers. No major changes in the tax system were introduced until 1977, when a reform plan was approved by the first democratic government. On the expenditure side, welfare payments and current transfers were the main items, accounting for 67 percent and 16 percent respectively.

Spain's fiscal situation during the third period of liberalization was drastically different from the previous episodes. After years of relatively small surpluses, Spain recorded continuous and increasing deficits after 1976. From 1977 to 1980 the annual public deficit was about 1.5 percent of GDP.

Revenues increased at an average annual rate of 25.6 percent, while current and capital expenditures increased at average annual rates of 28.1 percent and 22.2 percent respectively. As a result, the share of total revenues in GDP increased from 27.1 to 30.4 percent, while total annual expenditures rose from 27.6 to 32.6 percent of GDP.

The rise in government expenditures after 1977 reflected a deterioration in economic circumstances that led to a large expansion of current transfers, mainly welfare and unemployment payments and subsidies to public agencies. This expansion of current transfers retarded public investment, since the government chose to hold down the deficit by postponing capital outlays. Despite the 1977 tax reform, revenues grew more slowly than they had before 1977. Tax reform was intended to create greater equity in taxation and to curb tax evasion. Prior to 1978, the system obtained revenue chiefly through indirect taxes. (In 1976, for example, indirect taxes accounted for more that 60 percent of all revenue.) Direct taxes were levied without considering the income of the taxpayer and fraud was widespread. The most important change in 1977 was modification of the personal income tax, which was imposed on all incomes at progressive rates ranging from 15 to 40 percent. Reform also included the establishment of a wealth tax, some surcharges on luxury taxes, and minor changes in the corporate tax. Despite reform, however, revenues increased at a decreasing rate. By 1979, direct taxes accounted for 50 percent of total tax revenues.

The emergence of a public deficit in 1976 marked the beginning of a new disequilibrium that would prove difficult to eliminate; by 1982 the deficit had reached 5.4 percent of GDP. A high proportion of the deficit was monetized. In 1982 the deficit accounted for 117 percent of the increase in the monetary base, compared with only 38.5 percent in 1975.

Exchange Rate Policy

Spain's exchange rate was fixed from 1939 until 1948, when a system of multiple rates was introduced. An attempt to reunify the exchange rate structure was made in 1957, when a formal rate of 42 pesetas per US dollar was established. This rate could not be maintained, however, since in the free market of Tangiers the rate was 59 pesetas to the dollar. Hence, multiple rates were again introduced, and a complex structure of export premiums and import taxes emerged. Export rates ranged from 31 to 57 pesetas per US dollar and import rates from 25.5 to 127.7 pesetas per US dollar, although rates higher than 50 pesetas per US dollar were infrequent. A major component of the 1959 stabilization plan was the introduction of a unified exchange rate which set the par value at 60 pesetas per US dollar. This new formal parity meant a devaluation of more than 40 percent.

Spain, like many other countries, followed a policy of fixed exchange rates from 1959 to 1973, with minor adjustments in 1967, when the pesetas was devalued again the dollar by an average of 14.1 percent, and between 1970 and 1973, when the peseta appreciated against the dollar. The most important feature of the second period of fixed exchange rates was continuous appreciation in the real exchange rate of the peseta.

Table 3.6 and figure 3.1 show that Spanish authorities never used exchange rates as a tool to promote exports. In fact, they allowed real exchange rates to appreciate, reintroducing the anti-export bias created by the existing structure of protection.

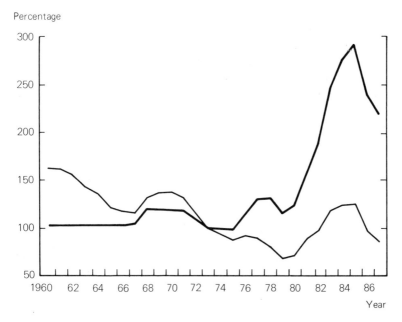

Figure 3.1 Exchange rate policy with respect to the US dollar, 1960–1987: ————, nominal exchange rate (pesetas per US dollar); ————, purchasing power parity adjusted exchange rate (pesetas per US dollar)

Table 3.6 Indicators of exchange rate policy with respect to the US dollar, 1960–1984

Year	Nominal exchange rate (pesetas per US$)	Nominal effective exchange rate (imports)	Nominal effective exchange rate (exports)	Real exchange rate (pesetas per US$)	Real effective exchange rate (imports)	Real effective exchange rate (exports)
1960	60.0	88.1	75.2	225.9	237.9	203.0
1961	60.0	88.7	75.6	224.5	238.1	203.0
1962	60.0	88.0	76.2	214.7	225.9	195.6
1963	59.9	87.2	76.7	199.5	208.4	183.3
1964	59.9	88.5	77.5	189.3	200.6	175.6
1965	59.9	87.3	79.8	169.8	177.6	162.2
1966	59.9	88.7	81.0	164.5	174.5	159.5
1967	61.7	90.8	82.9	161.8	172.3	157.5
1968	69.7	101.6	94.5	183.5	191.8	178.5
1969	69.9	102.1	95.8	189.9	199.0	186.7
1970	69.7	100.8	95.2	190.1	197.1	186.2
1971	69.2	99.9	95.8	181.8	188.2	180.4
1972	64.3	93.0	89.7	160.9	167.0	161.1
1973	58.3	83.9	81.3	139.2	143.7	139.2
1974	57.7	81.1	80.0	132.2	133.2	131.3
1975	57.4	80.5	80.4	122.6	123.3	123.1
1976	66.9	95.0	92.9	128.4	130.7	127.9
1977	76.0	107.9	107.0	124.7	127.1	125.9
1978	76.7	109.1	107.7	113.1	115.5	113.9
1979	67.1	95.5	94.0	95.3	97.2	95.7
1980	71.7	100.0	100.0	100.0	100.0	100.0
1981	92.3	128.8	129.1	124.0	124.1	124.3
1982	109.9	154.5	154.3	136.9	138.0	137.9
1983	143.4	200.7	200.9	164.5	165.1	165.2
1984	160.8	225.0	226.2	172.7	173.3	174.2
Rate of change						
1961	0.0	0.7	0.6	−0.6	0.1	0.0
1962	0.0	−0.8	0.8	−4.4	−5.1	−3.6
1963	−0.2	−0.9	0.7	−7.1	−7.8	−6.3
1964	0.0	1.5	1.0	−5.1	−3.7	−4.2
1965	0.0	−1.3	3.0	−0.3	−11.5	−7.6
1966	0.1	1.5	1.5	−3.1	−1.7	−1.7
1970	−0.2	−1.3	−0.6	0.1	−1.0	−0.2
1971	−0.7	−0.8	0.6	−4.3	−4.5	−3.1
1972	−7.2	−6.9	−6.3	−11.5	−11.3	−10.7
1973	−9.3	−9.8	−9.4	−13.5	−14.0	−13.6
1974	−1.0	−3.4	−1.6	−5.1	−7.3	−5.7
1975	−0.5	−0.7	0.6	−7.2	−7.4	−6.3
1977	13.5	13.6	15.1	−2.9	−2.8	−1.5
1978	0.9	1.1	0.7	−9.3	−9.1	−9.5
1979	−12.4	−12.5	−12.7	−15.8	−15.9	−16.0
1980	6.8	4.7	6.3	4.9	2.9	4.5

Sources: Banco de España, various years; own calculations

This view continued until 1980, even though the government was forced to allow greater and more frequent devaluations of the peseta. In 1976 the peseta was devalued by 16.5 percent, and again in 1977 by 13.5 percent, to halt appreciation in the real exchange rate. Capital inflows in 1978 and 1979 put pressure on the nominal exchange rate, which appreciated strongly. The evolution of the exchange rate was perceived as inconsistent with liberalization, and measures aimed at reducing capital inflows were adopted. The second oil shock in 1979 put an end to this nominal

Table 3.7 Indicators of exchange rate policy with respect to European Economic Community currencies, 1970–1984

Year	Nominal exchange rate (pesetas per US$)	Nominal effective exchange rate (imports)	Nominal effective exchange rate (exports)	Real exchange rate (pesetas per US$)	Real effective exchange rate (imports)	Real effective exchange rate (exports)
1970	129.0	124.3	131.6	222.7	214.8	227.3
1971	127.5	123.1	128.4	214.0	206.8	215.7
1972	129.6	124.8	129.4	210.1	202.4	209.9
1973	131.5	127.4	131.4	206.0	199.6	206.0
1974	136.3	135.2	137.0	208.0	207.2	210.1
1975	132.0	131.2	131.3	195.5	194.4	194.6
1976	122.9	120.7	123.4	168.2	165.3	169.0
1977	109.0	106.9	107.9	130.4	128.0	129.1
1978	98.8	96.7	98.0	106.5	104.3	105.7
1979	107.6	105.5	107.1	110.1	108.0	109.6
1980	100.1	100.0	100.0	100.0	100.0	100.0
1981	91.9	91.8	91.6	88.6	88.5	88.4
1982	86.5	85.8	85.9	78.6	78.0	78.1
1983	72.3	72.0	71.9	61.6	61.4	61.3
1984	71.0	70.7	70.4	57.3	57.1	56.8
Rate of change						
1971	−1.2	−1.0	−2.4	−3.9	−3.7	−5.1
1972	1.7	1.4	0.8	−1.8	−2.1	−2.7
1973	1.5	2.1	1.6	−1.9	−1.4	−1.9
1974	3.6	6.1	4.3	1.4	3.8	2.0
1975	−3.1	−3.0	−4.2	−6.4	−6.2	−7.4
1976	−6.9	−8.0	−6.0	−13.9	−15.0	−13.2
1977	−11.3	−11.4	−12.6	−22.5	−22.6	−23.6
1978	−9.4	−9.5	−9.1	−18.3	−18.5	−18.1
1979	9.0	9.1	9.2	3.4	3.5	3.7
1980	−7.0	−5.2	−6.6	−9.2	−7.4	−8.8
1981	−8.2	−8.2	−8.4	−11.4	−11.5	−11.6
1982	−5.8	−6.5	−6.2	−11.2	−11.9	−11.6
1983	−16.5	−16.1	−16.3	−21.7	−21.3	−21.5
1984	−1.7	−1.7	−2.1	−7.0	−7.0	−7.4

Sources: Banco de España, various years; own calculations

appreciation and paved the way for a strong depreciation of the peseta against the dollar in the early 1980s.

Spanish exchange rate policy has been largely geared to accommodate the evolution of the trade-weighted exchange rate with the EEC. The main purpose of this policy seems to have been to accommodate through nominal devaluations the inflation differential between Spain and the EEC countries. Table 3.7 shows the evolution of the nominal and the consumer-price-adjusted exchange rates of the peseta versus a basket of EEC currencies.

Export Promotion Policy

The devaluation of 1959 had a favorable impact on exports. Because of the devaluation, the nominal and real effective exchange rates for exports increased substantially and stayed relatively high during 1960 and 1961. Nevertheless, as already indicated, exchange rate management was not an important aspect of export promotion in the 1960s. Despite steady appreciation of the peseta, the exchange rate was not modified until 1967.

Other direct and indirect incentives, mainly for manufactured exports, were established early in the 1960s. The structure of incentives included refunds of indirect taxes on exports, tariff rebates on imported inputs used in the production of export goods, and the granting of export credits and insurance of exports. In addition, the government organized other promotional activities, such as market research, commercial trade missions, and international trade fairs, to assist Spanish exporters.

The refund of indirect taxes on exports (*desgravación fiscal*) was introduced in 1960 as a border fiscal adjustment to avoid double taxation and to make goods produced in Spain competitive in foreign markets. But the refund process also included an element of subsidy. The rate of rebate was, in general, equal to the border tax (ICGI) on identical or equivalent imported goods, which overvalued the burden of indirect taxes on domestic goods. For that reason, the tax rebate was not neutral; it granted an effective subsidy to exports. Administration of the refund system was the responsibility of the Ministry of Finance and involved a great deal of discretion, that is, the refund was not granted automatically. Ministry officials determined the amount of the rebate and the goods that were eligible. The list of such goods was gradually lengthened, and by 1962 covered approximately 75 percent of Spain's industrial exports and a few of its agricultural goods.

Several special customs regimes (*Tráfico de Perfeccionamiento*) were used for the purpose of granting tariff exemptions or refunds on imported raw materials and intermediate inputs incorporated into, or used in the production of, exports. The special regimes were as follows:

1   Temporary admission: this system permitted producers to import, free of duties and for a limited period of time, raw materials which were to be transformed by Spanish industries and reexported. Quantitative restrictions did not apply to import classified under this regime. The regime did not have much success. Although the value of imports subject to temporary admission increased from US$21 million in 1962 to US$54 million in 1972, their share of total exports fell from 5.3 to 1.8 percent.

2   Replacement of materials incorporated in exports: under this system, created in 1962, raw materials, semimanufactures, and finished pieces or parts of the same kind or with characteristics similar to those embodied in previously exported goods could be imported free of duties. This system was more flexible than the previous one, and imported goods subject to this regime increased from 0.5 percent of imports in 1962 to 6 percent in 1972. Textiles and metal products accounted for almost 75 percent of total imports under this regime.

3   The temporary import system: This system, which was established in 1960, allowed certain specified goods to be imported duty free on condition that they were reexported within a fixed period of time. In the case of imported goods incorporated into an export product, the imported goods could not be modified. That implied the simple assembly of finished parts and the exclusion of raw materials. Metal industries were the chief user of this sytem. By 1970, temporary imports accounted for more than 40 percent of total imports.

4   In 1965 the general principles of an *export refund*, or *drawback*, system were established by law, but they did not play a significant role during the three liberalization periods under study here.

Although export credits had existed in Spain since 1929, when the Banco Exterior de España was created to administer them, they only acquired relevance in the 1960s. Export credits include diverse types of benefits offered by both private and official banking institutions. The most important were those used to finance the manufacture of goods for export, the construction and export of ships, heavy equipment, and machinery, the construction of warehouses for storing goods, working capital requirements, and the establishment or acquisition of marketing services abroad. The terms and conditions of these lines of export credit were very favorable. Normally, the rate of interest was below the prevailing Central Bank rate, and the repayment period was 5–10 years for exports of heavy equipment and for the construction of warehouses for export goods.

Export credits were made available through commercial banks that enjoyed automatic rediscounting facilities with the Central Bank and through official credit institutions, mainly the Banco de Crédito Industrial.

From 1965 to 1968 export credits to Spanish firms were supplied about equally by official and private banks. After 1970 there was an abrupt shift, and export financing was left in the hands of private banks and the Banco Exterior de España. The volume of credits increased substantially, particularly after 1965, and the share of total exports aided by such credits rose from 2.4 percent in 1960 to 24.1 percent in 1968. The estimations that have been made do not show that this subsidy was very large during the first liberalization episode; effective devaluation for exports never exceeded 1 percentage point. Nevertheless, as in the case of tax rebates, they may have been important for some sectors, given the concentration of export credit devoted to heavy capital goods (mainly ships, textile machinery, and metal-working machinery).

In 1972 the old export credit system based on the opening of special rediscount lines with the Bank of Spain to financial institutions that granted credit facilities to exporters was reshaped. Public export credit was placed exclusively in the hands of the Banco Exterior de España. Most of these public funds consisted of resources originally allocated to the Instituto de Crédito Oficial (ICO). Commercial banks, savings, insitutions, and the Banco Exterior de España were also allowed to carry out export credit transactions. Funds were raised through compulsory "investment" coefficients (export credits eligible to fulfill the legal requirements). Between 1971 and 1982, commercial banks were required to allocate 3 percent of their eligible resources to export-credit-related transactions.

The only published data refer to the stock of credit that existed at the end of each year, and this information underestimates the real importance of this scheme. In 1972 the ratio of export credits to exports was around 26 percent; by 1975 it had risen to 34.6 percent.

The Banco Exterior de España provided about 18 percent of all export credits between 1971 and 1973, but its market share rose to 44 percent in 1975. Working capital was the most important type of credit, accounting for 51.5 percent of all export credit in 1975. Under this line of credit, funds were allocated chiefly to enterprises that habitually relied on export activity. The short-term nature and simple administrative procedures for working-capital credits induced commercial banks to concentrate on them, leaving more risky transactions to the Banco Exterior Credits for ship construction and export accounted for 24 percent of total credits in 1975, while machinery exports accounted for the remainder.

During the third episode there were no important changes in Spain's export promotion schemes, but funds channeled to export credits increased by a large amount, and at the end of the period the huge financial resources needed to maintain the system placed pressure on the ICO and the Banco Exterior de España. The percentage of total exports that received credit subsidies ranged from 37 percent in 1977 to 50 percent in 1982. Exports of capital goods financed by export credits increased even faster, and in 1982 accounted for 82 percent of such exports. Between 1976 and 1980 private and public credit institutions accounted for about the same share of exports, that is, 50 percent. However, by 1981 the system tax was unable to keep pace with financial necessities.

Domestic Controls

Price Controls

The stabilization plan of 1959 removed most of the price controls imposed by the government in 1956. To allow prices to reflect the true cost of public services, a general increase in the prices of railway transportation, telephone services, oil products, public water supply, tobacco, and other products and services was allowed. In addition, all price controls on products whose trade had been liberalized were removed.

Only basic products and services continued to be subject to price controls. These included foodstuffs (such as sugar and bread), industrial products (such as cement, steel, coal, and pharmaceuticals), public transport, tourist prices, and residential rents. The price controls that were maintained were implemented with a progressive degree of flexibility.

In October 1966, however, the Ministry of Commerce created a new system of price controls with six different levels: free prices, declared prices, regulated prices, maximum prices, negotiated prices, and special prices. This system did not go into effect until 1970. In the meantime, a general price freeze was imposed at the end of 1967 and renewed for another year in December 1968. Under the freeze, only 2 percent increases, to compensate in exceptional cases for the higher prices of imported inputs, were allowed.

When the new system of price controls was put into effect in 1970, the prices of goods in the consumer price index (CPI) were placed under one of four levels of regulation. Only 8 percent of the commodities covered in the CPI were classified as free price items, while 12 percent were placed under declared price status. The remaining goods were included on either the regulated price or maximum price lists. These prices could only be increased by formal authorization. A Price and Income Commission was entrusted with administering the system.

In 1971 the government and private enterprises in more than 20 sectors came to an agreement on prices. This arrangement eliminated competition and produced inefficiencies since most of the agreed prices were based on average prices.

A new price freeze was imposed from September to December 1973. Before the freeze ended, the government introduced a new system of price controls. A new commission called the Junta Superior de Precios was established, a prices fell into one of three categories: "authorized prices" that included regulated and maximum prices under the freeze; "specially supervised prices" that could not deviate much; "self-regulated prices" that had to be declared and in some cases justified. At least 22.2 percent of the goods included in the CPI were classified as authorized prices, while 45 percent were given free or self-regulated status. This system was developed throughout 1975 and 1976, but the introduction of a new CPI in 1977 made part of it obsolete.

The results of the system were far from positive among private sector firms. There was great confusion because of the large number of laws, decrees, orders, and regulations affecting prices. The government, meanwhile, found it difficult to monitor such a complicated system. Furthermore, the prices of agricultural products included in the CPI were then negotiated outside the system.

In January 1978 a more liberal system was put in place that substantially reduced the number of goods subject to price controls and decentralized the administrative system. The new system had two price categories: "authorized" and "declared or communicated." Prices in the first category required prior authorization; prices in the second category required only prior notification to the Junta Superior de Precios. In 1980 the authorized category covered only 16.6 percent of the goods in the new CPI, while the communicated group included only 2.6 percent. The rest were already free. Both categories covered 38 sectors (32 with authorized prices and six with communicated prices). The list of sectors was reduced to 34 in 1981 and to less than 20 in 1982. Further reduction of the list of controlled sectors proved to be difficult, since most of them were either public monopolies (gasoline, tobacco) or private oligopolies (electricity) or public services (railways, telephone, gas, etc.). Other authorized prices, especially those of some foodstuffs, responded to the fact that they were negotiated with the agricultural sector every year in order to maintain agricultural incomes.

Incomes Policy

Government intervention in labor relations was all-encompassing during the Franco era. Collective bargaining was performed by so-called trade unions that represented both employers and employees and had compulsory affiliation. The outcome of union elections was determined by the regime, and both strikes and lockouts were prohibited. When there was internal disagreement within a union, the government imposed a decision. If negotiated wages and salaries surpassed established ceilings, government approval was required. Employers had little authority to dismiss any employee.

Prior to 1959, the government normally interfered in the determination of union wages. But the first liberalization period between 1959 and 1966 was a period of strong economic expansion, and the government abstained from interfering in the determination of wages. After inflationary pressures and current account deficits reappeared in 1965, however, the government decided to establish an 8 percent ceiling on wage increases in 1966. But the ceiling did not hold. Wages increased by 15.3 percent in industry and by 11.3 percent in agriculture that year. In November 1967, to complement the devaluation of the peseta, wages and other incomes were frozen and collective bargaining was banned until 1969.

In that year the increase in union wages was limited to 5.9 percent. Limits continued to exist in 1970, although with more flexibility. The ceiling for annual agreements was put at 6.5 percent, and for biennial agreements at 8 percent. At the same time, and in clear contradiction, the government approved an increase in minimum wages of 18 percent, which undermined the established limits. The average wage increase in 1970 reached 15 percent, and in 1971, 1972, and 1973 the government again abstained from imposing ceilings.

In November 1973 a new policy on wages was introduced. Wage increases were indexed to CPI growth, although the government allowed an additional 5 percent in exceptional cases. The increases were related to the total payroll of the firm, and firms were allowed to distribute the increases freely, provided that the average payroll increase was contained within the limits. In 1974, however, increases in wages could not be held in check and rose by 50 percent or more. The government abolished wage indexation in October 1974 but reintroduced it in April 1975 and continued it thereafter, although the way indexation was calculated changed drastically in 1978.

Prior to 1978, indexation was based on past inflation in the CPI. This tended to boost inflation, however, since wages rose in accordance with the previous year's change in the CPI in combination with the rate of productivity growth. After 1978, indexation was based on the rise in CPI and productivity forecast for the current year. This system helped to reduce inflationary expectations.

After the democratic election of 1977, the Council of Ministers asked for "urgent negotiation of an agreement to moderate the growth of wages." The results of this negotiation were part of the Moncloa Pact. It was agreed that the maximum increase in the total national payroll would be 22 percent in 1978 and 15 percent in 1979. The increase in social security payments was limited to 18 percent. Although the 22 percent ceiling may appear to be high, payrolls at the time of the Moncloa Pact were growing at an annual rate of 28 percent; the average wage per hour was growing by 30 percent a year. The new wage policy was successful. The collective bargaining agreements concluded in 1978 showed an average increase per employee of 20.6 percent.

Efforts in 1979 to reach another incomes agreement failed, and the government restricted the growth of wages in 1979 to 80 percent of the increase in 1978. In 1980 the trade unions and the employers reached agreement on wage increases of 13–16 percent for 1980 and 11–15 percent for 1981.

Industrial Policy

Government intervention in industrial activity was extremely intense prior to 1959. Development of the public industrial sector was promoted by the INI, private industry was closely regulated, and incentives for industries that the government considered of national interest were developed. The 1959 stabilization plan produced important changes. First, the authorization of industrial investments was greatly liberalized, and the only regulation left in place was designed to prevent the construction of factories below optimum size. Second, the incentives were applied by sector or region instead of to individual firms. Both changes were clearly due to the fact that the excessive weight of small industrial firms and the high regional disequilibria were two of the main concerns of the government in those years.

Industrial policy focused on increased plant size. Incentives to expand were mainly fiscal (tax rebates) and financial (low interest credit). Between 1959 and 1965, nearly 600 firms shrank to less than 100 through mergers or takeovers. The results were more positive in sectors where there was a higher degree of oligopoly or firms of larger size, as in chemical industries, electric power production, and metal-working.

In 1964 the government introduced a First Development Plan, based mostly on French ideas and experience. The so-called "indicative plans" were compulsory in the public sector and advisory in the private sector. One of the main instruments of the plan in industry was "concerted action." Such actions were agreements between the government and the private sector under which the latter agreed to reach certain production targets while the former agreed to provide certain incentives. The sectors favored by the plan were iron and steel, coal, leather, paper, iron mining, shipbuilding, and electric power production.

Very soon after it began, however, the scheme of "concerted action" began to be affected by both external and internal developments. First, the chosen sectors were traditional ones where capital need was intensive, dependence on raw materials was high, and employees needed little training. These sectors soon began to encounter competition from the newly industrialized countries of the Far East. Second, production targets were too optimistic and overcapacity appeared within a few years. Third, administrative control was weak, leading to substantial discrimination in favor of certain firms.

Regional disequilibria were also a concern, and a series of incentives was approved to establish new industries in certain regions, provinces, or areas, called *polos* and *polígonos* of industrial development. This policy also failed to achieve what was expected of it. In some areas the absence of a basic infrastructure made the *polos* inefficient. In other areas the *polos* had greater success, but this success did not result in widespread economic development in the surrounding area.

A new development plan was created in 1972. The notion of establishing *polos* and *polígonos* was almost forgotten and the use of concerted action expanded, creating even greater overcapacity. Some targets were revised upward in 1973, only a few months before the oil crisis. The new plan also paid more attention to technological aspects that had been ignored earlier. A special department was created in the Ministry of Industry in 1973 to promote industrial innovation among private industries. At the same time, some "concerted research plans" between the government and industrial sectors were strengthened, although the results were not very significant.

In another development, public sector industries under the INI began to be used as a tool of industrial policy. In principle the idea made sense, since the INI seemed to be the logical instrument for restructuring and modernizing some sectors and for encouraging research. The reality proved otherwise, however. The belligerent attitude of the INI in some sectors resulted in its swallowing private firms that did not have any future.

The Moncloa Pact included a decision to issue, before the end of 1978, a plan to adapt the Spanish industrial sector to the first oil crisis. But because of the second oil crisis the plan did not materialize. The government started negotiating restructuring agreements with different firms on an *ad hoc* basis. This approach was eventually discarded in favor of a legal framework for industrial restructuring issued in June 1981. By then, three major other decrees had been issued that established special restructuring procedures for producers of electrical appliances, producers of special steel, and integrated iron and steel plants. The new industrial reconversion policy dealt with entire industrial sectors and established three types of incentives for sectors: fiscal measures (tax rebates and more flexibility in computing tax bases and in paying tax debts), financial incentives (low cost credit, public grants), and labor incentives (rebates and delays in making social security payments, more flexibility in labor contracting, more geographic mobility, etc.). Sectors affected by this policy included textiles, electrical equipment, shipbuilding, copper, electronic components, and crude steel. Some individual firms continued to receive *ad hoc* treatment.

Restrictions on the Movement of Capital Flows

Until 1959 virtually all international movement of capital in Spain was subject to severe restrictions. Along with import liberalization, however, Spain initiated policies at that time that were designed to attract foreign private capital, although exports of capital continued to be highly restricted.

This policy on capital movements was based mainly on balance-of-payments considerations. Controls on capital imports were relaxed to secure sufficient amounts of foreign capital to finance current deficits and to bolster Spain's reserves. Protection of certain activities and the government's desire to supervise capital movements generally were also important reasons for these regulations.

The liberalization decree of 1959 specified that the participation of foreign capital would be freely permitted in most Spanish industries. In certain activities, such as banking and insurance, foreign direct investment of up to 50 percent of the capital of enterprises was also automatically authorized. Investment in excess of 50 percent required the authorization of the Council of Ministers. In practice, such authorization was quite liberal. Foreign investment was normally allowed only in the defense, communications, and film industries and in certain public utilities. Portfolio investment in Spanish firms, foreign acquisition of real estate, and foreign commercial credits were also liberalized. Although restricted, foreign financial credits were authorized quite liberally.

External direct investments were judged on a case-by-case basis. They were granted liberally only when investment abroad was in the investor's own line of business and when it contributed to Spanish exports. To protect the domestic capital market, external portfolio investment and the insurance of foreign securities in the Spanish market were not normally allowed.

The framework for capital movements was substantially modified in 1979, when a new exchange control law was approved. Although the new law represented a clear move toward greater liberalization, capital inflows remained quite controlled. The main liberalization measures pertained to Spanish investment abroad. Direct investment was freely permitted, provided that the Spanish company shared at least 20 percent of the foreign company capital. Portfolio investment by Spanish residents abroad was not permitted except in the case of fixed-income securities denominated in foreign currencies and issued by private or public Spanish firms.

Although Spain, which had invoked the derogation clause of the OECD Capital Movements Code in 1959, was able to abandon the clause in 1972, there were still many regulations controlling outward capital movements as well as some kinds of inward capital flows. Large capital inflows in 1977–9 and subsequent upward pressure on the peseta forced the government to establish a non-interest-bearing deposit requirement equal to 25 percent of the value of all foreign loans and credits. The deposit was repayable to the borrower at the time of loan amortization. This deposit requirement was abolished in October 1979.

4

Economic Performance after Each Liberalization Episode

Each episode of trade liberalization in Spain was preceded by measures that created the stable macroeconomic environment needed for the introduction of liberalization. These stabilization measures had no substantially adverse effects on GDP growth during the period 1960–80. Until the first oil shock in 1973, the Spanish economy grew at a fast although declining pace: 7.3 percent during the first episode, 6.7 percent in the years 1967–9, 5.3 percent in the years of the second episode, and just 1.7 percent during the third liberalization episode. This low rate largely reflected the economic consequences of external shocks. Demand management was nonetheless rather successful in controlling inflation and equilibrating the balance of payments.

Both imports and exports grew at a very rapid rate during the initial liberalization period. These rates moderated during the second episode, with export growth easily exceeding growth in imports. This fairly successful export performance was due to increasing revenues from tourism and diversification of Spanish exports.

The Inflation Rate

Spain's accelerating inflation was halted in 1959 following the introduction of stabilization measures. Wholesale prices and the cost of living index, which had been growing at an annual rate of around 10 percent in the period 1954–8, were sharply reduced and remained stable until 1962, notwithstanding devaluation, a consequent increase in import prices, and the elimination of a number of price controls. Devaluation had little inflationary impact, given the ratio of imports of goods and services to GDP of around 10 percent. Furthermore, the rise in import prices was relatively low – about 6 percent in 1959. This rise was offset by the increase in competition resulting from import liberalization. The low level of demand following stabilization also helped to bridle inflationary pressures.

Prices remained stable from 1962 to 1965, although at higher levels than before. Seasonal factors were important during this period. The evolution of the indicators was primarily determined by a substantial price increase in agricultural and food products, which were heavily weighted in the indices. The sharp increase during 1965 can only in small part be explained by seasonal factors affecting agricultural prices, since the prices of nonfood items also increased considerably. It is unlikely that this increase can be attributed to a general excess of demand, since there was no evidence of supply bottlenecks. Furthermore, the current account was in surplus in 1964. The most important single factor was the policy of agricultural support, reinforced by wage pressures. The new orientation in agricultural policy, a standstill in guaranteed farm prices and an increase in food imports, together with monetary restraints, resulted in a substantial deceleration of inflation in 1966.

From 1966 to 1970 the inflation rate remained low and in 1969 it subsided to 2.2 percent. Thus the beginning of the second liberalization episode in 1970 was prefaced by a stable price environment. However, the inflation rate steadily increased between 1970 and 1975, especially after the 1973 oil shock. Huge increases in both import prices and nominal wages fueled price pressures, and in 1977 the CPI grew by 24.5 percent. The growing economic disequilibrium eventually led to the new stabilization program outlined in the Moncloa Pact. The introduction of a tighter macroeconomic policy and wage moderation made it possible to reduce inflation in subsequent years. Nonetheless, price increases were substantial during the third liberalization episode of 1977–80, averaging 18.9 percent a year. The continued policies of wage moderation and disinflation between 1982 and 1986 brought inflation down to 8.8 percent.

Figure 4.1 and table 4.1 show the evolution of the CPI during the period 1955–86.

Wages

Because of legal constraints on dismissing redundant workers, enterprises that faced economic difficulties in periods of recession reacted primarily by curtailing the number of working hours and reducing overtime payments and incentive premiums. As a result, real wages decreased in 1959 by about 1 percentage point. After 1960, however, real wages increased at an average annual rate of about 8 percent.

The elimination of shortages of raw materials and semifinished goods after 1959, in combination with greater freedom to import, resulted in large productivity gains. Moreover, the high rate of investment during

Percentage

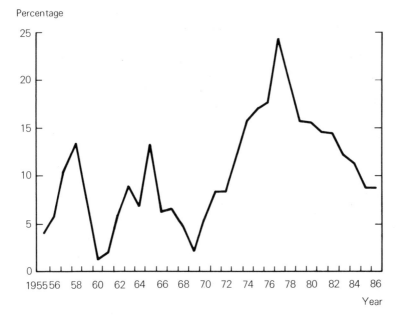

Figure 4.1 Inflation rate, 1955–1986

these years must have had important returns in terms of output per man-hour. Thus the increase in productivity attained during the period 1959–66 probably equaled the sharp increase in wages.

During the second episode, and despite the wage control mechanism created in 1970, nominal wages grew at a very fast pace, especially in 1974 and 1975 when the average rate of growth was about 25 percent. For the period 1970–5 as a whole, real wages grew by 6.9 percent annually. The acceleration in wage growth at the end of the episode was mainly a result of the unstable political atmosphere during Franco's final years.

Nominal wages outpaced the increase in prices during the third episode as well, although to a lesser degree. Real wages in industry grew by 5.7 percent from 1977 to 1980.

Modification of the wage determination system in 1977 helped to moderate wage increases, as did a rise in unemployment in the late 1970s. After 1980, wage settlements showed a downward trend as a result of a more reasonable stance by the trade unions in the bargaining process.

Table 4.2 depicts the evolution of nominal and real industrial wages during the period under analysis.

Table 4.1 Inflation rate, 1955–1986

Year	Index (1976 = 100)	Rate of inflation
1955	18.2	4.1
1956	19.3	5.9
1957	21.4	10.8
1958	24.3	13.4
1959	26.0	7.3
1960	26.4	1.3
1961	26.9	2.0
1962	28.5	6.0
1963	31.0	8.9
1964	33.2	6.8
1965	37.6	13.2
1966	39.9	6.3
Average, 1959–66		6.5
1967	42.5	6.6
1968	44.5	4.8
1969	45.5	2.2
1970	48.1	5.7
1971	52.1	8.2
1972	56.4	8.3
1973	62.8	11.4
1974	72.7	15.7
1975	85.0	17.0
Average, 1970–5		11.0
1976	100.0	17.6
1977	124.5	24.5
1978	149.1	19.8
1979	172.5	15.7
1980	199.3	15.6
Average, 1977–80		18.9
1981	228.4	14.5
1982	261.3	14.4
1983	293.1	12.2
1984	326.1	11.3
1985	354.8	8.8
1986	386.1	8.8

Source: Instituto Nacional de Estadística, various years

Table 4.2 Nominal and real industrial wages, 1956–1986

Year	Index of nominal wages (1970 = 100)	Rate of growth (%)	Index of real wages (1970 = 100)	Rate of growth (%)
1956	20.4	14.2	50.7	7.7
1957	23.2	14.0	52.2	2.8
1958	25.3	9.1	50.1	− 4.0
1959	26.9	6.2	49.7	− 0.7
1960	28.5	6.0	51.9	4.4
1961	30.7	7.9	55.0	5.9
1962	36.0	17.1	60.8	10.5
1963	41.1	14.1	63.7	4.8
1964	47.2	14.9	68.5	7.6
1965	55.2	16.9	70.7	3.2
1966	64.5	16.8	77.7	9.9
Average, 1959–66		12.5		5.7
1967	73.2	13.5	82.8	6.6
1968	79.1	8.0	85.4	3.1
1969	88.1	11.4	93.1	9.0
1970	100.0	13.6	100.0	7.4
1971	113.0	13.0	104.4	4.4
1972	130.9	15.8	111.6	6.9
1973	153.7	17.4	117.7	5.4
1974	193.0	25.5	127.7	8.5
1975	245.4	27.2	138.9	8.8
Average, 1970–5		18.7		6.9
1976	314.2	28.0	151.2	8.8
1977	437.4	39.2	169.0	11.8
1978	550.6	25.9	177.7	5.1
1979	672.9	22.2	187.7	5.6
1980	780.3	16.0	188.3	0.3
Average, 1977–80		25.8		5.7
1981	939.3	20.4	197.9	5.1
1982	1,069.3	13.8	196.9	− 0.5
1983	1,027.5	12.9	198.3	0.7
1984	1,309.4	8.4	193.2	− 2.6
1985	1,453,9	11.0	197.1	2.0
1986	1,588.8	9.3	198.0	0.4
Average, 1981–6		12.6		0.9

Sources: Banco de España, various years; own calculations

Interest Rates

Throughout the first episode Spain kept interest rates low and stable in order to spur economic growth and a high level of private investment. Though the declared intentions of the Spanish monetary authorities were to make interest rates more flexible and to allow them to play their natural role as an allocative mechanism, the fact is that a system of direct regulation was built up. This intervention was geared to assure low rates and to protect the banking system from market pressures and competition. All interest rates were subject to legal ceilings below market rates, and a large segment of all financial transactions was governed by compulsory investment ratios that channeled funding either to low-yielding public and private bonds or to long-term credit for specific sectors.

Between 1958 and 1964 the maximum legal rate on a one-year deposit never exceeded 3 percent. Loan rates, meanwhile, had legal minima which were set by a committee representing banking institutions. Despite frequent changes in individual interest rates, the structure itself remained complex and rigid over the whole period, with nominal rates ranging from 4 to 6 percent and real rates generally being negative.

Interest rates were liberalized somewhat in 1969. Rates became a varied mixture of free, fixed, and regulated rates, depending on the nature of the asset. Most public securities and bonds were issued at fixed rates largely independent of market conditions. However, a majority of all interest rates were linked to the basic rediscount rate of the Bank of Spain. Although this reform was a considerable advance over the previous system, the interest rate structure as a whole remained largely isolated from actual market conditions.

A major step toward liberalization of the financial system was achieved in 1977, when the authorities decided to gradually let the market determine interest rates and ceilings on interest rates were removed. Only long-term interest rates were affected initially, but in 1986 the last ceilings were abolished. Real interest rates, after being negative for many years, turned positive in 1983.

The Trade Sector

Imports

The stabilization measures of 1959 had an immediate impact on the external sector. Imports started to decelerate in the third quarter of the year, and from July to December they fell by about 18 percent compared with the same period of 1958. The decline in import growth continued in

1960. It was the short-term result of devaluation, the imposition of a 25 percent advance deposit on imports, and contraction in demand.

From 1961 to 1966, however, Spain's imports increased substantially. In the period 1961–6, real imports of goods and services showed average rates of growth of 27 percent. However, the devaluation of 1967, combined with the lowest rate of real GDP growth for the decade, then caused real imports to recede. All in all, the ratio of imports to GDP increased from about 8 percent in 1959 to more than 13 percent in 1968 (table 4.3 and figure 4.2).

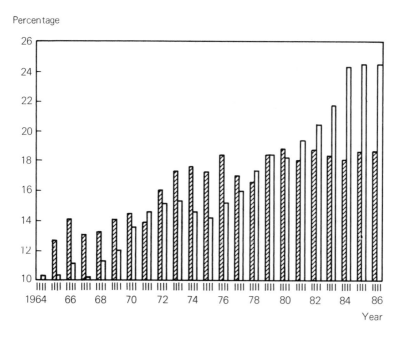

Percentage

Figure 4.2 Degree of openness, 1964–1986: shaded columns, imports as a percentage of gross domestic product; unshaded columns, exports as a percentage of gross domestic product

The prices of imported goods relative to domestic goods declined by about 20 percent between 1961 and 1966. This drop, combined with very high growth in real GDP and substantial import liberalization, partly explains the rapid increase in imports during these years. Several studies of the determinants of imports, using GDP to reflect the behavior of real economic activity and several proxies for relative prices as the main explanatory factors, have shown an income elasticity of about 1.17 and a price elasticity of between − 0.9 and − 1.3, with a likely value of around unity. According to such studies, changes in real income were probably the

Table 4.3 Indicators of trade performance, 1959–1986

Year	Current account[a] (billion pesetas)	Imports as percentage of GDP	Real growth of imports (%)	Exports as percentage of GDP	Real growth of exports (%)	Exports and imports as percentage of GDP
1959	−5.3	7.9	8.0	7.0	26.8	14.9
1960	18.2	8.3	4.8	11.3	64.5	19.6
1961	3.5	10.5	39.8	11.0	8.6	21.5
1962	−9.4	12.4	34.1	11.3	13.1	23.7
1963	−26.1	13.2	23.2	10.5	3.7	23.7
1964	−16.9	13.6	13.1	12.0	25.3	25.6
1965	−50.6	12.7	33.1	10.4	6.9	23.1
1966	−58.7	14.1	19.0	11.1	15.2	25.2
Average, 1959–66	−18.1		21.9		20.5	
1967	−55.1	13.1	−3.3	10.2	−4.7	24.3
1968	−4.7	13.2	8.1	11.3	18.4	24.5
1969	−64.8	14.0	15.8	12.0	15.5	26.0
1970	−40.6	14.4	7.0	13.5	17.4	27.9
1971	6.2	13.8	0.7	14.5	13.0	28.3
1972	−13.1	16.0	24.7	15.1	12.2	31.1
1973	−47.9	17.2	16.4	15.2	9.0	32.4
1974	−243.6	17.6	7.7	14.5	0.8	32.1
1975	−236.6	17.2	−1.1	14.2	−1.5	31.4
Average, 1970–5			11.3		8.5	
1976	−291.2	18.3	10.1	15.1	10.1	33.4
1977	−194.3	16.9	−4.7	15.9	8.5	32.8
1978	80.3	16.5	−0.7	17.3	10.7	33.8
1979	17.7	18.4	11.5	18.4	6.4	36.8
1980	−391.9	18.8	3.8	18.2	0.6	37.0
Average, 1977–80	−122.0		2.5		6.5	
1981	−354.4	18.0	−3.5	19.4	6.9	37.4
1982	−357.2	18.7	4.8	20.5	6.7	39.2
1983	−133.7	18.3	−0.3	21.7	8.3	40.0
1984	559.4	18.0	1.1	24.4	15.1	42.4
1985	633.8	18.6	5.4	24.5	2.9	43.1
1986	754.0	18.6	3.0	24.5	3.0	43.1

Source: Instituto Nacional de Estadística, various years

most important factor in the rise in imports, with relative prices playing only a marginal role (Bonilla, 1978; Mauleón, 1985).

The structure and annual rate of change of commodity imports by major category are shown in tables 4.4–4.8. In the 1960s intermediate products and equipment goods accounted for more than 60 percent of total imports, reflecting the intense process of modernization that was taking place. The decline in the share of intermediate goods between 1959 and 1968 is mainly explained by the fall in imports of intermediate goods for agriculture, while imports of such goods for industry increased. Imports of consumer goods increased steadily, but by 1966 they were still small in comparative terms.

Between 1970 and 1975 – the second liberalization episode – imports of goods and services grew in real terms by 10.1 percent annually. Nevertheless, there were substantial fluctuations. The austerity program of the

Table 4.4 Imports by major category, 1959–1968 (percent)

Year	Food	Oil	Intermediate goods	Capital	Consumer goods	Total
1959	10.6	16.1	49.4	22.3	1.5	100.0
1960	12.1	17.0	45.1	22.8	2.9	100.0
1961	16.2	12.3	47.9	20.2	3.4	100.0
1962	18.3	11.7	39.4	27.3	3.2	100.0
1963	22.0	9.5	36.1	27.9	4.5	100.0
1964	16.5	12.7	37.2	27.7	5.9	100.0
1965	17.5	10.0	39.9	26.8	5.8	100.0
1966	16.3	9.7	40.2	27.3	6.5	100.0
1967	15.8	12.4	36.6	28.0	7.3	100.0
1968	13.8	15.4	38.4	25.4	7.0	100.0

Sources: Dirección General de Aduanas, various years; Secretaria de Estado de Comercio, various years

Table 4.5 Nominal annual rate of growth in imports, 1960–1968 (percent)

Year	Food	Oil	Intermediate goods	Capital	Consumer goods	Average
1960	−4.1	−10.8	−23.2	−14.0	55.0	−15.9
1961	116.3	16.6	99.2	43.9	92.3	62.0
1962	51.6	28.6	10.6	81.7	31.6	34.3
1963	55.0	4.4	17.5	31.1	76.0	28.2
1965	41.9	5.6	43.2	29.3	30.1	33.6
1966	10.9	14.3	19.8	21.2	34.9	18.4
1967	−5.0	25.9	−10.4	0.9	9.5	−1.7
1968	1.5	45.1	22.1	5.6	13.1	16.4

Sources: Dirección General de Aduanas, various years; Secretaria de Estado de Comercio, various years

mid-1970s induced a stagnation of imports, while the recovery of 1972–3 brought about impressive growth that only slowed down in the last two years of the episode. As a result, the import-to-GDP ratio of 14.4 percent in 1970 rose to 17.2 percent in 1975. Spain's imports were biased toward semimanufactures and capital goods, which accounted for 30.6 percent and 27.7 percent respectively of total imports in 1970. Agricultural products and energy imports represented about 13 percent of foreign purchases, while manufactures were 15.5 percent. After the first oil shock, these percentages changed substantially. The strong dependence of the Spanish economy on imported oil raised energy imports to 25.6 percent of total imports in 1975. The percentages of agricultural and manufactured imports remained roughly the same as in 1970, while semimanufactures and capital goods accounted for 23 percent of 1975 imports.

Table 4.6 Imports, 1970–1986 (million US dollars at average annual exchange rate)

Year	SITC 0	SITC 1	SITC 2	SITC 3	SITC 4	SITC 5	SITC 6	SITC 7	SITC 8	SITC 9	Total
1970	482.9	72.9	813.7	630.1	27.5	502.0	761.6	1,227.1	217.0	33.1	4,767.8
1971	563.1	101.7	871.3	820.7	26.7	531.6	605.4	1,214.7	254.7	28.0	5,018.0
1972	733.0	111.1	1,170.2	978.5	39.4	743.8	813.4	1,803.9	381.0	33.7	6,808.0
1973	1,202.5	146.1	1,546.5	1,248.4	49.1	1,039.9	1,183.4	2,627.3	532.4	60.2	9,635.8
1974	1,653.2	167.9	2,359.5	3,898.0	59.5	1,552.9	1,748.1	3,213.7	663.0	89.9	15,405.6
1975	1,861.0	180.1	2,231.3	4,182.1	161.6	1,384.7	1,766.6	3,555.5	747.2	168.3	16,238.2
1976	1,524.1	230.6	2,431.2	5,097.4	71.5	1,601.1	1,918.3	3,585.7	842.6	176.7	17,479.2
1977	1,861.5	242.3	2,508.1	5,033.1	80.4	1,605.9	1,781.5	3,507.1	961.2	198.1	17,779.3
1978	2,002.6	298.0	2,706.2	5,291.7	128.8	1,835.1	1,676.5	3,617.9	1,023.1	83.8	18,663.8
1979	2,543.6	325.0	3,617.1	7,659.6	128.8	2,543.8	2,379.5	4,795.7	1,328.7	63.5	25,385.3
1980	2,747.4	391.6	4,268.5	12,998.1	129.9	2,512.8	2,815.8	6,002.2	1,688.3	254.2	33,809.1
1981	2,409.6	369.6	3,520.0	13,643.6	116.3	2,423.1	2,361.0	5,591.4	1,558.1	182.2	32,174.8
1982	2,531.8	419.1	3,246.0	12,536.7	78.2	2,351.2	2,580.4	6,036.5	1,597.8	284.2	31,641.9
1983	2,366.0	445.7	3,108.6	11,660.6	66.1	2,244.1	2,084.4	5,436.0	1,418.3	281.3	29,111.0
1984	2,136.0	469.4	3,401.6	10,840.2	86.5	2,356.2	2,126.0	5,824.9	1,317.4	234.9	28,793.1
1985	2,187.6	426.5	3,322.3	10,640.0	89.9	2,513.1	2,429.2	6,464.7	1,551.7	209.9	29,834.8
1986	2,398.5	507.3	3,341.1	6,653.5	116.1	3,908.0	4,230.5	10,158.9	2,537.2	71.1	34,922.2

SITC, UN Standard International Trade Classification.

Sources: Dirección General de Aduanas, various years; Secretaria de Estado de Comercio, various years

Table 4.7 Distribution of imports by category, 1970–1986

Year	SITC 0	SITC 1	SITC 2	SITC 3	SITC 4	SITC 5	SITC 6	SITC 7	SITC 8	SITC 9	Total
1970	10.1	1.5	17.1	13.2	0.6	10.5	16.0	25.7	4.6	0.7	100.0
1971	11.2	2.0	17.4	16.4	0.5	10.6	12.1	24.2	5.1	0.6	100.0
1972	10.8	1.6	17.2	14.4	0.6	10.9	11.9	26.5	5.6	0.5	100.0
1973	12.5	1.5	16.0	13.0	0.5	10.8	12.3	27.3	5.5	0.6	100.0
1974	10.7	1.1	15.3	25.3	0.4	10.1	11.3	20.9	4.3	0.6	100.0
1975	11.5	1.1	13.7	15.8	1.0	8.5	10.9	21.9	4.6	1.0	100.0
1976	8.7	1.3	13.9	29.2	0.4	9.2	11.0	20.5	4.8	1.0	100.0
1977	10.5	1.4	14.1	28.3	0.5	9.0	10.0	19.7	5.4	1.1	100.0
1978	10.7	1.6	14.5	28.4	0.7	9.8	9.0	19.4	5.5	0.4	100.0
1979	10.0	1.3	14.2	30.2	0.5	10.0	9.4	18.9	5.2	0.3	100.0
1980	8.1	1.2	12.6	38.4	0.4	7.4	8.3	17.8	5.0	0.8	100.0
1981	7.5	1.1	10.9	42.4	0.4	7.5	7.3	17.4	4.8	0.6	100.0
1982	8.0	1.3	10.3	39.6	0.2	7.4	8.1	19.1	5.0	0.9	100.0
1983	8.1	1.5	10.7	40.1	0.2	7.7	7.2	18.7	4.9	1.0	100.0
1984	7.4	1.6	11.8	37.6	0.3	8.2	7.4	20.2	4.6	0.8	100.0
1985	7.3	1.4	11.1	35.7	0.3	8.4	8.1	21.7	5.2	0.7	100.0
1986	9.7	1.5	9.6	19.1	0.3	11.2	12.1	29.1	7.3	0.2	100.0

SITC, UN Standard International Trade Classification.

Sources: Dirección General de Aduanas, various years; Secretaría de Estado de Comercio, various years

Table **4.8** Rate of annual real growth of imports, 1971–1986

Year	SITC 0	SITC 1	SITC 2	SITC 3	SITC 4	SITC 5	SITC 6	SITC 7	SITC 8	SITC 9	Average
1971	10.7	32.4	4.9	13.2	-4.7	7.2	-28.9	-11.5	14.3	-17.6	-0.7
1972	20.2	0.9	24.3	9.3	36.4	37.9	23.5	36.4	27.0	2.1	26.4
1973	14.4	-8.3	-7.9	7.2	-13.1	10.9	25.7	25.8	13.6	45.5	11.7
1974	23.4	3.1	14.2	8.7	-9.4	-2.5	27.8	5.9	10.6	32.5	7.1
1975	4.5	-0.5	1.9	-3.4	192.9	-12.3	-17.6	-9.8	-7.6	53.5	-2.5
1976	-15.6	31.9	17.4	16.6	-52.3	34.2	4.9	-2.5	23.0	14.6	11.0
1977	1.2	-12.9	-12.3	-6.4	-4.4	-5.4	-9.9	-5.1	5.6	3.7	-6.3
1978	5.0	20.0	5.9	-0.8	57.2	-2.4	-21.8	-14.3	-11.9	-65.0	-5.3
1979	14.0	-2.2	11.9	11.7	-16.3	19.7	23.6	15.5	13.2	-33.9	13.9
1980	-1.9	9.5	7.2	2.1	-8.4	-18.3	9.5	15.8	14.7	261.1	3.7
1981	-7.7	-0.7	-11.4	-5.5	-3.8	4.2	-12.2	-2.4	-3.4	-25.0	-5.4
1982	11.2	20.0	2.0	-2.1	-25.6	0.6	7.6	7.2	4.7	59.3	3.3
1983	-3.8	9.5	1.0	3.5	-10.9	5.4	-14.8	-5.7	-7.9	2.6	-0.8
1984	-13.6	0.8	0.2	-2.9	19.9	7.5	5.7	11.1	-2.6	-12.4	0.8
1985	7.2	-4.9	6.9	1.7	13.8	6.9	16.0	12.6	19.2	-9.6	7.0
1986	23.0	-5.8	2.4	-1.7	31.5	34.3	39.6	25.9	27.7	-73.5	15.8

SITC, UN Standard International Trade Classification.

Sources: Dirección General de Aduanas, various years; Secretaria de Estado de Comercio, various years

During the third episode of liberalization (1977–80), aggregate imports of goods and services grew at an average annual real rate of 2.5 percent. The import-to-GDP ratio reached 18.8 percent in 1980, compared with 16.9 percent in 1977. The import structure continued to be dominated by energy imports, which accounted for roughly 40 percent of the total. Agricultural and manufactured imports accounted for 12 percent of the total, while capital goods and semimanufactures were 21 percent and 16 percent respectively.

Exports

Tables 4.9–4.13 show the evolution of exports of goods and services. As in the case of imports, the devaluation and the restrictive policy of 1959 had an immediate impact on the behavior of exports. Real exports of goods and services increased by more than 60 percent in real terms by 1960, an exceptional increase that would not be attained again. Exports of commodities increased more than fivefold, whereas services did even better. From 1960 to 1966 the cumulative average real rate of growth was 20.5 percent for all exports and 16 percent for exports of goods alone.

However, export behavior was quite irregular. Years of very rapid growth alternated with years of stagnation. This irregularity can be attributed mainly to seasonal factors, since Spanish exports in the 1960s depended strongly on agricultural and food products which accounted for about 50 percent of all exports. Slowness in the implementation of export promotion measures was probably another reason for the fluctuations. As mentioned earlier, the real effective exchange rate for exports declined steadily until 1967, and export promotion was not enough to offset the real appreciation. The beneficial effect on exports that is usually attributed to

Table 4.9 Structure of exports by major category, 1959–1968

Year	Food	Oil	Intermediate goods	Capital	Consumer goods	Total
1959	59.9	0.3	26.7	1.3	11.8	100.0
1960	50.0	0.5	36.1	2.3	11.2	100.0
1961	57.5	0.6	24.3	3.6	13.9	100.0
1962	57.4	1.6	21.0	7.3	12.8	100.0
1963	49.8	3.2	24.8	8.4	13.9	100.0
1964	52.6	5.1	21.7	8.6	12.2	100.0
1965	46.8	3.9	23.7	10.0	15.7	100.0
1966	43.3	4.5	19.9	15.9	16.4	100.0
1967	44.8	5.9	20.3	12.3	16.7	100.0
1968	36.4	8.7	21.8	14.3	18.8	100.0

Sources: Dirección General de Aduanas, various years; Secretaria de Estado de Comercio, various years

Table 4.10 Nominal rate of growth of exports, 1960–1968

Year	Food	Oil	Intermediate goods	Capital	Consumer goods	Average
1960	24.6	128.5	124.0	154.7	40.8	49.2
1961	9.7	9.4	−35.8	−80.9	18.9	−4.6
1962	4.5	174.3	−9.7	111.5	−4.1	4.7
1963	−12.0	111.4	19.8	14.6	10.5	1.4
1965	9.8	−19.9	10.3	17.8	20.9	7.3
1966	19.8	47.4	15.0	108.9	34.8	29.5
1967	16.4	47.4	15.0	−13.0	15.4	12.7
1968	6.9	93.8	41.1	53.1	47.4	31.4

Sources: Dirección General de Aduanas, various years; Secretaria de Estado de Comercio, various years

import liberalization takes some time to be effective, particularly in an economy just relinquishing its autarkic views and where experienced exporters are not abundant. Export promotion did not provide enough incentives for consolidating export growth where domestic activities, particularly the industrial sector, were still sheltered through tariffs and other measures.

The situation changed after 1966, when commodity exports increased by 26 percent in real terms. Exports of capital goods were the most dynamic component, growing at a rate exceeding 80 percent. Devaluation at the end of 1967 and a restrictive domestic policy helped to sustain the expansion in exports. Although total exports declined in 1967, the real rate of growth of commodity exports was 11 percent. Real growth in exports continued to be higher and more sustained until 1973. Other explanatory factors were intensive export promotion and the rapid economic growth of other industrial countries. As a result, the ratio of exports to GDP increased from 7 percent in 1959 to 11.3 percent in 1968.

Empirical evidence has generally shown that the evolution of world trade is the most important factor in explaining export growth, followed in importance by fluctuations in domestic economic activity and changes in the relative prices of exports to domestic goods. Estimates of export elasticities range from 1.8 to 2.2 percent for world income, and from − 0.7 to − 0.9 percent for relative prices.

Tables 4.9 and 4.10 present data on the distribution and rates of change of exports by major category for the period 1959–68. Agricultural and food products exports declined by almost 50 percent over the period, while equipment and consumer goods exports increased substantially, accounting together for more than 33 percent of total exports in 1968.

During the second liberalization episode (1970–5) export behavior was quite dynamic. Exports of goods and services grew on average by

Table 4.11 Exports, 1970–1986 (million US dollars at average annual exchange rate)

Year	SITC 0	SITC 1	SITC 2	SITC 3	SITC 4	SITC 5	SITC 6	SITC 7	SITC 8	SITC 9	Total
1970	620.1	80.6	94.0	131.6	141.0	125.9	412.6	467.7	320.4	3.4	2,397.3
1971	642.0	94.2	101.7	127.1	179.6	143.1	597.3	628.4	453.7	3.2	2,970.3
1972	840.0	140.3	111.6	138.0	85.0	171.5	815.9	826.7	682.2	4.0	3,815.2
1973	1,091.9	222.6	153.3	243.6	206.8	237.9	1,127.1	1,120.7	783.4	6.4	5,193.7
1974	1,177.9	262.1	233.9	478.6	259.2	534.8	1,520.2	1,578.5	1,017.0	10.0	7,072.3
1975	1,344.0	238.8	236.3	252.3	120.7	401.1	1,974.3	1,967.9	1,117.0	16.9	7,669.3
1976	1,482.5	291.7	273.4	324.3	179.0	521.8	2,237.4	2,144.4	1,239.4	25.5	8,719.5
1977	1,645.3	286.5	312.8	377.5	222.0	653.0	2,766.5	2,609.6	1,309.9	23.3	10,206.5
1978	1,966.6	313.6	376.5	328.2	287.5	871.9	3,930.4	3,335.6	1,623.6	29.4	13,063.4
1979	2,799.5	483.5	484.2	346.4	403.4	1,389.3	5,340.0	4,812.3	2,111.5	23.2	18,193.2
1980	2,727.4	475.8	648.2	797.4	466.8	1,511.8	6,301.3	5,353.8	2,069.9	40.5	20,393.1
1981	3,037.5	410.7	650.3	1,073.6	331.3	1,457.6	6,143.1	5,165.1	2,129.5	56.1	20,454.8
1982	2,599.6	400.6	582.4	1,458.4	286.4	1,469.8	5,761.3	5,603.6	2,110.7	65.1	20,344.8
1983	2,428.7	353.5	583.4	1,760.0	318.6	1,516.0	5,479.5	5,177.2	2,037.8	99.1	19,753.8
1984	2,840.3	343.2	664.6	2,085.7	4.8.5	1,819.1	6,238.4	6,247.7	2,348.0	180.7	23,206.0
1985	2,740.6	377.8	721.1	2,258.5	472.0	2,048.0	6,392.4	6,550.2	2,443.8	131.4	24,135.7
1986	3,556.8	489.0	862.9	1,711.9	336.4	2,269.0	6,443.1	8,371.9	3,002.1	92.1	27,135.2

SITC, UN Standard International Trade Classification.

Sources: Dirección General de Aduanas, various years; Secretaría de Estado de Comercio, various years

Table 4.12 Distribution of exports by category, 1970–1986

Year	SITC 0	SITC 1	SITC 2	SITC 3	SITC 4	SITC 5	SITC 6	SITC 7	SITC 8	SITC 9	Total
1970	25.9	3.4	3.9	5.5	5.9	5.3	17.2	19.5	13.4	0.1	100.0
1971	21.6	3.2	3.4	4.3	6.0	4.8	20.1	21.2	15.3	0.1	100.0
1972	22.0	3.7	2.9	3.6	2.2	4.5	21.4	21.7	17.9	0.1	100.0
1973	21.0	4.3	3.0	4.7	4.0	4.6	21.7	21.6	15.1	0.1	100.0
1974	16.7	3.7	3.3	6.8	3.7	7.6	21.5	22.3	14.4	0.1	100.0
1975	17.5	3.1	3.1	3.3	1.6	5.2	25.7	25.7	14.6	0.2	100.0
1976	17.0	3.3	3.1	3.7	2.1	6.0	25.7	24.6	14.2	0.3	100.0
1977	16.1	2.8	3.1	3.7	2.2	6.4	27.1	25.6	12.8	0.2	100.0
1978	15.1	2.4	2.9	2.5	2.2	6.7	30.1	25.5	12.4	0.2	100.0
1979	15.4	2.7	2.7	1.9	2.2	7.6	29.4	26.5	11.6	0.1	100.0
1980	13.4	2.3	3.2	3.9	2.3	7.4	30.9	26.3	10.2	0.2	100.0
1981	14.8	2.0	3.2	5.2	1.6	7.1	30.0	25.3	10.4	0.3	100.0
1982	12.8	2.0	2.9	7.2	1.4	7.2	28.3	27.6	10.4	0.3	100.0
1983	12.3	1.8	3.0	8.9	1.6	7.7	27.7	26.2	10.3	0.5	100.0
1984	12.2	1.5	2.9	9.0	1.9	7.8	26.9	26.9	10.1	0.8	100.0
1985	11.4	1.6	3.0	9.4	2.0	8.5	26.5	27.1	10.1	0.5	100.0
1986	13.1	1.8	3.2	6.3	1.2	8.4	23.7	30.9	10.1	0.3	100.0

SITC, UN Standard International Trade Classification.

Sources: Dirección General de Aduanas, various years; Secretaría de Estado de Comercio, various years

Table 4.13 Rate of annual real growth of exports, 1971–1986

Year	SITC 0	SITC 1	SITC 2	SITC 3	SITC 4	SITC 5	SITC 6	SITC 7	SITC 8	SITC 9	Total
1971	−2.5	10.0	8.6	−22.3	27.8	21.5	30.3	20.9	39.7	−7.7	19.5
1972	12.1	27.7	−0.5	11.2	−57.0	7.1	22.6	18.1	34.1	11.6	14.0
1973	−2.0	19.6	8.7	−7.9	92.3	−6.0	17.3	15.1	−1.8	36.6	5.7
1974	−8.9	−0.5	13.2	−6.3	−7.0	71.4	23.8	29.3	11.5	35.5	10.0
1975	5.3	−15.9	−3.0	−44.6	−55.3	−24.8	8.8	4.5	−2.4	49.9	2.4
1976	21.0	34.0	23.3	34.1	58.0	43.0	11.6	7.3	10.6	50.0	19.6
1977	1.1	−10.5	4.3	15.9	13.1	20.3	19.1	17.2	−3.6	−16.6	8.7
1978	−2.7	−10.9	15.8	−22.0	24.6	28.0	23.1	10.8	6.9	9.0	12.5
1979	10.4	19.5	6.9	−26.5	16.3	25.5	13.6	20.6	6.9	−35.4	11.7
1980	−9.1	−8.2	13.8	49.9	−1.3	−2.9	4.4	−1.6	−10.8	59.3	0.1
1981	33.3	3.3	−1.4	16.0	−30.3	8.4	3.9	2.8	10.0	47.9	10.0
1982	−7.9	5.0	−0.3	84.3	−4.1	4.9	−6.3	8.4	1.7	19.0	4.2
1983	2.4	−3.3	13.1	17.0	26.0	17.5	3.2	0.3	7.5	69.5	7.3
1984	17.3	−2.7	5.4	19.6	27.3	16.0	16.9	23.9	15.6	82.9	16.5
1985	−4.2	9.3	11.2	11.2	10.4	12.6	−2.2	0.1	1.0	−29.4	2.6
1986	4.0	3.7	0.1	28.2	−40.4	−6.7	−23.0	−2.4	−7.7	−47.3	−4.2

SITC, UN Standard International Trade Classification.

Sources: Dirección General de Aduanas, various years; Secretaria de Estado de Comercio, various years

8.5 percent in real terms each year. This growth slowed at the end of the period, however. Exports almost stagnated in 1974, and in 1975 they decreased by 1.5 percent. Extremely expansive domestic policies, real appreciation of the exchange rate, and deceleration in foreign demand after the first oil shock were the main reasons. Nevertheless, the ratio of exports to GDP increased from 13.5 percent in 1970 to 14.2 percent in 1975 (tables 4.11–4.13).

Manufactured goods accounted for 35 percent of total exports in 1975, while capital goods sharply increased their participation in foreign sales to 31.5 percent in 1975 as against 23.9 percent in 1970. Agricultural exports decreased to 11.4 percent. Semimanufactures and energy retained their relative importance, accounting for 18.8 percent and 3.3 percent respectively.

During the third liberalization episode (1977–80) trade policy reinforced the effects of depreciation and restrictive domestic policies. As a result, aggregate exports of goods and services grew on average by 6.5 percent in real terms. The ratio of exports to GDP was 18.2 percent in 1980, 2.3 percentage points more than in 1977. Between 1977 and 1982, capital goods exports outpaced manufactured exports. In 1982 the former accounted for 34 percent of total exports, while the latter accounted for around 26 percent. Five years earlier the percentages were roughly the other way around. Transport equipment exports, including cars, were the main factor behind the structural change. Semimanufactures represented about 25 percent of total exports, while agriculture and energy accounted for 8.3 percent and 6.7 percent respectively.

The Balance-of-payments Position

As a result of the 1959 program, an import surplus appeared in 1960. From 1961 onward, following the rapid increase in domestic demand and appreciation in the real exchange rate, imports expanded at a higher pace than exports. That expansion was reflected in a continuously increasing trade deficit.

The behavior of the balance in services, transfers, and capital were instrumental in supporting the dynamism of imports and in financing the increasing external gap. Net services and transfers registered a continuous surplus, basically as a result of development of tourism and worker remittances. The growth of tourism was dramatic. The sector's receipts increased by more than 130 percent in 1960, and from 1961 to 1968 the cumulative average rate of growth of the net balance was about 18 percent. After 1963, however, the current balance was in deficit. That deficit decelerated after 1966 as a result of devaluation, an end to import liberalization, and the larger role assigned to export promotion.

Table 4.14 Balance of payments, 1959–1986 (million US dollars)

	Imports	Export	Trade balance	Net services	Net transfers	Current account balance	Long-term capital	Private capital	Public capital	Banking system	Overall balance	Short-term capital	Change in foreign assets	Change in value	Errors and omissions
1959	758.5	523.3	-235.1	134.0	72.9	-28.2	97.6	43.6	54.0	0.0	69.3	0.0	-69.7	0.0	0.3
1960	688.1	745.2	57.1	246.1	90.1	393.3	126.1	106.5	19.6	0.0	519.4	0.0	-459.8	0.0	-59.6
1961	1,037.9	759.2	-278.7	337.4	162.6	221.3	210.3	191.2	19.1	0.0	431.6	0.0	-354.3	0.0	-77.3
1962	1,438.2	800.3	-637.9	467.3	221.1	50.5	120.9	107.5	13.4	0.0	171.4	0.0	-205.7	0.0	34.2
1963	1,798.6	785.9	-1,012.6	569.0	257.8	-185.8	218.7	214.1	4.6	0.0	32.9	0.0	-104.8	0.0	71.8
1964	2,075.5	1,005.3	-1,070.2	782.4	320.8	33.8	254.7	268.1	-13.4	0.0	287.7	0.0	-326.5	0.0	38.8
1965	2,777.8	1,019.1	-1,758.7	912.5	359.9	-486.3	308.8	322.4	-13.6	0.0	-177.5	0.0	130.8	0.0	46.7
1966	3,300.0	1,308.3	-1,991.7	1,008.9	418.7	-564.1	343.6	302.5	41.1	0.0	-220.4	0.0	187.5	0.0	32.9
1967	3,199.9	1,418.7	-1,781.2	875.6	450.3	-456.3	535.1	502.0	33.1	0.0	78.9	0.0	136.2	0.0	-215.0
1968	3,242.3	1,667.1	-1,575.2	885.7	447.7	-241.8	581.2	436.2	145.0	0.0	339.4	0.0	-71.0	0.0	-268.4
1969	3,864.9	1,994.3	-1,870.6	945.1	532.0	-393.5	505.7	481.3	24.4	0.0	112.2	0.0	230.2	0.0	-342.4
1970	4,357.2	2,438.5	-1,873.7	1,293.4	658.9	78.5	669.4	696.9	-27.4	0.0	747.9	0.0	-812.9	0.0	65.3
1971	4,577.4	2,978.4	-1,599.0	1,687.8	767.3	856.1	498.9	601.7	-102.7	0.0	1,355.1	0.0	-1,257.3	0.0	-97.8
1972	6,236.5	3,920.2	-2,316.3	2,021.3	886.0	571.0	940.3	934.2	-2.6	8.7	1,511.3	-55.4	-1,367.4	-124.9	-36.4
1973	8,947.7	5,402.4	-3,545.3	2,688.2	1,414.0	556.9	837.2	810.1	-45.3	72.4	1,394.1	354.2	-1,691.0	-2.6	-54.6
1974	14,334.2	7,265.1	-7,069.1	2,678.9	1,145.6	-3,244.6	2,627.9	1,615.9	53.1	958.9	-616.7	-138.7	793.3	0.0	-38.0
1975	15,192.6	7,806.9	-7,385.7	2,754.6	1,143.3	-3,487.8	2,585.7	1,788.2	14.8	782.7	-902.1	119.4	754.6	0.0	-7.9
1976	16,316.8	8,989.8	-7,327.0	1,891.1	1,142.2	-4,293.7	2,707.4	1,447.4	570.4	689.6	-1,586.3	37.3	1,071.4	0.0	477.4
1977	16,811.9	10,611.8	-6,200.1	2,621.7	1,414.0	-2,164.4	3,706.1	1,746.0	1,276.8	683.3	1,541.7	703.1	-1,145.7	0.0	-1,099.1
1978	17,504.7	13,480.3	-4,024.4	4,000.5	1,656.4	1,632.5	-967.3	2,113.2	-394.9	249.0	3,599.8	154.6	-3,856.7	0.0	102.3
1979	24,022.2	18,351.4	-5,670.8	5,014.2	1,782.1	1,125.5	4,523.2	2,834.5	381.8	1,306.9	5,648.7	196.6	-3,512.2	0.0	-2,333.3
1980	32,305.5	20,580.6	-11,724.9	4,488.6	1,048.4	-5,187.9	4,792.4	4,020.4	174.1	597.9	-395.5	456.7	547.8	0.0	-609.0
1981	31,086.0	20,970.8	-10,115.2	3,442.6	1,692.1	-4,980.5	4,300.8	3,597.8	638.5	64.5	-679.7	1,165.1	1,321.5	0.0	-1,806.9
1982	30,513.0	21,332.1	-9,180.9	3,475.5	1,580.9	-4,124.5	1,846.3	763.2	1,009.4	73.7	-2,278.2	717.5	3,154.8	0.0	-1,594.1
1983	27,543.4	19,870.9	-7,672.5	3,814.0	1,179.9	-2,678.6	3,124.4	2,152.8	953.4	18.2	445.8	355.1	931.5	160.7	-1,893.1
1984	27,062.6	23,022.6	-4,040.0	5,225.9	1,179.9	2,365.8	3,111.1	2,799.4	532.1	-220.4	5,476.9	506.0	-3,093.2	0.0	-2,827.7
1985	27,857.0	23,478.0	-4,379.0	5,895.3	1,137.3	2,653.6	-2,654.2	-1,374.0	-71.5	-1,208.7	-0.6	71.2	1,257.0	0.0	-1,327.6
1986	32,937.3	26,600.6	-6,336.7	9,374.1	1,093.7	4,131.1	-3,306.2	680.1	-2,193.5	-1,792.8	824.9	611.0	-1,718.9	0.0	283.0

Source: Secretaría de Estado de Comercio, various years

As shown in table 4.14, the flow of private foreign capital into Spain increased substantially after 1959. Before that time, because of restrictive controls, it was negligible. Deterioration in Spain's external position in the mid-1950s had to be financed with imports of official capital, mainly US aid. Liberalization of capital imports in 1959 reversed this trend. Total net capital inflows increased from about US$91 million in the period 1959–62 to more than US$300 million in 1963–5. Between 1963 and 1968, Spain was the largest net importer of capital among the OECD members.

The trade balance deficit persisted during the period 1970–5. As a ratio of GDP, the deficit ranged from 3.8 percent in 1971 to 7.9 percent in 1974. The positive behavior of net services meant that the current account registered small surpluses from 1970 to 1973. The international economic crisis of 1973 and high domestic demand for imports led to increasingly larger deficits. As a percentage of GDP, the current account shifted from a surplus of 2.1 percent in 1971 to a 3.6 percent deficit in 1975. The overall balance registered surpluses from 1970 to 1973, but deficits reappeared in 1974 and 1975. As a consequence of the policies developed to cushion the economic effects of the crisis, Spain's external debt more than doubled between 1973 and 1975. Outstanding debt in 1975 reached US$8.4 billion, or 61 percent of total Spanish exports of goods and services that year. Debt service amounted to US$1.7 billion, or 12 percent of total exports, of which US$529 million was interest.

The relative magnitude of the trade balance deficit decreased in 1978–9, and services and transfers helped to shift the current account into surplus. Favorable long-term capital inflows led the overall balance to a surplus that accounted for above 2 percent of GDP. The stock of foreign reserves rose to US$13 billion.

From 1979 onward the heavy burden imposed by the second oil shock accelerated deterioration of the trade balance, which as a percentage of GDP reached around 5 percent. The current account deficit remained around 2 percent of GDP and, although net capital inflows accelerated, the overall balance registered small deficits until 1983.

Foreign reserves declined to US$11.5 billion in 1982, while Spanish foreign debt nearly doubled between 1977 and 1982 to reach the unprecedented level of US$29 billion in 1982 – more than 86 percent of Spain's total annual exports of goods and services, and more than 15 percent of GDP. Debt service payments represented 14.8 percent of total exports. This increase in foreign indebtedness declined after 1984, however, and never had a major effect on the creditworthiness of the country.

Output

The devaluation and other measures of 1959 had a temporary but spectacularly positive effect on the balance of payments, but they also had an important recessionary impact. Consumption contracted substantially and productive investment fell by 18 percent. Agriculture expanded in 1959 because of good harvests, but it declined in 1960. The manufacturing sector stagnated in 1959 but recovered by the end of 1960. Services, construction, and the metal industries were the sectors hit hardest by the recession.

Real GDP expanded by an average of 7.3 percent per year between 1960 and 1966 (table 4.15), which was an unprecedented rate of growth. Manufacturing, with an average growth rate of around 11.6 percent, was the most dynamic sector; services and agriculture expanded by 8.8 percent and 3.7 percent respectively. Increasing domestic demand and the creation of better facilities to import capital and other industrial goods gave the industrial sector the incentives it needed to expand and modernize. This process explains the high rates of growth of industrial output, and subsequently of exports, in these years. For industry, this was a period of easy growth in which practically all sectors participated. The most important contributors to growth in manufacturing were nontraditional activities, such as transport equipment, metal industries and machinery, and chemical products. Transport equipment, the leading sector, maintained an average annual growth rate of 19.3 percent between 1960 and 1966. The

Table 4.15 Real rate of growth in demand and gross domestic product (percent)

Year	Private consumption	Public consumption	Investments	Exports	Imports	GDP
1965	7.0	3.7	18.0	6.9	33.1	6.3
1966	6.9	1.7	12.6	15.2	19.0	7.1
1967	6.0	2.3	0.2	− 4.7	− 3.3	4.3
1968	6.0	1.9	6.8	18.4	8.1	6.8
1969	7.0	4.2	17.1	15.5	15.8	8.9
1970	4.2	5.3	− 1.2	17.4	7.0	4.1
1971	4.9	4.7	− 1.9	13.0	0.7	5.0
1972	8.3	5.5	16.1	12.2	24.7	8.1
1973	8.0	6.7	12.6	9.0	16.4	7.9
1974	5.2	8.3	10.6	0.8	7.7	5.7
1975	2.4	5.2	− 3.6	− 1.5	− 1.1	1.1
1976	4.7	5.3	− 1.4	10.1	10.1	3.0
1977	2.5	4.1	− 4.0	8.5	− 4.7	3.3
1978	1.3	5.5	− 6.4	10.7	− 0.7	1.8
1979	1.2	4.2	− 1.1	6.4	11.5	0.2
1980	1.3	4.4	3.9	0.6	3.8	1.5
1981	− 0.9	1.5	− 4.8	6.9	− 3.5	0.4
1982	0.7	6.5	− 3.3	6.7	4.8	0.9
1983	0.7	4.7	− 3.4	8.3	− 0.3	2.1
1984	− 0.5	2.9	− 5.1	15.1	1.1	2.7
1985	1.8	4.4	3.9	2.9	5.4	2.2
1986	3.6	4.0	12.0	1.1	1.6	3.0

Sources: Instituto Nacional de Estadística, various years; Banco de España, various years

growth rate in light industries, such as textiles, leather and clothing, and food products, lagged behind rates for manufacturing as a whole.

On an annual average basis, GDP grew by 5.3 percent during the second liberalization episode. In the first years of the period, when liberalization was at its highest, GDP increased by around 6.2 percent, but by 1975 the rate of growth decelerated as liberalization lost momentum. The driving force behind GDP growth was domestic demand, mainly private consumption. Gross capital formation fell sharply in the first two years of the liberalization episode but soon recovered. From 1972 to 1974 investment rose in real terms by an average 13.1 percent.

GDP growth during the period 1970–5 was mainly the result of expansion in the industrial and services sectors. The average real GDP increase was about 7.5 percent in industry and about 5.6 percent in services. However, in 1975 the Spanish industrial sector registered negative real growth of − 0.6 percent, which marked the beginning of a phase of slow industrial development (table 4.16).

The path of the agricultural sector was rather uneven. Although the average real increase was around 3.4 percent, the years of strong growth,

Table 4.16 Sources of gross domestic product (annual growth, percent)

Year	Agriculture	Industry	Construction	Services	GDP
1965	− 5.5	11.6	11.8	5.3	5.8
1966	5.7	10.3	11.9	5.6	7.4
1967	3.9	5.5	3.3	5.1	4.9
1968	0.1	8.0	13.6	5.7	6.3
1969	1.7	13.6	6.6	8.3	8.9
1970	− 0.9	8.1	− 0.1	5.2	4.9
1971	10.6	6.2	− 1.1	5.1	5.5
1972	0.2	14.7	9.2	6.6	8.6
1973	3.7	10.7	8.5	7.2	8.1
1974	7.3	6.2	4.5	5.7	5.9
1975	− 0.2	− 0.6	− 4.0	3.9	1.3
1976	4.4	3.4	− 3.9	4.0	3.3
1977	− 4.3	4.7	− 2.0	4.4	3.1
1978	6.7	2.0	− 4.7	3.0	2.5
1979	− 4.1	− 0.1	− 3.6	1.7	0.2
1980	8.8	0.4	− 1.7	1.2	1.5
1981	− 9.5	− 0.2	− 0.2	1.2	− 0.2
1982	− 1.5	− 1.2	2.7	2.5	1.2
1983	6.2	1.6	0.1	1.8	1.9
1984	10.7	0.8	− 4.7	2.5	2.1
1985	1.3	2.1	1.8	2.0	1.9
1986	− 9.0	3.5	6.0	4.4	3.3

Sources: Instituto Nacional de Estadística, various years; Banco de España, various years

such as 1971 and 1974, were followed by stagnation in 1972 and decline in 1975. Construction advanced by an average of 2.8 percent, but that average also incorporated an uneven path of growth.

In short, Spain's economy continued to grow very quickly for a couple of years after the 1973 oil shock, and stagnation did not appear until 1975.

The evolution of GDP during the third liberalization episode (1977–80) was in sharp contrast with its path during the two previous liberalizations. The average annual GDP increase between 1977 and 1980 was just 1.7 percent. Although private consumption retained its crucial role, gross capital formation declined in real terms over the period (− 1.9 percent). Imports only increased by an annual 2.5 percent, but exports grew on average by 6.5 percent each year. The services sector showed the greatest growth rate (2.6 percent), while agriculture and industry grew by an average of 1.8 percent. Construction declined by 3.0 percent.

Employment

The first period of liberalization was marked by an initial rise in unemployment during the second half of 1959, an intensification of unemployment in 1960, and a distinct rise in 1961. Construction, agriculture and the food industries, and the wood and metal industries were the most affected sectors. As in the case of output, however, employment steadily increased after 1961.

It was during this period of the early 1960s that the industrial sector became the most important employer in Spain, surpassing agriculture. From 1960 to 1968 growth in industrial employment occurred at a rate of 2.6 percent per year, compared with a 0.7 percent rise in total employment. Agriculture lost a million workers, and farm employment declined at an average rate of − 3.4 percent.

Among the manufacturing subsectors, those which showed the greatest gains were the metal industries, machinery, and transport equipment. These industries accounted for about 50 percent of all new jobs in manufacturing. Employment growth in manufacturing all told, however, was substantially lower than growth in value added, reflecting large gains in labor productivity. After 1961, unemployment was not a serious problem, fluctuating around 1–2 percent. Although new employment opportunities in industry and services were not sufficient to absorb all the workers leaving agriculture, there was an important safety valve: the emigration of Spanish workers abroad, which rapidly increased over these years. The unemployment rate was also kept down by the relatively low participation of females in the labor force. Although open unemployment was not an important problem, substantial underemployment existed as a result of labor legislation inhibiting the discharge of redundant workers.

Table 4.17 Overview of labor market, 1978–1987 (millions)

Category	1978	1979	1980	1981	1982	1983	1984	1985	1986	1987
Total labor force	12,965.5	12,987.8	13,003.7	13,045.0	13,205.9	13,353.1	13,436.7	13,541.6	13,781.2	13,988.0
Male	9,241.4	9,227.9	9,249.1	9,292.8	9,332.5	9,349.2	9,400.8	9,449.1	9,530.3	9,573.6
Female	3,724.0	3,759.9	3,754.6	3,752.2	3,873.4	4,003.9	4,035.9	4,092.4	4,250.9	4,414.4
Total employed	12,049.5	11,855.2	11,502.4	11,171.6	11,061.1	10,984.1	10,668.2	10,570.8	10,820.5	10,976.7
Male	8,626.0	8,465.2	8,233.7	8,028.1	7,921.0	7,812.7	7,576.2	7,516.9	7,657.3	7,739.9
Female	3,423.4	3,390.1	3,268.7	3,143.4	3,140.2	3,171.4	3,092.0	3,053.9	3,163.2	3,236.8
Total unemployed	916.0	1,132.5	1,501.4	1,873.4	2,144.8	2,369.1	2,768.5	2,970.8	2,960.8	3,011.3
Male	615.4	762.7	1,015.4	1,264.7	1,411.5	1,536.5	1,824.6	1,932.3	1,873.0	1,833.7
Female	300.6	369.7	485.9	608.8	733.2	832.6	943.9	1,038.5	1,087.8	1,177.6
Total unemployment rate	7.1	8.7	11.5	14.4	16.2	17.7	20.5	21.9	21.5	21.5
Male	6.7	8.3	11.0	13.6	15.1	16.4	19.4	20.4	19.7	19.2
Female	8.1	9.8	12.9	16.2	18.9	20.8	23.4	25.4	25.6	26.7

Source: Instituto Nacional de Estadística, various years

Unemployment was not a problem during the second period of liberalization. The unemployment rate between 1970 and 1975 was less than 2 percent. However, growth in the rate of employment began to decelerate in 1975. Migration to other European countries declined, many earlier migrants returned to Spain, and the nationality boom of the 1950s and 1960s created the conditions for an increase in the unemployment rate between 1977 and 1986. Table 4.17 shows statistics on the Spanish labor market from the beginning of the third liberalization episode in 1977 up to 1986. The number of people over 16 grew at around 1.4 percent yearly, and the potential labor force increased by an average of 0.8 percent. Employment fell by − 1.8 percent from 1978 to 1985. The escalation of the unemployment rate has been dramatic: it grew from 5.3 percent in 1978 to 21.9 percent in 1985, although there is some evidence that the real unemployment rate was 4–15 percentage points lower.

The structural change in employment that began in the 1960s continued during the 1970s and 1980s. Agriculture, which still accounted for 21.6 percent of total employment in 1975, accounted for less than 15 percent by 1985. As in the years 1960–8, the farm sector again lost around a million workers. Industry's share of the workforce also declined between 1977 and 1985, from 26.8 percent in 1977 to 23.8 percent in 1985. This represented a loss of around 500,000 jobs. However, in sharp contrast with the previous period of expansion, the services sector was unable to absorb all the workers who had lost jobs in agriculture and industry. Between 1977 and 1986, around 600,000 jobs were created in the services sector, whose share of total employment rose to around 43 percent (table 4.18).

Table 4.18 Rate of change in major labor market indicators, 1978–1987 (percent)

Category	1978	1979	1980	1981	1982	1983	1984	1985	1986	1987
Total labor force	0.2	0.2	0.1	0.3	1.2	1.1	0.6	0.8	1.8	1.5
Male	0.0	− 0.1	0.2	0.5	0.4	0.2	0.6	0.5	0.9	0.5
Female	0.9	1.0	− 0.1	− 0.1	3.2	3.4	0.8	1.4	3.9	3.8
Total employed	− 1.7	− 1.6	− 3.0	− 2.9	− 1.0	− 0.7	− 2.9	− 0.9	2.4	1.4
Male	− 1.6	− 1.9	− 2.7	− 2.5	− 1.3	− 1.4	− 3.0	− 0.8	1.9	1.1
Female	− 1.7	− 1.0	− 3.6	− 3.8	− 0.1	1.0	− 2.5	− 1.2	3.6	2.3
Total unemployed	33.8	23.6	32.6	24.8	14.5	10.5	16.9	7.3	− 0.3	1.7
Male	29.3	23.9	33.1	24.5	11.6	8.9	18.8	5.9	− 3.1	− 2.1
Female	44.0	23.0	31.4	25.3	20.4	13.5	13.4	10.0	4.7	8.3

Source: Instituto Nacional de Estadistica, various years

Investment

Economic activity – and particularly investment – slowed down substantially as a consequence of the stabilization measures of 1959. However, investment started to expand rapidly in 1961, especially in the manufacturing industries. The gradual removal of internal and external controls, and incentives designed to attract foreign investment, were undoubtedly important contributing factors. The ratio of total gross domestic investment to GDP increased from 22 percent in 1961 to more than 26 percent in 1966, growing in real terms at an average rate of about 7 percent annually. Then, under the impact of restrictive measures implemented in 1967–8, private investment declined substantially.

The structure of investment changed significantly during the 1960s. Industrial investment increased substantially, both in absolute and relative terms, whereas housing investment dropped markedly. A rapid increase in domestic demand, massive imports of new capital goods, and an increase in foreign competition were the chief factors in the steady upward trend of gross investment in manufacturing in the period 1960–6 when such investment almost quadrupled in value.

Annual gross investment in dwellings represented, on average, about 25 percent of total fixed-asset formation, although the share declined as the 1960s progressed. The boom in construction paralleled the rapid process of urbanization that took place after 1960, but in the mid-1960s the authorities curtailed incentives for construction in the belief that the boom had become excessive. In the second half of 1968, however, when the sector experienced the lowest level of activity of the whole decade, the authorities again took steps to stimulate construction.

Investment in transportation and equipment (around 18 percent of total investment) was linked to Spain's efforts to modernize its rail and road infrastructure. Finally, investment in agriculture showed a low and relatively stable ratio to GDP of about 2 percent. This was clearly insufficient for a sector that still accounted for a third of the total labor force and a sixth of GDP. The low profitability of the sector, along with the rigidities in agricultural price policy that frequently led to excess supply of certain basic goods, may explain the low level of agricultural investment.

During the second episode (1970–5) investment initially declined and then recovered in 1972–4, when it grew by 13.1 percent a year. Unfortunately, information about the distribution of investment by sector is not readily available.

The most remarkable feature of the evolution of investment during the third episode was its continuous decline. Gross capital formation in real terms between 1977 and 1980 fell by around 1.9 percent, while the investment-to-GDP ratio declined from 25.5 to 21.1 percent. This trend continued during the years 1981–4, causing a strong decrease in capital stock.

5

Sectoral Impacts of Trade Liberalization

In this chapter we discuss sectoral changes and identify the sectors favored by trade policy during the three liberalization episodes.

Table 5.1 presents estimates of effective protection rates in 1962 and 1966 (no information is available for previous years). Sectors are ranked in the table according to their level of effective protection relative to the all-industry average in 1962. The favored sectors include all those with higher than average protection in that year. All sectors in the favored group – mainly intermediate products and capital goods – experienced a substantial reduction in effective protection between 1962 and 1966. Among the nonfavored sectors, however, effective protection increased. The result, of course, was to narrow the degree of dispersion in relative protection. By 1966 the pattern of sectoral incentives was less distorted. The structure of protection did not change meaningfully between 1962 and 1966 (the rank correlation coefficient for relative effective protection in both years was 0.818, which is statistically significant at the 99 percent level of confidence) when trade policy aimed at fostering the development of industries producing intermediate inputs and capital goods.

It was not possible to use a similar sectoral method of classification for the second and third episodes. Both the level of sectoral aggregation and the methodology used for the analysis of favored industries in the 1970s are different. The sectoral breakdown follows Spain's National Accounts classifications. Sectoral trade policy measures are captured through effective exchange rates $[e/(1 + t)](1 + ICGI)$ for imports and $e/(1 + d)$ for exports where e is the formal exchange rate, t is the nominal sectoral tariff, ICGI is the equalization tax on imports, and d is the export tax rebate. The formal rate is a trade-weighted exchange rate, and an increase indicates an appreciation. Effective exchange rates for imports do not include quantitative restrictions; effective exchange rates for exports do not take export credit subsidies into account. In addition, effective exchange rates do not capture the net protective effect on sectors in the way that effective rates of

Table 5.1 Effective protection during the first liberalization episode

	Relative effective protection			Effective protection (percentage change)
	1962	1966	Change, 1962–6	
Favored sectors				
Textiles	1.58	1.34	−15.2	−23.8
Synthetic fibers	1.55	1.31	−15.5	−24.3
Plastics	1.44	1.25	−13.2	−21.8
Shoes and leather	1.42	1.10	−22.5	−0.2
Transport equipment	1.26	0.98	−22.2	−27.1
Electrical machinery	1.07	1.02	−4.7	−14.1
Paper products	1.01	1.00	−1.0	−11.2
Average	1.33	1.14	−14.3	−21.8
Nonfavored sectors				
Metal products	0.97	0.99	2.1	−8.4
Lumber products	0.96	1.00	4.2	−5.9
Raw chemicals	0.94	0.92	−2.1	−12.7
Shipbuilding	0.89	1.03	15.7	4.2
Nonelectrical machinery	0.88	0.81	−8.0	−17.7
Iron and steel	0.87	1.27	46.0	30.9
Other chemicals	0.82	0.99	20.7	9.2
Stone, clay, and glass products	0.81	0.96	18.5	6.2
Nonferrous metals	0.77	0.92	19.5	7.4
Miscellaneous	0.64	0.73	14.1	2.0
Printing and publishing	0.58	0.71	22.4	8.6
Rubber products	0.53	0.62	28.3	15.5
Average	0.81	0.92	13.6	3.3
Total effective protection	1.59	1.43	−10.1	

Sources: Gamir, 1972; own data

protection do. Therefore the effective exchange rate estimates are not an accurate measure of the absolute level of sectoral import protection or export incentives, even though their evolution is quite useful for comparisons across sectors.

Tables 5.2 and 5.3 present by sector the evolution of real effective exchange rates for imports (REEMs) and exports (REEXs) during the second and third episodes of liberalization. Changes in real bias are included. Real bias is defined as the ratio of the real effective exchange rate for exports to that for imports. The higher the bias is, the higher is the level of protection relative to export incentives granted to a specific sector. Favored sectors include those that enjoyed higher rates of import protection in 1971. The higher the rate of protection or export subsidy granted to a sector is, the lower is its effective exchange rate for imports or exports.

Table 5.2 Real effective exchange rates: second liberalization episode

	Imports			Exports		
	1971	1975	Percentage change	1971	1975	Percentage change
Favored sectors						
Plastics	55.7	66.8	19.9	66.9	78.3	17.0
Nonmetal products	59.1	70.5	19.3	68.0	80.4	18.2
Shoes and apparel	59.3	71.3	20.2	69.4	80.6	16.1
Textiles	60.0	69.1	15.2	68.5	78.5	14.6
Transport equipment	60.3	74.2	23.1	68.9	80.1	16.3
Miscellaneous	60.9	74.3	22.0	70.2	83.2	18.5
Machinery	61.4	73.7	20.0	68.9	80.4	16.7
Paper and printing	62.8	78.5	25.0	68.1	80.2	17.8
Chemicals	63.0	75.5	19.8	69.5	81.8	17.7
Nonfavored sectors						
Metal products	66.2	81.6	23.3	69.1	82.2	19.0
Food and beverages	69.0	84.5	22.5	72.4	79.4	9.7
Wood and furniture	69.9	80.0	14.5	73.1	84.9	16.2
Agriculture	73.3	84.5	15.3	73.2	85.2	16.4
Mining	73.7	85.2	15.6	73.2	85.8	17.2

Table 5.3 Real effective exchange rates: third liberalization episode

	Imports			Exports		
	1977	1980	Percentage change	1977	1980	Percentage change
Favored sectors						
Plastics	62.4	77.9	24.4	74.6	85.5	14.6
Nonmetal products	69.7	82.9	18.9	79.1	90.7	14.7
Shoes and apparel	70.5	81.5	15.6	78.4	87.6	11.7
Textiles	70.1	79.6	13.6	70.4	86.3	22.6
Transport equipment	64.4	81.1	25.9	75.2	87.8	16.8
Miscellaneous	74.4	87.1	17.1	78.7	93.0	18.2
Machinery	70.7	80.1	13.3	78.7	86.9	10.4
Paper and printing	74.8	86.0	15.0	77.7	87.3	12.4
Chemicals	73.9	85.9	16.2	80.0	90.8	13.5
Nonfavored sectors						
Metal products	77.9	87.3	12.1	78.9	86.9	10.1
Food and beverages	82.1	90.2	9.9	85.2	92.9	9.0
Wood and furniture	76.9	89.3	16.1	81.5	92.5	13.4
Agriculture	84.1	83.8	11.5	86.4	96.6	11.8
Mining	84.6	94.5	11.7	85.2	94.8	11.3

The formal exchange rate appreciated during the second episode in both nominal and real terms. In this context, the real effective exchange rate for imports will appreciate more than the formal rate when imports are liberalized or export subsidies are increased, while the real effective exchange rate for exports will appreciate less. As shown in table 5.2, those sectors with higher than average import protection experienced a greater liberalization than nonfavored activities. Nominal protection decreased in all favored sectors except textiles, while in the nonfavored group it increased in agriculture, mining, and wood and furniture. Export incentives followed a different pattern – that is, they increased relatively more in nonfavored activities. In fact, export subsidies for favored sectors decreased, except for textiles, shoes, machinery, and transport equipment. As a result of these developments, real bias decreased in most sectors in both favored and nonfavored groups.

The pattern of trade policy changes during the third episode was similar. Nominal protection and export subsidies decreased in all favored sectors (see table 5.3) except shoes and machinery, where export tax rebates increased. In contrast, nominal protection and export incentives increased in nonfavored activities.

As in the 1960s, the two liberalization attempts of the 1970s were relatively successful in reducing import protection and the bias against exports. Nevertheless, the structure of sectoral incentives for exports and imports did not experience any substantial change and continued to favor the production of intermediate inputs, certain labor intensive products such as textiles, shoes and apparel, and equipment goods. Rank correlation coefficients between the structure of the nominal effective exchange rate for imports in 1971 and 1980 and between the nominal effective exchange rates for imports and exports in 1971 and in 1980 were 0.88, 0.83, and 0.84, all statistically significant at the 99 percent level, indicating that the pattern of trade incentives was fairly stable during the 1970s and that export promotion was also higher in sectors with relatively high protection against imports.

The Time Pattern of Sectoral Response

The liberalization measures of the first episode (1959–66) began to be introduced at the same time that a stabilization program was implemented. After a short recession in 1959–60, the economy started to grow at a very high rate and the liberalization program developed in a very favorable environment.

Table 5.4 summarizes at the sectoral level the evolution of major economic variables between 1962 and 1966. Real industrial output and employment grew by 12.9 percent and 3.4 percent respectively, there was a

Table 5.4 Change in major economic variables, 1962 and 1966 (percent)

	Imports	Exports	Output	Employment	Capital intensity	Apparent labor productivity
Favored sectors						
Textiles	39.6	16.5	1.8	−0.4	11.7	2.2
Synthetic fibers	48.0	7.2	24.4	3.0	13.2	20.7
Plastics	25.4	8.3	29.9	17.0	8.1	1.0
Shoes and leather	52.7	23.6	10.0	2.0	7.8	7.9
Transport equipment	12.7	62.1	19.4	6.9	12.1	11.7
Electrical machinery	35.6	22.4	26.6	8.6	−9.3	16.5
Paper products	25.6	61.9	15.7	−1.8	20.9	17.7
Average	34.2	28.9	18.3	5.0	9.4	12.6
Nonfavored sectors						
Metal products	31.6	32.7	15.5	9.5	−3.3	5.5
Lumber products	24.3	21.6	10.5	1.9	16.9	8.4
Raw chemicals	16.9	12.6	12.0	−1.6	22.7	13.8
Shipbuilding	47.5	37.7	18.8	0.2	34.4	18.5
Nonelectrical machinery	22.8	30.0	18.8	4.1	20.4	14.1
Iron and steel	25.5	−10.2	14.8	−2.4	15.7	17.7
Other chemicals	26.1	7.1	9.7	1.5	11.0	8.1
Stone, clay, and glass products	32.2	10.0	16.6	4.4	10.5	11.7
Nonferrous metals	35.6	15.3	17.7	3.8	26.3	13.2
Miscellaneous	19.3	43.8	20.6	9.1	25.6	10.5
Printing and publishing	21.6	9.6	7.4	2.7	16.8	4.6
Rubber products	13.9	52.5	16.1	5.1	14.6	10.5
Average	26.4	21.9	14.9	3.2	17.6	11.4
Total	29.3	24.5	16.1	3.9	14.6	11.8

substantial expansion in trade flows, and the economy became more capital intensive, especially in nonfavored sectors.

Favored sectors showed better economic performance, on average, than nonfavored sectors. In the former, real output increased by about 18.3 percent, and only textiles, shoes and leather, and paper products registered lower than average rates of growth. The group of nonfavored activities performed relatively poorly, but only a few sectors – lumber products, raw and other chemicals, and printing and publishing – grew below average. Employment growth was also more dynamic in favored sectors. In general, sluggish expansion or decline in employment was observed in sectors with lower than average output growth or in activities marked by technological innovation and greater capital investment (synthetic fibers, paper products, shipbuilding, and iron and steel).

This episode entailed a substantial increase in import and export shares. Import expansion (29.3 percent) was higher than export growth (24.5 percent), and both were, on average, greater in favored than in nonfavored sectors. Import shares increased in all sectors except plastics, transport equipment, miscellaneous, and paper and printing, while export share declined in synthetic fibers, plastics, iron and steel, other chemicals, glass products, and nonferrous metals.

The evolution of major economic aggregates during the second and third episodes is depicted in tables 5.5 and 5.6. The pattern is very similar to that of the first episode. Growth in foreign trade, output, and employment was greater in favored than in nonfavored sectors.

Table 5.5 Sectoral changes during the second liberalization episode, 1971–1975 (percent)

	Imports	Exports	Output	Employment
Favored sectors				
Plastics	65.0	77.9	32.6	14.3
Nonmetal products	35.0	100.2	94.1	7.8
Shoes and apparel	128.8	42.3	−6.5	8.6
Textiles	48.9	37.4	7.2	−1.7
Transport equipment	111.2	76.7	24.8	18.1
Miscellaneous	61.4	56.7	94.2	−23.9
Machinery	54.1	78.9	64.7	37.1
Paper and printing	51.8	45.2	59.4	38.5
Chemicals	21.0	31.4	45.7	6.7
Nonfavored sectors				
Metal products	44.0	62.6	12.1	11.6
Food and beverages	104.5	−11.6	18.9	28.6
Wood and furniture	35.6	29.4	51.4	14.7
Agriculture	30.6	19.5	11.2	−16.6
Mining	51.0	−27.9	−24.8	−8.1

Table 5.6 Sectoral changes during the third liberalization episode, 1977–1980 (percent)

	Imports	Exports	Output	Employment
Favored sectors				
Plastics	45.1	13.3	21.8	14.1
Nonmetal products	38.5	43.1	14.9	−3.4
Shoes and apparel	19.5	−12.3	−36.9	−19.4
Textiles	2.4	11.8	20.6	−3.9
Transport equipment	86.7	33.2	−1.9	−4.1
Miscellaneous	29.5	13.0	−28.3	−2.5
Machinery	1.7	37.3	14.9	−7.8
Paper and printing	20.5	50.8	5.7	−4.4
Chemicals	24.9	63.4	6.2	−6.5
Nonfavored sectors				
Metal products	11.1	104.6	−1.1	−9.3
Food and beverages	−31.9	−4.0	3.5	−8.5
Wood and furniture	8.7	21.5	18.0	−13.8
Agriculture	27.3	35.9	11.4	−15.8
Mining	8.5	26.6	−0.4	−19.9

In the favored group, only three sectors experienced low output growth during the second episode: transport equipment, textiles, and shoes and apparel. The first, however, includes shipbuilding, a sector strongly hit by the recession and the emergence of new competitors. If this subsector is excluded, output growth would have been very high, mainly because of fast development in the Spanish automobile industry. Textiles, shoes, and leather were also affected by increasing international competition. In addition, the underground economy in these sectors was large, and it is very unlikely that the available statistics accurately reflect performance. Textiles, together with miscellaneous, registered a fall in employment; nonmetal industries, shoes and leather products, and chemicals recorded only small increases. Import and export performances were stronger in favored sectors, but because of high rates of growth in sectoral output, import and export shares declined in miscellaneous, machinery, paper and printing, and chemicals. Output and employment growth in nonfavored sectors were relatively weak, and export performance was not much better. Instead, import shares (except in wood and furniture) increased. In terms of output and employment the behavior of nonfavored sectors was determined by changes in agriculture and mining, and it is very likely that liberalization did not play a major role since both agriculture and mining tend to shrink as industrialization grows stronger.

During the third liberalization episode the major change in the economic environment was a continuous decline in employment. This general feature was again more acute in nonfavored sectors despite better output and smaller increases in imports. The favored sectors were relatively less dynamic in output and in export growth.

Correlation between Policy and Trade

The next step in our investigation of sectoral economic responses during liberalization was to determine whether there was any systematic relationship between changes in trade policy and actual trade flows by sector. For this purpose, we estimated Spearman's rank correlations for each of the three liberalization episodes. The results are summarized in tables 5.7 and 5.8.

Table 5.7 Spearman's rank correlation coefficients between changes in trade policy and trade flows

	M	MS	X	XS
First episode (1962–6)				
EPR	0.402*	0.525*	0.202	0.593*
Relative EPR	0.407*	0.531*	0.231	
Absolute EPR	0.449*	0.393*	0.189	
Second episode (1971–5)				
NEEM	0.499*	0.204		
REEM	0.481*	0.204		
NEEX			− 0.358	0.059
REEX			− 0.367	0.073
Level NEEX			0.749**	0.512**
Level REEX			0.815**	0.314
Third episode (1977–80)				
NEEM	0.556*	0.477*		
REEM	0.521*	0.385		
NEEX			− 0.347	− 0.330
REEX			− 0.073	− 0.279
Level NEEX			− 0.349	0.037
Level REEX			− 0.103	0.121

M, MS, percentage change in real imports or import shares.
X, XS, percentage change in real exports or export shares.
EPR, percentage change in effective protection.
NEEM, REEM, percentage change in nominal or real exchange rates for imports.
NEEX, REEX, percentage change in nominal or real exchange rates for exports.
In the first episode of liberalization, M, MS, X, and XS indicate percentage changes in the period 1962–8. In addition, the correlation coefficient between XS and EPR is found for a smaller sample than for the other variables (17 sectors instead of 19).
* Coefficients are statistically significant at the 95 percent confidence level.
** Coefficients are statistically significant at the 99 percent confidence level.

Table 5.8 Spearman's rank correlation coefficients between changes in trade flows and other related variables

	Y	L	X	XS
First episode (1962–8)				
M	− 0.05	0.011	0.363	
MS	− 0.525*	− 0.365		− 0.318
	(− 0.605*)	(− 0.479*)		(0.121)
X	0.414*	0.568*		
XS	0.02	0.237		
Y		0.763*	0.628*	
Second episode (1971–5)				
M	− 0.116	0.385	0.196	
MS	− 0.776*	0.165		0.473*
X	0.499*	0.224		
XS	0.473*	0.024		
Y		0.253		
Third episode (1977–80)				
M	− 0.068	0.512*	0.213	
MS	− 0.631**	− 0.152		0.788**
X	0.086	− 0.015		
XS	− 0.701**	0.077		
Y		− 0.327		

Y, L, percentage change in real output or employment.
M, MS, percentage change in real imports or import shares.
X, XS, percentage change in real exports or export shares.
The correlation coefficients for the period 1962–6 were not statistically significant except for the values in parentheses.
* Coefficients are statistically significant at the 95 percent confidence level.
** Coefficients are statistically significant at the 99 percent confidence level.

Liberalization ordinarily decreases the relative price of imports with respect to exports and nontradeable goods, and is very likely to lead to an increase in both imports and exports. Reductions in protection during the first liberalization episode were positively related to increases in imports and import shares. The rank correlation coefficients for changes in effective protection rates in 1962–8 were statistically significant at the 95 percent level. The same result applied to changes in absolute levels of relative effective protection rates. The correlations were also statistically significant for imports, but in general not for import shares, during the second and third liberalization episodes. Nominal and real effective exchange rates for imports were used as a proxy for changes in trade policy for the latter two episodes.

The results of the investigation to determine the relation between changes in trade policy and changes in exports were less clear. No meaningful correlation was found between changes in effective protection during the first episode and changes in exports and export shares for the whole sample. For a reduced sample of 17 sectors that excluded synthetic and artificial fibers and rubber products, however, the changes in effective protection between 1962 and 1966 were highly correlated with changes in export shares for 1962–6 and 1962–8. Investigation of changes in nominal or real effective exchange rates for exports during the second and third episodes and changes in exports or export shares did not reveal any significant correlation, but export behavior was strongly related to the level of the effective exchange rate for exports, indicating that the greater the export incentives granted to a sector (and, by definition, the lower the sectoral effective exchange rate), the greater the growth in export shares. This result was not obtained for the third episode, however.

Import expansion during a period of liberalization ordinarily has a negative effect on the rates of output growth and employment, while increases in exports work in the opposite direction. The relations between changes in imports and changes in output were not statistically significant for the three episodes. However, changes in import shares were negatively and significantly related to changes in output. Export growth was also positively related to output changes, except during the third episode. In contrast, changes in export shares were negatively correlated with output changes in the second and third episodes. Since changes in import and export shares were positively correlated in both episodes, this striking result may indicate that sectors facing high import competition intensified their propensity to export in order to offset their weakened performance in domestic markets.

Investigation of the relation between trade flows and changes in employment yields less convincing results. Except for the period 1962–6, sectoral changes in share of imports or exports are not negatively correlated with changes in employment. In addition, the coefficient was positive and statistically significant during the third liberalization episode. Export growth and employment, as well as output growth and employment, were positively and significantly correlated only during the first episode.

In short, the statistical evidence drawn from rank correlations over the three periods under study is, in general, consistent with the behavior expected in major economic aggregates during liberalization episodes. In general, reductions of protection and increases in export incentives resulted in better import and export performance. The increase in imports was associated with deceleration in output growth, but this effect was partially offset by export expansion. However, rank correlations do not definitely indicate a significant relationship between changes in import competition and employment behavior.

Imports and Employment

The deterioration of the employment situation in Spain since 1974 has been dramatic. In the 1960s and early 1970s the country experienced one of the lowest rates of unemployment among OECD members. After the first oil shock, however, unemployment in Spain rose from between 1 and 2 percent annually to about 22 percent in 1986. It is possible that Spain has a larger informal economy and more fraud in unemployment registration, and that these factors, together with definition procedures, explain some of the increase.

During the period from 1960 to 1974, unemployment was kept low by the large migration of workers to other countries. However, after 1974, as output growth began to slow down, the labor flow reversed direction. Moreover, as a result of the baby boom of the 1960s and the increase in the female employment rate, the growth rate of the labor force increased just as demand decelerated.

Our hypothesis is that trade liberalization and employment were not closely related, and that greater rigidity in the Spanish labor market explains the difference between the unemployment figures of Spain and those of the other OECD countries (Dolado and Malo de Molina, 1985). The evolution of industrial labor costs in Spain and the other OECD countries is presented in table 5.9. The absence of flexibility in the Spanish labor market is reflected in real wages after 1974.

Table 5.9 Real unit labor costs in various countries, 1975, 1979, and 1982 (1970 = 100)

	Spain	United Kingdom	Belgium	Denmark	France	West Germany	Italy	Holland
1975	123.10	102.10	117.30	95.20	110.20	104.30	132.80	112.60
1979	154.20	101.30	115.30	95.00	110.80	105.40	120.20	103.90
1982	141.60	106.80	110.60	79.70	115.20	104.20	115.20	91.80

Source: Banco de España, 1985

The absence of real wage adjustments despite intense external shocks was on indication of wage rigidity. Labor costs per unit of output in Spanish industry increased more than in any other OECD country after 1974. Although real wages continued to increase after 1979, the fall in employment explains why the index decreased until 1982. The existence of generalized indexation schemes since the early 1970s, the increase in social security taxes, and a reduction in wage structure dispersion were the main factors that led to a continuous increase in the real price of labor. This was compounded by a surge in trade union activity after 1975.

Table 5.10 Real wage rigidity in Spain

	1	2	3	4	5	6
	Elasticity of nominal wages				Real wage rigidity	
	Unemployment rate	Short term prices	Long term prices	Unemployment	Short term	Long term
Global economy						
1970–84	8.18	0.59	1.00	0.27	2.18	3.70
1976–84	12.10			0.18	3.24	5.50
1984	20.60			0.11	5.51	9.34
Industrial sector						
1970–84	5.28	0.88	1.00	0.36	2.44	2.78
1976–84	8.12			0.24	3.59	4.07
1984	15.05			0.13	6.50	7.35

Column 5 is column 2 divided by column 4; column 6 is column 3 divided by column 4.

Source: Dolado and Malo de Molina, 1985

Table 5.10 presents additional indicators of wage rigidity. The elasticity values were obtained by estimating wage equations by means of the Phillips curve. The short-term elasticity of nominal wages with respect to inflation is a measure of "nominal inertia." The higher is its value, the higher is the real wage rigidity. The values in Spain were quite high as a result of indexation. However, elasticity with respect to the unemployment rate was quite low and decreasing, indicating that the responsiveness of nominal wages weakened as unemployment increased. Columns 5 and 6 present a synthetic measure of rigidity. The values for Spain were higher than for any other OECD country for the period 1974–86.

Wage rigidity was reinforced by a high degree of employment rigidity. During the Franco years, labor contracts were extended indefinitely and the costs of dismissing workers were high. As a result, labor was a quasi-fixed production factor. These circumstances did not change after 1974. Adjustment costs increased and were substantially higher than in most of the other industrialized countries. Empirical evidence, obtained from econometric estimations of labor demand functions, points to the existence of a significant adjustment costs. The long-term elasticity of labor demand with respect to real labor costs was quite similar to that of other OECD countries, but the average lag in the response was very high.

Figure 5.1 shows the positive correlation between wage rigidity and unemployment. With respect to both the industrial sector and the total economy, Spain showed the highest index of real wage rigidity and also the highest increase in unemployment. The absence of real wage flexibility

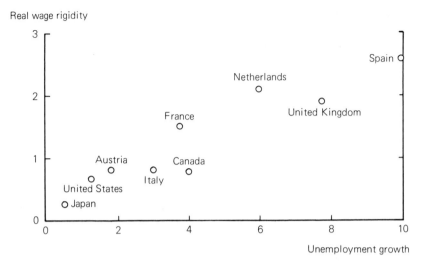

Figure 5.1 Labor market rigidities and unemployment growth

despite external disturbance leads to an increase in structural unemployment for a given level of aggregate demand and inflation. Table 5.11 presents estimations of the nonaccelerating inflation rate of unemployment (NAIRU) for Spain and other OECD countries. All countries experienced an increase in the rate of structural unemployment after 1973, but Spain showed the highest increase, which after 1979 was similar to the observed rate of unemployment. Changes in aggregate demand, social security taxes, the real costs of imported inputs, and the intensity of trade union pressure, together with other minor influences, explained about 95 percent of employment growth over the period.

Measuring the Effects on Employment of Changes in Foreign Trade

An increase in competing imports indicates trade liberalization. In the short run, imports will compete with domestic production and therefore employment may fall. A rise in unemployment will thus be the major cost borne during the transition period. Obtaining a rough estimation of the order of magnitude of this impact may be decisive in determining the appropriate timing, sequencing, and probability of success of liberalization. Determining the link between changes in employment and trade liberalization is not an easy task, however, since any change in employment levels is the result of the interaction of several factors.

Table 5.11 Estimates of the nonaccelerating rate of unemployment

	Period	Average unemployment rate	OECD estimates	Other studies
West Germany	1971–5	1.80	3.30	1.80
	1976–80	3.60	2.40	3.70
	1981–3	6.30	3.70	6.70
Canada	1970–3	5.90	4.70	0.00
	1974–9	7.20	5.80	0.00
	1980–3	8.50	7.40	0.00
Spain	1970–3	0.90	0.00	0.90
	1974–9	3.40	0.00	6.60
	1980–4	18.40	0.00	11.30
United States	1970–3	5.40	5.40	5.80
	1974–81	6.90	6.50	7.10
	1982–3	9.70	6.10	6.80
France	1971–5	2.70	4.50	3.00
	1976–80	5.20	4.80	5.30
	1981–3	8.30	7.70	7.30
Italy	1971–5	5.80	5.40	5.80
	1976–80	7.10	5.20	7.10
	1981–3	9.10	5.40	0.00
Japan	1972–5	1.50	1.20	0.00
	1976–80	2.10	1.90	0.00
	1981–3	2.20	2.30	0.00
United Kingdom	1971–5	3.00	4.20	2.80
	1976–80	5.40	7.60	5.50
	1981–3	10.60	9.40	10.80

Source: Dolado and Malo de Molina, 1985

In this section an accounting procedure of the constant-market-share type is used to estimate the contributions of domestic demand, labor productivity, and foreign trade to change in sectoral employment growth rates (Krueger, 1980).

By definition,

$$C_{it} = Y_{it} + M_{it} - X_{it}$$

where C is domestic consmption, Y is gross output, M is imports, and X is exports, all measured in constant prices, and i and t indicate sector and time period. If $Y_{it}/L_{it} = A_{it}$ is the average product of labor and $Y_{it}/C_{it} = S_{it}$ is the ratio of domestic output to domestic consumption, and if A_{it}, S_{it}, and C_{it} increase at constant rates r_1, r_2, and r_3,

$$A_t = A_0 \exp(r_1 t)$$
$$S_t = S_0 \exp(r_2 t)$$
$$C_t = C_0 \exp(r_3 t)$$
$$\begin{aligned} L_t &= A_t^{-1} S_t C_t \\ &= A_0^{-1} \exp(-r_1 t) \, S_0 \exp(r_2 t) \, C_0 \exp(r_3 t) \\ &= L_0 \exp[(r_2 + r_3 - r_1)t] \end{aligned}$$

The rate of change in employment can be interpreted as the result of changes in apparent domestic consumption r_3, the share of domestic output in domestic consumption r_2 (a proxy for the contribution of the foreign sector), and labor productivity r_1. If we define domestic consumption alternatively as $Y + M$ and $Y + M - X$, we can differentiate between the role of changes in import penetration ratios and the offsetting effects of export expansion. By maintaining domestic output as a constant share of domestic consumption during two consecutive years while keeping domestic consumption and labor productivity at the second-year levels, a rough estimate of the likely impact of imports, or the net trade balance, on employment can be obtained.

A major shortcoming of this approach is that neither domestic demand nor labor productivity are affected by changes in import-to-output or export-to-output ratios. It might be thought that, by keeping the import share constant and ruling out import competition, labor productivity would increase at a slower pace. In that case the estimates would not be an indication of an upper bound. However, it can equally be argued that slower growth of labor productivity is the origin of more rapid import growth. Finally, note that with a lower rate of productivity change the price of domestic goods will be higher if import competition does not increase, and thus domestic consumption might have grown less.

Result of Liberalization on Employment

In this section we present estimates of r_1, r_2, and r_3 for each episode of liberalization and try to isolate the impact of changes in import and export shares on changes in sectoral employment in terms of both rate of growth and number of workers affected.

Employment: First Episode

Analysis of the first episode was constrained by data limitations. In order to have a compatible disaggregated set of data, we had to rely on input–output tables for the 1960s. This meant narrowing the scope of the study to the period 1962–6 and describing the evolution of the period based on information for the first and last years.

Table 5.12 shows the contributions of demand, labor productivity, and import share to the rate of change of sectoral employment. In order to concentrate on the specific role of import competition, we included exports as a component of domestic demand in column 3, a constraint that is relaxed in column 4. In column 3 we show the rate of growth of domestic consumption plus exports. Column 2 gives the rate of change of labor productivity, and column 5 gives the rate of growth of domestic output in domestic consumption. Column 1 presents the observed rates of employment change, which by definition are equal to the sum of columns 2, 4, and 6 when we use imports plus output as a proxy for demand growth, and to the sum of columns 2, 3, and 5 when we use output plus imports minus exports as a proxy for demand growth.

All sectors experienced an increase in labor productivity. Import competition in general was also greater, since the share of domestic output in consumption decreased for all sectors except food and beverages, rubber, and petroleum products. The effects on employment of changes in the import share are quite uniform except for synthetic fibers and capital goods, in which the rates differ by 3 to almost 7 percentage points. However, these effects are comparatively small in relation to the impact of changes in demand and labor productivity.

Columns 4 and 6 present estimates based on changes in the net trade balance. The rates of change in labor productivity were not affected, and the only modifications refer to the behavior of apparent consumption and the share of domestic output in domestic demand.

Compared with the previous results, half the sectors experienced a significant reduction in the negative impact on employment, which was offset (partially or totally) by export expansion. The sign changed from negative to positive in shoes and leather products, transport equipment, shipbuilding, and oil products. The estimates for the other sectors were not affected significantly by differential treatment of exports.

In columns 7–10 we use the previous information to obtain an estimate of the maximum likely impact of changes in import and export shares on the number of jobs. Columns 7 and 8 give the rates at which employment would have changed had the share of domestic output in domestic consumption (including and excluding exports respectively) remained constant. Columns 9 and 10 translate these growth rates into number of jobs. Textiles was the only sector in which employment would have increased instead of declined if the import share had been kept constant. For the other sectors there is a change in sign, and all of them experience a higher employment gain, or lower decline, except food, beverages, and petroleum products. In fact, the import share of these three sectors declined.

Table 5.12 Imports and employment in the first liberalization episode, 1962–1966

Sector	Actual employment change (thousands)	Y/L	Y + M	Y + M − X	$\dfrac{Y}{Y+H}$	$\dfrac{Y}{Y+H-X}$	Employment change (thousands)			
							if import share is constant	if net trade balance is constant	because of change in import share	because of change in net trade balance
Food and beverages	0.6	− 8.8	8.6	9.4	0.8	0.0	− 0.2	0.6	− 4.8	0.0
Other food products	− 3.5	− 9.2	5.9	5.9	− 0.2	− 0.2	− 3.3	− 3.3	2.0	2.0
Textiles	− 0.4	− 2.2	2.5	2.3	− 0.7	− 0.5	0.3	0.1	12.4	8.6
Shoes and leather products	2.0	− 7.9	10.7	9.8	− 0.8	0.1	2.8	1.9	8.6	− 0.7
Lumber products	1.9	− 8.4	11.2	10.8	− 0.9	− 0.5	2.8	2.4	10.9	6.0
Paper products	− 1.8	− 17.7	17.1	16.8	− 1.2	− 0.9	− 0.6	− 0.9	1.7	1.3
Printing and publishing	2.7	− 4.6	7.8	7.6	− 0.5	− 0.3	3.2	3.0	1.9	1.1
Raw chemicals	− 1.6	− 13.6	13.3	13.4	− 1.1	− 1.2	− 0.5	− 0.4	1.6	1.7
Synthetic and artificial fibers	3.0	− 20.7	30.5	31.2	− 6.8	− 7.5	9.8	10.5	5.6	6.2
Rubber products	5.1	− 10.5	15.6	15.2	0.0	0.4	5.1	4.7	0.1	− 0.5
Plastics	17.0	− 11.0	29.9	29.9	− 1.9	− 1.9	16.9	18.9	4.3	4.3
Other chemical products	1.5	− 8.1	10.5	10.6	− 0.9	− 1.0	2.4	2.5	3.9	4.3
Petroleum byproducts	10.3	− 3.7	13.5	16.5	0.5	− 2.5	9.8	12.8	0.0	1.3
Iron and steel	− 2.4	− 17.7	16.1	16.4	− 0.8	− 1.1	− 1.6	− 1.3	2.8	3.8
Nonferrous metals	3.8	− 13.2	20.3	20.7	− 3.3	− 3.7	7.1	7.5	6.9	7.8
Electrical machinery	8.6	− 16.5	28.4	28.5	− 3.3	− 3.4	11.9	12.0	15.1	15.6
Nonelectrical machinery	4.1	− 14.1	20.8	20.4	− 2.6	− 2.2	6.7	6.3	13.7	11.5
Transport equipment	6.9	− 11.7	18.7	18.2	− 0.1	0.4	7.0	6.5	2.9	− 1.8
Shipbuilding	0.2	− 18.5	18.8	14.1	− 0.1	4.6	0.3	− 4.4	0.2	− 8.8
Metal products	9.5	− 5.5	17.1	16.7	− 2.1	− 1.7	11.6	11.2	39.6	33.1
Miscellaneous manufacturing	9.1	− 10.5	20.3	20.0	− 0.7	− 0.4	9.8	9.5	2.0	1.5
Stone, clay, and glass products	4.4	− 11.7	17.8	17.9	− 1.7	− 1.8	6.1	6.2	13.5	14.3
Total									144.9	112.8

Y/L, change in labor productivity; Y + M, Y + M − X, demand growth; Y/(Y + M), change in import share; Y/(Y + M − X), change in net trade balance.

The number of jobs lost as a result of the change in the share of domestic output in domestic consumption was estimated to be 144,900 or 112,800, depending on whether imports only or net trade balance was used in the definition of domestic demand. These figures amounted to 4.9 percent and 3.8 percent respectively, of total industrial employment in 1966. In relation to total employment, these rates declined to 1.2 percent and 0.9 percent respectively. The job loss in five sectors – textiles, lumber products, electrical and nonelectrical machinery, metal products, and stone, clay and glass products – accounted for about three quarters of the total.

Employment: Second Episode
A different source of information on production sectors was used to gauge the change in employment during the second and third episodes. The data are based on National Accounts figures and the authors' own calculations. Agriculture and mining were included in the sectoral breakdown, and the manufacturing sector was more aggregated than for the first episode. The inclusion of agriculture and mining, which experienced a secular decline in employment, adds an additional argument to the reasons for the likely overestimation bias of this approach.

The results for the second episode are shown in table 5.13. As before, the primary determinants of employment behavior found elsewhere than in import competition. All sectors except mining and shoes and leather experienced a substantial increase in domestic demand and labor productivity that, in general, exceeded the impact of change in the share of domestic output in domestic consumption, which decreased in all sectors except miscellaneous.

The sectoral effects of changes in the import share upon employment do vary considerably, however. In mining, transport equipment, textiles, and wood and furniture they were higher than 1 percent. Explicit consideration of exports introduced several significant differences. In two sectors, chemicals and shoes and leather, the external effect on employment changed from negative to positive, while in transport equipment, textiles, and plastics the negative impact was substantially reduced. Among the remaining sectors the changes were either nil or reinforced the negative impact. The estimated decline in employment due to increased import competition amounted to 139,600 jobs, which in 1974 represented 2.2 percent of total employment and 2.4 percent of industrial employment. As in the first episode, the impact was highly concentrated: machinery, transport equipment, textiles, wood and furniture, and paper and printing accounted for 84 percent of the total effect in the industrial sector. There are also the sectors which register a higher displacement of workers because of imports.

The results do not change much when the net trade balance is used. The affected workers numbered 137,600, or 2.1 percent of total employment.

Table 5.13 Imports and employment in the second liberalzation episode, 1971–1975

Sector	Actual employment change (thousands)	Y/L	Y + M	Y + M − X	$\frac{Y}{Y+H}$	$\frac{Y}{Y+H-X}$	Employment change (thousands)			
							if import share is constant	if net trade balance is constant	because of change in import share	because of change in net trade balance
Agriculture	-3.60	-7.50	4.40	4.70	-0.50	-0.70	-1.30	-2.90	51.90	70.40
Mining	-3.90	5.40	-1.90	-1.30	-7.40	-8.00	3.50	4.10	13.00	14.20
Metal industries	3.30	-7.20	11.10	11.40	-0.60	-0.90	3.90	4.20	1.80	2.60
Nonmetal industries	2.40	-21.10	23.70	24.20	-0.20	-0.80	2.60	3.20	1.70	5.70
Chemical industries	1.20	-13.00	14.20	13.80	-0.10	0.40	1.30	0.80	0.70	-1.80
Machinery	11.70	-5.60	17.60	17.70	-0.30	-0.40	12.00	12.10	20.00	22.20
Transport equipment	4.90	-2.60	9.10	8.10	-1.60	-0.70	6.50	5.60	14.40	6.70
Food, beverages, and tobacco	8.20	2.00	6.40	6.40	-0.20	-0.20	6.40	8.40	7.00	6.90
Textiles	-1.70	-2.00	1.50	0.50	-1.20	-0.30	-0.50	-1.40	9.70	2.70
Shoes and leather	2.20	4.50	-2.00	-3.50	-0.20	1.30	2.40	0.90	2.10	-14.70
Wood and furniture	3.70	-15.00	19.90	20.20	-1.20	-1.50	4.90	5.20	10.00	12.50
Paper and printing	11.90	-12.10	24.70	25.70	-0.90	-1.80	12.70	13.60	8.60	13.70
Plastic and rubber	3.80	-8.10	12.70	12.00	-0.80	0.00	4.60	3.80	2.40	0.10
Miscellaneous	-4.80	-23.20	16.50	16.60	1.80	1.80	-6.60	-6.60	-3.70	-3.70
Total									139.60	137.60

These figures suggest that the offsetting role of export expansion was not very great and was in fact lower than during the first liberalization period. If the industrial sector alone is considered, though, the impact of exports is much more significant. The negative effect of increased import penetration falls from 2.4 to 1.7 percent of industrial employment.

Employment: Third Episode

Table 5.14 shows the results of the analysis for the period 1977–80. The employment situation during this third episode differed greatly from that during the previous liberalization episodes. Employment declined steadily instead of rising. All sectors except shoes and leather and miscellaneous recorded increases in domestic demand and labor productivity. In general, import penetration increased as the share of domestic output in domestic consumption declined in all sectors except agriculture, machinery, food, textiles, and wood and furniture. The highest negative impacts on employment, both in absolute numbers and in relative terms, were in chemicals, transport equipment, shoes and leather, and miscellaneous products. The number of jobs negatively affected by changes in the import share was 31,500, which represented 0.62 percent of total employment and 0.95 percent of industrial employment.

When we treat exports separately and consider the effects of changes in the net trade balance, the results are drastically changed. Except for mining, plastics, and miscellaneous products, the negative impact was offset (totally or partially) by export expansion. In terms of number of workers, the impact changed from a decline of 31,500 to an increase of 70,800, or 1.6 percent of total employment in the industrial sector. The negative impact of import penetration, in short, was estimated to have been smaller than in the two previous liberalization attempts and was more than offset by expansion.

Estimate of Output Losses

The estimated effects of liberalization on employment are used here to obtain estimates of the transitory output losses associated with changes in import competition and the compensating effects of export expansion.

For any particular sector, the total loss in domestic production will be the result of output displacement attributable to changes in employment and other productive factors. We assume that the sectoral average wage is a reasonable proxy for the marginal productivity of labor, that the utilization of nonlabor factors changes at the same rate as employment, and that their marginal product is also the same.

Given these assumptions, we estimate the output loss as the product of the absolute number of workers displaced by changes in import competi-

Table 5.14 Imports and employment in the third liberalization episode, 1977–1980

Sector	Actual employment change (thousands)	Y/L	Y + M	Y + M − X	$\frac{Y}{Y+H}$	$\frac{Y}{Y+H-X}$	Employment change (thousands) if import share is constant	if net trade balance is constant	because of change in import share	because of change in net trade balance
Agriculture	−5.60	−9.80	4.10	3.70	0.10	0.50	−5.70	−6.10	2.90	−22.30
Mining	−7.10	−7.50	1.00	0.40	−0.60	0.00	−6.50	−7.10	1.00	0.30
Metal industries	−3.20	−2.90	0.20	−4.60	−0.50	4.30	−2.70	−7.50	1.40	−10.00
Nonmetal industries	−1.10	−5.90	5.00	4.10	−0.20	0.70	−0.90	−1.80	1.50	−4.00
Chemical industries	−2.20	−4.40	3.10	1.70	−0.90	0.50	−1.30	−2.70	4.90	−2.30
Machinery	−2.70	−7.60	4.00	3.00	0.90	1.90	−3.60	−4.60	−16.40	−34.50
Transport equipment	−1.40	−0.70	1.20	−0.60	−1.90	0.00	0.50	−1.40	16.70	−0.10
Food, beverages, and tobacco	−2.90	−4.20	0.70	0.90	0.60	0.40	−3.50	−3.30	−6.10	−3.80
Textiles	−1.30	−7.80	6.20	6.40	0.40	0.10	−1.70	−1.40	−2.80	−0.60
Shoes and leather	−6.90	7.80	−13.70	−15.20	−1.00	0.50	−5.90	−7.40	12.20	−2.20
Wood and furniture	−4.80	−11.00	5.50	5.40	0.70	0.80	−5.50	−5.60	−3.90	−4.70
Paper and printing	−1.50	−3.40	2.20	−0.90	−0.30	1.00	−1.20	−2.50	1.50	−4.70
Plastic and rubber	4.50	−2.20	7.00	7.40	−0.30	−0.70	4.80	5.20	1.40	2.80
Miscellaneous	−0.80	9.80	−2.60	−3.40	−8.00	−7.20	7.20	6.40	17.20	15.30
Total									31.50	−70.80

tion and average wage. The contribution of nonlabor factors is measured in the same way, but the ratio of nonlabor to labor income in value added is used instead of the average wage. Finally, the potential offsetting impact of export growth is evaluated by means of the same approach.

Tables 5.15, 5.16, and 5.17 give the result (in millions of constant pesetas) for each of the three episodes of liberalization. The information on sectoral average wages and nonlabor income, as well as value added, was drawn from input–output tables for 1966, 1975, and 1980.

During the first liberalization episode the overall gross output loss due to import competition was estimated at 4.7 percent of value added in the industrial sector and 1.3 percent of value added in the whole economy. Nine sectors – textiles, synthetic fibers, plastics, nonferrous metals, electrical and nonelectrical machinery, metal products, stone, clay and glass, and miscellaneous products – accounted for about three quarters of the

Table 5.15 Gross loss in output in the first liberalization episode, 1962–1966 (million 1962 pesetas)

	(1)	(2)	(3)	(4)	(5)	%GDP	(6)	%GDP
Food and beverages	−252.0	0.0	−604.8	0.0	−858.8	3.2	0.0	0.0
Other food products	124.0	124.0	260.4	260.4	384.4	0.9	384.4	0.9
Textiles	737.8	523.6	1,032.9	733.0	1,770.7	2.8	1,256.6	2.0
Shoes and leather products	180.6	−14.7	162.5	−13.2	343.1	3.4	−27.9	0.3
Lumber products	395.7	217.8	474.8	261.4	870.5	3.7	479.2	2.0
Paper products	157.2	120.2	267.3	204.4	424.6	4.8	324.7	3.7
Printing and publishing	123.3	71.4	111.0	64.3	234.3	2.1	135.6	1.2
Raw chemicals	204.3	217.1	429.1	455.9	633.4	4.7	673.0	5.0
Synthetic and artificial fibers	636.2	704.3	763.4	845.2	1,399.6	31.5	1,549.5	34.8
Rubber products	7.0	−35.2	9.2	−45.8	16.2	0.3	−81.0	1.3
Plastics	467.0	46,467.0	840.6	840.6	1,307.5	13.5	1,307.5	13.5
Other chemical products	207.1	228.3	414.2	456.7	621.3	3.9	685.0	4.3
Petroleum byproducts	0.0	69.5	0.0	584.2	0.0	0.0	653.8	12.4
Iron and steel	324.8	440.8	324.8	440.8	649.6	3.5	881.6	4.3
Nonferrous metals	244.9	276.9	832.8	941.5	1,077.8	14.3	1,218.4	16.2
Electrical machinery	2,012.8	2,079.5	603.8	623.8	2,616.7	15.7	2,703.3	16.2
Nonelectrical machinery	1,313.8	1,102.8	788.3	661.7	2,102.1	11.2	1,764.6	9.4
Transport equipment	243.6	−151.2	219.2	−136.1	462.8	1.2	−287.3	0.8
Shipbuilding	17.1	−750.6	13.6	−600.5	30.7	0.4	−1,351.2	16.8
Metal products	1,362.2	1,138.6	953.6	797.0	2,315.8	10.6	1,935.7	8.9
Miscellaneous manufacturing	419.2	314.4	670.7	503.0	1,089.9	4.3	817.4	3.2
Stone, clay, and glass products	900.4	953.8	900.4	953.8	1,800.9	7.5	1,907.6	7.9
Total	9,827.0	8,098.3	9,467.8	8,832.1	19,295.1	1.2	16,930.5	0.9

1, due to employment effects of changes in M share.
2, due to employment effects of change in trade balance.
3, due to capital effects of change in M share.
4, due to capital effects of changes in trade balance.
5, Total = (1) + (8).
6, Total = (2) + (4).
Source: The authors

Table 5.16 Gross loss in output in the second liberalization episode, 1971–1975 (million 1975 pesetas)

	1	2	3	4	5	6	7	8
	Gross loss in output due to employment effects of changes in		Gross loss in output due to capital effects of changes in		Total of columns 1 and 3	Column 5 as a percentage of GDP	Total of columns 2 and 4	Column 7 as a percentage of GDP
Sector	Import share	Trade balance	Import share	Trade balance				
Agriculture	15.90	21.60	37.70	51.10	53.60	1.00	72.70	1.30
Mining	12.80	14.00	20.80	22.70	33.60	14.10	36.70	15.40
Metal industries	6.30	9.00	4.70	6.70	11.00	1.20	15.60	1.70
Nonmetal industries	2.30	7.70	1.30	4.20	3.60	0.40	11.90	1.40
Chemical industries	1.10	-3.00	1.00	-2.80	2.20	0.20	-5.70	-0.60
Machinery	42.30	46.90	9.90	11.00	52.20	1.60	57.90	1.80
Transport Equipment	25.20	11.70	8.40	3.90	33.60	2.90	15.60	1.40
Foods, beverages, and tobacco	7.40	7.30	7.00	7.00	14.40	0.90	14.30	0.90
Textiles	12.20	3.40	4.80	1.40	17.00	2.10	4.80	0.60
Shoes and leather	2.80	-19.80	1.40	-10.00	4.30	0.30	-29.80	-2.20
Wood and furniture	12.40	15.50	4.90	6.10	17.30	2.10	21.60	2.60
Paper and printing	19.10	30.50	7.60	12.20	26.70	2.70	42.70	4.30
Plastic and rubber	5.30	0.30	2.30	0.10	7.60	1.40	0.40	0.10
Miscellaneous	-5.10	-5.10	-2.10	-2.10	-7.20	-2.70	-7.20	-2.70
Total	160.10	140.00	109.70	111.50	269.700	1.40	251.50	1.30

Table 5.17 Gross loss in output in the third liberalization episode, 1977–1980 (million 1980 pesetas)

	1	2	3	4	5	6	7	8
	Gross loss in output due to employment effects of changes in		Gross loss in output due to capital effects of changes in		Total of columns 1 and 3	Column 5 as a percentage of GDP	Total of columns 2 and 4	Column 7 as a percentage of GDP
Sector	Import share	Trade balance	Import share	Trade balance				
Agriculture	1.00	−7.80	2.70	−20.70	3.70	0.10	−28.50	−1.10
Mining	2.80	0.90	3.00	1.00	5.80	2.70	1.80	0.90
Metal industries	6.10	43.55	5.00	−36.20	11.10	1.70	−79.70	−12.00
Nonmetal industries	2.80	−7.50	1.80	−4.90	4.70	0.70	−12.40	−2.00
Chemical industries	11.90	−5.40	12.70	−5.80	24.60	2.90	−11.20	−1.30
Machinery	−36.20	−76.30	−17.70	−37.30	−53.90	−2.60	−113.70	1.80
Transport equipment	41.50	−0.10	1.50	0.00	53.00	5.80	−0.20	1.40
Foods, beverages, and tobacco	−11.70	−7.30	−12.10	−7.60	−23.80	−1.60	−14.90	−1.00
Textiles	−3.60	−0.80	−2.50	−0.60	−6.10	−1.20	−1.40	−0.30
Shoes and leather	14.40	−2.50	7.40	−1.30	21.80	3.90	−3.80	−0.70
Wood and furniture	−4.70	−5.60	−2.30	−2.70	−7.00	−1.60	−8.30	−1.90
Paper and printing	2.70	−8.60	1.80	−5.70	4.40	0.90	−14.30	−2.90
Plastic and rubber	2.80	5.60	1.70	3.30	4.50	1.20	9.00	2.50
Miscellaneous	16.10	14.30	9.60	8.60	25.70	27.30	22.90	24.20
Total	45.90	−144.80	22.60	−109.90	68.50	0.10	−254.70	0.50

total effect. In general, the largest losses were found in sectors which also suffered a larger impact in terms of employment change. Discrepancies in the rankings of sectors were due mainly to differences in the relative sectoral shares of labor and value added. If changes in the net trade balance instead of changes in imports are considered, the global impact is slightly reduced and the ranking of the most affected sectors does not change. In shoes and leather products, rubber, transport equipment, and shipbuilding, however, the results were significantly different. In these sectors the effect of import penetration was completely offset by export expansion.

The transitory losses for the second liberalization episode are presented in table 5.16. The total output loss was estimated to be around 1.4 percent of total value added. Agriculture, mining, machinery, transport equipment, and paper and printing experienced the largest losses and accounted for 75 percent of the total. These estimates are quite similar to those for the first episode, but the impact on the industrial sector appears to have been significantly smaller. If agriculture and mining are eliminated from the sectoral breakdown, the value of the output loss represents 1.3 percent of industrial GDP, less than a third of what it was in the period 1962–6. Similarly, the compensating role of export expansion was weaker, and chemicals and shoes and leather were the only two sectors that experienced a reversal of the negative loss.

During the third liberalization episode the magnitude of output loss was even lower (table 5.17). The estimates range from 0.15 to 0.59 percent of industrial value added, or from 0.15 to 0.54 percent of total GDP. As when we estimated the effects of liberalization on employment, export expansion totally compensated for changes in import penetration, turning a loss into a gain.

6

Trade Liberalization in Spain: Conclusions

Spain is a country where the process of liberalization occurred over a long period of time. Its long-term tendency toward a more liberal trade regime was punctuated by major upswings in 1959–60, 1970–1, and 1977–8, followed by short periods of time during which liberalization did not progress. The chief characteristics of the episodes were tariff cuts, loosening of the quantitative restriction system, and improvement of export promotion schemes. International influences were also important, since multilateral trade agreements reinforced the liberalization measures. A summary of the trade liberalization process in Spain is presented in table 6.1.

In the first liberalization episode (1959–66), the memoranda sent by Spanish economic authorities to the IMF and the OEEC contained the core of the new strategy, and some rather clear targets were established. Although the degree to which the targets were met cannot be quantified, liberalization went further than expected.

The second episode (1970–5) was guided by two different policies. Some degree of liberalization was achieved following the signing of the 1970 preferential agreement with the EEC. The agreement, in effect, led to pre-announced and multistage liberalization episode with a timetable for the implementation of certain reforms. The second phase included unilateral tariff cuts and the elimination of some quantitative restrictions. The driving force behind this policy was concern over rising inflation. Unsettled political conditions between 1972 and 1975 ruled out the use of a tight macroeconomic policy to fight inflation, as had been done in 1967 and 1970. The use of unilateral liberalization measures ended after 1975 as economic conditions, including the balance of payments, deteriorated.

The third episode (1977–80) had some of the attributes of the previous episode. The expectation that Spain would soon become a full member of the EEC influenced to a great extent the decision to take further steps toward liberalization. Concern about inflation also played a role in the 1979 concertina operation. There was no timetable for the implementation of reforms, and the authorities never defined the proposed extent of the next phase of liberalization.

The third episode involved domestic and external liberalization measures conceived of as voluntary to prepare Spain for joining the EEC. After the second oil shock, Spain's economic record worsened. A current account imbalance, together with sticky inflation rates, increasing public sector deficits, and an unemployment rate of around 17 percent, raised serious doubts about further tariff cuts and reductions in quantitative restrictions. In addition, the political climate deteriorated. Because of these constraints, further liberalization was delayed until integration into the EEC became a fact.

People in Spain believe in the existence of an "iron law" that reads as follows: "No economic reform can be implemented while the balance of payments is in surplus or in equilibrium." The "law" might be more accurately stated as follows: "The level of foreign currency reserves has been the decisive factor in the implementation of all important economic reforms in Spain in the last 50 years." The levels of unemployment or public sector deficits have never been as important as the level of reserves. That is a characteristic feature of countries, such as Spain, that have been largely isolated from the rest of the world. During the first episode, fear of the outside world and of economic "dependence" led the regime to be very careful about the level of reserves. But the realization that economic development required a higher level of imports made the availability of foreign currency reserves a key factor in designing development strategy.

When trade liberalization becomes a matter of interest, the "iron law" is transformed to read as follows: "Only when the level of reserves is high enough and the balance of payments is in surplus or equilibrium is it possible to implement trade liberalization in Spain."

Economic reform has only arrived in Spain after a worsening of economic conditions. "Bad economic conditions" usually means a low level of reserves. Economic reform consists of a strong devaluation followed by fiscal and monetary tightening. Only when the balance of payments recovers and the level of reserves is adequate does trade liberalization make its appearance. After a few years of liberalization there is a worsening in the trade sector, a reversal of orthodox policy, and the whole process starts again.

Spain's economic condition was perilous prior to the first liberalization episode. Reserves were nil, and only the threat of insolvency forced Franco to accept liberalization. The first steps were a devaluation of the peseta and monetary restraint. By mid-1960, when the balance of payments had improved dramatically, trade liberalization intensified.

The second liberalization episode (1970–5) was preceded by adjustment measures introduced in 1967. Another devaluation occurred, and a new economic policy was introduced to support devaluation. Spain's foreign

Table 6.1 Summary of liberalization, 1959–1980

	1959–66 episode	1970–5 episode	1977–80 episode
Broad nature	From QRs to tariffs. Unified exchange rate. New tariff legislation and tariff reduction	Loosening of QRs. Tariff reductions and higher export incentives. EEC preferential agreement	Loosening of QRs, tariff reduction, and improving export schemes. EFTA agreement and GATT Tokyo Round
Size: duration; pace	Large: about 7 years; gradual	EEC agreement; large; substantial; gradual. Autonomous measures; large; short; gradual	Large: about 10 years; concentrated in first years
Stages and targets	No clear stages planned after 1960, but a continuous increasing liberalization intended	Yes, for EEC agreement	No, though the intention was to prepare for integration with EEC
Economic circumstances			
Real GDP growth	High	High	Moderate, declining
Inflation rate	High and increasing	Low, decreasing	High, rapidly increasing
Balance of payments	Current account deficit, rapid deterioration	Current account deficit, steady	Current account deficit, increasing
Budget deficits	Surplus	Surplus	Increasing deficit
Unemployment	Low	Low	Increasing
Political circumstances			
Stable, strong government	Yes, despite changes in cabinet	No, deterioration of political climate	No, transition to democracy
Ideological shift	Yes	No	Yes
Ministries responsible	Commerce, finance, and Central Bank	Commerce	Commerce
International influence	IMF, OEEC	EEC	EEC, indirect influence

Other policies			
Monetary policy	Restrictive first, expansive later	Expansive	Restrictive
Fiscal policy	Surplus	Surplus	Expansive, deficit
Exchange rates	Fixed parities Devaluation first, real appreciation	Real appreciation Managed floating from 1973	Managed floating 1977 devaluation, real appreciation
Export promotion	Several incentives	Increased	Increased
Domestic controls			
Capital movements	Inflows encouraged, but outflows restricted	Inflows encouraged, but outflow restrictions continue	Inflows encouraged and also liberalization in outflows
Prices	Reduction in controls, but high	Reduction in controls, but high	Reduction in controls, but high
Wages	High	High	Declining
Interest rates	Controlled	Controlled	Slow liberalization
Implementation of trade liberalization	Fully implemented, but liberalization did not continue after 1966	EEC commitment fully implemented Reversal of autonomous measures after 1975	Multilateral agreements maintained Autonomous measures also maintained, but liberalization did not continue after 1981
Economic performance			
Real GDP	Short recession, high rate of growth afterwards	High, deceleration at the end of the episode	Low, declining
Inflation rate	Low and accelerating	High, accelerating	High, decelerating
Balance of payments	Improving until 1962, increasing current accounts deficits afterwards	Surplus until 1973, large deficits afterwards	Improving, surplus in 1978-9 and large deficit in 1980
Budget deficits	No	No	Yes
Unemployment	Low	Low	Rapidly increasing
External shocks	No	Yes	Yes
Real wages	Increasing	Rapidly increasing	High, moderaton

QR quantitative restrictions; EFTA, European Free Trade Agreement; GATT, General Agreement on Tariffs and Trade; IMF, International Monetary Fund; OEEC, Organization for European Economic Cooperation.

currency reserves increased in 1969 for the first time since 1964 and reached US$1.0 billion in 1970 and US$6.8 billion in 1971.

The third liberalization episode (1977–80) started when a new devaluation of the peseta (June 1977) and a comprehensive stabilization plan (the Moncloa Pact) transformed a US$5 billion current account deficit into a surplus.

Deceleration or reversal of liberalization, however, has always been associated with weakness in the balance of payments. The pattern can be clearly grasped by inspection of figure 6.1, which plots the evolution of the current account balance against the index of trade liberalization. As figure 6.1 shows, periods of trade liberalization coincide with better performance in the current account. The success of liberalization in Spain has been largely due to the fact that it has always been preceded by a major devaluation and an economic stabilization program.

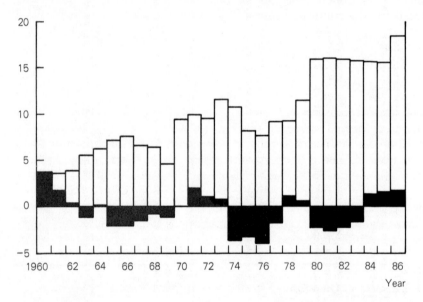

Figure 6.1 Trade liberalization and the current account, 1960–1986: unshaded columns, trade liberalization index; shaded columns, current account as a percentage of gross domestic product

One-stage Liberalization versus Multistage Liberalization

The Spanish experience suggests the superiority of a gradual and multistage liberalization over a one-stage process. This conclusion is based mainly on the relative success of the liberalization episodes of the last 30 years. This gradual approach has been more influenced by international agreements than by the preferences of Spain's economic authorities.

The 1959 liberalization episode was planned as a gradual and multistage process. Given Spain's long history of protectionism and government intervention, an instantaneous liberalization was both inconceivable and politically unfeasible. However, the attempt turned out so well that it became possible to go much further than expected. The same can be said about the 1970 episode, which was centered on a preferential agreement with the EEC whose effects would be felt only gradually. After the first oil shock Spain's voluntary liberalization was reversed, but its commitment to the EEC continued. The third episode in 1977 was decided on a unilateral basis, but the goal of integration into the EEC played a major role. Although liberalization did not make further progress after 1980, neither was it reversed. The preference for gradualism was based not on a need to minimize adjustment costs, but on international agreements that normally incorporated a multistage approach as a standard feature.

The Length of the Liberalization Process

Above, we argued in favor of gradualism. But we also believe that liberalization measures not linked to any international agreements should have been carried out more quickly than they were. This conclusion is based on the absence of significant adjustment costs. Liberalization could have been deeper if implemented faster. In addition, when a strong political commitment to liberalize is absent, a faster process may minimize the possibility of reversal. Also, as the 1959 episode shows, the first step toward liberalization in a country that has historically embraced protectionism should be a drastic one in order to reinforce the credibility of the move toward liberalization.

Replacement of Quantitative Restrictions by Tariffs

The replacement of quantitative restrictions by tariffs took place during the first episode, and we believe that this was beneficial and desirable. This step made the structure of protectionism more transparent. Simultaneously, it minimized adjustment costs during the transition period and set the stage for future tariff reductions. The change was also important in improving the performance of the economy as the availability of essential imported inputs was substantially increased. The success of this initial stage made the idea of liberalization more acceptable and paved the way for future removal of trade barriers.

The Desirability of Export Promotion Schemes

Given the role played by the evolution of the balance of payments on the fate of trade liberalization in Spain, export expansion seems to be crucial to the success of liberalization. Exports grew substantially during the three liberalization episodes, thus helping to alleviate losses in employment. Export promotion schemes were steadily intensified during the whole period under analysis, but no significant relationship was found between these efforts and export performance except in the second episode. In addition, the export promotion schemes contained elements that helped to reduce sectoral anti-export biases. In the long term, however, they did not contribute to efficient reallocation of resources.

An important issue is whether measures to foster export growth should precede import liberalization. In Spain, export promotion was always enhanced when the current account was in deficit. Except in the first episode, it usually preceded import liberalization. Nevertheless, the evidence from the Spanish experience is not clear enough to support the idea that such a sequence is either necessary or desirable.

Uniform versus Differential Treatment of Sectors

The Spanish experience is one of differential treatment. The pattern of liberalization and export promotion in each sector was different, both as a result of industry lobbying and because of the targets of development. While it can be argued that a uniform process of liberalization is superior to a differential process, the latter may also contribute to smooth adjustment costs by tailoring liberalization to the capacity of each sector. The risk of this strategy is that some sectors may remain indefinitely sheltered from foreign competition.

Appropriate Economic Circumstances Preceding Liberalization

The balance of payments has had a major influence in determining the timing of Spain's episodes of liberalization. Although severe disruption was a necessary stimulus for planning, implementation only took place when the balance-of-payments position had improved and foreign exchange reserves were large and increasing.

Sustainability of Liberalization

Liberalization has been sustained in Spain since 1959. Although there have been temporary pauses in the process, there have been no major reversals. Thus sustainability is strongly linked to a stable macroeconomic environment. In Spain, trade liberalization was always preceded by currency devaluation and the implementation of a stabilization program. After the start of each episode, the loosening of other macroeconomic policies gave rise to new disequilibria (higher inflation, appreciation of the real exchange rate, etc.) that weakened Spanish competitiveness in the trade sector and the country's balance of payments. This pattern, seen clearly in the first episode, was affected in the second and third episodes by the first and second oil shocks. The first shock slowed Spanish liberalization, while the second eventually led to postponement of any further liberalization measures. However, liberalization was encouraged by other elements, such as international commitments.

Trade and Domestic Employment

Trends in the labor market changed completely between 1975 and 1977. Employment grew, although at a declining rate, from 1960 to 1974. In 1977, when the third episode began, Spain was suffering a generalized and sharp decline in employment. Neither trade liberalization nor trade flow, however, was the main force underlying this decline. Rigidity in the market, typified by slow and costly adjustments in the labor force of individual companies and excessive growth in real wages, was the main cause of the relatively poor unemployment level after 1974. The oil shocks gave a large boost to the unemployment rate. The end of the dictatorship and the transition to democracy helped to reinforce labor market rigidities, since increases in real wages and greater job security were used to alleviate political and social tensions.

The links between trade flows and changes in employment are not easily discovered through bivariant analysis. A negative and significant correlation between changes in imports and changes in employment was found only for the period 1962–6. With respect to the other liberalization episodes, either no correlation was found or it had the wrong sign. The same can be said for all three episodes with regard to the relationship between exports and employment.

However, the results obtained from analysis of the impact of changes in import and export shares on employment were more helpful. According to our results, the negative effects of increased import penetration on employment were not negligible, especially during the first episode. Capital goods, textiles, and other light manufacturing sectors apparently experienced the largest employment losses. However, export expansion, particularly during the first and third episodes, had compensating positive effects on employment.

In any case, the effects of trade flow on employment seem to have been secondary, given the general economic context. Employment problems during the first and second episodes were eased by a climate of generalized economic growth, while the rise in unemployment during the third episode was so steady and unrelieved that economic agents could not attribute it entirely to trade liberalization.

The "Invisibles" Factor

Spain's trade balance is normally negative. The country has had only 16 annual trade surpluses over the past 100 years. Those years of surplus coincided with exceptional events, such as two World Wars and the Korean War. In recent years, however, the trade deficit has been balanced to some extent by a surplus in the balance of services. During the period 1960–84 the trade balance ran a deficit every year, but the current account showed a surplus in 11 of those years, thanks mainly to the services sector.

Tourist receipts and unrequited transfers by migrant workers are the two items that have compensated for the trade balance deficit. During the 25 years under study, tourist receipts have covered, on average, 77 percent of the trade balance deficit. Unrequited transfers have been less important, covering an average of 28 percent of the trade balance.

Receipts of invisibles, in short, have often allowed Spain to achieve surplus in its current account. These surpluses served as buffers against the oil shocks, thus making them of great importance to the introduction and success of the liberalization episodes. This does not mean that liberalization could not have occurred without the income from services and invisibles. Without it, however, Spain would have found it necessary to pursue different policies which would probably have involved a much greater degree of specialization in labor intensive exports. But services and invisibles gave Spain a unique opportunity to develop a more capital intensive industrialization that assisted the country in sustaining liberalization.

References

Anderson, C. W. (1970) *The Political Economy of Modern Spain – Policy Making in an Authoritarian System*. Madison, WI: University of Wisconsin Press.

Banco de Bilbao (1978) *Renta Nacional de España 1955–75*. Madrid: Banco de Bilbao.

Banco de España (1985) *Boletín Económico*, February.

Banco de España, *Boletín Estadístico*, monthly, Madrid.

Banco de España, *Informe Anual*, various years. Madrid.

Boletín de Información Comercial Española, *Legislación Comercial y Arancelaria*, monthly. Madrid: Ministerio de Comercio.

Bonilla, J. M. (1978) "Funciones de importación y exportación para la economía española." Madrid: Banco de España, Estudios Económicos no. 14.

Chamorro, S., R. Comendador, J. J. Dolado, R. Repullo, and J. Rodríguez (1975) "Las balanzas de pagos de España del período de la autarquia." *Información Comercial Española*, 502, June.

Comin, F. (1985) "Fuentes cuantitativas para el estudio del sector público en España 1801–1980." Madrid: Instituto de Estudios Fiscales, Monograph 40.

Dirección General de Aduanas, *Estadísticas del Comercio Exterior de España*, annual. Madrid: Ministerio de Hacienda.

Dolado, J. J. and J. L. Malo de Molina (1985) "Desempleo y rigidez del mercado de trabajo en España." *Boletín Económico del Banco de España*, September.

Donges, J. B. (1971) "From an autarchic towards a cautiously outward-looking industrialization policy: the case of Spain." *Weltwirtschaftliches Archiv*, 107.

Fondo para la Investigación Económica y Social de las Cajas de Ahorros Confederadas (1979) *Tablas Input–output de 1975 y Análisis de la Interdependencia de la Economía Española*. Madrid: Cajas de Ahorros Confederada.

Gamir, L. (1972) "El proteccionismo arancelario en la España actual." *Información Comercial Española*, 463, March.

González, M. J. (1979) *La Economía Política del Franquismo 1940–1970, Dirigismo, Mercado y Planificación*. Madrid: Tecnos.

IMF (International Monetary Fund), *Annual Report on Exchange Restrictions*, various issues.

Instituto de Estudios de Planificación (1975) *Tablas Input–output de la Economía Española, 1970*. Madrid: Ministerio de Planificación del Desarrollo.

Instituto Nacional de Estadística (1986) *Encuesta Industrial 1978–1986*. Madrid: INE.

Instituto Nacional de Estadística, *Anuario Estadístico de España*, annual. Madrid.

Instituto Nacional de Estadística, *Contabilidad Nacional de España*, annual (base year 1970), Madrid.

Krueger, A. O. (1980) "Protectionist pressures, imports and employment in the United States." New York: National Bureau of Economic Research, Working Paper no. 461.

Macrométrica (1978) *Cifras de la España económica*. Madrid: Fondo Editorial Standard Eléctrica.

Martínez Méndez, P. (1982) "El proceso de ajuste de la economía española: 1973–1980." Madrid: Banco de España, Estudios Económicos no. 14.

Mauleón, I. (1985) "Una función de exportaciones para la economía Española," Madrid: Banco de España, Working Document no. 8507.

Ministerio de Comercio (Secretaría General Técnica) (1977) *Legislación Básica sobre Comercio Exterior*, Madrid: Ministerio de Comercio.

Ministerio de Comercio, *La Balanza de Pagos de España*, annual. Madrid.

Ministerio de Economía (1977) *Programa de Saneamiento y Reforma Económica: Pacto de la Moncloa*. Madrid: Secretaría General Técnica.

Ministerio de Hacienda (1969) *La Contabilidad Nacional de España, Años 1954 a 1964*. Madrid: Instituto de Estudios Fiscales.

Ministerio de Hacienda, *Cuentas de las Administraciones Públicas*, various years. Madrid.

OECD (Organization for Economic Cooperation and Development) (1971) *The Capital Market, International Capital Movements, Restrictions on Capital Operations in Spain*. Paris: Committee for Invisibles Transactions.

OECD, *Economic Surveys: Spain*, various issues. Paris.

Organización Sindical Española, *Tablas Input–output de la Economía Española, 1962, 1968*.

Schwartz, P. (ed.) (1977) *El Producto Nacional de España en el Siglo XX*. Madrid: Instituto de Estudios Fiscales.

Torres, A. and L. Gamir (1986a) "Política arancelaria." In *Política Económica de España*. Madrid: Alianza Universidad Textos, 112.

Torres, A. and L. Gamir (1986b) "Política de comercio exterior." In *Política Económica de España*. Madrid: Alianza Universidad Textos, 112.

Viñas, A. et al. (1979) *Política Comercial Exterior en España (1931–1975)*. Madrid: Banco Exterior de España.

Part III

Turkey

Tercan Baysan
Middle East Technical University, Ankara
George Washington University, Washington D.C.
The World Bank, Washington, D.C.

Charles Blitzer
Massachusetts Institute of Technology
The World Bank, Washington, D.C.

Contents

List of Figures

List of Tables

Introduction

Four episodes of trade liberalization occurred in Turkey during the period 1950–84. The first three were characterized mainly by once-and-for-all changes in exchange rates, relaxation of import restrictions, and increased incentives for exports. These episodes, however, were not undertaken as parts of a deliberate plan to establish a full-fledged liberal trade regime. In contrast, the liberalization of January 1980 was an integral component of what appears to have been a fundamental change in Turkey's development strategy. On the trade side, policy has shifted away from indiscriminate import substitution and toward export-oriented development. This liberalization will extend beyond foreign trade to encompass the economy as a whole. Because of a lack of detailed data for the 1950s, only the two most recent episodes – those that began in 1970 and in 1980 – are studied here.

Our conclusion is that the 1970 episode was not a true attempt at trade liberalization but rather a short-term response to high inflation, balance-of-payments deficits, and a poor foreign exchange position. The relatively weak measures taken in 1970 had no permanently liberalizing effects on Turkish trade. Those measures, however, did achieve the relatively limited objectives for which they were designed.

To set the scene for the broad economic reforms initiated in 1980, we trace the deterioration of economic and political conditions during the 1970s. Unlike the 1970 measures, the 1980 reforms constituted an effort by Turkey to achieve permanent economic change and trade liberalization by reducing or eliminating protectionist measures. A domestic austerity program was put into place, state-controlled enterprises were reformed, and government control over domestic and monetary structures was loosened. Although there were flaws and uncertainties, and although it is too early to say whether the 1980 program will succeed in the long run, there are several early indications that favorable long-term and large-scale results may accrue if Turkey continues its present course.

This study is divided into five chapters. The first is a background chapter that traces development in key economic and social variables since the early 1950s. The second chapter continues with a review of the pre-1962 economy and an examination of the macroeconomic and trade policy trends of the past two decades.

Chapter 3 is a careful examination of the economic measures instituted in 1970, while chapter 4 is devoted to a similarly detailed examination of the 1980 episode. With the help of a substantial body of statistical evidence, we weigh such factors as export and import controls and sectoral production; exchange rate, monetary, and fiscal policies; and socio-economic and political conditions in order to assess the background motivation, and success of these two attempts at reform.

The general issues of trade liberalization are dealt with in chapter 5. We examine how the sequencing of policies affects the success of liberalization. We then draw inferences from Turkey's experience to provide practical suggestions for other nations attempting to liberalize their external sector.

1

Economic Background

Although it may be unwise to call any country "typical" of a large group, Turkey in many respects is a typical middle income developing country. Table 1.1 shows several basic indicators of economic progress in middle income developing countries, all developing countries, and the 17 other developing countries originally included in this project.[1] Turkey lies near the mean in geographic area, population growth, per capita income and growth, life expectancy, and trade deficit as a share of gross domestic product (GDP). However, Turkey is more "dualistic" than most middle income countries, coming closer to the average for all developing countries in the categories of literacy and share of agricultural employment.

Turkey is typical of middle income developing countries in other ways as well. In the political sphere, for example, Turkey has experienced considerable instability during the past 25 years. There have been numerous changes in the ruling coalitions, three constitutions, and three episodes of military intervention. Ideologically, government policy is consistently nationalistic, with economic policy ranging from mildly leftist to moderately rightist. While generally supporting other developing countries on international economic issues, Turkey has remained an active member of the North Atlantic Treaty Organization (NATO) and the Organization for Economic Cooperation and Development (OECD). During the past decade, however, Turkey has moved into closer alignment with other Islamic countries. Although there has been some revival of Islamic consciousness in the country, economic factors are the principal explanation for these improved relations. Turkey is attempting to take advantage of the increased wealth in the Middle East to expand its export markets and to find new sources of credit and investment.

Political instability has carried over into economic policy. While all Turkish governments have been interventionist and nationalistic – by which is meant that the state has tried to direct the pattern of investment

1 Because it is a high income country, New Zealand is not included in this comparison.

Table 1.1 Comparison of basic indicators

Countries	Population 1984 (millions)	Population growth 1973–84 (%)	Area (× 1,000 km²)	Per capita GNP 1984 (US$)	Per capita GNP growth 1965–84 (%)	Adult literacy rate 1980 (%)	Life expectancy at birth 1984	Average inflation rate 1973–84 (%)	Population employed in agriculture 1980 (%)
Turkey	48.4	2.2	781	1,160	2.9	60.0	64	42.4	58.0
All LDCs[a]	37.3	2.1	767	589	3.1	56.4	60	29.4	61.4
Middle-income countries[a]	19.8	2.4	717	1,250	3.1	65.0	61	38.0	44.0
Countries in this study[b]	39.6	1.7	1,090	2,276	3.2	81.3	68	40.3	30.4

LDC, less developed country; GNP, gross national product.
[a] Weighted averages.
[b] Arithmetic averages.

Source: World Bank, 1986

while limiting foreign ownership and management – there have been many changes in emphasis over the years. For instance, rightist governments have been more willing to rely on the private sector and to reduce trade restrictions, while the left has placed more emphasis on social welfare programs and economic autarky.

However, the more important effects of political instability have been a tendency to use the government's economic power (in terms of both price intervention and operation of State Economic Enterprises (SEEs)) for explicitly political purposes and an inability to formulate or implement a consistent set of economic policies. Although the reforms of 1980 were significant, Turkey remains an economy in which the public sector accounts for about 60 percent of national investment, owns and operates about 40 percent of all manufacturing enterprises, and dominates the minerals sector. This pattern is not uncommon among developing countries.

Turkey also lies close to the mean among middle income developing countries in terms of production, expenditure, and trade. Table 1.2 shows certain key indicators for Turkey and other groups of countries. Turkey is more dualistic than most other middle income countries, relying more on exports of primary products and earning more national income from agriculture. At the same time, agriculture has grown much more slowly than manufacturing.

What most distinguishes Turkey from the other developing countries in this project is how little it relies on trade. Merchandise exports constituted only 12 percent of GDP in 1984, while the median for the group was 24 percent. In setting trade policy, however, Turkey has usually behaved like other developing countries. With the exception of the period since 1980, the objectives of trade policy have been increases in government revenues to promote domestic manufacturing and reduction of balance-of-payments imbalances through import restrictions. Policymakers have taken a strange view of the notion of comparative advantage. While they believe that Turkey can produce new products efficiently, their policies also reflect the belief that domestic industries cannot compete internationally. This ambivalence is reflected in Turkey's uncertain approach toward membership of the European Economic Community (EEC).

As with most countries studied in this project, inflation and foreign debt have become increasingly significant problems for Turkey since the 1970s (see table 1.2). Turkey was hit particularly hard by the oil price increases of the 1970s. As higher oil prices contributed to inflation, the government tried to limit the immediate impact by taking steps to hold down energy prices and by borrowing heavily in the Eurodollar market. As a result, Turkey was compelled to undertake major debt rescheduling in 1978–9, largely through the OECD.

Table 1.2 Comparison of the structure of production and foreign trace (percent)

Countries	Agriculture		Manufacturing			Investments share of GDP 1984	Exports share of GDP 1984	Primary exports share of all exports 1981	Debt-service ratio 1984	Trade deficit share of GDP 1984
	1984 share of GDP	Average growth 1973–84	1984 share of GDP	Average growth 1973–84						
Turkey	19.0	3.3	24.0	4.0	20.0	12.0	63.0	22.8	7.4
All LDCs[a]	20.0	3.3	20.1	4.5	22.1	20.6	55.1	16.8	0.4
Middle income countries[a]	14.0	2.7	22.0	5.5	21.0	25.0	57.0	17.2	−0.6
Countries in this study[b]	14.9	2.6	22.5	4.9	22.1	23.8	55.1	19.2	4.1

LDC, less developed country.
[a] Weighted averages.
[b] Arithmetic averages.

Source: World Bank, 1986

Economic Structure and Performance

Table 1.3 summarizes the composition of national income and growth by sector for selected years between 1950 and 1985. The most striking change is the steady decline in agriculture's share from about 45 percent in 1950 to less than 17 percent in 1985. Meanwhile, manufacturing's share of national income doubled and that of utilities quadrupled. Trade, transportation, and financial and other services all grew faster than aggregate GDP. The average share of indirect taxes remained approximately constant, but net factor income grew rapidly, turning from negative to positive in the mid-1960s as workers' remittances became important.

Table 1.3 Gross national product by type of economic activity for selected years, 1950–1985 (million 1968 lira)

Activity	1950	1958	1964	1970	1976	1982	1985
Agriculture	15,618	25,675	28,698	32,017	42,732	48,202	51,251
Agriculture and livestock	15,471	25,403	28,222	31,211	41,483	46,515	49,344
Forestry	100	160	323	593	874	954	1,018
Fishing	47	112	153	213	375	733	889
Industry	4,154	8,831	13,136	22,669	39,165	46,015	57,423
Mining and quarrying	595	1,031	1,414	1,887	3,169	3,931	4,561
Manufacturing	3,373	7,262	10,809	19,392	33,115	37,669	47,440
Electricity, gas, and water	186	538	913	1,390	2,881	4,415	5,422
Construction	2,109	4,055	5,436	8,155	11,164	13,000	13,718
Services	12,908	22,105	31,627	49,412	81,069	97,553	112,716
Wholesale	2,766	5,033	8,044	13,428	25,170	30,281	37,253
Transportation and communications	1,860	3,839	5,828	10,393	17,836	18,856	21,808
Financial institutions	402	1,070	1,475	2,572	4,158	5,195	5,647
Ownership of dwellings	2,839	3,714	4,419	5,735	8,492	10,461	11,348
Business and personal services	1,763	3,098	4,032	5,766	8,856	10,239	11,796
Government services	3,277	5,352	7,830	11,518	16,558	22,521	24,864
GDP at factor cost	34,789	60,666	78,896	112,252	174,130	204,770	35,108
Net factor income from rest of world	− ,92	− 463	− 163	1,477	2,544	1,075	623
GNP at factor cost	34,697	60,203	78,734	113,729	176,674	205,845	235,731
Less subsidies	1	131	463	1,322	1,661	2,471	3,761
Indirect taxes	3,810	5,772	9,349	13,018	20,738	21,170	26,245
GNP in purchasers' price	38,506	65,844	87,619	125,426	195,751	224,544	258,215

Source: State Institute of Statistics (SIS), *Statistical Yearbook of Turkey*,various issues

Distribution of gross national products (GNP) by expenditure category through 1985 is summarized in table 1.4. As noted above, the shares are not very different from those for all lower middle income developing countries as shown in recent *World Development Reports* issued by the World Bank. The principal difference between 1958 and 1985 is the increase of about 5 percent in investment as a share of GNP. About half

Table 1.4 Gross national product by type of expenditure for selected years, 1950–1985 (share of gross national product at purchasers' prices)

Type of expenditure	1950	1958	1964	1970	1976	1980	1982	1985
Government final consumption	11.8	9.6	12.1	12.7	15.8	12.3	10.7	8.5
Private final consumption	78.0	77.3	74.6	68.9	65.9	71.9	71.2	74.0
Change in stocks	n.a.	n.a.	0.7	1.2	0.7	1.9	1.5	0.4
Gross fixed capital formation	11.0	14.0	14.6	18.3	22.6	19.5	18.8	19.0
Gross domestic demand at purchasers' prices	100.8	101.0	102.0	101.1	105.1	105.5	102.1	101.9
Foreign balance	− 0.8	− 1.0	− 2.0	− 1.1	− 5.1	− 5.5	− 2.1	− 1.9
GNP at purchasers' price	100.0	100.0	100.0	100.0	100.0	100.0	100.0	100.0

n.a., not available.

Sources: SIS, National Income and Expenditure of Turkey, 1948–72; SIS, Statistical Yearbook of Turkey, various issues; World Bank Country Data Series, 1986

this increase was financed by reduced private consumption and about half by additional foreign borrowing. However, it appears that the investment share has declined considerably during the current period of austerity from its high values in the late 1970s.

Arguably the most important governmental economic interventions are made through the public investment budget. The government has accounted for 40 percent or more of national investment as far back as data are available. In 1962, the year preceding the first five-year plan, public investment was 47 percent of the total. Since then, it has been lower than private investment in only three years. As a share of GDP, public investment rose from about 8 percent in the early 1960s to between 9 and 11 percent during the first and second plan periods (1963–73), to between 12 and 15 percent from 1975 to 1980, and to between 17 and 19 percent since 1981. The government directly controls virtually all infrastructure investment and about half of investment in manufacturing, to a total of about 61 percent.

Indirect control over private investment is exercised in several ways. Large projects (particularly when foreign financing is involved) require approval from the State Planning Organization (SPO). The government also has the power to grant partial or absolute protection from imports, and often has done so before investment decisions were made. In addition, the government influences investment through its large share of ownership in the banking sector.

Despite its diminishing share of GDP, agriculture remains a very important sector in Turkey. It accounts for about 55 percent of all employment, and its raw products are the basis for most of the country's exports. Thirty percent of total exports in 1985 were of raw or semi-processed agricultural products, and another 30 percent were goods manufactured mostly from agricultural raw materials (textiles etc.). By far the most important crop is wheat. Other important domestic crops are barley, maize, and sugar beet. The major export crops are tobacco, cotton, and hazelnuts.

Turkey's agricultural problems are much like those of many developing countries. Agriculture grew rapidly in the 1950s as the amount of land under cultivation increased by 50 percent. Since the early 1960s, however, the cultivated area has grown by only 15 percent, and there has been a slight decline in cultivated area in the last decade. Thus increased value added must come either from higher yields or from planting larger amounts of higher-valued crops. Increases in yields have been elusive because of infrastructure problems, poor use of credit, and the high costs of additional irrigation, fertilizers, and pesticides. Although it is clearly possible to improve the crop mix, government pricing policies have been designed chiefly to encourage additional exports of food crops and livestock.

During this period, government policies of subsidized credit, price and quantity protection, and heavy public investment have been used to assist the manufacturing sector. It is therefore not surprising that the sector's growth has far exceeded that of GDP (see table 1.3). About half of manufactured output (in terms of value of gross output) is consumer goods; the share of consumer goods in value added and employment is considerably larger. Although manufactured investment goods represent only 10–15 percent of sectoral value, they have been growing more quickly than any other sector, largely because of public investment (often at low or negative real rates of return).

The manufacturing sector can be divided into three subsectors: public, large-scale private, and small-scale private. The public sector (SEEs) dominates heavy industry, receives the lion's share of investment, and pays the highest wages while accounting for the smallest share of employment. Large-scale private industry has been supported by the government through allocation of credit and almost complete protection from imports. However, it has been held back by the even more favorable treatment afforded the SEEs, and large public sector deficits have sometimes caused the large-scale private sector to be crowded out of capital markets.

Private small-scale manufacturing comes closest to being an internally competitive sector. Wages and capital-to-labor ratios are lower, and entry is easier. Growth has been checked, however, by the sector's difficulty in tapping credit markets.

The major objectives of the present government are to help the manufacturing sector by (a) encouraging exports, (b) promoting private investment, (c) lowering capital-to-output and capital-to-labor ratios, and (d) improving the efficiency of the SEEs.

The economy's average annual aggregate growth rate for the period 1950–85 was 5.7 percent, although there was significant variation within subperiods. The periods of most rapid growth were 1950–8 and 1970–6, while the period of slowest growth was that from 1976 to 1980. To a considerable degree, however, the rapid growth in the mid-1970s was illusory, since it was paid for by rapidly rising trade deficits and additional debt. The slow growth of the late 1970s was the result of Turkey's inability to finance trade deficits at previous relative magnitudes, structural adjustments associated with changing global factor prices, and macroeconomic stabilization policies.

Foreign Trade

Summary data on foreign accounts are presented in tables 1.5–1.7. From the early 1950s until the late 1970s, imports grew considerably faster than exports. As shown in table 1.5, imports exceeded exports by only 8 percent in 1950, but the margin grew to 30 percent by the early 1960s, 50 percent by 1970, and 161 percent by 1976. The financial crisis of 1979 forced the government to take strong action to reduce this deficit, and by 1985 imports exceeded exports by only 42 percent. Although growth in the amount of imports has slackened considerably in the past several years, export growth was the major factor in the turnaround.

Table 1.5 Merchandise imports and exports for selected years, 1950–1985 (million current US dollars)

	1950	1958	1964	1970	1976	1982	1985
Imports	285	315	542	886	5,129	8,731	11,344
Exports	263	247	411	589	1,960	5,746	7,958
Trade deficit	22	68	131	297	3,169	2,985	3,386
Import-to-export ratio	108	128	132	150	262	152	143

Source: SIS, Statistical Yearbook of Turkey, various years

Until recently, Turkey had succeeded (largely by fiat) in reducing imports of consumption goods almost to zero. In 1983, 70 percent of all imports were intermediate goods, with crude oil accounting for more than half. The remaining 30 percent were investment goods, mainly machinery. Crude oil is imported from Iran, Iraq, Libya, and Saudi Arabia, with the bulk of other imports coming from EEC countries. This pattern has changed very little since oil prices increased.[2]

There have been more substantial changes on the export side. Since 1977, and especially since 1980, manufacturing exports have risen very rapidly. As shown in table 1.7, export growth has been especially rapid in processed foods, textiles, chemicals, cement, glass, metals, and electronic

2 In 1985, consumer goods represented about 6 percent of total merchandise imports.

Table 1.6 Merchandise imports by category and source for selected years, 1958–1985 (million current US dollars)

	1958	1964	1970	1976	1980	1982	1985
Category							
Food and live animals	12.4	9.0	69.0	57.7	150.8	125.9	375.3
Live animals	0.1	0.4	1.1	2.7	5.8	4.3	n.a.
Cereals and cereal preparations	4.9	6.1	56.2	4.1	2.5	105.3	n.a.
Fruits and vegetables	n.a.	0.2	0.2	0.3	0.5	0.8	n.a.
Sugar, sugar preparations, and honey	n.a.	n.a.	6.3	10.6	130.5	0.4	n.a.
Coffee, tea, cocoa, and spices	4.3	2.1	5.0	21.7	5.0	14.0	n.a.
Other	3.1	0.2	0.2	18.3	6.5	1.1	n.a.
Beverages and tobacco	n.a.	n.a.	n.a.	1.2	0.3	0.4	n.a.
Crude material (except fuels)	25.7	35.5	49.3	208.5	299.6	382.6	624.4
Raw hides, skins, and furs	1.6	1.8	1.6	3.6	4.9	5.9	n.a.
Rubber	14.4	6.7	13.4	21.1	40.9	49.0	n.a.
Pulp and waste paper	0.3	0.8	2.1	18.4	16.1	28.2	n.a.
Textile fibers	3.5	21.2	19.3	48.9	54.4	82.3	n.a.
Crude fertilizers and crude minerals	5.9	2.2	3.6	54.5	59.8	74.4	n.a.
Metalliferous ores and metal scrap	n.a.	1.1	4.4	43.6	116.2	137.0	n.a.
Other	n.a.	1.7	4.9	18.4	7.3	5.8	n.a.
Mineral fuels and lubricants	40.3	67.7	66.6	1,127.0	3,909.8	3,850.2	3,687.8
Coal, coke, and briquettes	n.a.	0.2	0.7	18.2	40.9	97.7	n.a.
Petroleum and petroleum products	40.3	67.5	63.4	1,076.9	3,698.6	3,628.8	3,611.6
Gas (natural and manufactured)	n.a.	n.a.	2.5	31.9	170.3	123.7	n.a.
Animal and vegetable oils and fats	20.0	27.5	4.8	85.9	117.3	102.2	194.9
Chemicals	38.0	60.6	153.9	730.4	1,218.2	1,020.3	1,558.4
Chemical elements and compounds	12.8	21.5	61.3	348.2	483.5	582.2	n.a.
Dyeing and coloring materials	5.5	9.0	14.2	66.1	51.2	71.3	n.a.
Manufactured fertilizers	2.5	4.6	31.1	96.8	391.5	51.0	n.a.
Plastic materials and cellulose	2.7	8.7	16.6	97.4	114.9	159.5	n.a.
Other	14.5	16.8	30.7	121.9	177.1	156.3	n.a.
Manufactured goods classified mainly by raw materials used	63.1	102.6	155.6	791.2	689.9	878.4	1,467.5
Paper, paperboard, and products	8.7	6.0	12.9	28.8	55.7	55.2	n.a.
Textiles, yarns, and fabrics	7.1	15.7	17.4	58.4	79.5	103.3	146.0
Iron and steel	23.8	42.5	65.3	462.2	340.0	456.5	1,059.8
Nonferrous metals	4.4	8.7	22.1	84.3	76.9	101.2	223.9
Other	19.1	29.7	37.9	157.5	137.8	162.2	n.a.
Machinery and transport equipment	105.7	225.0	364.6	1,895.4	1,371.3	2,314.1	3,026.9
Machinery (other than electrical)	61.8	144.7	204.6	1,238.0	869.2	1,407.4	1,550.5
Electrical machinery	20.8	37.2	72.0	307.8	307.3	411.8	663.5
Transport equipment	23.1	43.0	88.0	349.6	194.8	494.9	812.9
Miscellaneous manufactured articles (furniture, travel goods, clothing, footwear, etc.)	9.9	14.1	22.0	95.7	56.8	119.1	408.4
Nonclassified materials	n.a.	n.a.	n.a.	n.a.	0.7	0.3	0.3
Source							
OECD countries	229.2	413.6	681.9	3,565.4	3,583.4	4,434.2	6,360.6
Eastern Europe	23.9	42.0	115.0	299.6	757.4	427.8	653.0
Middle Eastern countries	10.0	36.8	46.7	1,008.7	2,985.2	3,571.7	3,400.7
Other countries	52.0	49.6	42.2	254.9	583.4	300.7	929.3
Total	315.1	542.0	885.5	5,128.6	7,909.4	8,731.4	11,343.6

n.a., not available.

Sources: SIS, *Statistical Yearbook of Turkey*, various issues; World Bank, 1986

Table 1.7 Merchandise exports by category and destination for selected years, 1964–1985 (million current US dollars)

	1964	1970	1976	1980	1982	1985
Category						
Agriculture and livestock	319.9	442.6	1,254.3	1,671.7	2,141.2	1,719.4
Cereals and pulses	10.2	9.8	70.6	181.0	337.3	234.4
Nuts, fruits, and vegetables	86.2	137.5	375.2	753.9	648.6	560.6
Hazelnuts	50.2	84.0	203.2	394.8	240.7	255.4
Raisins	17.0	21.0	52.6	130.3	100.3	74.9
Other	19.0	29.5	119.5	228.7	307.6	230.3
Industrial crops	184.9	258.7	728.2	605.9	741.6	659.3
Tobacco	90.1	78.6	251.3	233.7	348.3	330.1
Cotton	92.3	171.3	434.2	322.6	296.6	169.8
Other	2.5	8.8	42.7	49.6	96.7	159.4
Forestry products	2.3	2.8	5.3			
Livestock products	36.3	33.8	75.0	108.2	389.7	244.2
Fishery products				22.7	24.0	21.0
Mining and quarrying products	14.1	39.5	110.0	191.0	175.3	243.8
Industrial products	76.6	104.6	595.8	1,047.4	3,429.4	5,994.8
Agriculture-based processed	46.2	41.4	86.8	190.2	568.2	646.6
Textiles	4.6	25.9	272.7	439.8	1,056.3	1,789.5
Forestry products	0.9	2.8	5.6	8.1	33.4	105.8
Hides and leather products	0.2	4.6	59.9	49.5	111.4	484.4
Chemicals	3.2	7.3	46.7	91.9	208.3	373.5
Petroleum products	7.7	0.6	16.2	38.5	343.9	372.0
Cements		2.7	16.3	39.6	206.6	43.7
Glass and ceramics	0.8	1.4	20.9	35.9	103.7	189.6
Nonferrous metal	12.8	14.7	16.9	18.3	44.6	115.5
Iron and steel	0.0	0.3	15.4	33.9	362.2	968.8
Metal products and machinery	0.1	2.1	16.5	29.8	143.0	450.4
Electrical appliances		0.3	1.1	11.5	75.2	118.9
Motor vehicles	0.0	0.5	9.3	50.3	110.2	146.6
Other			11.5	10.1	62.4	189.5
Destination						
OECD countries	324.3	429.7	1,483.2	1,679.7	2,556.0	4,106.2
Eastern Europe	37.7	83.8	157.2	490.6	323.2	334.5
Middle Eastern countries	27.0	45.7	116.0	494.8	2,540.1	3,238.2
Other countries	21.8	29.3	203.8	245.0	326.7	279.3
Total	410.8	588.5	1,960.2	2,910.1	5,746.0	7,958.1

Sources: data supplied by SPO; SPO, 1979; SIS, *Statistical Yearbook*, various issues; World Bank, 1986

machinery. Export growth has been promoted by explicit incentives to manufacturers to compensate them from reduced domestic demand.

There has also been a dramatic change in the destination of exports. In 1977, 70 percent of Turkey's export went to OECD countries and less than 8 percent went to Middle Eastern countries. Since then, exports to the

Middle East have increased more than twentyfold, and now account for about 40 percent of all merchandise exports. Exports to the OECD countries increased by only 145 percent between 1980 and 1985.

Natural Resources

Turkey comprises 780,000 km^2 of which 97 percent lie in the Asia Minor land mass (Anatolia) and the remainder lie on the European side of the Dardanelles and the Bosphoros. Northern Turkey, which abuts the Black Sea, enjoys considerable rainfall, moderate summers, and cool winters. The Aegean and Mediterranean coasts have milder winters, warmer summers, and less rainfall. Fruit and vegetables are grown throughout the country, with tobacco being the major export crop of the Aegean region and cotton the major export crop of the Mediterranean area. Most of central Anatolia is a high, rather arid, and treeless plateau with a fairly harsh climate. Wheat, barley, and livestock are the principal agricultural products.

For a country of its size, Turkey is only moderately endowed with mineral resources. Among her most important minerals are coal, lignite, petroleum, iron ore, chrome, and boron. Other minerals found in Turkey include sulfur, copper, magnesite, barite, marble, mercury, and zinc. Although petroleum is Turkey's most economically valuable mineral, domestic production accounts for only 12 percent of total consumption. Turkey also imports a small amount of coal for energy use (and a larger amount for coking purposes) and about 60 percent of its iron ore requirements. The mining sector accounts for less than 2 percent of GDP and less than 1 percent of employment. These proportions have not changed substantially since 1959.

Potential growth in mining is problematic. Costs have been high in the past, in part because of the inefficiency of the SEE that dominates coal mining. The government also controls prices and often sets them below recovery costs and border prices. Consequently, the apparently low level of mineral reserves may be more a reflection of how government controls have limited private sector investment in exploration and development than of actual reserve levels. The present government hopes that its liberalization of pricing and investment regulations will result in substantial new investment in mineral exploration and production.

Although it has been many centuries since much European and Asian trade moved through Anatolia, Turkey is beginning to take greater advantage of its favorable location. In the past ten years, particularly since the start of the war between Iran and Iraq, Turkey's exports to the Middle East have increased dramatically and now account for about 40 percent of export earnings. In addition to merchandise exports, service exports to the

Middle East have also risen substantially. Iraq exports about a million barrels of oil daily through a pipeline in Turkey, and a second pipeline is planned. Turkey is now a major competitor for medium-sized construction projects in Libya and the Persian Gulf countries. Tourism from the Middle East is also rising rapidly. Whether the flow of trade through Turkey will increase significantly in the next decade will depend largely on how firmly the liberalization program takes hold.

Population, Labor Force, and Employment

Turkey's population has grown rapidly since the end of World War II and is now about 50 million. The principal reason is public health measures, which have led to reduced infant and adult mortality.

The government has followed a passive population policy. Birth control devices are readily available, but they are not distributed by the government. Although there are some tax rebates for large families, they are not large in absolute terms or relative to the incomes of poor families.

Nevertheless, there has been a distinct fall in population growth since 1975. This may be due to increased female literacy, which correlates negatively with birth rates. However, even if the number of children per mother continues to decline sharply, the population will continue to increase rapidly because half the population is under 20 years old. No matter what policies are followed, it will be virtually impossible to hold the population below 100 million by early in the next century.

The other key demographic factor is urbanization. The urban population has quadrupled since 1950, while the rural population has increased by about two thirds. Although the major cities – especially Istanbul – have grown very rapidly, the urban population is less concentrated than in most developing countries. Since 1965, medium-sized cities throughout Turkey have grown even faster than large cities. There are no pronounced regional differences. The Black Sea and western Anatolia regions increased somewhat more slowly than the average, while Thrace and the Mediterranean coast grew faster.

The labor force has grown more slowly than the population as a whole. The reason for this is that female participation is much higher in agriculture than in other sectors and the population is becoming more urbanized. The general population has become somewhat younger, but this is not reflected in the labor force because an increasing proportion of children are in school.

Differences between rates of urban and rural participation in labor are pronounced. Participation by both sexes is higher in the rural sector, but the difference is larger for women. School attendance is more than three times higher in urban areas, and only 13 percent of all urban women over

11 work. In the rural sector, women from all but the wealthiest families are engaged in field work.

Universal free primary education has been national policy since the Ataturk regime in the 1930s. Illiteracy, however, is still fairly common. It is highest in the villages, among the elderly, and among women. Even among girls under 15 the rate of illiteracy is above 25 percent, more than twice the rate for boys that age. In urban areas, educational differences are reflected less in literacy rates and more in years of schooling.

By 1980 the nonagricultural labor force was literate, with almost a third having some secondary education. A relatively high percentage of women have secondary or college-level education, and a large number of teachers are female. Strikingly, almost half the agricultural labor force remains illiterate.

Occupational trends since 1970 are summarized in table 1.8. The most significant changes have been the decline in the proportion of farmers and the increase in the proportion of skilled, administrative, and technical workers. Technical and administrative occupations rely heavily on persons with a secondary school education. Service, sales, and urban productive labor generally have primary school education. Agricultural labor is split approximately evenly betwen the illiterate and those with primary education. The educational system is not precisely correlated with the demand for labor. For instance, about a third of university-educated persons work in jobs that require only a secondary education or less.

Table 1.8 Skill structure of labor force 1970–1980

Occupation	Workers (thousands (%))						Annual growth 1970–80 (%)
	1970		1975		1980		
Technical, professional, and related	555	(4.0)	640	(4.0)	833	(4.8)	4.2
Managerial, administrative, and related	85	(0.6)	76	(0.5)	161	(0.9)	6.6
Clerical	346	(2.5)	532	(3.3)	621	(3.6)	6.0
Salesmen and related	459	(3.3)	564	(3.5)	794	(4.6)	5.6
Service	545	(3.9)	577	(3.6)	920	(5.3)	5.4
Craftsmen, production workers and repairmen, and related	2,900	(20.6)	3,516	(22.0)	3,591	(20.7)	2.2
Farmers, fishermen, and related	9,157	(65.2)	10,092	(63.1)	10,442	(60.1)	1.3
Total	14,048	(100.0)	15,995	(100.0)	17,363	(100.0)	2.1

Source: SIS, Census of Population, various issues

As shown in table 1.9, employment growth in the 1970s was most rapid in financial services, personal services, and trade. Employment growth in manufacturing and construction was relatively high until 1975 and then slowed considerably. Between 1980 and 1985, total nonagricultural employment increased by 14 percent. Figure 1.1 shows how employment

Table 1.9 Employment by sector 1970 and 1980

Sector	1970 Workers (thousands)	1970 Share of nonagricultural labor force (%)	1980 Workers (thousands)	1980 Share of nonagricultural labor force (%)	Average annual growth 1970–80 (%)
Agriculture	10,231	—	11,105	—	0.8
Mining	111	2.3	132	1.8	1.8
Manufacturing	1,288	26.3	1,976	26.6	4.4
Utilities	15	0.3	33	0.4	8.5
Construction	431	8.8	765	10.3	5.9
Transportation	360	7.4	531	7.2	4.0
Trade	673	13.8	1,084	14.6	4.9
Finance	146	3.0	294	4.0	7.3
Service	1,865	38.2	2,603	35.1	3.4
Total	15,119	—	18,522	—	2.1

—, not applicable.

Source: SIS, *Census of Population,* various issues

Percent of national total

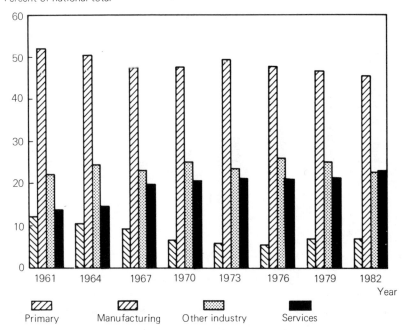

Figure 1.1 Sectoral employment shares (insured workers only)

shares (insured workers only) have changed among the major sectoral categories. There has been some decline in manufacturing's share as more service workers have appeared.

Data on the wages of Turkish workers are scarce. One reason is that a large proportion of the labor force (even outside agriculture) are either self-employed or employed by small firms that do not participate in the social security system. However, the available data indicate that real wages grew by about 50 percent from 1960 to 1970. The next spurt was between 1974 and 1977, when real wages went up by about 40 percent. Since 1981, however, the trend has been downward.

Figure 1.2 shows trends in relative sectoral wages since 1961. The most striking trend is the reduction of differences between the sectors. In 1961 nonagricultural primary products workers (mostly miners) earned about 25 percent less than the average for all insured workers, while workers in services earned 30 percent more than the average. By 1982 the earnings of primary sector workers were about 8 percent higher than the average, while those of service workers were about 5 percent below the average. There is also a systematic difference between public and private sector wages. Public sector firms paid higher wages throughout this period. There

Difference from average (percent)

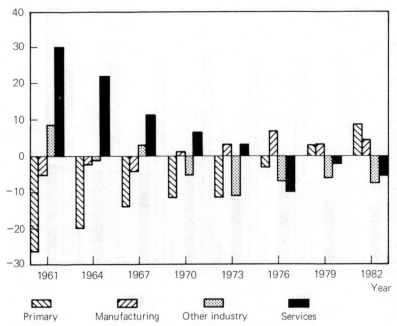

Figure 1.2 Relative sectoral wages (insured workers only)

is little question that this premium is not due to the greater efficiency of public sector firms.

Labor unions have been active in Turkey during the past 25 years, particularly in large manufacturing firms. One feature of the 1960s and 1970s was an extreme form of inter-union competition for membership. Strikes, particularly in the private sector, increased in the late 1970s as the economic situation worsened. Union activities were restricted after the military takeover of September 1980, and strikes were banned until recently. The more leftist unions have been disbanded, and only government-approved unions are allowed to operate.

Turkey has been a net exporter of labor, mainly to West Germany and other northern European countries, since the early 1960s. This has had several effects. Workers' remittances comprise a very significant fraction of Turkey's foreign exchange earnings, labor migration has helped ease domestic unemployment, and the domestic labor force has been strengthened by the skills of returning workers. It is difficult to estimate accurately the number of workers abroad, because most do not find jobs through official channels. However, it is likely that between 600,000 and a million Turks have been working in Europe since the mid-1970s. The total number varies with unemployment trends in Europe. In the past ten years, labor migration to Middle Eastern countries has become increasingly significant. Official figures indicate that as many as 45,000 Turks are now working in those countries.

2

Foreign Trade Policy: 1950–1984

Turkey's foreign trade policy during the period 1950–84 is described in this chapter. This is done with the help of an index representing the various degrees of liberalization of the economy, and by extension the intensity of the government's commitment to such policies. The scale of the index ranges from 1 to 20, with 1 corresponding to the most highly controlled and restrictionist trade regime, bordering on autarky, and 20 corresponding to the ideal of completely free trade policies.

The 10–20 range is reserved for "outward-oriented" trade regimes that allow or encourage specialization according to a country's comparative advantage, whereas the 1–9 range is used to identify restrictionist trade regimes that (a) support an import-substituting industrialization strategy and (b) restrict imports in response to chronic balance-of-payments difficulties caused by continuously overvalued exchange rates.

The chart showing the levels of the index by year is presented in figure 2.1. This graph serves as a reference scale as Turkey's foreign trade policies are discussed and evaluated.[1] To emphasize important changes in Turkish foreign trade policy and to distinguish periods in which economic performance and the quality of policymaking changed noticeably, the 34-year period is divided into four phases or subperiods. These are described briefly here and in greater detail below.

What is most apparent in figure 2.1 is a recurring "spike-slope" pattern, with each period lasting roughly ten years. In 1950, 1958, 1970, and 1980, steps were taken to reduce trade and other economic distortions. However, at least in the first three subperiods, the tide soon switched and trade policy became even more distorted than previously. The post-1980 liberalization period is different in two respects. Not only is it too early to tell whether the policy trends will again reverse, but in sharp contrast with the earlier episodes the government has made permanent liberalization a

---

1 In setting the annual levels of the index, qualitative and quantitative indicators of trade liberalization were used whenever possible. Inevitably, the index reflects the authors' subjective judgment.

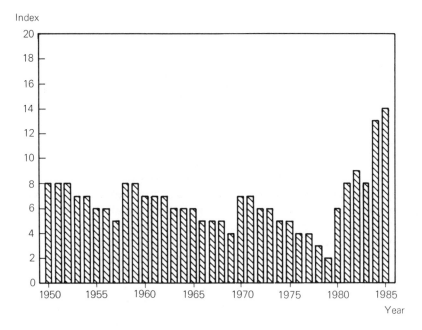

Figure 2.1 Trade liberalization index

central political and economic goal. It is this commitment that raised the index above the 10 level for the first time.

In the first subperiod, 1950–62, economic policy was essentially inward looking, but it was based neither on an explicit economic theory nor on formal planning. Policy was made mostly on an *ad hoc* basis, and there was a general lack of interest in coordinating economic policies. Insufficient understanding of economic principles and relationships by policy-makers – and their disregard of domestic as well as international advice – helped push the economy to the point of international bankruptcy by the late 1950s. Economic mismanagement was also an important contributory factor in the coup that overthrew the Democratic Party in May 1960.

The 1963–73 period can be called the period of "planned industrialization," characterized by strong central planning and import substitution trade policies. Coincidentally, it was also a period of reasonably successful economic performance, at least in terms of aggregate growth.

The third subperiod, 1974–9, can best be described as one of "external shock, domestic turmoil." The aftermath of the first oil price shock coincided with a time of weak coalition governments following Turkey's intervention in Cyprus. During this period, economic performance and policymaking deteriorated drastically, and the distortions in the economy (including trade distortions) became increasingly costly, culminating in a major debt crisis.

The most recent period, which can be called "economic liberalization," dates from January 1980, when the government announced its intention to move from highly interventionist planning and import substitution to a more market-oriented system. Present policies are focused explicitly on export promotion, liberalization of the import regime, and liberalization of foreign capital transactions.

The "spike–slope" pattern can also be seen as a reflection of a recurring cycle in the political economy of Turkey. The cycle starts with overly expansionist macroeconomic policy, leading to accelerating inflation and currency overvaluation. The inevitable balance-of-payments crisis brought about by unsustainable current account deficits has always been dealt with by a combination of fiscal austerity, devaluation, and trade controls to stimulate exports and ration imports.

The political costs of the adjustments required to break each crisis have been severe, with military intervention occurring in 1960, 1971, and 1980. After a few years, the military relinquishes power to a parliamentary government which becomes increasingly weak as economic performance falls short of expectations. The desire to meet expectations, and thereby retain political power, is what leads to renewed looseness in fiscal and monetary policy and the start of a new cycle. This cycle, which has averaged ten years in length, is illustrated in each of the subperiods discussed in this chapter. In constructing the liberalization index, significant weight has been given to the credibility of trade policies or the expectation, at the time, of policy reversals. This emphasis on a "forward-looking" rather than a "static" index is important to capture the linkage between current trade policies and investment-allocation behavior. Ultimately, it is through redistribution of investment that the impact of a more liberal regime will be felt.

Whether or not the trade policy changes of 1970 represented a "liberalization episode" is a semantic question best left to the reader to answer. However, we have interpreted the facts as indicating that no long-run changes in resource allocation were intended and that investment decisions were made throughout the period on the assumption that Turkey's inward orientation would continue indefinitely. The 1980 episode, in contrast, aimed at changing expectations. For these reasons, among others, the index was affected more in 1980 than in 1970.

Ad Hoc Economic Nationalism: 1950–1962

The Democratic Party's rise to power after the May 1950 elections led to a short-lived reversal of the government's previous economic policies. The

Democrats promised liberalized economic policies, increased encouragement to the private sector, and increased resources for agriculture. This program was in sharp contrast with the highly interventionist industry-biased anti-market inward-oriented "etatist" policies of the Republican People's Party, which had ruled the country since the days of Ataturk and the establishment of the Turkish Republic in 1923.[2]

Following the elections, the government did introduce some liberal domestic and foreign trade policies. As the economic situation deteriorated, however, economic policies changed quickly. Starting in September 1953, the trade and payments regime became increasingly restrictive in response to growing balance-of-payments difficulties, and the consequent developments culminated in the *de facto* devaluation of the Turkish lira in August 1958. These difficulties were mainly due to overly ambitious investment programs that required funds exceeding those available from domestic sources.

On the whole, the foreign trade regime of the 1950–62 period was highly restrictionist, and was characterized by constantly changing controls, regulations, and multiple exchange rates. Trade policy did not reflect any long-term purpose or strategy. Instead, it became increasingly restrictionist as a result of *ad hoc* measures introduced in response to the growing balance-of-payments deficit. Moreover, the initial experiment with a liberal trade policy (1950–3) was not an attempt to embark on a permanent course toward free trade. Rather, it resulted from a number of factors.

First, the government wanted to fulfill some of the election pledges made after a long period of economic restrictions. Second, after joining several international organization (European Payments Union (EPU), Organization for European Economic Cooperation (OEEC), International Monetary Fund (IMF), General Agreement on Tariffs and Trade (GATT), and International Bank for Reconstruction and Development (IBRD)) that were promoting international economic cooperation and freer trade, Turkey decided to implement the policy changes required by its membership in these organizations. Hence the new government followed the example of other European countries by abolishing a large number of import quotas in September 1950. Third, favorable world prices for Turkey's primary exports during the Korean War, bumper crops from 1951 through 1953, and considerable amounts of foreign aid received in the late 1940s and early 1950s encouraged the government to implement a fairly ambitious investment program and a somewhat more liberal trade policy.[3]

2 During the 1930s and 1940s, Turkey followed an industrialization strategy known as etatism, in which the state governed industrial activity. The government concentrated its efforts on the establishment of state-owned enterprises. Foreign trade and domestic market activities were highly controlled, and active encouragement of private industry almost ceased.
3 Hershlag (1968, p. 151) reported that American aid financed half the increase in imports in the late 1940s and early 1950s, as well as 40 percent of the increase in investment spending.

The trade liberalization index averaged 7.1 for the entire 13-year period. This reflects the reality that, except for a few years in the early 1950s, the trade regime was inward oriented and restrictionist. The annual levels of the index are listed in the first row of table 2.1. The other rows present important components of trade policy, and changes in these components are indicated whenever possible. Thus the information given in each column, below the indices, provides some support for the annual level of the index chosen for a specific year in relation to that of the preceding year.[4]

1950–1952

The annual level of the index for 1950, 1951, and 1952, is 8. A level higher than the average index for the entire subperiod was chosen to reflect the attempt to implement a more liberal trade policy. During these three years only a small number of import commodities were subject to quota restrictions, and import licenses were issued automatically. Export prohibitions were limited to only a few items, and export license requirements were applied only to tobacco, chrome, copper, opium, wool, pistachios, butter, and a few other commodities.[5]

Commodity trade showed an expansion in these years. Imports increased from US$286 million in 1951 to US$556 million in 1952, and then fell to US$533 million in 1953. Export earnings increased from US$263 million in 1950 to US$396 million in 1953, showing an increase of 51 percent in three years. Meanwhile, the share of imports in GNP rose from 8.3 percent in 1950 to 9.6 percent in 1953 (at current prices), while the share of exports remained at 7.6 percent. The faster increase in imports led to growing deficits in commodity trade accounts, which were mostly financed by the foreign loans, grants-in-aid, and short-term credits extended by the exporters of the EPU countries.[6]

4 Data limitations compelled the authors to rely on the indicators listed in table 2.1 in determining the annual levels of the index. Thus unavailability of disaggregated data on output levels and trade flows for the 1950s made the calculations of sectoral (weighted) average nominal tariff rates impossible. To our knowledge, there are no available estimates of effective protection rates and domestic resource costs for the 1950s.

5 The purpose of export licensing was to prevent reexport of these commodities by countries with whom Turkey traded through bilateral agreements. In these cases, trade in both directions was usually based on artificially high prices. In accepting such deals, Turkish exporters were motivated by the premiums accorded. Krueger (1974) notes that these "switch deals" were widespread in the mid-1950s.

6 Between 1950 and 1953, according to Cohn (1970), Turkey received US$224.4 million in economic aid from the United States, 64 percent as grants-in-aid, and the remainder as long-term loans. Turkey received US$50.9 million from the World Bank during the period 1950–6 (Hershlag, 1968, p. 152). Foreign private investment during the period 1950–3 was only US$27 million, while importers' credit totalled US$89 million (Ministry of Finance, 1983, p. 44). For details, see Baysan and Blitzer, 1988, appendix table 2.1.

It soon became obvious, however, that Turkey could not sustain such high trade deficits. Debt-servicing obligations had increased rapidly, and there were already sizable amounts in arrears.[7] What made the payments situation even worse was that huge amounts of short-term debt accumulated as Turkish importers made heavy use of suppliers' credit. Thus, by 1953 a serious balance-of-payments problem had emerged. At the same time, inflationary pressures that had been eased by increased imports again became a threat to economic stability.

1953–1957

In response to the worsening of the balance of payments, the government took steps to make the trade regime more restrictive, starting with measures introduced in September 1953. Therefore the index declined continuously in these years. The annual levels of the index were 7, 7, 6, 6, and 5 for the years 1953–7.

On September 1, 1953, the government issued a decree tightening its control over foreign trade. "Strict" licensing was to be required for all imports, with many import commodities transferred to the quota list. Some imports were put on a newly established list to which foreign exchange allocations were to be provided only under "special circumstances." Further, all importers were required to possess an "importer's certificate." Those importers who were already in place were allocated an initial share of 40 percent from the global quota, while new applicants were allocated an initial share of 30 percent. The remaining 30 percent was to be distributed according to the amounts of foreign exchange demanded in the applications. Guarantee deposit requirements were set at 4 percent. Surcharges ranging from 25 to 75 percent were imposed on "luxury" imports on a separate list. Through these increased exchange controls, expanded quantitative restrictions (QRs), and exchange surcharges, the government hoped to reduce demand for imports and thereby ease the balance-of-payments problem.

At the same time, exchange premiums were introduced for certain marginal exports, such as fresh fruits and vegetables, olives, wine, rugs, and a few other goods. The premium rate was 25 percent for exports paid in bilateral account currencies, 40 percent for exports paid in sterling and in currencies of the EPU countries, and 50 percent for export earnings of

---

7 By the end of 1950, according to the World Bank (1951, pp. 243–4), Turkey's total foreign debt was TL730 million (or US$261 million at the official exchange rate of TL2.80 per US dollar), amounting to 7.5 percent of GNP. It is unclear whether or not this included the arrears resulting from the suppliers' credit received until this date. The World Bank report also indicates that the foreign debt generated TL15 million in interest payments, plus TL37 million in amortization for 1950, giving a debt service ratio of 7 percent *vis-à-vis* Turkey's actual exports in 1950.

Table 2.1 Index of liberalization and changes in the trade regime, 1950–1962

	1950	1951	1952	1953	1954	1955	1956	1957	1958	1959	1960	1961	1962
Index of liberalization	8	8	8	7	7	6	6	5	8	8	7	7	7
Import regime	Liberal			From Sep 1953 highly restrictive		Increasingly restrictive			First import program		Partial liberalization		
Customs duties	At 1946 level			Changed to *ad valorem* basis, generally raised									
Other taxes													
(i) Production tax		15% throughout the period					Altered and raised						
(ii) Municipality share		2.5%											
(iii) Wharf tax													
Other surcharges				25%–75% surcharge on luxury imports				From Mar 1, 1957, 40% exchange tax on many imports					
Guarantee deposits													
(i) Rates (%)				4	4	10	10	10	10–20	?	?	?	?
(ii) Duration (months)				3	3	5	5	5	5	?	?	?	?
QRs		Reduced		Many items to quota list		Most items stayed on quota list							
Prohibitions		Existed		From Sep 1953 number of items increased									
Regulations		Licenses automatic		Strict licensing									
Nominal EERs (TL per US$)													
(i) Capital goods				3.22	3.48	4.02	4.72	5.97	16.15	12.55	12.11	12.55	12.54
(ii) Consumer goods				5.60	6.09	6.37	6.54	7.47	22.26	18.58	18.66	18.66	15.78
Export regime		Throughout the period few items were subject to export prohibitions											
		Liberal application of regulations		Strict application of export licensing and price controls									
Subsidies				20%–50% exchange premium on nontraditional exports				Number of exports eligible for exchange premium increased					

Regulations	Licensing and price controls	Applied liberally	Number of commodities subject to licensing increase / strict price controls							
Nominal EERs (TL per US$)										
(i) Traditional exports			2.80	2.85	2.89	2.91	2.94	5.14	6.77	9.00 · 9.00 · 9.00
(ii) Nontraditional exports			3.92	4.48	4.50	5.00	5.00	9.00	9.00	9.00 · 9.00 · 9.00
(iii) Weighted average			2.84	2.89	2.96	3.15	3.17	5.87	7.61	9.00 · 9.00 · 9.00
Foreign exchange regime			From Sep 1953 multiple exchange rates							
Controls	Existed		Foreign exchange controls tightened							
Official exchange rate (TL per US$)	2.80								(from Aug 1960) 9.00	
Other de facto rates (TL per US$)										
(i) Tourists and invisibles			2.80		2.80	2.80 / 5.75	2.80 / 5.75	9.00	9.00	9.00 · 9.00
(ii) Capital transactions			2.80		2.80	2.80	2.80	9.00	9.00	9.00 · 9.00
Devaluations			August 1958 nominal devaluation of 220%							
Black-market rates (TL per US$)					12.0	9.6–11	12.5	May = 17		
Foreign debt (year-end disbursed)	$280 million							$1,011 million		
Foreign investment regulations	Law 5821		Law 6224							

EER, effective exchange rate.

Sources: Krueger, 1974; World Bank, 1951; Official Gazette, various issues; Herschlag, 1968

"free" dollars. The objective was to partially compensate exporters for the overvalued exchange rate. Since traditional exports were excluded, however, it is doubtful that this measure was effective. A second measure affecting exports was an increase in the number of commodities subject to export licensing.

In late 1953 the coverage of the import surcharge was extended, and the issuance of import licenses was restricted to "essential" imports only. A system of multiple exchange rates was also inaugurated.

These steps notwithstanding, the trade regime became even more restrictive in the following years. This was in response to continuing balance-of-payments difficulties caused by huge international indebtedness and falling export earnings.[8] The overvaluation of the Turkish lira also increased steadily. Black-market rates far exceeded the official exchange rate of TL2.80 per US dollar, reaching TL12 per dollar in 1955 and TL17 per dollar in May 1958 (Krueger, 1974, p. 54).

In 1954 Turkey replaced specific tariff rates with *ad valorem* rates. At the same time, tariff rates were raised in general (see Baysan and Blitzer, 1988, appendix table 2.2, for a sample of 1954 tariff rates). On average, tariff rates were much higher on consumer goods (mostly in the 75–100 percent range for luxury items) and competing imports (in the 50–100 percent range).

The September 1953 measures and the changes in tariffs introduced in 1954 provide the basis for setting the annual levels of the index at 7 for 1953 and 1954. The reduction from the 1952 level of 8 reflects the increased restrictiveness of the trade regime and the tariff changes. The index values for 1955, 1956, and 1957 were reduced mainly because of the increase in the overvaluation of the lira and because of additional measures undertaken to restrict imports.[9]

While no major policy changes were announced in 1955, Turkey signed bilateral trade agreements with EPU countries that year in an effort to

---

8 After reaching a peak of US$396 million in 1953, export earnings steadily fell (except in 1957) until 1958, when proceeds from exports amounted to US$247 million, the lowest level in the 1950s. Poor export performance can be explained partly by the sharp fall in agricultural production in the mid-1950s, which in turn was due to weather factors and the overvalued exchange rate. EERs for traditional exports were maintained almost at the official exchange rate (TL2.80 per US dollar) until August 1958.

9 Turkey's inflation rate far exceeded the global average during the mid-1950s and late 1950s. According to official indices (biased downward because of government-controlled prices), the rate of inflation was 10 percent in 1954, 8 percent in 1955, 17 percent in 1956, 19 percent in 1957, 15 percent in 1958, and 20 percent in 1959 (SPO, 1962, p. 21). One major cause was the government's persistence in implementing large and economically unsound investment projects, which were financed through money creation. Efforts to check inflation through price controls and by setting below-cost prices for SEE products led to further increases in the money supply, thus intensifying inflation.

repay part of its mounting short-term debt through export revenues.[10] During 1955–6, the number of exports eligible for exchange premiums was increased and premium rates were altered in an effort to boost foreign exchange inflow. In October 1956 a 35 percent exchange premium was given to cotton exports paid for in "free" dollars or EPU currencies, and exporters of manganese and chromium were allowed to retain 100 percent of their foreign exchange earnings to pay for imports of equipment and materials. At the same time, effective exchange rates (EERs) were raised from TL2.80 per US dollar to TL5.75 per dollar for sales of foreign exchange by foreign tourists through a 105 percent premium, and to TL5.25 per dollar for purchases of foreign exchange by Turkish nationals for travel abroad through a surcharge of 87.5 percent.

In 1957 the government imposed a 40 percent exchange tax ("Treasury's share") on foreign exchange allocated for purchases of various imports, including iron, steel, cement, rubber, machinery, and equipment. This change, aimed at restricting imports, explains the reduction in the liberalization index in 1957.

1958–1962

Despite exchange controls and other restrictive measures, the trade deficit remained a major source of disequilibrium for the Turkish economy. Cuts in imports of raw materials and capital goods severely affected domestic production. As the government tried to control prices, shortages of a wide range of commodities became apparent. Black-market activities flourished. (In 1957 the black-market rate for the US dollar was at least four times higher than the official rate.) The multiple exchange rate system introduced in September 1953 became increasingly distortionary and biased, since effective rates changed constantly and large discrepancies emerged between the rates applicable to exports and imports. Meanwhile, the real EER for traditional exports fell continuously. Krueger's (1974) estimates of price-level-deflated EERs (PLD-EERs) show that the PLD-EER for traditional exports fell by about 44 percent between 1953 and 1957 (see also Baysan and Blitzer, 1988, appendix table 2.3).

Adverse developments in the domestic economy and the worsening trade and payments situation reached a climax in early 1958. Unable to

10 For further details, see Hershlag (1968, p. 183) and Krueger (1974, p. 31) It should be noted that in the mid-1950s the volume of trade with Turkey's bilateral agreement partners (mostly Eastern European countries) expanded as Turkey tried desperately to find new markets for its exports and new sources of import supply in the face of dwindling exports to Western countries. Turkey's share of imports originating from the bilateral agreement countries increased from 7 to 29 percent between 1953 and 1955. During the same period, its share of exports to the same countries rose from 14 to 32 percent (Krueger, 1974, p. 39).

Table 2.2 Index of liberalization and changes in the foreign trade regime, 1963–1973

	1963	1964	1965	1966	1967	1968	1969	1970	1971	1972	1973
1 Index of liberalization	6	6	6	5	5	5	4	7	7	6	6
2 Import regime		Inward-oriented foreign trade policies		Increasingly restrictionist				Devaluation			
		Highly protectionist									
2a Customs duties	1954 schedule	1964 schedule (new rates)									
2b Other taxes											
Production tax (%)	15.0										
Municipality share (%)	2.5										
Wharf tax (%)					5.0						
Stamp duty (%)	5.0				10.0	15.0	25.0	10.0 Rates-down (after Aug)			
Guarantee deposits											
Rates (%)	10–30	10–30	10–100	10–100	10–125	10–125	20–150	50 (Aug)	20–50	20–50	5–50
Duration (months)	4	4	5	5	5	5	8	8 (until Aug)			
QRs											
Prohibitions	The quota list enumerated commodity categories subject to quota restrictions										
Regulations	Existed and gradually increased										
	Import procedures had been fairly complex and involved obtaining "importer's" and "permission" certificates for applying to the Central Bank for import licences; price controls were in effect but applied liberally										
2c Nominal EERs (TL per US$)								(after Aug)			
Capital goods	12.99	12.99	15.5	15.5	15.29	12.26	13.16	19.68			
Consumer goods	16.23	16.26	17.75	17.75	18.5	18.79	19.69	30.00			
Competing imports	19.41	19.41	23.01	23.01	23.46	21.96	21.98	35.50			

3 Export regime											
3a subsidies	Indirect tax rebates increased gradually; number of eligible items also increased										
3b Regulations	Export licensing was required for some commodities					Export credits			Strict		
	Rebates					Import Replenishment Program			price controls		
	Price controls were enforced through price registration										
3c Nominal EERs (TL per US$)											
Traditional exports	9.00	9.00	9.00	9.02	9.02	9.02	9.37	10.69	12.62	13.19	13.60
Nontraditional exports	9.62	9.62	10.09	9.72	9.72	10.28	11.37	14.97	18.44	17.69	17.28
Weighted average	9.04	9.04	9.06	9.06	9.06	9.09	10.15				
4 Foreign exchange regime											
Controls	Existed			Became more strict							
4a Official exchange rate (TL per US$)	9.00							Aug 15.00	Dec 14.00		
Other de facto rates (TL per US$)											
4b Tourists: buying	9.02	9.02	9.02	9.02	9.02	12.00	12.00	14.85			
selling	13.50	13.50	13.50	13.50	13.50	13.50	13.50	15.00			
4c Workers' remittances	9.00	9.00	11.43	11.43	11.43	12.00	12.00	15.00			
4d Devaluations/revaluations								Aug 66.7% devaluation	Dec revaluation		
4e Bias against exports (EERe/EERm)	0.58	0.58	0.51	0.51	0.51	0.53	0.55	0.57	0.58		
5 Foreign debt (year-end disbursed)					$1,441 million			$2,528 million			
6 Foreign investment regulation	Law 6624 regulating foreign private investment in effect since 1954										

Sources: *Official Gazette*, various issues; Krueger, 1974; authors' esimates

stabilize the economy or meet debt obligations, the government belatedly agreed on a stabilization program prepared with the assistance of the IMF and the OEEC. The stabilization program, announced on August 4, 1958, introduced major changes in foreign trade and domestic economic policies.

The most important component was a *de facto* devaluation of the lira. Turkey also moved to a more unified exchange rate system, abolishing the complex system of exchange surcharges and premiums. A single selling rate was established at TL9.025 per US dollar; this was applicable to imports, all invisible transactions, capital transfers, and tourists. It was accomplished by imposing a uniform exchange tax of TL6.225 per US dollar on the official exchange rate, which was maintained at TL2.8 per dollar until August 1960.

Three different buying rates were announced. The effective exchange rate for opium, tobacco, copper, and chrome exports was set at TL4.90 per US dollar; these products were granted an exchange premium of TL2.10 per dollar. The premium for exports of figs, raisins, and hazelnuts was fixed at TL2.80 per dollar, giving an effective rate of TL5.60 per dollar. The buying rate for other exports, invisible transactions, and capital transfers was set at TL9.00 per dollar with a premium of TL6.20 per dollar.

The devaluation plan also included the consolidation and rescheduling of Turkey's outstanding commercial debt. Negotiations were held after the announcement of the stabilization program, and the parties reached an agreement on a debt repayment schedule in 1959 (Krueger, 1974, pp. 76–7). The consolidated debt in 1959 amounted to US$422 million, and the official debt – including the consolidated debt – was estimated to be US$690 million by the end of 1961 (Krueger, 1974, p. 76).

As part of the stabilization agreement, Turkey received large amounts of foreign loans. The US government extended US$259 million in grants and loans, the OEEC countries provided US$75 million, and another US$25 million was made available by the IMF. These credits were crucial in bringing some degree of rationalization and liberalization to the import regime.

New import and export regulations and foreign trade procedures were announced after the devaluation. The many separate lists of imports were replaced by import programs, which stated import regulations and procedures and also indicated the rates of advance deposit requirements. Since their inauguration in 1958, the import programs have continued to be a major instrument of import control. The first (quarterly) import program appeared in the *Official Gazette* on September 23, 1958. This first program contained only a quota list. For each commodity category the global quota allocation and the shares of industrialists and importers were specified in dollars. In subsequent import programs a liberalized list was also included. The second and third programs were announced in February and August

1959. Licenses were issued automatically and, although the prices of imports were monitored, this monitoring was fairly relaxed.

Export licenses were still required for some commodities. However, export price controls became more realistic; minimum prices (which had been set at high levels) were aligned to international levels, and price checks were made after export. These adjustments introduced a considerable element of liberalization.

Following the August 1958 devaluation, imports increased by a half in the first year, and from US$315 million in 1958 to US$470 million in 1959, but sagged to US$468 million in 1960. Thereafter, imports rose to US$507 million in 1961 and US$619 million in 1962. Increases in EERs after 1958 had some positive impact on export earnings, which increased from US$247 million in 1958 to US$354 million in 1959, US$321 million in 1960, US$347 million in 1961, and US$381 million in 1962.

The foregoing brief description of developments between 1958 and 1962 gives a basis for determining the annual level of the index for these years. The index number chosen for 1958 is 8. The 3 point increase from the 1957 level reflects the August 1958 devaluation package. However, the index is kept below 10, since the August 1958 measures were essentially correctional (domestic inflation had been much greater than that observed in the Western countries) and were not aimed at permanently setting up a more liberal trade regime. It is true that the devaluation package had some distortion-reducing elements, but the bias against exports was maintained. This disparity in the EERs between exports and imports indicates that the trade regime continued to be inward looking. After 1958 the index declined slowly as a result of overvaluation of the lira after 1958.[11] Indeed, the rate of inflation in 1959 was nearly 20 percent.

Planned Industrialization: 1963–1973

In the aftermath of the 1960 military coup, Turkey entered an era of planned economic development. Much of the support for the coup stemmed from dissatisfaction with the country's economic performance, and the framers of the new constitution created a strong planning apparatus, the SPO, as a means of insuring more rapid development. The consensus was that the state should have a leading role in promoting development and that Turkey should industrialize as rapidly as possible. While the planners had little theoretical objection to exports, they felt that

11 The trend toward increasing overvaluation was partially compensated by some steps taken to liberalize imports and increases in EERs granted to some traditional exports.

free-trade policies inevitably would leave Turkey a producer of agricultural products, with few possibilities for industrial growth.

During this period, two five-year plans (1963–7 and 1968–72) were implemented. These plans (as well as a third five-year plan developed in 1971–2) had similar objectives. They were (a) economic growth, (b) structural change by setting higher growth targets for manufacturing industries, and (c) development of import-competing industries and diversification of exports. The role of trade policy would be to provide protection to domestic industries and to allow the import of capital goods and raw materials deemed essential to achieving the three objectives. To this end, trade policy was to be coordinated with industrialization policy.

A New Import Regime

Since their inauguration in 1958, import programs have become Turkey's major instrument for regulating imports. Their preparation involves the SPO, the Central Bank, the Ministries of Finance, Commerce, and Industry, and the Union of Chambers of Commerce and Industry. Each program is published in the *Official Gazette* and contains the import regulations and procedures that importers must follow to obtain import licenses. Until 1980 commodities eligible for import were listed on either the liberalized list or the quota list. The liberalized list contained commodities considered essential for the achievement of plan objectives, including most capital goods and raw materials. The quota list contained "less essential" goods (for example consumer goods) along with competing imports.

Commodities were frequently reshuffled between the two lists, but during most of this period the quota list grew. As soon as domestic production of an import-competing product began, the import was transferred from the liberalized to the quota list. If potential domestic production was large enough to meet domestic demand, local producers applied for complete protection and the authorities usually granted this by removing the item from the quota list.

In addition, there was a bilateral quota list. This list specified the commodities that could be imported from the bilateral agreement countries. Goods from these countries constituted only a small part of total imports. Capital goods and US Public Law 480 imports, which were directly financed through aid programs, appeared in a category called "self-financed imports."

Until recently, importers had to go through a complex set of procedures. For example, industrialists and wholesalers first had to obtain an "importer's certificate" from their local chamber and then a ministerial "permission certificate" from the designated ministry (when required) before they could apply to the Central Bank for an "import license" (permit). Applicants were also required to present a "letter of credit" and to place a specified interest-free "guarantee deposit" with their commercial bank.

For quota list items, importers were also required to obtain a "requirement certificate" from a designated ministry.[12] It was only after these procedures had been completed that importers could place actual orders. Commodities arriving at Turkish ports were compared with their descriptions and prices as reported in the application.[13] Imports were not cleared until after the payment of all duties and taxes. The length of time an applicant had to wait for an import license depended on the availability of foreign exchange. Long delays were not uncommon particularly for items on the liberalized list.

Import taxes were an important policy instrument throughout this period. While the government relied heavily on QRs and import prohibitions to protect domestic industries, taxes were also used extensively to restrict imports.[14] In addition to customs duties, taxes on imports included the "municipality share," a wharf tax, a stamp duty, and a production tax. Tariff duties and the stamp duty are levied on the cost, insurance, and freight (c.i.f.) value of imports on an *ad valorem* basis. The 5 percent stamp duty introduced in 1963 was raised to 10 percent in 1967, 15 percent in 1968, and 25 percent in 1969. It was lowered to 10 percent after the August 1970 devaluation. Tariff duties, however, have not changed significantly since an across-the-board adjustment in 1964.

The remaining import taxes have cascading structures. The municipality share, first levied in July 1948, is 15 percent of the customs duty. The wharf tax has been levied on goods arriving by ship since 1951. It is calculated by taking a percentage of the sum of the c.i.f. value, the customs duty, the municipality share, and landing costs. The wharf tax was 2.5 percent until 1967 and has been 5 percent since then. Commodity-specific production taxes were levied on imports throughout the period. They ranged from 5 to 30 percent, and were calculated on a base that included landed cost inclusive of c.i.f. value plus all other taxes and landing charges.

12 "Requirement certificates" were issued according to existing plant capacities, and are different from "permission certificates."
13 Krueger (1974, p. 153) reported that, in contrast with the 1950s when price checks were strict, in the 1960s they were fairly relaxed. Overinvoicing was believed to be widely practiced owing to overvaluation of the lira. She also points out that, after the change of government in 1971, price checks were applied more forcefully.
14 Apart from restricting imports, import taxes were an important source of government revenue. In the 1960s, import taxes amounted to about a quarter of total annual tax revenues.

The Export Regime

A series of export controls were put in place during the 1960s and 1970s. These are determined by a decree on foreign trade regulation prepared annually by the Ministry of Commerce and published in the *Official Gazette*. The principal instruments of control are price registration and export licensing. The purpose of price registration is to prevent under-invoicing by exporters. Commodities subject to export licensing by the Ministry of Commerce are listed annually. The purpose of licensing is to prevent sharp increases in domestic prices, particularly for commodities that are considered essential to Turkish consumers, such as wheat and meat.

The most important policy intervention is the tax rebate system, introduced in 1963 as an incentive for exports. Law 261 (June 27, 1963) authorized the Council of Ministers to set rates for tax rebates such that import taxes and other indirect taxes included in the cost of manufactured export goods could be partially or fully refunded after export. Some specific rates set in 1963 were converted to an *ad valorem* basis in 1964. Over the years, the number of eligible commodities and the rebate rates have both increased. Exports benefiting from rebates amounted to TL250 million in 1967, TL248 million in 1968, and TL1,427 million in 1969, whereas rebates paid in the same years amounted to TL25 million, TL58 million, and TL208 million. These amounts imply average rebate rates of 10 percent in 1967, 23 percent in 1968, and 15 percent in 1969. The fall in the rate in 1969 was caused by the inclusion of certain agricultural and processed food commodities which received low rebate rates (Ticaret Bakanligi, 1974, p. 19).

Other export promotion measures were less effective than the tax rebate system. These included "export credits" at subsidized rates of interest and an "import replenishment" program that involved provision of foreign exchange for the importation of inputs. Krueger (1974) reported that in the late 1960s the export credit scheme proved ineffective because commercial banks were not willing to extend credits at subsidized rates. The replenishment program was doomed to failure from the start, since only US$2 million was allocated for the program.

1963–1969

Whereas trade policy during the 1950s lacked any long-term strategy and became increasingly restrictionist in response to balance-of-payments difficulties, there was a deliberate attempt during the period 1963–73 to use trade policy to promote import-substituting industrialization. Heavy reliance was placed on controlling imports through QRs and prohibitions.

The average level of the index of liberalization for the 1960s and early 1970s was therefore set at 5.6, somewhat below the average for the 1950s. At the same time, note that overall macroeconomic performance improved substantially between 1963 and 1973.

The annual levels of the liberalization index during the period 1963–73 are listed in table 2.2, row 1. The index for 1963 is 6. In 1964 tariff rates were changed across the board and generally were raised (see Baysan and Blitzer, 1988, appendix table 2.2, for a sample of the 1954 and 1964 tariff rates).[15] The rates applicable to consumer goods and competing imports increased in most cases. Under the same law, the rates of the production tax, which had been levied on both imports and domestically produced substitutes, were increased on a large number of commodities. It is possible that increases in tariff duties sometimes reduced the "rents" caused by QRs. The continuing decline in the liberalization index until 1970 reflects both the increased overvaluation of the Turkish lira and the additional protective and restrictive measures introduced as a consequence of overvaluation. Throughout this period, the economy became increasingly domestically oriented, and relative prices became more distorted until corrective steps (including a major devaluation) were taken in 1970.

A number of quantitative data support this trend. These include estimates of sectoral effective protection rates (EPRs) and domestic resource costs (DRCs). The data give an overall picture of the degree of protection provided by the trade regime, its indiscriminate support of import-substituting industries, and the extent of inefficient resource-allocation costs that the regime inflicted upon the economy. First some of the piecemeal evidence will be reviewed, beginning with some of the findings reported by Krueger (1974).

Krueger's examination of import programs in the 1960s, based on samples of commodities and import lists, showed that by 1966 " . . . the value of permissible imports for quota items fell sharply . . . ," and there was a " . . . gradual shift toward quota lists (as domestic production began) and the 'prohibited list' (as domestic production was deemed adequate to meet domestic demand) . . . " (Krueger, 1974, p. 165). The first observation is illustrated by the fact that, while actual levels of imports under the quota list fell from US$218 million in 1966 to US$181 million in 1969 and were still below the 1966 level in 1970, the number of commodity categories on the quota list increased from 418 to 471 in the same period. This implies that the average value of permissible imports fell. The increase in the number of quota categories is also indicative of a shift

15 Domestic production of some commodities classified as import substitutes (MS) by Krueger (1974) had not yet started in 1954. Examples include rubber tires and manmade fibers.

toward reliance on the quota list (Baysan and Blitzer, 1988, appendix tables 2.4 and 2.5).

Results based on a sample of commodity categories are summarized in table 2.3. Out of 110 commodity categories, 32 appeared on the liberalized list in 1962 and only 24 in 1968. In contrast the number of commodity categories on the quota list increased from 32 to 36, and the number of prohibited commodities rose from 46 to 50.

Table 2.3 Distribution of a representative sample of 110 commodities by import category, 1962–1968

Year	Liberalized list	Quota list	Prohibited commodities	Total
1962	32	32	46	110
1965	32	33	46	110
1968	24	36	50	110

Source: Krueger, 1974

Other import taxes and guarantee deposits were also raised in the second half of the 1960s in response to mounting balance-of-payments difficulties, which are summarized by Baysan and Blitzer (1988, appendix table 2.6). Table 2.2, rows 2a and 2b, lists some of the restrictive measures introduced by the government. The 5 percent stamp duty, first levied in 1963, was increased to 10 percent in 1967, 15 percent in 1968, and 25 percent in 1969. The wharf tax doubled in 1967. These changes, together with sharp increases in guarantee deposit rates, explain the continued fall in the index through 1969; guarantee deposit rates rose continuously between 1963 and 1970 (see table 2.4).

Both the rates of change in deposit rates and the levels reflected a strong bias against items on the liberalized list. One plausible explanation is that, in the absence of quantitative limits, the authorities attempted to discourage import demand for liberalized list items by making them more costly, and intensified their efforts as the balance-of-payments situation worsened.

The other bias worth noting is that higher deposit rates were set for items on the liberalized list II. This list contained some competing imports. Hence the higher rates were probably intended to protect domestic industries.

The other important aspect of guarantee deposits was the length of time during which they were held: about four months in 1963 and 1964, and about five months from 1965 through 1968. As dwindling supplies of foreign exchange led to longer delays in the issuance of import licenses, the period during which guarantee deposits were held increased to eight

Table 2.4 Guarantee deposit rates, 1963–1973 (percent)

	Liberalized list I		Liberalized list II		Quota list	
	Industrialists	Importers	Industrialists	Importers	Industrialists	Importers
1963	10–30	10–30	—	—	10	10–20
1964	30	30	30	30	10	30
1965	70	70	100	100	10	30
1966	70	70	100	100	10	30
1967	70	70	100–25	100–25	10	30
1968	70	70	100–25	100–25	10	30
1969	90	90	120–50	120–50	20	50
1970[a]	90	90	150	150	20	50
1971	45	45	60–75	60–75	10	25
1972	45	45	60–75	60–75	10	25
1973	25–50	25–50	10–20	10–20	5	10

—, not applicable.
[a] Pre-devaluation rates.
Sources: Krueger, 1974; World Bank, 1982

months in 1969 and early 1970. Since these deposits did not receive any interest, importers incurred a cost, which increased the longer the funds were held.[16]

Despite these restrictive measures, excess demand for foreign exchange did not fall, and overvaluation of the Turkish lira increased because of both growth and the resulting inflation.[17] Some evidence to the contrary was found by Krueger when she calculated the "ratio of value of license applications to licenses issued by quota categories" for several years. In the late 1960s and 1970 (before devaluation), the ratios were much higher for a larger number of categories than in earlier years. For example, while the ratio ranged between 4 and 10 for 29 quota categories in 1962, there were 45 quota categories in 1968 and 52 in 1970 for which application values exceeded values of licenses issued by a factor of 4–10. Part of these excess demand resulted from speculative motives as the premium (that is, "scarcity rents") on import licenses increased continuously from TL4–6 per US dollar in 1964–5 to TL9–15 per dollar in 1968–9.

While the import regime became more restrictive, the bias against exports kept pace. Table 2.2 gives nominal EERs for different export and

16 As Krueger (1974, p. 289) observes, the implicit cost also "varied with the ratio of the value of license applications to receipts . . . ."
17 During the period 1963–70 the average annual rate of inflation was approximately 8 percent. Over the same period the maximum rate of inflation in the EEC countries was 4.5 percent (France) and the minimum was 2.3 percent (West Germany) (IMF, *International Financial Statistics*, December 1973).

import categories. The ratios of export-to-import EERs, derived from the latter values of EERs, are given in row 4e. They range between 0.50 and 0.58. In a sense, the export incentives of the 1960s were just large enough to match the incremental protection granted to import-substituting industries but not large enough to reduce the bias of the regime.

1970–1973

When the increased trade restrictions and foreign exchange controls failed to remove the main causes of the disequilibrium in the balance of payments, and as the foreign exchange situation became more severe, the government was forced to announce a devaluation in August 1970. As in 1958, the devaluation was part of a stabilization program put into effect at the same time. The nominal devaluation was 66.7 percent, raising the parity rate from TL9 to TL15 per US dollar. At the same time, the stamp duty on imports was lowered from 25 to 10 percent. In addition, guarantee deposit rates were reduced by about half, with the new rates ranging from 10 to 75 percent.

However, uniform exchange rates did not apply to all trade transactions. For example, a lower rate of TL12 per US dollar was applied to nine items, mostly traditional exports.[18] This rate was subsequently raised, as promised by the government, to TL13 per dollar in 1971. Furthermore, rebates ranging from 25 to 40 percent were granted for exports exceeding $1 million, and 30 percent or less for exports of less than $1 million. The objectives were to encourage the consolidation of smaller export firms and to promote larger export volumes. Policymakers, motivated by "elasticity pessimism," thought that consolidation would help to prevent price cuts and thus prevent losses in export revenues. Additional measures, including the establishment of two funds designed to expand export credits, were introduced in August 1970 to increase the effectiveness of the export credit scheme.

Effective devaluation rates varied among export and import categories, since the devaluation package included (in addition to lower exchange rates for traditional exports) alterations in surcharges, the rebate system, and guarantee deposit rates. For the most part, the new effective devaluation rates were less than the nominal devaluation.

The short-term effects of devaluation on the balance of payments were impressive. Export revenues increased from US$588 million in 1970 to US$1,317 million in 1973. The response of workers' remittances was also very strong. Remittances rose to a peak of US$1,183 million in 1973 from US$273 million in 1970. Imports more than doubled, expanding from US$948 million in 1970 to US$2,086 million in 1973.

18 Cotton, tobacco, hazelnuts, raisins, dried figs, olive oil, oil cakes, molasses, and fig cakes.

After the devaluation, however, inflationary pressures also accelerated, thus helping to undermine its long-term success. The rate of inflation was 16 percent in 1971, 18 percent in 1972, and 20 percent in 1973, according to official figures (which are likely biased downwards). The causes of this inflationary cycle and the parallel changes in domestic economic policies announced as part of the 1970 stabilization program will be discussed later. Here it suffices to say that by 1973 the real exchange rate had fallen by at least 10 percent.

It must be stressed that the August 1970 devaluation was taken as a once-and-for-all step to reduce the overvaluation of the lira and to bring some uniformity to the EERs, which even the most ardent advocates of "planned industrialization" agreed had become too distorted. Neither the exchange rate alignments nor the partial relaxation of import restrictions should be considered as an attempt at establishing permanently a more liberal outward-oriented trade strategy. There was no sequencing involved in the devaluation package, as all changes were put into effect in August 1970. The only time-phased change was related to the exchange rates of traditional export commodities. Those rates were raised gradually, and the time phasing was motivated by macroeconomic considerations.

In 1970 the index of liberalization was raised to 7 from its low level of 4 in 1969. This was on the grounds that the August 1970 changes, including the stamp duty and advance deposit rate reductions, reduced the restrictiveness of the import regime and narrowed the disparities between the incentives for export and import-substituting production to a range comparable with those observed in the first half of the 1960s. For 1971 the index was again set at 7, but it was reduced by 1 in 1972 and 1973 to reflect the reemergence of overvaluation associated with increased domestic inflation.

Effective Protection Rates and Domestic Resource Costs

Estimates of sectoral EPRs and DRCs also provide evidence that foreign trade policy was highly restrictive and heavily biased toward import-substituting industries during this period. Moreover, the trade distortions inflicted heavy costs due to resulting inefficiencies in resource allocation. Estimates of sectoral EPRs are available for 1967 in a study by Baysan (1974) and they were calculated for 1973, the most recent year for which an input–output table is available. Sectoral nominal tariff rates wer derived from commodity-specific tariff rates (inclusive of all import taxes) and export subsidies at the six-digit level using weights. Adjustments were made in the weighted sectoral nominal tariff rates in order to remove biases caused by the weighting method and to account for the implicit tariff resulting from QRs. The two sets of EPR estimates are presented in the third and fourth columns of table 2.5. Corden's approach was used to

Table 2.5 Estimates of effective protection rates and domestic resource costs by sector

Industry	Sector of classification	1967–8 EPRs (%)	1973 EPRs (%)	1973 DRCs (TL per US$)
Cotton	E		-2.7	14.5
Tobacco	E		-1.0	14.7
Other industrial crops	ME	-2	-0.4	14.8
Olives	ME		-1.7	14.7
Other oil seeds	ME		-2.7	14.5
Wheat	ME		-8.7	13.5
Other cereals and animal feeds	ME	2	-10.0	13.2
Rice	MS		73.8	25.9
Citrus fruits	ME	2	-1.0	14.7
Grapes	ME		-1.6	14.6
Other fruits	ME	5	-1.5	14.7
Nuts	E	-3	-2.2	14.5
Chick-peas and lentils	ME		13.2	16.8
Tomatoes – other pulses	ME	-7	-1.3	14.7
Dry beans, potatoes, and onions	ME		-11.2	13.2
Sheep and goat	ME		-0.7	14.8
Poultry	ME		4.8	15.6
Cattle and buffalo	ME	4	5.2	15.6
Other animals	ME		9.0	16.2
Forestry	ME	24	20.5	17.2
Fishing	ME	2	-3.0	14.3
Coal mining	MS	8	12.6	16.5
Crude oil and natural gas	MS	467[a]	124.2[a]	33.3
Iron ore mining	ME	8	-7.7	13.3
Nonferrous ore mining	ME		-1.9	14.4
Mining of nonmetallic minerals	ME	18	6.8	15.5
Stone quarrying	ME		14.6	16.5
Meat slaughtering and processing	ME	5	10.4	15.2
Canning fruits and vegetables	ME	-4	13.1	15.7
Vegetable, animal oils, and fats	ME	18	7.9	15.2
Grain mill products	MS		Very large	negative[b]
Sugar	MS	Very large	416.9	80.1
Manufacturing other food products	ME	4	1.6	14.1
Alcoholic beverages	MS	313	223.2	48.2
Soft drinks	ME		0.4	14.3
Tobacco	E	41	-2.9	14.3
Ginning	E		29.6	18.5
Manufacturing of textiles	ME		20.2	17.2
Cotton	ME	38		
Wool	MS	98		
Knitting	ME	21		
Other	ME	21		
Wearing apparel	MS	161	17.1	17.1
Leather and fur products	ME		8.5	15.4
Footwear	MS	26	35.1	19.9
Wood and wood products	MS		29.6	18.5

Table 2.5 (continued)

Wooden furniture products	MS	108	22.8	17.4
Paper and paper products	MS	155	154.2	36.8
Fertilizer	MS	132	112.6	31.1
Drugs and medicines	MS		139.9	34.8
Other chemical products	MS	250	121.7	32.5
Petroleum refineries	MS		124.1	33.4
Petroleum and coal products	MS	336	50.7	21.3
Rubber products	MS	b	117.5	31.6
Plastic products	MS		358.2	68.7
Glass products	MS	23	51.3	21.9
Cement	MS	154	27.0	17.4
Other nonmetal products	MS	23	75.2	25.3
Iron and steel basic industries	MS	163	203.9	45.5
Nonferrous basic industries	MS	98	79.5	25.7
Fabricated metal products	MS	190	95.7	28.5
Machinery (except electrical)	MS		108.6	30.8
Agricultural equipment	MS	132	103.1	29.7
Electrical machinery	MS	163	133.6	34.3
Shipbuilding and repairing	MS		101.8	29.8
Railroad equipment	MS		29.8	19.2
Motor vehicles	MS	184.0	93.9	28.4
Other transportation equipment	MS		89.5	28.1
Other manufacturing industries	MS		105.7	29.6
Variance		12,002.3	6,746.8	156.5
Mean		86.7	55.3	22.8

Sectors are classified according to whether they were producing traditional exports (E), nontraditional exports (ME), or import substitutes (MS).

[a] Nominal protection accorded to the crude petroleum industry was reduced from 423 percent in 1967 to 124 percent in 1973.

[b] Negative international value added results if the international value of inputs exceeds the international value of output. Similarly, negative DRCs may result if foreign exchange costs of inputs (direct and indirect) are larger than the international value of the product.

Sources: Baysan, 1974; authors' calculations, 1973 (unpublished)

calculate both set of EPRs. Hence the EPRs give the ratio of the difference between the domestic and international value added to the international value added per unit of production (Corden, 1966, pp. 221–37).

There are 41 sectors in the 1967 set and 65 for 1973, all producing tradeable commodities. Both sets show that the foreign trade regime provided high levels of protection to the import-substituting industries. Indeed, for manufacturing industries like crude petroleum, petroleum refineries, pharmaceuticals, chemicals, paper products, fertilizers, rubber and plastic products, metal products, iron and steel products, nonelectrical machinery, and sugar, EPRs were extremely high (generally above 100 percent).

In the last two rows of table 2.5 the unweighted means of all sectoral EPRs and their variance around the mean are given for both sets of estimates.[19] Despite the negative or extremely low EPRs for a large number of export sectors (which obviously reduced the mean), the values of the mean suggest that the foreign trade regime was highly protectionist. When only import-substituting sectors are considered, the values of the mean are much higher, reflecting the bias of the regime toward the latter group and its strictly inward-oriented structure. The bias of the regime against traditional as well as nontraditional export sectors is obvious from the relatively low EPRs. In fact, the results show that the trade regime caused negative protection for many export sectors, including such traditional exports as cotton, tobacco, and hazelnuts.

With such an effective protection structure, the trade policies no doubt created incentives that favored import-competing industries. It has been widely argued in the literature that in the general equilibrium context, when we consider input substitution, EPRs cannot be used as indicators of the direction of the resource pull effects of tariffs. Nevertheless, EPRs provide a better picture of protection afforded to various production activities in the presence of tariffs on imports of intermediate inputs and, as such, they are better indicators of the incentive effects of the commercial policy. The variance of EPRs around the mean reflects the nonuniformity of the tariff structure. However, there is no reason to believe that the prevailing nonuniform tariff rates were "made to measure."[20] In fact, excessive reliance on QRs and prohibitions suggests the contrary.

Two sets of DRC estimates are presented.[21] The first set, given in table 2.6, includes Krueger's estimates of DRCs for the second half of the 1960s, which are based on firm-specific data. Only the sectoral means and variances of DRC estimates are listed. After a ranking of sectoral DRCs is

19 Values of the means are reduced, since two observations from the first set and one observation from the second set were left out. In one case, negative "international value added" was encountered, and in the other two cases EPRs were extremely large (due to negligible denominators). Their inclusion would have distorted the results.

20 A "made-to-measure tariff" will be low enough not to allow any profits. Thus it would also eliminate the possibility of "fragmentation of production." However excessive tariff protection or QRs can easily allow several firms to operate even when the domestic market is too small for each to operate at minimum efficient scale. As one example, currently there are three automobile plants in Turkey, operating profitably despite a small domestic market. For a more thorough discussion of the "made-to-measure tariff" concept, see Corden (1974, pp. 219–23).

21 DRC is a measure of the social opportunity cost of earning (or saving) a unit of foreign exchange through exporting (or through import substitution). DRCs are usually derived by calculating the shadow-price value of all domestic factors of production used (directly and indirectly) per unit of foreign exchange earned or saved.

Table 2.6 Estimates of the means and variances of sectoral domestic resource costs

| | | DRC (TL per US$) | |
Sector	Years	Mean	Variance
Food and beverages	1965–9	14.11	46.06
Textiles	1966–9	13.48	43.77
Forest products	1968	10.44	n.a.
Leather products	1966	10.24	n.a.
Paper products	1965–8	13.69	67.40
Rubber products	1965–8	45.59	890.49
Plastics	1965–9	37.05	843.90
Chemicals	1965–9	14.56	16.92
Cement	1966–9	14.80	6.26
Stone and clay products	1968	10.62	n.a.
Glass and ceramics	1965–8	10.80	28.34
Iron and steel	1965–9	13.68	29.70
Iron and steel products	1966–9	93.87	43,737.12
Other metal products	1965–9	14.17	22.89
Machinery and parts	1965–9	21.81	139.27
Transport equipment	1966–9	27.78	278.88

n.a., not available.
Years indicate dates of data sources.

Source: Krueger, 1974

obtained, information on the "equilibrium" exchange rate is necessary as a reference point to distinguish high cost (import-competing) and low cost (exporting) industries. Since the official exchange rate was TL9 per US dollar in the late 1960s – and if we assume TL15 per dollar to closely approximate the equilibrium exchange rate (as assumed by Krueger) – the following observations are applicable. Almost all import-substituting industries had a mean DRC higher than TL15 per dollar. These included paper products, rubber products, plastic, iron and steel products, machinery parts, and transport equipment. Estimates show that the mean DRCs were much lower for the export-oriented industries. Just to mention a few, they were TL10.24 per dollar for leather products, TL10.44 per dollar for forest products, and TL10.62 per dollar for stone and clay products.

Krueger's estimates of firm-specific DRCs, and the sectoral means and variances of these DRC, clearly indicate that in the 1960s Turkey's trade regime led to the development of a wide range of high cost import-substituting industries. Despite statements in the five-year plans that encouragement of import-competing industries would be selective, the variances in DRCs between industries indicate that this was not true in practice. In fact, Krueger mentions cases where low and high cost firms were involved in the same activity. This shows that the trade regime was not only indiscriminate but also caused "fragmentation of production" by providing excessive protection. Estimates of the resource-allocation costs indicate that protection costs were of the order of 7.8 to 9.8 percent of the international value of Turkish GNP in 1967 (Baysan, 1974, p. 288).

The second set of DRC estimates is given in the fifth column of table 2.5. These are *ex post facto* estimates representing sectoral averages, and as such do not reveal any information about intrasectoral variations in the DRCs. (*Ex ante* estimates of DRCs could be obtained if we used data supplied in the investment project proposals submitted to development banks.) These estimates are based on data from 1973 Turkish input–output table and shadow prices obtained from a multisector programming model.[22] These sectoral DRCs show that most of the import-substituting industries had DRCs exceeding TL20 per US dollar in 1973, and that they varied by large margins. If we assume that the exchange rate of TL20 per dollar approximates the equilibrium exchange rate for 1973 these results support Krueger's findings that the trade regime promoted high cost import substitution and did so indiscriminately.

Relationship between the European Economic Community and Turkey

Before we proceed to the 1974–9 period, it is important to mention that Turkey became an associate member of the EEC in 1963 with the signing of the Ankara Agreement. This agreement provided for a preparatory stage, a transitional period, and then full membership of the EEC.

During the preparatory period, which was to cover 1963–73, the EEC granted unilateral concessions to Turkey in the form of financial assistance (US$175 million over the period 1964–9) and preferential tariffs on Turkey's traditional exports of tobacco, dried figs, raisins, and hazelnuts.

Turkey's associate membership in the EEC did not necessitate any changes in the country's foreign trade regime until 1971. After that, bilateral concessions began as part of the transitional period. In September 1971, Turkey reduced tariffs on imports from the EEC countries by 10 percent for goods that would be liberalized over 12 years and 5 percent for goods to be liberalized over 22 years. A second reduction of equal magnitude, as stipulated in the 1970 protocol, was carried out in January 1976. The EEC's concessions to Turkey included tariff reductions on cotton textile exports and some agricultural products, extension of intra-EEC status to some agricultural and industrial products, and financial assistance amounting to US$195 million. Moreover, it was agreed that free

---

22 Since fixed input–output coefficients are used, the possibility of falling average costs due to economies of scale is excluded. Similarly, dynamic externalities (for example, "learning by doing") are also ignored.

movement of workers would be gradually established between December 1, 1976, and December 1, 1986.

Since the mid-1970s, however, disagreements over Turkey's textile exports and, in particular, over the free movement of Turkish workers in Europe have continued to strain relations. On January 1, 1977, Turkey postponed the first planned alignment of her external tariff with that of the EEC *vis-à-vis* third countries. Turkey also postponed the third (10 percent) reduction, which was due in January 1978, of her customs duties on imports originating from the EEC. Thus, in effect, relations between Turkey and the EEC were frozen from 1977 until recently. Attempts are being made on both sides to revitalize the relationship.

Indeed, following the full entry into the EEC of Greece, Spain, and Portugal in the 1980s, the Turkish government has intensified its efforts to make it clear that Turkey will apply for full membership soon. However, the issue of the free movement of Turkish workers in Europe appears to be one of the major obstacles to Turkey's full membership, though the EEC countries have recently started emphasizing the "pace of democratization" in Turkey as another important issue.

External Shock and Domestic Turmoil: 1974–1979

The period 1974–9 was one of external shocks, expansionary macro-economic policies, and political instability. Economic policymaking was not consistent, nor stable, nor very rational. In a period when global growth was low, in part owing to adjustment to much higher energy costs, the Turkish economy was slow to adjust. Despite unfavorable external circumstances, successive Turkish governments attempted to maintain or even accelerate the aggregate economic growth rates achieved during the first two five-year plans.[23] For a brief time, in the heyday of oil profits "recycling," they were successful. Growth exceeded 7 percent in the three years immediately following the first oil price shock.

Because it was based on inflationary policies, heavy borrowing, and postponement of the structural adjustments called for by changing world factor prices, the growth process soon proved to be temporary. Economic performance – as measured by high trade deficits, debt, inflation, and employment, and low or negative real growth – rapidly deteriorated after 1976, culminating in a foreign debt crisis in 1979. During these years, oil import costs rose from US$222 million in 1973 to US$1,126 million in 1976

23 Between October 1973 and September 1980, seven governments took office, all of them coalitions. One government was in office for only ten days, and the longest term in office was 14 months.

and to US$1,662 million in 1979, while the share of oil imports in total imports went from 11 to 33 percent.

Meanwhile, rapid inflation eroded the real exchange rate very quickly. According to a World Bank report, the index of the real exchange rate *vis-à-vis* the US dollar fell from 100 in 1973 to 94.2 in 1974, 86.8 in 1977, 85.3 in 1978, and 75 in 1979. A similar trend was also observed in the index of the real exchange rate *vis-à-vis* the currencies of Turkey's eight largest trading partners (World Bank, 1982, vol. II, p. 8).

As the extent of overvaluation of the Turkish lira increased (despite small devaluations in 1975 and 1976 and larger ones in 1978 and 1979), Turkey's export earnings showed little real growth. In fact, exports fell in 1975 and 1977, and grew by less than 50 percent in nominal dollars in the high inflation period 1974–9. Rapid increases in imports and poor export performance created huge deficits in the commodity trade account, which reached a record level of US$4,061 million in 1977. These deficits were partially offset by workers' remittances and partly financed through large amounts of short-term borrowing and, to a lesser extent, long-term foreign borrowing (Baysan and Blitzer, 1988, appendix table 2.7).

Workers' remittances were US$1,426 million in 1976, and then stabilized around US$950–1,000 million in 1976–8 as Turkish emigrant workers held onto their earnings in the expectation of large devaluations. They also resorted to other channels (both legal and illegal) to transfer part of their remittances.[24] The large devaluation of June 11, 1979, and accompanying increases in interest rates were successful in attracting larger amounts of remittances as pent-up and normal savings were transferred. As a result, remittances rose to US$1,624 million in 1979.

The strategy followed in foreign borrowing is perhaps the best indicator of how badly the economy was being managed. Successive governments assumed a great deal of financial risk by relying heavily on short-term commercial borrowing, especially through Convertible Turkish Lira Deposit Accounts, at terms that became increasingly costly. The total external (disbursed outstanding) debt was US$3,496 million at the end of 1974, of which short-term debt accounted for only a small fraction (US$216 million). By the end of 1978, however, the total foreign debt had increased to US$14,126 million, while the short-term component had increased to US$7,469 million. Following two debt-rescheduling arrangements in 1978 and 1979, short-term debt was reduced to US$4,492 million in 1979.

---

24 It is widely believed that in the second half of the 1970s there was a parallel foreign exchange market, which was supplied by remittances. Turkish importers financed their underinvoiced imports using this unofficial market. Estimates of the volume of transactions in the parallel market are not available. However, its flourishing existence was an indication of overvaluation of the Turkish lira and foreign exchange stringency.

Table 2.7 Index of liberalization and changes in the foreign trade regime, 1974–1979

	1974	1975	1976	1977	1978	1979
Index of liberalization	5	5	4	4	3	2
Import regime						
Stamp duty (%)	9–9.5				22.5–25	25–40
Guarantee deposits (%)	5–10		10–20		5–15–30	From Jun 11
Export regime		From 1975			From Mar 2	
Indirect tax rebates (%)	10–20–30–40	5–10–20–25–30			10–15–20–	5–10–15–20
					25	5–10–15
					5–10–15–20	
Foreign exchange						
Official rate and		From Oct 28	From Apr 2	From Sep 21	From Mar 1	From Jun 11
devaluations (TL per US$)	13.85	15.30	16.40	19.25	25.50	47.10
Real exchange rate *vis-à-vis*						
US$ (1973 = 100)	92.8	92.8	93.3	89.5	85.3	75.0
Foreign debt (year-end)						
Total debt (outstanding						
and disbursed only)						
(million US$)	3,496	4,734	7,313	11,405	14,126	15,791
Short-term debt (million US$)	216	1,398	3,441	6,600	7,469	4,492

Sources: Official Gazette, various issues; World Bank, 1980, 1982

Annual Levels of the Index

The basic nature of the foreign trade regime did not change in 1974–9. After the brief experience with liberalized import and export regulations in 1974–6, controls were intensified and additional measures were undertaken to restrict imports in response to severe balance-of-payments difficulties. Throughout this period, but especially in the second half, the extent of overvaluation was much greater than in the period 1963–73. This created an even greater bias in favor of import-substituting industries by raising implicit nominal protection.

Therefore an index average of 3.8 is considered to be appropriate for the entire period. Increased overvaluation of the Turkish lira and increased import restrictions in the second half of the 1970s warrant lower values of the index than in either the 1950s or the 1960s. The successive reductions (or slope) of the index reflect increasing overvaluation as well as the explicit policy measures of the late 1970s aimed at restricting imports.

Table 2.7 summarizes some of the important foreign trade policy changes. No major changes were effected in the tariff schedule or in the tax rebate system for exports. The stamp duty was raised to 25 percent in 1978 from its previous level of 9–9.5 percent. Guarantee deposit rates were generally increased in 1978, although the bias against the liberalized list categories was maintained. In 1979 the latter rates were raised once more and, in addition, one bias was removed by subjecting quota list items to new high rates of 25–40 percent. Minor changes were introduced in the indirect tax rebates for exports in 1975, 1978, and 1979. Ironically rates were reduced by about 5 percentage points on each occasion, thus lowering existing EERs for exports.

The Turkish lira was devalued by small amounts in 1975, 1976, and 1977. On March 1, 1978, the rate was changed to TL25.50 per US dollar from its previous rate of TL19.25 per dollar, set on September 21, 1977. After a small devaluation on April 10, 1979, a major devaluation was announced on June 11, 1979. The exchange rate of TL47.10 per dollar was applied to all transactions. Crude petroleum and fertilizer imports were subject to a lower rate of TL35.70 per dollar, and the rate was set at TL35.00 per dollar for traditional exports.

Quantitative Indicators

Data prepared by the SPO on realized imports under the liberalized list and the quota list were used to calculate the average value of imports per commodity category to find the pattern of permissible imports. The results are presented in table 2.8. The values of actual imports are given in the second and fifth columns, and the number of commodity categories

Table 2.8 Imports, 1974–1979, and number of commodity categories under each import list

Year	Liberalized lists I and II			Imports (million US$)	Quota list	
	Imports excluding oil	Number of commodity categories	Average value of each category (million US$)		Number of commodity categories	Average value of each category (million US$)
1974	1,761	1,530	1.151	697	383	1.820
1975	2,108	1,541	1.368	1,163	456	2.550
1976	2,193	1,571	1.396	1,143	445	2.569
1977	2,591	1,537	1.682	1,160	383	3.029
1978	1,859	1,487	1.250	784	368	2.130
1979	1,735	1,620	1.071	973	345	2.820

Sources: SPO, Annual Program, various issues; Official Gazette

included in the liberalized list (I and II) and the quota list are listed in the third and sixth columns respectively. (Oil imports were excluded from the liberalized list so as not to distort the results.)

The figures show a general expansion in imports between 1974 and 1977, when both the total and average values of permissible commodity categories increased. However, as import restrictions intensified, the trend reversed in 1978 and 1979. A fall in the average value of permissible commodity categories under the liberalized list was observed in both years, whereas the average value of quota list categories increased in 1979. The ratio of the value of quota list imports to liberalized list imports was 0.55 in 1975 and 0.52 in 1976. The ratio fell to 0.45 in 1977 and 0.42 in 1978, and then rose to 0.56 in 1979. Thus the data do not show any apparent shift in the value of imports in favor of quota list items except in 1979.

To determine whether there was any shift toward the quota list, the experiment that Krueger conducted for the 1960s was repeated using the same sample of 110 commodity categories. The import programs of 1973, 1975, 1977, and 1979 were examined to trace the distribution patterns of these 110 categories. Table 2.9 presents the results. They do not show any shift toward the quota list. Instead, the number of commodities placed on the liberalized lists increased from 31 in 1973 to 38 in 1977. It seems that this happened because goods that were split between the two categories were often transferred to the liberalized lists completely (see table 2.9, fourth column), whereas the number of commodity categories on the quota list fell from 17 in 1973 to 13 in subsequent years. Out of 110 commodity categories, 46 were prohibited between 1973 and 1977. The 1979 results show a sharp increase in the number of commodity categories that were prohibited. Some categories were removed from the liberalized lists.

Table 2.9 Distribution of a representative sample of 110
commodities by import category, 1973–1979

Year	Liberalized lists I and II	Quota list	Liberalized and quota lists	Prohibited commodities	Total
1973	31	17	16	46	110
1975	37	13	14	46	110
1977	38	13	13	46	110
1979	32	13	11	54	110

The reduction in the number of permissible commodity categories substantiates the earlier statement that in 1979 the import regime became highly restrictionist.

Evaluation of the trade regime based on estimates of sectoral EPRs and DRCs for 1973 also holds for the 1974–9 period. This is because there were no major changes in the latter period to alter the protective nature of the tariff structure. If anything, highly protected industries were accorded additional "nominal" protection through the increase in the stamp duty in 1978. Implicit nominal protection levels were still much higher owing to continued application of QRs and prohibitions.

Available estimates of the sectoral (weighted) average nominal tariff rates also show that the structure of tariff rates did not change over the period 1974–9. The unweighted economy-wide average nominal tariff rate was about 60 percent for imports from non-EEC countries and 49 percent for imports originating from the EEC, the latter being reduced as a result of the 1973 and 1976 tariff cuts (Baysan and Blitzer, 1988, appendix table 2.8).

Economic Liberalization: 1980–1984

As Turkey's economic and political problems intensified in 1979, the need to undertake immediate and substantial reforms in economic management became crucial. Turkey's creditors were insisting on steps to reduce the trade deficit and to improve efficiency in resource use. The government also became convinced that fundamental changes were required.

The short-term objectives were to reduce the rate of inflation and improve the balance-of-payments situation. Since 1980, a series of reforms have reduced subsidies to the SEEs, tightened the public budget, and eased bureaucratic controls on foreign exchange transactions. The government is also attempting to promote private investment (domestic and foreign), in part through reductions in public investment and central planning.

The January 1980 program and subsequent measures indicated a definite and determined shift toward an outward-oriented strategy. For the first time, the government made trade liberalization a major policy priority. That is why, for the first time, the level of the liberalization index increased to 10 and above in the post-1980 period.

By 1979 the index had sunk to its lowest level, 2. In light of the devaluation of January 1980 and the government's decision to establish a more liberal trade regime, the index increased to 6 for the year 1980. The index was not set higher because the government preferred not to announce any time schedule for further reforms (thus raising doubts about the credibility of the government's commitment) and because no significant import liberalization steps were announced in 1980.

The government decision to devalue the lira from TL47.10 to TL70 per US dollar occurred on January 24, 1980. The new rate applied to all international transactions except imports of fertilizers, for which the rate was set at TL55 per dollar. In subsequent months the lira depreciated further, and by December the exchange rate was about TL90 per dollar. Thus, by the end of 1980, the lira had depreciated in real terms by 3 percent against the US dollar and by 5 percent *vis-à-vis* the currencies of Turkey's eight largest trading partners compared with its 1973 level. This took place despite a rate of inflation in excess of 100 percent.

At the same time, exporters were granted tax exemptions on raw materials and intermediate products imported under the foreign exchange allocation scheme. Indirect tax rebate rates were also reduced across the board. The only important change immediately affecting imports was the reduction of guarantee deposit rates by 10 percent for liberalized list I items, and by 15–20 percent for the commodity categories under liberalized list II and the quota list. Meanwhile, the number of commodity categories on the quota list was reduced from 345 in 1979 to 312 in 1980. These measures constituted only a limited relaxation of import restrictions.

The increase in the index to 8 for 1981 reflects additional liberalization measures. In January 1981 the quota list was abolished, and most of its commodity categories were transferred to liberalized list II. (Some – amounting to a tenth of the total value of the quota list in 1980 – were transferred to liberalized list I.) At the same time, some transfers were made from liberalized list II to liberalized list I. Thus liberalized list I items increased from 653 in 1980 to 942 in 1981, and liberalized list II items fell from 958 in 1980 to 835 in 1981. Simultaneously, the guarantee deposit rates for liberalized list I commodity categories were reduced from 15–30 to 10–20 percent. On the export side, incentives were granted, including income tax reductions and reduced (subsidized) interest rates on credits for export-oriented investments. Indirect tax rebate rates were increased by 5–10 percentage points in May.

The Turkish lira depreciated still further in early 1981 with biweekly adjustments in exchange rates, and daily adjustments have been in effect since May of that year. The adjustments, in principle, compensate for fluctuations in "purchasing power parity."[25] By December the official exchange rate exceeded TL130 per US dollar. Consequently, between the third quarter of 1980 and the third quarter of 1981 the lira depreciated in real terms against the US dollar by 17 percent but appreciated *vis-à-vis* the currencies of Turkey's major trading partners by about 10 percent.

Because the pace of reform slowed after 1981, the index increased by only 1 in 1982. In that year there were no major changes in the foreign trade regime. The number of commodities on liberalized list II was reduced from 835 to 821, and duty exemptions were granted to 11 commodity categories, including corn, rice, soybeans, oil cakes, ferro-alloys, and arc electrodes. The duty rate on common plate glass was reduced to 20 percent. At the same time, the latter groups of commodities, plus animal oils and fats, coffee beans, vegetable oils, cocoa, and cast iron, became subject to a newly introduced commodity-specific import surcharge.[26] Export incentives remained unchanged, except for some increases in indirect tax rebate rates.

The index is set at 8 for 1983, a reduction of one point from 1982. This reflects an increasingly stringent foreign exchange situation and resulting delays in the issuance of import licenses. In 1983 there was a relaxation of the austerity measures before the general elections in November; these intensified inflationary pressures and increased the overvaluation of the Turkish lira. Consequently, the balance-of-payments situation worsened. The continuous daily adjustments were not large enough to compensate for Turkey's higher inflation rate, then in excess of 40 percent. The 1983 import program contained only minor changes, including reductions in the guarantee deposit rates ranging from 2.5 to 5 percentage points and the addition of several more items to the list of commodities subject to import surcharges.[27]

In November 1983 the first general election was held since the military intervention of September 12, 1980. The Motherland Party, after winning a majority in Parliament, formed a government that took office under the leadership of Prime Minister Turgut Ozal. The new government declared its determination to pursue the outward-oriented foreign trade policy initiated in 1980 (when Ozal was deputy prime minister for the economy). The government also announced that additional measures would be taken to integrate Turkey into the global economy.

The import and export programs for 1984 were issued on December 10, 1983. Although there were no major changes in the export regime, the

---

25 A trade-weighted basked of currencies has been used to calculate daily adjustments. However, the weights have never been announced publicly.

26 A new import list was introduced in 1982 that included 23 commodity categories that were subject to the payment of commodity-specific import taxes (called the "fund").

27 These included hides, merino wool, power cells, batteries, and video cassettes.

Table 2.10 A sample of 1984 changes in customs duty and production in tax rates

Product	Old rates Customs duty	Old rates Production tax	New rates Customs duty	New rates Production tax
Lanolin	40	0	30	0
Fatty acids	40	15	20	12
Glycerol	40	15	20	12
Sodium chloride	15	15	10	12
Carbon black	30	18	10	12
Nitric acid	40	18	20	12
Boric acid	30	18	10	12
Ammonium	25	18	20	12
Sodium	15	18	20	12
Sodium perborate	50	18	10	12
Nitrous hydrocarbons	50	18	20	12
Sorbitol and mannitol	15	18	10	12
Acetone	35	18	20	12
Acetic acid	50	18	15	12
Citric acid	30	18	15	12
Dyes (except indigo)	40	15	20	12
Ink	9	15	30	12
Insecticides	40	15	20	10
Laminated products	50	25	0	0
Polypropylene	50	25	15	18
Rubber tires and tubes	40	8	50	5
Kraft paper	35	20	30	15
Tracing paper	15	20	5	15
Writing paper	60	20	30	15
Viscose rayon	50	12	25	12
Woollen textiles	100	18	20	12
Unfinished synthetics	25	12	30	20
Finished synthetics	150	18	50	12
Silk and cotton knits	125	18	40	12
Glass envelopes	50	15	0	0
Fabrics of glass yarns	100	15	20	15
Blister copper	30	30	1	20
Copper foil	45	30	10	5
Copper tubing	40	30	10	20
Aluminium sheets	20	30	10	20
Flash and water heaters	60	25	75	18
Dishwashing machines	25	8	60	18
Radio transmitters	50	25	30	10
Transistors	10	18	0	0
Mine detectors	50	25	0	0
Battery carbons	35	25	30	18
Electron microscopes	15	25	1	5
Electro-therapy equipment	28	25	20	0
Sound recorders	60	20	20	15
Recorder tapes	60	20	30	10
Turntable cartridges	40	20	10	10
Arithmetic average	43.74	18.91	20.48	11.35
Weighted average	44.22	18.03	23.12	10.65

Source: Official Gazette, December 29, 1983

1984 import program included some alterations in the import lists and tariff rates. These were a major step toward liberalization in the import regime.

Liberalization lists I and II were abolished, and a negative list system was introduced. The negative system included a prohibited list (List I) and a list of import commodities subject to permission (List II). The prohibited list contained some 219 commodity categories, mostly exports, consumer goods, and antiques. The permission list included mostly import substitutes. Commodities not on either list I or list II were automatically considered as liberalized (free) import commodities.

However, about 77 liberalized import commodities were subject to a commodity-specific import surcharge. These taxes, which have been imposed on a limited basis since 1982, effectively increased the total import tax on most of these commodities. Commodities subject to these taxes were mostly consumer goods, including dairy products, seed oils, vegetable oils, animal fats, corn, coffee beans, and household appliances. Customs duties and production tax rates were also altered for a large number of commodity categories. Rates were reduced simultaneously for about 331 commodity categories, mostly at the six-digit level of disaggregation. The production tax rate was lowered for another 56 import commodities.

Reductions were granted to a wide range of commodities, including consumer goods and import substitutes. The new and old rates of customs duties and production taxes for a representative sample of imports are compared in table 2.10. Tariff reductions ranged from 5 to 100 percent, which is substantial. Average reductions were about 20 percent for customs duties and 8 percent for production taxes. At the same time, customs duty rates were raised on 62 commodity categories, mostly consumer durables. Note, however, that most goods in the latter group had earlier enjoyed absolute protection through import prohibitions. Hence the increase in their tariff rates might be interpreted as a move toward eventual greater reliance on price policy to protect domestic industry.

These substantial reductions in duties and production tax rates, and the explicit listing of prohibited commodities, represented important steps toward further liberalization of the import regime. Given both these recent changes and the new government's declaration that the outward orientation of trade policy will continue, the liberalization index for 1984 was set at 13, a full 5 points above the 1983 level and by far the highest in recent Turkish economic history. The increase to 14 for 1985 reflects continuation of import liberalization but at a somewhat slower pace.

3
The 1970 Devaluation and its Aftermath

In August 1970 a series of economic reforms was announced in Turkey. The basic objective was to overcome balance-of-payments problems, which had become increasingly severe. The centerpiece was a substantial devaluation, which raised the parity rate by 66.7 percent from TL9 to TL15 per US dollar. This can be considered a liberalization episode in the sense that it might have both changed the domestic terms of trade between exportable and importable goods and reduced excess demand for foreign exchange.

In addition to the devaluation there were also a number of changes in trade policy which were designed to minimize the inflationary impact of the devaluation and to reinforce the incentives for exports. The 1970 events were also a liberalization in that, prior to devaluation, a multiple exchange rate system had existed through a subsidy tax system that created several official *de facto* rates affecting different balance-of-payments transactions.

These reforms, however, were not intended to constitute a major change in the inward-looking nature of the Turkish economy. Nor did they signify a policy shift toward increased reliance on the private sector. There was no major reshuffling of commodities between the liberalized lists (I and II) and the quota list. In fact, the import regime retained its basic feature of heavy reliance on explicit QRs, implicit QRs through import licensing, and outright import prohibitions to protect import-competing industries.

As with the devaluation of 1958, the 1970 actions occurred in the context of a stabilization program intended to correct imbalances. Neither the 1970 package nor government pronouncements suggested that the government intended to liberalize foreign trade activities or that the devaluation was to be the first step on the road to a major restructuring of economic management policies.[1]

---

1 In interviews with former SPO officials, the authors were told that the Demirel government had intended to reduce the bias against exports and export sectors and that, as a part of the long-term objective to diversify export industries, the SPO intensified its efforts to prepare export-oriented investment projects to be presented to the World Bank as early as 1967. The interviews also revealed that the customs duties were not reduced in 1970 because Turkey wanted to retain bargaining leverage in its forthcoming negotiations with the EEC.

Despite this fact, the conditions under which the August 1970 devaluation package was undertaken make examining the post-devaluation period a worthwhile exercise. We refer to the continuous and heavy reliance on QRs for protection and import restriction purposes (perhaps unique among Mediterranean Basin countries) both before and after the devaluation. Note that the relative price effects (and therefore the resource-allocation effects) of a devaluation undertaken concurrent with QRs are quite different from those of a devaluation undertaken concurrent with QRs are quite different from those of a devaluation undertaken in the absence of QRs. In the latter case, we would normally expect the relative domestic prices of tradeables to increase *vis-à-vis* nontradeables. In the former case, if the devaluation succeeds in expanding foreign exchange earnings and thus allows more imports into the country, the size of "scarcity rents" received by importers may decrease as implicit protection for import-competing products falls. Other things being equal, that would increase the domestic relative prices of exports in relation to imports. Under such conditions we could not predict the direction of changes in the domestic prices of tradeables relative to nontradeables, since that would depend on relevant demand and supply elasticities and on the tradeable input intensities of nontradeable commodities.

Hence the possibility of such a relative price effect after the 1970 devaluation is the major reason for examining the early 1970s. This serves the objectives of the project, one of which is to identify those industries producing tradeables that show strong production and employment responses to relative price changes.

Economic Circumstances when the Policy was Introduced

The causes of the severe balance-of-payments difficulties of the late 1960s lie in the domestic economic policies of that period. A 7 percent growth target, coupled with the import-substituting industrialization strategy, increased the demand for raw material and capital goods imports. Actual imports increased by 11.5 percent in 1968, while export proceeds fell by 4.6 percent in the same year (table 3.1). To reduce the pressure on the balance of payments, the government, rather than adjusting the exchange rate, chose in the late 1960s to adopt a more restrictive import regime. The stamp duty on imports rose from 5 percent in 1963 to 10 percent in 1967, and the wharf tax from 2.5 to 5 percent. As the foreign exchange situation worsened, the stamp duty was further raised to 15 percent in 1968 and to 25 percent in 1969. Simultaneously, the import advance (or guarantee) deposit rates were increased several times between 1967 and August 1970, rising in range from 10–100 percent of the c.i.f. values of imports to 20–150 percent. Import growth held at 4.8 percent in 1969, while the

Table 3.1 Commodity trade, net aid flows, and external debt, 1967–1970 (million US dollars)

	1967	1968	1969	1970
Imports	685	764	801	948
Exports	520	496	537	588
Balance	−165	−268	−264	−360
Aid flow	221	272	321	479
Debt service	133	106	152	205
Net aid flow	88	166	169	274
Workers' remittances	93	107	141	273
External debt (outstanding and disbursed)	1,441	n.a.	n.a.	1,911
Trade price indices (dollar prices, 1968 = 100)				
Exports	n.a.	100	100.5	99.2
Imports	n.a.	100	101.4	102.5
Terms of trade	n.a.	100	99.1	96.8
Real GDP growth of Turkey's major trading partners (%)				
United States	5.78	9.20	8.12	5.15
United Kingdom	2.83	4.19	1.38	2.11
West Germany	−0.16	6.00	7.45	5.13
France	4.76	4.21	6.95	5.74
Italy	7.12	6.65	6.08	5.30
Black-market price of US$ as a proportion of the official price	Dec 1.41	Dec 1.52	Dec 1.53	Mar 1.54

n.a., not available.

Sources: SPO, Annual Program, 1980; IMF, 1981a, b, 1984; Pick Publishing Corporation, 1972

growth of real GDP that year was 5.7 percent (Baysan and Blitzer, 1988, appendix table 3.1).

The authorities, through various measures, also tried to encourage foreign exchange earnings. The tourist buying rate and the rate applicable to workers' remittances were raised from TL9 and TL11.43 per US dollar in 1967 to TL12 per US dollar in 1968. The SPO expanded the number of nontraditional exports eligible for tax rebates and at the same time announced increases in the rebate rates in February, April, and September 1968. In addition, an export credit program and an import replenishment scheme were introduced in September 1968. Export earnings, responding to higher EERs, increased by 8.3 percent in 1969. Despite the measures taken to discourage import demand and to expand foreign exchange earnings, the balance-of-payments situation continued to deteriorate. As the foreign exchange shortage became increasingly acute, the premium on import licenses increased continuously from TL4–6 per US dollar in 1964–5 to TL9–15 per dollar in 1968–9. Delays in the issuance of import licenses were about five months from 1965 through 1968, and then as long as eight months in 1969 and early 1970. There were also long delays in foreign exchange transfers, even after import licenses had been issued.

Rumors of a devaluation began as early as 1967, and by 1969 there was open debate on the issue as overvaluation of the lira increased and its external value began to fall.[2] The ratio of the black-market rate to the official exchange rate increased from 1.41 in December 1967 to 1.52 in December 1968, 1.53 in December 1969, and 1.54 by the end of March 1970 (table 3.1). Because of its importance in overall export performance, it is worth noting that agricultural output stagnated in 1967 and grew only by 1.4 percent in 1968 and 1.1 percent in 1969. Even if Turkey had experienced greater agricultural growth in the late 1960s, it would still be difficult to determine whether export proceeds from traditional exports (which amounted to about 61–5 percent of commodity export earnings during the late 1960s) would have been larger. Even if they had been, the increment would not have been large enough to resolve Turkey's balance-of-payment difficulties. The size of the increase would have been limited by strong domestic demand, unfavorable EERs for traditional exports, and low income elasticities of foreign import demand for these products (mainly cotton, tobacco, hazelnuts, and raisins).

External factors in the second half of the 1960s were, if anything, favorable. Turkey's major trading partners experienced fairly high growth rates during this period (table 3.1). Terms of trade worsened, but not enough to account for the economic difficulties that Turkey experienced in the period.

Political Circumstances

The pre-devaluation period was dominated by social unrest and political instability. Under the leadership of Prime Minister Demirel, the Justice Party returned to power in October 1969 with a comfortable majority in the Parliament. However, the government faced both severe economic problems and serious social unrest. Clashes between right-wing and left-wing extremists, the closing of universities, and street demonstrations were widespread. Political violence continued through 1970 and into early 1971. Severe social unrest, allegations of corruption, continuing violence, and internal opposition within the Justice Party all began to weaken the Demirel government. The proposed 1970 budget was defeated in Febru-

2 The ambitious economic growth targets exceeded what could be reached without deficit financing. The government increasingly resorted to deficit financing. Money supply (M1) increased by 13.7 percent in 1968 and by 16.7 percent in 1969. Although the official figures show increases of 7.8 percent, 3.2 percent, and 7.2 percent in wholesale prices in 1967, 1968, and 1969 respectively, it was widely believed that the latter figures (heavily biased downward owing to prevailing price controls) failed to reflect the actual extent of inflation.

ary; some Justice Party duties (opposing Demirel's economic program and his bid for a devaluation) voted against it. A temporary budget went into effect, and after 25 Justice Party deputies defected and formed a new party Demirel formed a new government. The government's tax proposal was vetoed by the president. Thus, by spring 1970 the political situation was extremely unstable, and the government's economic program was in jeopardy.

Although the IMF and the OECD had been pressuring the Demirel government to devalue the lira, the timing of the devaluation in 1970 was probably more influenced by political developments in the post-election period. Demirel had been expected to announce a devaluation after the October 1969 elections, but apparently faced serious opposition from within his own party and did not. However, when the 1970 devaluation was announced, it provoked little reaction because attention was focused almost entirely on the political situation.

The August 1970 Devaluation Package

Exchange Rate and Other Trade Policy Changes

The most important component of the 1970 program was the nominal devaluation, which raised the parity rate from TL9 to TL15 per US dollar. A uniform exchange rate system for almost all foreign transactions replaced the existing multiple exchange rates. However, a lower rate of TL12 per dollar was applied to nine traditional export items. These were cotton, tobacco, hazelnuts, raisins, dried figs, olive oil, oil cakes, molasses, and fig cakes. This special lower rate for traditional exports was gradually raised and in August 1973 was aligned with the basic official rate, thus eliminating the temporary (incremental) bias against traditional exports.[3] Given that several official exchange rates existed prior to the devaluation, the effective nominal devaluation ranged from about 11 percent for purchases of foreign exchange by Turkish citizens for travel abroad to 66.7 percent for commodity trade transactions.

3 Of these, cotton, tobacco, hazelnuts, and raisins are major export items, proceeds from which amounted to 61 percent of total merchandise export earnings in 1969 and 1970. In defending the lower rate set for the nine agricultural exports, officials argued that, even at this overvalued exchange rate, Turkey would continue to retain its competitive edge in traditional exports. Yet a lower exchange rate for traditional exports would prevent the realization of large windfall gains by traders and farmers, thus avoiding additional inflationary pressures. However, the government had promised to gradually align the special export rate with the basic official rate.

The Import Regime

The 1970 program did not include any major change in the import regime. Except for duty exemptions granted to some iron and steel products, customs duty rates remained the same. However, there were two alterations. The stamp duty, levied on the c.i.f. value of imports, was lowered from its 1969 level of 25 percent to 10 percent. Also, advance deposit rates, applicable to the Turkish lira equivalent of the c.i.f. value of imports, were cut by about half from their 1969 range of 20–150 percent. Both changes were intended to lower the landed cost of imports and to relax an import regime that had become extremely restrictive in response to the balance-of-payments crisis of the late 1960s.

Export Promotion Policy

The changes in export promotion that accompanied the 1970 devaluation included (a) a simplification of the tax rebate system (b) additional measures to increase the effectiveness of the export credit scheme (c) the establishment of two funds to support the export credit program and (d) allocating more foreign exchange for the import of inputs by manufacturing exporters. These changes notwithstanding, the tax rebate system continued to be the major aspect of the export promotion scheme in the post-devaluation period.

There were doubts about the effectiveness of the new export credit scheme from the beginning.[4] Although the new system allowed large subsidies to lending banks and to borrowing exporters, and two funds were established in support of these measures, it was not clear exactly when and how the banks were to receive the subsidies, how the borrowers were to be classified, or how much credit was to be made available through the funds. Under the new subsidy scheme the lending banks were accorded a subsidy of 0.7 percentage points, thus raising the lending rate to 12.2 percent, as opposed to the nonpreferential short-term credit rate of 11.5 percent. The 0.7 point difference would hardly have been an incentive for the banks to extend export credits, particularly considering the potential delays they faced before receiving the subsidies.

Moreover, the banks could receive returns higher than the legal maximum rate allowed on preferential loans through hidden charges. Therefore the incentive margin of 0.7 is rather deceptive. Whatever export credits were actually extended during the 1970s by the banks probably included some hidden charges – either that, or state banks rather than private banks were the main lenders.

---

4 See, for example, Fry (1972, pp. 118–21) and Yaser (1972, pp. 12–15).

Owing to small alterations in the import surcharges and the export tax rebate system, changes in the import and export EERs effected by the August 1970 program were less than the increase in the official parity rate. EERs for imports increased by 54 percent as the stamp duty on imports was reduced from 25 to 10 percent, and EERs for exports increased, on average, by 65.5 percent owing to a slight reduction in the tax rebate rates.

Domestic Policy Changes

Two changes in fiscal policy were introduced in the 1970 devaluation. The first was the announcement of changes in some indirect tax rates and the introduction of new taxes. The second was a new law on government employees.

The production tax on some petroleum products and on the assembly industries was raised, as were the stamp duties levied on contracts, deeds, petitions, securities, and so forth. Legal fees and the prices of official documents (such as identity cards, passports, and notary papers) also rose. Alterations were introduced in the real estate purchase tax and the inheritance tax.

A number of new taxes were introduced at the same time. These included a vehicle purchase tax, an enterprise operating tax imposed on sales of certain services and luxury goods, a real estate appreciation tax, a soccer pool tax, and a tax on new construction.

A new personnel law, which became effective in December 1970, raised the salaries of civil servants substantially. Indeed, there is reason to believe that the tax measures introduced in August were undertaken to expand public sector revenues to (at least partially) finance anticipated increases in current expenditures, such as rises for civil servants.

In the monetary sphere, some changes in interest rates were announced in August 1970, and these became effective in September. Interest rates on loans were increased across the board by 1–1.5 percent, from the 8–10.5 percent to the 9–11.5 percent range. The only exception was a 3.5 percent increase, from 7 to 10.5 percent, for medium- and long-term agricultural credit. Simultaneously, a complex system of subsidies payable to both banks and borrowers in priority sectors were announced. The new system had 28 types of subsidies. Note also that the preferential export and agricultural credits were exempted from taxes and stamp duties normally payable by borrowers. The aim was to encourage banks to use their own resources in selected credit areas. The government did not make clear how the new interest rates were determined, nor why it preferred to institute a complicated subsidy scheme that was bound to create administrative difficulties.

Changes in maximum interest rates on deposits also became effective in September. The sight deposit rate for individuals was held constant at

3 percent but lowered from 2 to 1 percent for government, commercial, and interbank deposits. Time deposit rates were increased substantially. The rate on time deposits of 6–12 months was raised from 5–6 percent, and on time deposits of more than 12 months from 6–6.5 to 9 percent.

Finally, some price increases were also announced. These included increases in the prices of sugar, sugar beet, and fertilizers, and increases in the support prices for cotton, wheat, hazelnuts, raisins, figs, olive oil, and pistachio nuts. The latter increases ranged from 2.6 percent for wheat to 29.3 percent for hazelnuts.

Leaving aside the issue of whether the salary and price increases were warranted, the extent and timing of these increases were somewhat unfortunate and naturally raised some doubts about the government's intention to pursue noninflationary policies, since the same government also made a commitment, through official pronouncements, that measures would be taken to control inflation. It was emphasized by the government that the prices of SEE products would not be increased, and that all available means would be used to discourage manufacturers and importers from "baseless" price increases.

The policy changes described above were implemented in a matter of a few months. There is no evidence that implemented magnitudes and planned magnitudes differed. The severity of the QR system was reduced after the devaluation. In the immediate post-devaluation period, devaluation-related foreign aid inflows and the fairly quick response of workers' remittances allowed the authorities to be more liberal in issuing import licenses. Merchandise exports responded strongly, and remittances continued to grow. Thus it was the improved foreign exchange situation which encouraged the government to relax import controls. However, it is important to remember that the structure of the QR system did not change, nor was it intended to change.

Street violence continued throughout 1970 and in the early part of 1971, undermining the government's authority, and there was military intervention in March 1971. The forced resignation of the Demirel government was due in large measure to social unrest rather than devaluation. However, political events of this period did have an effect on overall economic performance and the rapidity with which the benefits of the devaluation eroded. Between March 1971 and October 1973 four coalition governments took office, each announcing intentions to implement major economic reforms. Although the violence stopped after martial law was imposed in March 1971, political instability continued.

Economic Performance Following the August 1970 Actions

Prices

The general price level rose very sharply after devaluation. Annualized increases in wholesale prices were approximately 21 percent within three months of the devaluation, 26 percent within six months, and 23 percent within a year. The consumer price index and the GDP deflator showed similar price movements (table 3.2). Although there was a slowdown in inflation in 1972, perhaps partly because of a 30 percent real increase in imports, inflation accelerated again in subsequent years, reaching rates in excess of 20 percent.

Table 3.2 Annualized percentage change in general price levels following the 1970 devaluation (annualized percentage changes)

After Jul 1970	Consumer prices	Wholesale prices	Year	GDP deflator
In 3 months	29.5	20.8	1970	11.8
In 6 months	26.4	26.2	1971	18.3
In 9 months	19.6	22.8	1972	16.3
In 1 year	27.7	23.3	1973	22.0
In 2 years	23.5	22.5	1974	28.5

Sources: Central Bank, Annual Report, various issues; IMF, 1981a

Several demand–pull and cost–push factors contributed to inflationary pressures in the post-devaluation period. The government's current expenditure increased by 46.4 percent in 1971 over the 1970 level, and when collective bargaining with SEE workers resulted in wage increases, government payments to SEEs also increased. The price increases announced in August 1970 were followed by other increases in the spring of 1971. In May, June, and July the government announced the following price increases for SEE products: 115 percent for industrial coke, 7–22 percent for cement, 7 percent for fuel, 45 percent for electricity to municipalities, 12–22 percent for steel, and 25–50 percent for paper. The price increases must have caused some cost–push inflation in the early 1970s. Also in 1971, agricultural support prices were increased once again. Some of the increases were 18.5 percent for cotton and olive oil, 13.3 percent for hazelnuts, 17.5 percent for dried figs, 6.3 percent for wheat, and 4.3 percent for raisins. These increases, coupled with an unusually good harvest in 1971, also contributed to inflation.[5] To finance large agricultural purchases

5 Real agricultural output increased by 13 percent.

and other payments to SEEs, the government resorted to large borrowings from the Central Bank. Public sector borrowing reached TL3,574 million in 1971, an increase of 43 percent over the 1970 level.

The other factor that might have increased inflationary pressures in this period was a substantial increase in workers' remittances, which in 1971 increased by 94 percent over 1969, reaching a level of US$273 million. Remittance inflow continued to increase at rates of 72.5 percent, 57 percent, and 60 percent in 1971, 1972, and 1973 respectively. It is likely that Turkish lira counterparts of these remittances increased consumer demand, thus putting upward pressure on prices.

Monetary expansion was substantial and large enough to sustain high rates of inflation in the post-devaluation period. As the authorities chose not to sterilize Turkish lira counterparts of remittances and relied on Central Bank borrowing to finance deficits, the money supply expanded dramatically. Within one and two years of the devaluation, the cumulative increases in M1 were 29.4 percent and 58.8 percent respectively.

However, it should also be pointed out that the larger inflow of remittances, while augmenting domestic demand and thereby contributing to inflationary pressures, allowed imports to increase and thus helped dampen these pressures. Another factor contributing to the containment of inflationary pressures was the large spread between the Central Bank's selling price of TL15.15 per US dollar and the buying price of TL12 per dollar set for traditional exports.

The inflationary undertakings of the government during the post-devaluation period provide some grounds for arguing that the August 1970 devaluation itself was not the cause of high rates of inflation in the early 1970s. Obviously, the devaluation increased the landed costs of imports. However, the increased availability of foreign exchange in the post-devaluation period permitted substantial increases in real imports: 17 percent in 1970, 16 percent in 1971, and 30 percent in 1972. Thus, whereas scarcity premiums on import licenses were as large as TL9–15 per US dollar prior to the devaluation, these more or less disappeared after the devaluation. Also, the ratio of black-market to official exchange rate, a good indicator of foreign exchange stringency and the average extent of scarcity rents, fell from 1.53 in December 1969 to the range 1.01–1.08 in the post-devaluation period. Therefore there is reason to believe that the domestic prices of imported goods did not rise much because scarcity premiums were squeezed owing to increased supplies. Also, the disappearance of "rents" on imported raw materials and intermediates probably reduced the extent of devaluation-related cost–push effects in the domestic industries that used those inputs. In addition, those industries that depended heavily on imported materials, and therefore had experienced low capacity utilization in the late 1960s owing to severe foreign exchange stringency, were probably able to improve their capacity utilization rates and thereby to reduce average costs in the post-devaluation period. Indeed, there is some indirect evidence that import-competing industries showed relatively lower price increases during the period 1970–3 than those producing exportables.[6] Price increases were lower in import-competing industries, such as rubber products, electrical machinery, and transport equipment, than in such export-oriented manufacturing industries as textiles and apparel, leather products, and food and beverages. Note also that the first oil shock and expenditures related to the Cyprus intervention in 1974 led to the larger price increases in 1973 and 1974.

Changes in Exchange Rates after August 1970

Nominal Exchange Rates

After the August 1970 devaluation, two things occurred that affected nominal exchange rates. The first was related to the gradual alignment of the special export rate of TL12 per US dollar with the offical rate. The rate, which was applicable to exports of nine agricultural products including Turkey's traditional exports, was changed, as promised by the government, to TL13 per US dollar in January 1971 for tobacco, and on July 9, 1971, for the rest. Subsequently, the special exchange rate was raised to TL14 per US dollar for hazelnuts on March 31, 1972, and on August 1, 1973, for the rest.

The second change involved a revaluation of the Turkish lira against the US dollar. Following the devaluation of the dollar against major currencies in the latter part of 1971, Turkey announced a new parity rate of TL14 per US dollar in December 1971, with a spread of TL0.3 between the buying and selling rates.

While revaluation of the Turkish lira in late 1971 reduced EERs for both exports and imports,[7] the gradual increases in the special export rates for

6 The government's price intervention in the agriculture, mining, utilities, tobacco, paper, chemicals, petroleum products, and transport equipment industries makes an analysis of price movements in the early 1970s rather difficult. See Baysan and Blitzer (1988, appendix table 3.2) for producer price trends from 1969 to 1974.

7 In order to avoid any misinterpretation, it is perhaps worth repeating the definition of "effective exchange rate" (EER) adopted in this study. Import EERs refer to the official selling rate adjusted for import taxes and "scarcity rents" resulting from QRs. However, in the actual estimation of import EERs for the early 1970s, no attempt was made to incorporate scarcity rents as this would have required direct price comparisons. In any event, there is reason to believe that these scarcity premiums were negligible in the post-devaluation period until 1974. EERs for exports refer to the official buying rates after adjustment for export incentives. In estimating the latter rates, only the export tax rebates were taken into account. Omission of other export incentives should not distort the results because, as explained earlier, the remaining incentive measures were rather ineffective during this period.

the nine agricultural products removed the temporary incremental discrimination against agricultural exports introduced in August 1970. Nevertheless, throughout this period the biases of the trade regime were maintained. For example, on the export side, even after the alignment of the special export rate with the official rate, the ratio of nominal EERs for nontraditional (mainly manufactured) exports and traditional exports was still 1.27 in 1973, slightly higher than the 1.21 observed in 1969 (see table 3.3). Since the August devaluation package did not introduce any change in the coverage of export incentives, agricultural products (with the exception of fresh fruit and vegetables) continued to be ineligible for the export incentives in the early 1970s, and therefore EERs for traditional exports remained at par with the special export rate. Manufacturing sector exports, however, have always benefited from export incentives. After the introduction of a simplified export tax rebate system in August 1970, the new system of four basic rebate rates coupled with the provision of an additional rebate of 10 percentage points for exports exceeding US$1 million continued to maintain what was essentially a nonuniform EER system for manufactured exports, though disparities remained small (nominal export EERs for manufacturing industries over the period 1969–73 are given in table 3.4). After the devaluation, the unweighted average EER for manufactured exports was about 25 percent higher than the official exchange rate and, in general, import-competing industries

Table 3.3 Nominal effective exchange rates, 1969–1973

Rate	1969	Annual average 1970	After devaluation 1970	1971	1972	1973
Nominal EERs						
TXEER	9.37	10.69	12.00	12.62	13.19	13.60
NXEER	11.37	14.97	18.82	18.44	17.68	17.28
XEER	10.15	12.36	14.66	15.18	15.30	15.55
MEER	17.90	22.98	27.59	27.17	26.05	26.01
Percent change from previous year						
TXEER		14.1	28.1	5.2	4.5	3.1
NXEER		31.7	65.5	− 2.0	− 4.0	− 2.3
XEER		21.8	44.4	3.5	0.1	1.6
MEER		28.4	54.1	− 1.5	− 4.1	− 0.2
Ratios						
NXEER/TXEER	1.21	1.40	1.57	1.46	1.34	1.27
MEER/XEER	1.76	1.86	1.88	1.79	1.70	1.67
MEER/NXEER	1.57	1.54	1.47	1.47	1.47	1.51

TXEER, EER for traditional exports; NXEER, EER for nontraditional exports, XEER, EER for all exports; MEER, EER for imports.

Table 3.4 Nominal effective exchange rates for manufactured exports, 1969–1973 (lira per US dollar)

Manufacturing industry	1969	Average for 1970	After Aug 1970	1971	1972	1973
Vegetables and fruit	9.97	13.22	16.63	16.45	15.05	n.a.
Food processing	9.61	13.09	16.46	18.11	16.93	16.82
Beverages	10.35	13.51	16.99	17.21	16.43	16.54
Textiles and clothing	12.05	15.14	19.04	18.12	17.38	16.90
Forestry products	10.25	14.64	18.41	17.47	16.40	16.17
Paper	n.a.	n.a.	n.a.	19.07	n.a.	n.a.
Leather products	11.09	14.96	18.82	18.86	17.77	17.27
Chemicals	11.21	15.56	19.58	19.66	19.14	18.46
Glass products	11.61	15.65	19.69	18.47	18.53	18.90
Ceramics	10.83	14.60	18.36	17.77	16.39	15.70
Iron and steel	10.37	15.39	19.36	18.65	17.59	17.14
Nonferrous metals	10.82	14.01	17.63	18.02	17.95	17.55
Metal products	11.90	17.77	22.35	18.28	18.31	17.37
Machinery production	13.35	17.94	22.57	19.64	18.83	17.56
Electrical machinery	12.30	15.63	19.66	19.37	18.24	16.55
Vehicle production	12.53	15.57	19.59	19.15	18.23	18.06
Cement	13.10	15.02	18.89	20.04	19.75	18.63
Plastics	n.a.	14.68	18.46	18.83	18.24	17.47
Tires	11.96	14.51	18.25	18.40	17.67	17.41
Agricultural machinery and equipment	n.a.	n.a.	n.a.	18.81	18.50	18.19
Clay and cement products	n.a.	n.a.	n.a.	17.92	17.69	17.30
Petroleum products	n.a.	13.46	16.93	17.29	16.27	15.68
Unweighted average EER	11.37	14.97	18.82	18.44	17.68	17.28
Variance of nominal EER	1.136	1.631	2.581	0.756	1.187	0.762

n.a., not available.

Sources: SPO, Annual Program, various issues; data supplied by Ministry of Commerce, 1974; SIS, Statistical Yearbook of Turkey, various issues; IMF, 1981

were afforded higher export EERs compared with export-oriented industries. For example, EERs for exports of import-competing machinery and metal products industries were the highest at TL22.57 and TL22.35 per US dollar respectively. In contrast, export-oriented processed fruit and vegetables and food-processing industries had the lowest export EERs of TL16.63 per dollar and TL16.46 per dollar respectively.

As pointed out earlier, the 1970 devaluation package was not intended to change the basic import-substituting bias of the trade regime. That this was the case is amply shown by the fact that EERs for imports remained well above those pertaining to exports (figure 3.1 shows the time pattern of EERs for imports and exports). Indeed, the ratio of the unweighted average EERs for imports and exports rose from 1.76 in 1969 to 1.86 in

Nominal FERs

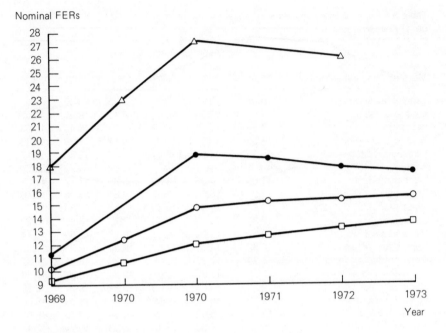

Figure 3.1 Time pattern of effective exchange rates, 1969–1973:
△, effective exchange rate for imports;
●, effective exchange rate for nontraditional exports;
○, effective exchange rate for all exports;
□, effective exchange rate for traditional exports

1970 and to 1.88 after August 1970 owing to the lower (buying) exchange rate set for traditional exports. Although this ratio subsequently fell as the special export rate was raised, it was still 1.67 in 1973 (see table 3.3 and figure 3.2). Note, however, that the ratio of EERs for imports and nontraditional (or manufactured) exports decreased from 1.57 in 1969 to 1.47 after the devaluation. This was brought about by the devaluation-related reduction in the import stamp duty from 25 to 10 percent and by falling scarcity rents.

Similar disparities between the import and export EERs also existed at individual industry levels; these are observable from industry-specific export and import EERs presented in tables 3.4 and 3.5. There were two important industries, however, where the disparity between import and export EERs was small and where export EERs slightly exceeded import EERs in the post-devaluation period. These were the textile and clothing

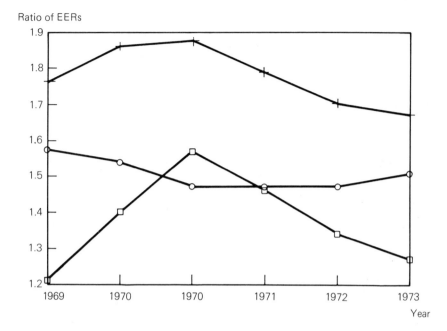

Figure 3.2 Ratios of effective exchange rates, 1969–1973:
+, ratio of effective exchange rate for imports to effective exchange rate for all exports;
○, ratio of effective exchange rate for imports to effective exchange rate for nontraditional exports;
□, ratio of effective exchange rate for nontraditional exports to effective exchange rate for traditional exports

and leather products industries, both of which have been favored export industries.[8]

To summarize, the time patterns of sectoral import and export EERs do not demonstrate any loosening of the protective structure or of the bias against export activities.

Real Exchange Rates

The success of a devaluation, especially in the long term, also depends on how well domestic inflation is controlled. Accelerating inflation can

---

8 Even in the case of these two industries, however, the apparent near neutrality of the trade regime needs to be interpreted with some care, because banned import items were not considered in estimating sectoral import EERs and because imports of finished textiles and leather products had been banned during the 1960s and 1970s.

Table 3.5 Nominal effective exchange rates for manufactured imports, 1969–1973 (lira per US dollar)

Manufacturing industry	1969	Average for 1970	After devaluation 1970	1971	1972	1973
Agriculture	13.26	16.79	19.85	19.55	18.73	18.71
Food processing	17.43	22.36	26.82	26.41	25.31	25.28
Beverages	35.96	47.09	57.72	26.85	54.48	54.41
Textiles and clothing	12.08	15.21	17.88	17.61	16.87	16.85
Forestry products	15.07	19.21	22.88	22.53	21.59	21.56
Paper	15.89	20.30	24.24	23.87	22.88	22.85
Leather products	12.26	15.45	18.18	17.90	17.16	17.14
Chemicals	15.71	20.06	23.94	23.57	22.59	22.56
Glass products	17.71	22.73	27.27	26.86	25.74	25.70
Ceramics	15.53	19.82	23.63	23.28	22.31	22.20
Iron and steel	15.16	19.33	23.03	22.68	21.74	21.71
Nonferrous metals	15.44	19.69	23.48	23.13	22.17	22.13
Metal products	19.79	25.51	30.75	30.29	29.03	28.99
Machinery production	15.89	20.30	24.24	23.87	22.88	22.85
Electrical machinery	15.62	19.94	23.79	23.42	22.45	22.42
Vehicle production	17.43	22.36	26.82	26.41	25.31	25.28
Cement	15.44	19.69	23.48	23.13	22.17	22.13
Plastics	34.59	45.27	55.45	54.61	52.34	52.26
Tires	18.98	24.42	29.39	28.94	27.74	27.70
Agricultural machinery	14.89	18.97	22.57	22.23	21.31	21.28
Clay and cement products	15.44	19.69	23.78	23.13	22.17	22.13
Petroleum products	24.24	31.45	38.18	37.60	36.04	35.99
Official exchange rate	9.08	12.12	15.15	14.92	14.30	14.28
Unweighted average EER	17.90	22.98	27.59	27.17	26.05	26.01
Variance of nominal EER	36.55	65.11	101.74	98.67	90.64	90.39

quickly erode any increment in real exchange rates effected by a devaluation, and balance-of-payments problems may reemerge.

The 66.7 percent nominal devaluation of August 1970 led to a 28.2 percent devaluation of the real exchange rate in 1970 over 1969, to a 53.5 percent depreciation of the real rate in 1971 over 1969, and to a 19.7 percent depreciation in 1971 over 1970. However, from 1971 to 1972 the real rate appreciated by 10.4 percent, and appreciation continued as accelerating inflation began to erode the real exchange rate in 1973 (table 3.6).

This pattern was also observable in real EERs for imports and nontraditional exports (see table 3.7). In terms of 1973 Turkish lira per 1973 US dollar, real EERs for imports increased from TL23.25 per US dollar in 1969 to TL34.06 per dollar after the devaluation – a 46 percent real devaluation. However, this was followed by a 10 percent appreciation in

Table 3.6 Real exchange rates, 1969–1974

Year	Nominal exchange rate (TL per US$)	Relative price index[a] vis-à-vis trading partners[b] (1973 = 100)	Real exchange rate (1973 TL per US$)	Change in real exchange rate (%)
1969	9.00	88.20	10.20	—
1970	11.50	87.90	13.08	28.2
1971	14.92	95.30	15.66	19.7
1972	14.15	100.90	14.02	−10.4
1973	14.15	100.00	14.15	0.9
1974	13.93	108.70	12.82	−9.4

—, not applicable.
[a] Domestic and foreign wholesale price indices.
[b] Belgium, France, West Germany, Italy, Switzerland, United Kingdom, and United States.

Source: World Bank, 1982

Table 3.7 Real effective exchange rates, 1969–1973

Rate	1969	Annual average 1970	After devaluation 1970	1971	1972	1973
PLD-EERs (deflator, wholesale prices)[a]						
PLD-TXEER (for traditional exports)	16.47	17.61	19.77	17.95	15.89	13.60
PLD-NXEER (for nontraditional exports)	19.98	24.66	31.00	26.23	21.30	17.28
PLD-XEER (for all exports)	17.84	20.36	24.15	21.59	18.43	15.55
PLD-MEER (for imports)	31.46	37.86	45.45	38.65	31.39	26.01
Real EERs (PLD-EERs inflated by export or import price indices)[b]						
Real TXEER	11.86	12.01	13.48	13.15	12.81	13.60
Real NXEER	14.39	16.82	21.15	19.21	17.17	17.28
Real XEER	12.85	13.39	16.47	15.81	14.85	15.55
Real MEER	23.25	28.37	34.06	30.88	25.79	26.01

For definitions, see table 3.3.
[a] Wholesale price index is set equal to 100 for 1973.
[b] Export and import price indices used to inflate domestic PLD-EERs based on US prices. All indices are set equal to 100 for 1973.

Sources: SPO, *Annual Program*, 1980; IMF, 1981a

1971 and a 20 percent apppreciation in 1972. The real EER for imports depreciated by only about 1 percent in 1973, and at TL26.01 per dollar it was only 12 percent higher than its 1969 level. Similarly, the August devaluation led to a 47 percent depreciation in the real EER for nontraditional exports compared with its 1969 level, and then inflation quickly eroded this gain with a 22 percent cumulative appreciation by 1973. Thus the latter real EER rose from TL14.39 per dollar in 1969 to TL17.28 per dollar in 1973, showing only a 20 percent cumulative depreciation. In contrast, the gradual increase in the special export rate accorded to traditional exports slowed the erosion of real EERs for this group to only 5 percent within two years following the devaluation.

The erosion of real exchange rates in the post-devaluation period contributed to a rapid expansion in Turkey's merchandise trade deficit in the early 1970s, thus undermining the long-term benefits of devaluation.

External Transactions

Merchandise Trade

The short-run balance-of-payments response to the August 1970 devaluation was impressive. The decision to devaluate permitted additional borrowing, and the inflow of workers' remittances increased dramatically. Official borrowing from bilateral and multilateral sources, net of debt servicing, amounted to US$155 million in 1970, and the total amount of remittances received during the August–December period of 1970 equaled US$172 million, larger than the US$141 million realized during the whole of 1969. In 1970, remittances amounted to US$273 million for the full year, showing a 94 percent increase over the 1969 level. These developments alone allowed the Central Bank both to issue import licenses and to transfer foreign exchange without the previously lengthy delays. During the following years remittances continued to grow substantially, and export proceeds also showed a healthy increase. Large supplies of foreign exchange, in turn, permitted the authorities to meet most of the license applications. Thus, although the government had not altered the basic structure of the protective regime and although QRs were still in place, merchandise imports rose sharply in the early 1970s.

Quarterly imports, in current dollars, were 50 percent larger in the fourth quarter than in the third quarter of 1970. Similarly, quarterly imports of 1971 exceeded those realized during the pre-devaluation period (Baysan and Blitzer, 1988, appendix table 3.3). The annual increase in merchandise imports, expressed in current US dollars, was 13.1 percent in 1970, 28.8 percent in 1971, 38.6 percent in 1972, 38.7 percent in 1973, and 81.4 percent in 1974. A large part of the 1974 increase was caused by increases in oil prices and by additional imports associated with the Cyprus intervention. The increase in imports was also large in real terms: 17.1 percent in 1970, followed by increases of 15.9 percent, 29.6 percent, 9.9 percent, and 9.3 percent respectively. The ratio of imports to GDP also increased continuously, jumping from 6.1 percent in 1969 to 11.1 percent in 1973 and to 14.1 percent in 1974.

The commodity composition of imports remained more or less the same over the period 1969–73. The share of both of investment good imports and of raw material plus intermediate goods imports in total imports showed only small variations (Baysan and Blitzer, 1988, appendix table 3.4). In 1974, however, the latter group's share temporarily rose to 62 percent while the former's fell to 34 percent. This was due to the factors stated in the preceding paragraph. The level of consumer goods imports increased from US$55 million in 1969 to US$157 million in 1974, but their share of total imports fell from 6.9 to 4.2 percent over the same period. This clearly indicates that the import regime remained highly protective. While the system continued to allow imports of (mostly noncompetitive) capital goods and intermediate, imports of competing consumer goods were prohibited. Permitted consumer goods consisted mainly of drugs and coffee beans.

Merchandise exports also responded strongly to the devaluation. Foreign exchange proceeds from commodity exports were 43 percent larger in the last quarter of 1970 than during the last quarter of 1969.[9] In annual terms, export proceeds expressed in current US dollars increased by 9.7 percent in 1970, 14.9 percent in 1971, 30.6 percent in 1972, 48.9 percent in 1973, and 16.7 percent in 1974 (Baysan and Blitzer, 1988, appendix table 3.5). In real terms the annual increases were 11 percent in 1970, 7.1 percent in 1971, 19.4 percent in 1972, 9.5 percent in 1973, and 5.7 percent in 1974.

Another important development observed on the export side in the post-devaluation period was a noticeable change in the composition of exports. While the share of traditional exports (cotton, tobacco, hazelnuts, and raisins) in total exports fell from 60.7 percent in 1969 to 43.5 percent in 1974, the share of all agricultural exports fell from 75.4 to 55.6 percent over the same period. The share of mineral exports increased from 6.5 percent in 1969 to 11.7 percent in 1971, and then fell to 5.7 percent in 1974. In contrast, the share of manufactured exports increased substantially, from 18.1 percent in 1969 to 38.6 percent in 1974.

Although the devaluation package contained a temporary incremental bias against traditional exports by setting a lower special exchange rate for manufactured exports, the observed structural change in the composition of exports during the early 1970s cannot simply be attributed to the August devaluation *per se*. Since its inception in the mid-1960s, the export incentive system had always favored the export-oriented manufacturing industries. The objective was to encourage further processing of agricultural products so as to increase the value-added content of exports through

---

9 Compared with the third quarter of 1970, export proceeds in the fourth quarter of 1970 rose by 138 percent. However, much of this increase was due to seasonal factors.

a deliberate emphasis on industries with export potential. These efforts and the ongoing industrialization process obviously started paying off in the early 1970s, and the devaluation probably contributed at the margin by providing the needed push in terms of higher EERs. There is, in fact, some evidence supporting the positive role of increases in EERs on Turkey's export performance. Krueger (1974), for example, performed a regression analysis on Turkey's exports in the later 1950s and 1960s. She found that, in cases where the government's intervention in export and domestic activities was minimal, exports were sensitive to changes in EERs. Two such cases were cotton exports and minor exports that also included manufactured goods.[10]

The factors listed above were important supply-side factors contributing to the strong export performance in the early 1970s. On the demand side, one important development which probably had some positive impact was the extension of duty-free entry status by the EEC to most of Turkey's manufactured exports in September 1971. Although key items such as cotton, yarn, cotton fabrics, machine-made carpets, woollen rugs, and kilims remained subject to certain tariff quotas, even for these items applicable tariffs were reduced by 75 percent for imports not exceeding predetermined global quotas. Moreover, Turkey's agricultural exports to the EEC were also accorded tariff reductions ranging from 50 to 75 percent. The EEC market had been important for Turkish exports, absorbing about 45 percent of them in the early 1970s. Therefore the favorable terms offered by the EEC to Turkey's exports in late 1971 must have played some role in the improved export performance, and especially in the rapid growth of manufactured exports in 1972 and 1973.[11]

Mineral exports showed fluctuating performance in the post-devaluation period (Baysan and Blitzer, 1988, appendix table 3.6). This simply highlights the fact that a satisfactory export performance in this sector required much more on the supply side than just an exchange rate adjustment. Indeed, Turkey's generally poor export performance in minerals can be traced to the government's mining policies. These had created so much uncertainty for the private sector that the development and exploitation of rich mineral deposits (particularly copper, chrome, and borate) slowed. High inland transportation costs and export price controls also adversely affected mineral exports.

10 Because the length of time during which the devaluation-related changes in real exchange rates remained uneroded was short, no attempt was made to perform a similar exercise for finding the extent of the causal link between the devaluation-led changes in real EERs and changes in export performance of different commodity categories.
11 The fact that several supply- and demand-side factors simultaneously affected Turkey's export performance in the post-devaluation period made any attempt to isolate the devaluation-related improvements rather difficult. For example, experiments with rank correlations produced no meaningful results.

Balance of Payments

In the post-devaluation period, reduced import restrictions and efforts to achieve the growth target of 7 percent led to much larger increases in import expenditures than in export earnings. Thus the deficit in "resource balance" (import surplus) increased from US$342 million in 1970 to US$674 million in 1972, and then jumped to US$2,060 million in 1974 (Baysan and Blitzer, 1988, appendix table 3.7). However, one extremely favorable development was the growth of workers' remittances, which increased from US$273 million in 1970 to US$471 million in 1971, US$740 million in 1972, US$1,183 million in 1973, and US$1,426 million in 1974 – increases of 73 percent, 57 percent, 60 percent and 21 percent respectively. This suggests that remittances were crucial in financing increasing amounts of imports in the early 1970s. In fact the current account in 1972 showed a surplus of US$15 million, and this surplus expanded to US$515 million in 1973. Parallel with these developments, net official reserves rose from US$105 million at the end of August 1969 to US$954 million by the end of August 1972, and passed the US$2 billion mark in August 1973 for the first time.

Obviously, many factors affect inflow of remittances. However, there is some ground for believing that the August 1970 devaluation had a significant positive impact during the early 1970s. While the number of Turkish workers abroad increased from 350,000 in 1969 to 809,000 in 1974, the annual amount of remittances per worker increased continuously from US$403 to US$1,762 over the same period.

Table 3.8 summarizes Turkey's external debt situation during the early 1970s. Turkey's short-term debt, in absolute terms and as a ratio of total external debt, was insignificant until the mid-1970s. The long-term debt (and thereby total outstanding debt) increased continuously in the early 1970s, expanding from US$2,052 million in 1969 to US$3,496 million in 1974 (an increase of 70 percent). However, as the export situation suggests, Turkey's capacity to repay its external debt and its ability to meet debt-servicing obligations also improved. The ratio of the stock of external debt to the flow of GDP fell from 0.165 in 1969 to 0.131 in 1974. Similarly, as seen in the lower part of table 3.8, debt service ratios also declined. The ratio of interest plus principal payments to merchandise exports fell from 0.244 to 0.149, and the ratio of the sum to aggregate foreign exchange earnings decreased from 0.153 to 0.064. Meanwhile, the debt service ratio with respect to GDP showed small variations (around 1 percent).

Table 3.8 External debt, 1969–1974 (million US dollars)

	1969	1970	1971	1972	1973	1974
External debt outstanding disbursed only (year-end)						
Long-term debt	2,052	2,207	2,466	2,519	2,984	3,280
Short-term debt	n.a.	n.a.	n.a.	19	279	216
Total[a]	2,052	2,207	2,466	2,538	3,263	3,496
Debt servicing						
Interest payments	44	47	60	62	59	102
Principal payments	87	146	75	117	72	126
Total	131	193	135	179	131	228
Foreign exchange earnings						
Exports of goods and NFS	713	754	875	1,153	1,799	2,123
of which: goods	537	589	677	885	1,317	1,532
Workers' remittances	141	273	471	740	1,183	1,426
Total	854	1,027	1,346	1,893	2,982	3,549
GDP at factor cost and current prices[b]	12,444	10,897	11,193	14,346	18,587	26,633
Debt service ratios (%)						
Ratio of interest + principal payment to merchandise expenditure	24.4	32.8	19.9	20.2	9.9	14.9
Ratio of interest + principal payment to aggregate foreign exchange earnings	15.3	18.8	10.0	9.5	4.4	6.4
Ratio of interest + principal payment to gross domestic product	1.1	1.8	1.2	1.2	0.7	0.9

n.a., not available.
[a] Short-term debt figures for 1969–71 were not available. Total external debt figures for the latter years therefore reflect long-term debt. This is not expected to create any problem in estimating debt service ratios since there is reason to believe that the short-term debt for the years mentioned was negligible.
[b] To obtain GDP expressed in US dollars, the official exchange rate was used. This causes some problems of interpretation owing to the devaluation of August 1970 and the relatively higher rates of domestic inflation while the exchange rate had been fixed. Therefore debt service as a proportion of GDP should be interpreted with care.

Source: SIS, Statistical Yearbook of Turkey, various issues; SPO, Annual Program, various issues; World Bank, 1980, p. 256, table 3.1, pp. 268–9

Time Pattern of Sectoral Responses

Unfortunately, it is easier to provide a theoretical argument for the possible resource-allocation effects of a devaluation undertaken in the presence of exchange controls and import rationing than it is to trace the actual resource-pull effects of such a devaluation. Indeed, the authors confronted this problem when examining post-devaluation economic performance. The problem was, of course, that sectoral data on actual output and employment reflected not only the possible responses to the devaluation-related relative price changes, but also the changes directly associated with expansion of the economy's production possibility frontier. The planned economic growth efforts continued unabated in the early 1970s, with the ongoing import-substituting industrialization strategy and prevailing supportive policies basically determining the sectoral pattern of economic growth.

In a real-life setting such as that of Turkey in the post-devaluation period, actual output, employment, investment, and trade flow are all affected by one another. It becomes very difficult to isolate static from dynamic resource shifts and therefore to attempt an attribution analysis. Bearing this in mind, in the following section we discuss the time pattern of sector responses in the post-devaluation period, identifying sectors that showed especially strong or weak responses.

Production Responses

Not surprisingly, analysis of post-devaluation economic performance shows that the manufacturing industries generally responded according to the prevailing incentive structure, which maintained the bias in favor of import-competing industries. Output responses were particularly strong in such import-competing industries as transport equipment, electrical machinery, petroleum and coal products, machinery, basic metals, paper, rubber products, and chemicals (Baysan and Blitzer, 1988, appendix table 3.8). After experiencing a slowdown in their production in the late 1960s as a result of severe foreign exchange shortages, these industries were also the ones benefiting from increased availability of foreign exchange following the August 1970 devaluation. Increases in imports of raw materials, other intermediate, spare parts for machinery, and equipment were particularly instrumental in the substantial post-devaluation output expansions experienced by the newly established assembly industries such as transport equipment, electrical machinery, and machinery. Over the period 1970–4 the annual average output growth rates were 33 percent in transport equipment, 32.4 percent in electrical machinery, and 19.6 percent in nonelectrical machinery.

Other manufacturing industries also showed output growth in the early 1970s, though at more moderate levels. For example, the export-oriented food and beverages and leather product industries experienced an annual average output growth of about 8 percent in the period 1970–4. The production level in the latter actually fell in 1972. Whatever the reason, this was obviously a temporary phenomenon, as shown by the resumption of output growth in this sector (and by sizable investment, which is discussed below). Textiles and apparel, the most important export-oriented manufacturing industry, showed a stronger output growth with an annual average of 15.3 percent. While all three industries had benefited from export incentives, the textile industry seems to have responded more quickly to the EEC's reduction of import barriers to Turkey's manufactured exports in September 1971 (indeed, textile exports increased by 98 percent in current dollar terms and by 79 percent in real terms in 1972, with the EEC accounting for most of the increase).

Nonetheless, import-competing industries in general continued to grow at higher rates in the early 1970s than the export-oriented sectors. Obviously, the devaluation package was not meant to generate a permanent shift in resource allocation and, whatever relative price changes it might have brought about in favor of exportables, these were perceived as temporary because of the continuation of import-substituting bias in the overall incentive structure.

Trade Ratios

As expected, the August 1970 devaluation and the accompanying relaxation of import restrictions led to increases in the trade ratios of most manufacturing industries. Specifically, the ratios of imports to domestic production generally rose in most import-competing industries (table 3.9). The most striking increases were shown by the chemicals, basic metals, machinery, and transportation equipment industries. For chemicals, the import ratio rose from 0.41 in 1969 to 1.16 in 1974. Similarly, in the basic metals, machinery, and transport equipment industries, the import ratio increased from 0.12 to 0.63, from 0.8 to 1.41, and from 0.26 to 0.45 respectively in the five years from 1969 to 1974. Note, however, that at the two- or three-digit level of industrial aggregation a rise in an import ratio does not necessarily imply that the corresponding domestic industry is facing greater import penetration. The import ratio of a broadly defined industry may also increase when less processed or noncompetitive items, normally classified under the same industry, are imported in greater quantities. This is most probably what happened in Turkey in the post-devaluation period. The existing QR system would not have allowed an increase in competing imports unless domestic production fell short of domestic demand, which was expanding rapidly in the early 1970s.

Industries producing exportables did not show much change in their import ratios over the period 1969–74, and these remained at fairly low levels. For example, the import ratio in the food and beverages industry rose from 0.02 in 1969 to 0.05 in 1974, and fell from 0.04 to 0.02 in the textiles and clothing industry and from 0.08 to 0.04 in the fur and leather products industries over the same period. Since the industries relied mostly on domestically available intermediates and since finished competing imports were prohibited, there is no reason why the August 1970 package should have led to any other outcome.

For most industries, the ratios of exports to domestic production remained at fairly low levels over the period 1969–74. In industries producing exportables, however, some increases were observed. For example, the export share of the food and beverages industry increased from 0.042 to 0.063 (table 3.10). Increases in the textiles and apparel industry and the wood products and furniture industry were even more impressive – from 0.017 to 0.132 and from 0.025 to 0.135 respectively. The export response of the fur and leather products industries was strong and rapid in 1970 and 1971, raising the latter's export ratio from 0.034 in 1969 to 0.412 in 1971. This ratio then fell to 0.083 by 1974 as export performance in leather products weakened. The sharp fall in this sector's output in 1972, coupled with rising domestic demand, might have caused this result.

Investment Responses

The size and direction of changes in sectoral capital stocks are perhaps the ultimate indicators of the pattern of industrialization and trade strategies pursued in an economy. Private sector investment would be directed to industries where the expected relative profitability is higher. This, in turn, depends on incentive structures created by government policies and on whether private firms perceive them to be temporary or permanent. Similarly, the distribution pattern of public sector investment in the medium and long term will indicate government's industrialization strategy.

Turkey's aggregate investment spending accelerated in the early 1970s, showing real increases of 7.9 percent in 1970, 10.1 percent in 1972, 17.5 percent in 1973, and 13.1 percent in 1974. In 1971, however, both private and public sector investments fell below 1970 levels. The military intervention in March 1971, and the coming to power of two caretaker "reformist" governments, no doubt led to postponements in public sector investments, and the resulting uncertainty about the government's economic program depressed investment in the private sector. The public sector's share in total fixed investment declined steadily during this period from 55.5 percent in 1969 to 47.6 percent in 1974.[12] Meanwhile, the percentage share of total fixed investment in GDP rose from 19.4 percent in 1969 to 20.9 percent in 1970, and the temporary fall in 1971 was followed by increases in subsequent years. In 1974 the percentage share reached 23.1 percent.

---

12 This decline, however, turned out to be a temporary phenomenon rather than a secular trend, as there were several reversals in the latter ratio in the second half of the 1970s.

As a consequence of the ongoing industrialization drive, the manufacturing sector had the largest investment share in the economy, and this share increased from 25.2 percent in 1969 to 30.8 percent in 1974. The agricultural sector's share in total investment fell from 12.2 percent in 1969 to 10.6 percent in 1974, despite this sector's 70 percent contribution to total merchandise export earnings. The mining sector remained neglected in this period, as evidenced by its fairly low and stable investment share of about 3.4 percent.

Import-competing industries, particularly petroleum and coal products, basic metals, machinery, electrical machinery, and transport equipment, experienced fairly high growth in their capital stock (Baysan and Blitzer, 1988, appendix table 3.9).

However, it is also worth noting that starting in the period 1971–2 investment activity speeded up in the export-oriented textiles, clothing, leather products, and food industries. While these industries remained favored in the allocation of export promotion incentives in the post-devaluation period, it is not possible to explain the increased investment activity in the latter industries totally by the devaluation-related temporary increases in real EERs for exports of these industries. Several other developments seem to have induced capital expansion in these industries:

Table 3.9 Ratio of imports to domestic production in manufacturing industries, 1969–1974

Manufacturing industry	1969	1970	1971	1972	1973	1974
Food and beverages	0.017	0.014	0.034	0.028	0.020	0.050
Tobacco and manufactures	0.000	0.000	0.000	0.000	0.000	0.000
Textiles and clothing	0.041	0.042	0.056	0.019	0.018	0.020
Wood products and furniture	0.016	0.074	0.069	0.011	0.012	0.021
Paper and paper products	0.200	0.116	0.292	0.139	0.136	0.176
Printing and publishing	0.000	0.000	0.000	0.065	0.045	0.055
Fur and leather products	0.082	0.076	0.121	0.008	0.008	0.040
Rubber products	0.023	0.016	0.027	0.062	0.073	0.120
Chemicals	0.409	0.431	0.602	0.810	0.924	1.159
Petroleum and coal products	0.043	0.038	0.057	0.070	0.023	0.049
Nonmetallic mineral products	0.053	0.032	0.051	0.113	0.084	0.074
Basic metals	0.118	0.199	0.356	0.294	0.371	0.629
Metal products	0.092	0.115	0.245	0.238	0.194	0.147
Machinery	0.802	0.776	1.316	1.330	1.248	1.410
Electrical machinery	0.592	1.051	0.832	0.751	0.645	0.483
Transport equipment	0.263	0.497	0.401	0.507	0.458	0.454

Calculations are based on flows valued at constant prices of 1965. Imports, expressed in current US dollars, were deflated by the US producer price indices (1965 = 100). These import figures were multiplied by the average exchange rates to express the latter flows in Turkish lira.

Sources: SIS, Foreign Trade Statistics, various issues; data supplied by SPO, December 1977; Economic Report of the President, 1985

(a) a clear indication by the government that these would continue to receive preferential treatment in the allocation of export incentives; (b) the EEC's lowering of trade barriers to Turkey's manufactured exports in late 1971; (c) the rapid increase in domestic demand.

A heavy concentration of investment in the import-competing segment of the manufacturing sector in the post-devaluation period strongly suggests, however, that the devaluation package was not intended as a move toward a neutral trade regime, and it was not perceived as such by the private sector.

Employment Responses and Labor Displacement

The post-devaluation employment responses of manufacturing industries appear to have been determined mainly by output expansion and, to a lesser extent, by substitution of capital for labor.[13]

In comparison with the 1969 employment levels, import-competing industries such as paper, chemicals, petroleum and coal products, basic metals, nonelectrical machinery, and transport equipment realized large increases in employment.[14] Exceptions were the metal products industry, in which employment fell by about 5 percent from 1969 to 1974, and the rubber products industry, which showed a moderate 21 percent increase in employment over the same period. The latter industry showed a delayed employment response starting in 1972, despite a rapid and strong output expansion. This might have been due to increased imports of raw materials after the devaluation, which allowed this industry to use existing capacity to increase output without expanding employment, but continuous expansion in the motor vehicles industry must have induced additional hiring after a time lag.

Among the export-producing industries, leather products increased its employment by 73 percent from 1969 to 1974. Over the same period, employment increased by 44 percent in the nonmetallic mineral products industry, 40.8 percent in wood products and furniture, 32 percent in food

13 The rank correlation coefficient calculated for changes in employment and production levels of the manufacturing industries over the period 1970–3 was statistically significant (0.753) and had the expected positive sign.

14 Available employment data cover all public sector enterprises and private sector firms which employed ten or more workers. Hence official employment figures reflected changes in employment levels of existing large private firms and of the state enterprises, as well the net contributions of those private firms that passed the ten-worker threshold in either direction. It is also worth noting that in 1970 value-added by "large" private sector firms accounted for 88 percent of total private sector value added in the manufacturing industries. Also, public sector employment dominated total employment in tobacco products (83 percent in 1972), paper (74 percent in 1972), petroleum and coal products (56 percent in 1972), basic metals (64 percent in 1972), and transport equipment (59 percent in 1972) (Baysan and Blitzer, 1988, appendix table 3.10).

and beverages, and 23.6 percent in textiles and apparel. Note that the latter two industries showed a relatively weaker employment response compared with their output growth. To some degree, this appears to have resulted from the substitution of capital for labor, as evidenced by the high investment activity. Indeed, some of the investment activity in manufacturing industries might have indicated the substitution of capital for labor rather than capacity expansion, since real interest rates became increasingly negative in the early 1970s.[15]

Information on the extent of industry-specific "unemployment" during the early 1970s could only be inferred from the available official employment figures. Accordingly, the tobacco, petroleum and coal, and electrical machinery industries had relatively large layoffs in 1970 concurrently with some production cuts, which could have been due to the production bottlenecks caused by the severe foreign exchange stringency in the first half of 1970. Similarly, some employment reduction was experienced in the metal products, tobacco, and chemicals industries in 1971, the petroleum–coal products and leather products industries in 1972, the paper

Table 3.10 Ratio of exports to domestic production in manufacturing industries, 1969–1974

Manufacturing industry	1969	1970	1971	1972	1973	1974
Food and beverages	0.042	0.036	0.053	0.073	0.088	0.063
Tobacco and manufactures	0.000	0.000	0.000	0.000	0.000	0.000
Textiles and clothing	0.017	0.029	0.050	0.077	0.125	0.132
Wood products and furniture	0.025	0.045	0.088	0.059	0.062	0.135
Paper and paper products	0.001	0.002	0.002	0.000	0.009	0.050
Printing and publishing	0.000	0.000	0.000	0.003	0.003	0.003
Fur and leather products	0.034	0.197	0.412	0.045	0.096	0.083
Rubber products	0.005	0.014	0.009	0.006	0.009	0.020
Chemicals	0.017	0.022	0.033	0.035	0.039	0.062
Petroleum and coal products	0.005	0.001	0.006	0.050	0.054	0.061
Nonmetallic mineral products	0.003	0.019	0.057	0.093	0.078	0.062
Basic metals	0.028	0.032	0.024	0.024	0.038	0.047
Metal products	0.002	0.002	0.006	0.010	0.016	0.026
Machinery	0.003	0.006	0.006	0.010	0.016	0.026
Electrical machinery	0.001	0.003	0.006	0.006	0.006	0.003
Transport equipment	0.000	0.003	0.001	0.001	0.002	0.010

Calculations are based on flows valued at constant 1965 prices. Exports, expressed in current US dollars, were deflated by the US producer price indices (1965 = 100). These export figures were multiplied by the average exchange rates to express the latter flows in Turkish lira.

Sources: SIS, Foreign Trade Statistics, various issues; SPO, December 1977; Economic Report of the President, 1985

15 Krueger and Tuncer (1982, p. 316) provide some evidence suggesting " . . . that much Turkish investment in the manufacturing sector was devoted to substitution of capital rather than to expanding capacity" during the period 1963–76.

industry in 1973, and the tobacco and rubber products industries in 1974. However, the large employment swings observed in the tobacco, petroleum and coal, and metal products industries were mainly due to fluctuations in the public sector segment of these industries. No specific explanation could be found for these frequent employment changes in the public sector. Given that it has been the government's policy to maintain employment in the SEEs and that employment in SEEs has been less sensitive to changes in relative factor prices, it is probable that noneconomic considerations led to the employment cuts of the early 1970s (Baysan and Blitzer, 1988, appendix table 3.10).

There is no evidence of labor displacement in the post-devaluation period which can be attributed to the expansion of imports. Since import quotas and prohibitions remained in place after the devaluation, these practically assured full protection to import-competing industries. Imports of consumer goods continued to be highly controlled, and restricted to drugs and noncompetitive items only. Raw materials, other intermediate goods, spare parts, and investment goods accounted for the large import expansion that followed the August 1970 devaluation, and these were mostly noncompetitive.

Factor Productivity Changes

There is some evidence that the August 1970 devaluation and the ensuing relaxation of import restrictions had a positive impact on total factor productivity in the manufacturing sector during the early 1970s.

Krueger and Tuncer conducted a study of "factor productivity growth" in Turkish manufacturing industries for the period 1963–76, and investigated two hypotheses: (a) both the continued drive toward import substitution and the apparently increasing costs of the restrictive trade regime would have resulted in a secular decline in the rates of productivity growth; (b) there was lower productivity growth in subperiods when the regime was more restrictive. To estimate the growth of total factor productivity (TFP) in each industry, the authors used the equation

$$\frac{dA_i}{A_{it}} = \frac{dX_i}{X_{it}} - \frac{\alpha_1 dV_1}{V_{1t}} - \cdots - \frac{\alpha_m dV_m}{V_{mt}}$$

where X_i is the output, the V_js ($j = 1, \ldots, m$) are inputs (primary as well as intermediate), and the α_js are input elasticities of output. Thus the growth dA_i/dA_{it} of factor productivity in industry i is calculated as a residual. Table 3.11 summarizes Krueger and Tuncer's results. They concluded that their estimates of factor productivity growth lend some support to the two hypotheses above. Indeed, as indicated in the bottom row of table 3.11, there was a secular decline in TFP growth over the period 1963–76 during which import substitution policies were in force.

Table 3.11 Total factor productivity growth, 1963–1976 (annual average growth, percent)

Industry	1963–7	1967–70	1970–3	1973–6	Total
Food processing	0.85	0.78	2.14	− 4.32	− 0.09
Beverages	16.32	− 8.64	5.02	− 1.18	3.16
Tobacco	6.68	3.02	8.50	2.93	7.44
Textiles	2.08	4.82	2.24	− 4.42	1.44
Wearing apparel and footwear	2.00	6.60	5.62	− 4.18	2.50
Wood and cork products	0.40	− 3.13	− 2.06	− 1.15	− 1.26
Furniture and fixtures	3.00	2.14	− 10.62	9.73	− 0.56
Paper and products	2.99	− 2.82	− 1.17	4.14	0.59
Fur and leather products	− 2.72	4.31	− 8.93	1.17	− 1.17
Rubber products	11.97	− 3.28	2.68	6.07	4.27
Chemicals	3.31	2.47	2.73	− 1.87	1.67
Petroleum and coal	9.27	− 8.30	− 0.66	− 7.90	0.24
Nonmetallic minerals	− 1.06	2.82	3.31	− 4.32	0.62
Basic metals	0.74	7.06	− 1.83	− 6.27	0.61
Metal products	2.23	− 3.48	8.08	− 0.29	2.39
Machinery	0.60	6.66	− 4.96	1.46	1.02
Electrical machinery	− 3.81	− 3.84	6.26	7.21	1.30
Transport equipment	5.77	− 6.44	9.35	3.25	1.42
Total	3.20	1.31	2.51	− 1.18	2.10

Source: Krueger and Tuncer, 1982

Also, TFP growth in the subperiods 1963–7 and 1970–3, when the import and exchange regimes were less restrictive, was higher than that observed in the subperiods 1967–70 and 1973–6, when the import and exchange regimes were highly restrictive.

Table 3.11 also shows that in the post-devaluation period, with the exception of the fur and leather products industries and the wood and cork products industries, there was TFP growth in industries producing export-ables: 2.14 percent in food processing, 2.24 percent in textiles, 5.62 percent in wearing apparel and footwear, and 3.31 percent in nonmetallic mineral products.

Productivity growth performance in the import-substituting industries was also mixed. Those showing high TFP growth included metal products (8 percent), electrical machinery (6 percent), and transport equipment (9 percent).

Income Distribution

Many government policies have affected income distribution in Turkey. Agricultural price support policies, trade and foreign exchange regimes, price controls, minimum wages, pricing policy for SEE products, credit rationing, the salary scales of civil servants, and other factors have been crucial in determining income distribution patterns among factors of production, between sectors, and between different socioeconomic groups. Some of these policies had offsetting effects on income distribution. Krueger, for example, concluded that during the 1950s and 1960s " . . . the effects of Turkey's trade regime on overall income distribution have probably been slight" (Krueger, 1974, p. 240) as the income distributional effects of import-substitution-biased trade and foreign exchange policies were at least partially offset by domestic policies, such as the agricultural support pricing and input subsidy policies, and export incentive policies.

In 1970, along with the devaluation, there were also changes in SEE product prices, agricultural prices, interest rates, indirect tax rates, civil servant salaries, and so forth. Therefore no attempt was made to quantify any incremental impact of the devaluation on income distribution, as this would have been rather difficult. However, whatever income distribution effect the devaluation might have had must have been limited in scope and temporary in nature. Commercial exporters probably captured some windfall gains. There is also reason to believe that the scarcity rents received by import license holders were largely diminished as a result of substantial expansion of imports in the post-devaluation period. The temporary incremental bias against traditional exports caused by the lower exchange rate was probably compensated for by the support price increases announced in August 1970 and in the spring of 1971. It is highly unlikely that the devaluation had any permanent effect on income distribution, given that the real exchange rate quickly eroded and relative price effects were temporary.

The Impact on the Government's Budget

The August 1970 devaluation package did not introduce any change in customs duty rates, apart from duty exemptions granted to some iron and steel products. However, the stamp duty, an across-the-board surcharge levied on the c.i.f. value of imports, was lowered from 25 to 10 percent. Because of this reduction, revenues from import taxes fell by 2.3 percent in 1970 over 1969, while import expenditures increased by 18.2 percent in current dollars. As a result, the share of import taxes in aggregate public sector revenues decreased to 11.5 percent in 1970 from 14.8 percent in 1969. Nonetheless, the loss of revenues from import surcharges in 1970 was probably more than offset by the large differential between the new parity rate of TL15 per US dollar and the Central Bank's lower buying rate of TL12 per dollar set for the proceeds from traditional exports. In any case, this loss of revenue from imports proved to be temporary. As import growth accelerated subsequently, both as a share of total revenues and in absolute terms, import tax revenues showed substantial expansion. From 1970 to 1971 revenues from this source increased by 83 percent, and by 51 percent between 1971 and 1973. These increases raised the share of import taxes to 17.2 percent in 1971 and to 18 percent in 1973. Obviously, the dramatic increases in imports more than compensated for the reduction in the stamp duty. These developments suggest that the external policy changes instituted in August 1970 did not cause any strain on the budget in the early 1970s.

Conclusion

The August 1970 devaluation achieved its immediate objectives. It encouraged remittances and permitted some additional borrowing. By substantially reducing the extent of overvaluation, bringing a certain degree of uniformity into the nominal exchange rate system, and lowering surcharges and advance deposit requirements, the devaluation package revitalized current account transactions. Merchandise exports and imports expanded rapidly. These developments contributed to an impressive short-run balance-of-payments correction.

However, the protective trade regime including the QR system, remained intact. Consequently, there was no permanent shift in resource allocation and trade patterns. Lack of discipline in macroeconomic management led to accelerating inflation, thereby causing a rapid erosion in the real exchange rate. Thus the early benefits of the devaluation started dissipating after a couple of years. Substantial increases in workers' remittances merely postponed the reemergence of balance-of-payments problem until the mid-1970s. At the same time, the first oil shock started dominating balance-of-payments developments, exacerbating the emerging trade deficit. Indeed, the government's failure to allow appropriate adjustments in relative energy prices and its continued commitment to higher growth targets despite changing domestic and global economic conditions quickly worsened the balance-of-payments situation.

Subsequent devaluations, starting right after the first oil shock and accompanied by a more prudent macroeconomic management and energy policy, might have prolonged the initial success, thus encouraging some permanent change in the trade regime in the mid-1970s. However, this did not happen, and Turkey, under several short-lived and weak coalition governments, entered an era of severe economic mismanagement which culminated in the debt crisis of the late 1970s.

4

Trade Liberalization in the 1980s

Turkey's next liberalization episode began in 1980. Unlike the 1970 episode, it marked the beginning of a major program of economic liberalization and trade reform. Like all Turkey's previous liberalization episodes, its roots lay in balance-of-payments difficulties. The late 1970s was a period when inflation was accelerating, unemployment was rising, shortages were common, and labor unrest had reached crisis proportions. Even worse, political violence was rampant throughout Turkey. All these problems were becoming increasingly severe owing to the economy's inability to adjust to higher world energy prices, a lack of incentives for exports, irrationality in the import-licensing system, poor performance by SEEs, and political instability. Also like earlier episodes, the liberalization of 1980 was characterized by a devaluation of the lira and the institution of a macroeconomic stabilization program. However, what distinguishes this episode from earlier liberalization attempts is that for the first time the Turkish government demonstrated that it would use economic policies to create a more liberal market-oriented economy.

The main objectives of the 1980 economic reforms can be summarized as follows: first, to stabilize the balance of payments through domestic austerity and export-encouragement programs; second, to encourage a more rational foreign exchange system by liberalizing the import-licensing system and allowing the exchange rate to equilibrate supply and demand levels; third, to encourage workers' remittances and direct foreign investment; fourth, to improve the efficiency of SEEs by allowing them to raise prices and at the same time exposing them to increased domestic and foreign competition; fifth, to increase the economic importance of the private sector by encouraging privatization and limiting some sectors dominated by public enterprises.

The explicit objectives of the 1980 liberalization included the dismantling of QRs, the maintenance of competitive exchange rates, the promotion of exports, and the elimination of direct import controls. In January 1980 the government devalued the lira from 47 to 70 per US dollar, and since then devaluation has by and large kept pace with domestic inflation. The exchange rate has been adjusted on a daily basis since May 1981.

In addition, major steps were taken to liberalize imports. Guarantee deposits were reduced in 1980. In 1981 the quota list was abolished, and a number of commodities were shifted from liberalized list II to liberalized list I. These lists were then abolished in 1984 and replaced by a simpler set of three lists. Tariffs were reduced, and measures were introduced to increase the effectiveness of a variety of export promotion schemes. These include tax exemptions, rebates, favorable credit terms, and foreign exchange retention. The government also negotiated a variety of bilateral trade agreements, the most important of which were with the neighboring Islamic countries.

In contrast with the 1970 episode, the government announced that the 1980 liberalization program would be gradual, with the ultimate objective of establishing an outward-looking economy, although timing strategies were not made explicit. Whether the long-run objective is to achieve completely free trade by removing all relative price distortions is not yet clear. In any case, this has been the most thoroughgoing and long-lasting liberalization episode in Turkey's history.

Economic Circumstances in 1980

Turkey's balance-of-payments difficulties in the late 1970s were rooted in both domestic and international conditions. After the first oil price shock, the government attempted to accelerate aggregate growth rates, mainly through increased foreign borrowing. Imports increased by 136 percent from 1977 to 1980, while exports grew by only 66 percent. The major component of the increased imports was oil, which accounted for 84 percent of the total.

In 1977 Turkey's trade deficit was US$4.1 billion. This deficit fell to US$2.3 billion in 1978 and then rose slightly to US$2.8 billion in 1979. As a result of rising debt and interest payments, the current account deficits deteriorated even more dramatically than the trade account. They rose from US$1.8 billion in 1978 to US$3.2 billion in 1980. External debt increased by almost US$12 billion in 1977–9, with short-term debt accounting for much of the increase.[1] In effect, Turkey was the first of the problem

---

1 Successive governments assumed a great deal of risk by allowing heavy short-term borrowing at terms that became increasingly costly. The major source was the Convertible Turkish Lira Deposits, which offered attractive terms and the Central Bank's full exchange risk coverage. Total external debt increased from US$3.5 billion at end-1974, of which only US$200 million was short term, to US$14 billion by the end of 1978, with US$7.5 billion at short term.

debtor countries. A crisis point arrived in 1979 and was resolved, at least temporarily, through a major debt rescheduling with official creditors.

As in the 1970 episode, the government tried to reduce pressure on the balance of payments by restricting imports. The stamp duty on imports was raised from 5–10 percent in 1974 to 22.5–25 percent in 1978. Guarantee deposit rates were increased from 10–20 percent in 1976 to 15–30 percent in 1978 and to 25–40 percent in 1979. Along with some attempts at fiscal stabilization, these measures brought some respite to the balance-of-payments problem in 1978, when imports fell by about 20 percent in nominal terms. In 1979, however, there was a substantial increase in imports, in part due to the rise in world oil prices.

The government encouraged foreign exchange earnings through various measures, although less strongly than in the late 1960s. The lira was devalued by 7 percent in 1976, 15 percent in 1977, 25 percent in 1978, and 45 percent in 1979. However, accelerating inflation substantially eroded the real exchange rate, which fell some 33 percent between 1973 and 1979. As overvaluation increased, export earnings showed little real growth. In 1979, exports actually fell slightly in nominal terms, while imports increased by over 10 percent.

Workers' remittances amounted to US$1.4 billion in 1976 but fell in response to the overvalued lira, averaging US$1.0 billion in 1977–8. Following the large devaluation in June 1979, remittances increased sharply and totaled US$1.6 billion for the entire year.

External factors had mixed effects on the Turkish economy in the second half of the 1970s. The most obvious were world oil prices. Since Turkey is a major oil importer, higher prices placed extreme stress on the economy. However, Turkey took no major steps to reduce its dependence on oil, and its inward-looking trade strategy was also significant. During a time when new markets were opening, especially in the Middle East, Turkey was slow to capitalize. Not until 1980 was significant attention given to expanding foreign exchange earnings from trade with other countries in the region.

Inflation accelerated in the late 1970s, in part owing to a rapidly increasing money supply. The average inflation rate in 1979 (measured by the wholesale price index) was 64 percent; the end-of-year rate was above 100 percent. The money supply (currency, sight, and time deposits) increased by 120 percent in 1979.

Production, meanwhile, was regularly disrupted by episodic violence, lack of labor discipline, and strikes. Almost 8 million workdays were lost in the first eight months of 1980, compared with about a million the previous year.

In most respects the protectionism immediately preceding the 1980 reforms was the same as that preceding the 1970 reforms. Both periods were characterized by heavy reliance on QRs, import prohibitions to protect domestic industries, and biases against exports.

Political Circumstances

The 1980 liberalization episode took place again the backdrop of the gravest political situation since the Turkish Republic was founded after World War I. Following the invasion of Cyprus in 1974, Turkey experienced a series of weak coalition governments led alternatively by the Republican People's Party of Bulent Ecevit and the Justice Party of Suleyman Demirel. Both parties could govern only with the participation of small parties on the right.

At the same time, there was serious conflict between rightists and leftists in urban working-class neighborhoods and in the universities. The failure of successive governments to quell the violence eroded their authority, concurrently reducing the possibility of their reforming economic policy.

Although the government was forced by debt renegotiations to commit Turkey to austerity measures in 1979, the scope of the reform package announced in January 1980 came as a surprise. Why the Demirel government appointed the framer of the 1980 reforms, Turgut Ozal, as the new economic czar, is not clear. Ozal, an engineer by training, headed the SPO under Demirel at the time of the 1970 devaluation but was not perceived at that time to be a strong supporter of liberal economic policies. Perhaps it was a last bold attempt to regain international credibility and with it an influx of desperately needed funds.

In any case, the military seized power ten months later and restored order. However, the new regime continued the economic liberalization policies instituted in January and retained Ozal as economic czar. A final political circumstance was the outbreak of war between Iran and Iraq in the fall of 1980. This was important because trade with Turkey became more attractive to both Iran and Iraq.

Post-1980 Liberalization Policies

Although explicit details of the liberalization strategy were not announced, some of the government's strategy can be inferred. The key elements were to use trade liberalization to address Turkey's most pressing macroeconomic problems and to allow affected industries adequate time to plan how they would adjust to a more competitive and outward-looking environment. Since neither macroeconomic nor industry adjustments could be predicted, the government felt that it did not make sense to announce either a timetable or a sequence of policy changes. Instead, a more pragmatic approach was adopted.

The main macroeconomic priority was to deal with the balance-of-payments problem. Therefore the initial steps of the liberalization program primarily were aimed at stimulating exports, reducing import demand, and attracting remittances. This explains the focus on export promotion schemes and devaluation. Initially, the government did little to reform the import-allocation system other than eliminate QRs.

Although import liberalization was an announced objective, this part of the program has proceeded more cautiously. A step-by-step approach was adopted to dismantling the quota and licensing system. The January 1980 steps included devaluing the lira to reduce excess demand for foreign exchange, allowing exporters to import intermediates and raw materials duty free, simplifying the export promotion system, and increasing the prices of many SEE goods. The principal change in the import regime was a reduction in the waiting period for import licenses and, once licenses had been granted, for foreign exchange.

Specific import quotas were eliminated in 1981, income taxes on new exports and interest rates on export-oriented investments were reduced, and rebate rates on exports were increased. Steps were taken to streamline the administration of the SEEs and to improve their financial position. The process accelerated in late 1983 and 1984 with greater reform of QRs and export promotion schemes. Prior to 1984, commodities not explicitly named on one of the lists could not be imported. However, in 1984 only commodities on the prohibited list could not be imported.

Exchange Rate Policy

The January 1980 reforms devalued Turkey's exchange rate by 48.6 percent, to an average rate of TL70 per US dollar.[2] This was followed by eight other devaluations in 1980, with an average rate for the year of TL78.6 per dollar. By late 1983, real devaluation was about 25 percent compared with early 1981. The total devaluation for 1981 was 46 percent, averaging TL111.5 per dollar. The average nominal rate was 162.6 in 1982, 225.5 in 1983, 366.7 in 1984, 522.0 in 1985, and 655.9 for the first eight months of 1986.

The 1980 devaluation was a substantial real devaluation. Based on trade weights and differential inflation rates and taking 1980's real EER as 100, the average devaluation rate for 1979 was 69. The year 1981 saw an additional 4 percent devaluation, and in 1982 the real rate reached 118. The index of the real exchange rate was 125 in 1983, 136 in 1984, and 136 in 1985.

---

2 A rate of TL55 per US dollar was maintained for fertilizer and associated raw materials. Note that prior to the January 1980 devaluation, in addition to the basic rate of TL47.10 per US dollar, a lower rate of TL35 per dollar was applied to certain transactions. Consequently, the rate of devaluation was higher for the latter groups in international transactions.

Export Promotion Policies

A variety of incentives have been used since 1980 to promote faster growth of exports. These include export tax rebates, credit subsidies, and foreign exchange allocations that allow for the duty-free import of intermediates and raw materials. The value of these direct subsidies averages about 20 percent of total exports, although they vary considerably across goods (World Bank, 1984). In general, rebates in the period 1981–3 were highest for capital goods (on average, in the 32–44 percent range), lowest for consumer goods (16–18 percent), and slightly higher for intermediate goods (18–29 percent). Since then, the proportionate value of these subsidies has changed considerably. Export credits were most important in 1981 (abut 60 percent of the total subsidy) but declined to about 30 percent in 1983. The tax rebate increased in importance, accounting for about 17 percent of the total subsidy in 1981 and nearly 50 percent in 1983. Duty-free imports accounted for about 20 percent. Table 4.1 shows total average subsidy rates for the period 1980–4 for some of the more important manufactured export commodity groups.

The value of export credit lies in the interest rate subsidy. The differential between the rates charged on general short-term credit and on export credits was over 30 percent in 1981 and down to 18 percent by end-1983. This decrease was due to reductions in the general rate and increases in the export rate, and reflects the government's desire to reduce interest rate differentials across the board.

Table 4.1 Subsidy rates on manufactured exports, 1980–1984 (percent)

Manufacturing industry	1980	1981	1982	1983	1984	Average 1980–4
Food and beverages	10.76	11.69	12.99	10.63	8.22	10.56
Textiles and clothing	20.33	19.32	18.56	21.66	13.55	17.84
Leather and fur	9.42	14.47	20.55	25.11	16.81	18.59
Paper and paper products	16.58	21.63	28.09	20.93	9.85	18.23
Chemicals	6.42	16.92	16.42	25.42	15.66	16.77
Rubber and plastics	36.47	24.94	29.64	21.24	20.01	23.98
Ceramics and glass	24.46	21.59	23.85	18.28	16.87	20.12
Cement and cement products	16.28	15.56	20.86	28.17	18.02	19.39
Iron and steel	16.70	15.27	23.91	29.17	21.02	23.50
Nonferrous metals	62.12	63.41	52.30	41.20	25.01	41.76
Fabricated metal products	71.13	70.18	101.48	159.46	69.71	98.64
Nonelectrical machinery	53.98	21.78	25.37	29.18	12.89	23.70
Electrical machinery	96.22	69.83	43.84	68.65	29.74	49.70
Transport equipment	57.58	47.04	31.69	28.71	25.33	35.13
Average	22.05	20.50	20.61	23.39	15.07	19.54

Source: Milanovic, 1986

Export tax rebates grew rapidly in the early 1980s, both in absolute terms and as a share of total exports. Commodities receiving rebates were grouped into ten lists, where rebate rates varied from zero to 20 percent. Higher rebates were granted to large exporters. The average tax rebate rose from 14 percent in 1981 to 23 percent in 1983 owing to increases in the rebate rates. The total coverage of the rebate system (measured by the share of exports eligible for rebates to total exports) rose from about two thirds to over three quarters. The average value for total manufactured exports rose from 3.6 percent of total manufactured exports in 1981 to 11.5 percent in 1983.

In late 1983 the government announced its intention to stimulate exports less through direct export subsidies and more through flexible exchange rates (devaluation) and import liberalization. Steps were taken in the near term to reduce the budgetary cost of export subsidies. The government hoped to reduce or eventually eliminate those subsidies. Although no changes were made in the system itself, the rebate rates were uniformly lowered by 20 percent in April 1984, and by an additional 25 percent in September. The cost of export credit rose four times in 1984, and maturities were shortened. Also, steps were taken to reduce red tape. The total average subsidy fell to 19.5 percent in 1984 compared with 23.2 percent in 1983.

Table 4.2 Real effective exchange rates for manufactured exports, 1980–1984

	1980	1981	1982	1983	1984	Average growth 1980–4 (%)
Food and beverages	110.8	116.0	133.2	138.7	147.3	7.4
Textiles and clothing	120.3	124.0	139.8	152.5	154.5	6.5
Leather and fur	109.4	118.9	142.1	156.9	159.0	9.8
Paper and paper products	116.6	126.4	151.0	151.6	149.5	6.4
Chemicals	106.4	121.5	137.3	157.3	157.4	10.3
Rubber and plastics	136.5	129.8	152.8	152.0	163.3	4.6
Ceramics and glass	124.5	126.3	146.0	148.3	159.1	6.3
Cement and cement products	116.3	120.1	142.5	160.7	160.6	8.4
Iron and steel	116.7	119.8	146.1	162.0	164.7	9.0
Nonferrous metals	162.1	169.8	179.6	177.0	170.1	1.2
Fabricated metal products	171.1	176.8	237.5	325.3	231.0	7.8
Nonelectrical machinery	154.0	126.5	147.8	162.0	153.6	− 0.1
Electrical machinery	196.2	176.5	169.6	211.5	176.6	− 2.6
Transport equipment	157.6	152.8	155.3	161.4	170.6	2.0
Average of manufactured exports	121.1	125.2	142.2	154.7	156.6	6.4
Average real exchange rate	100.0	103.9	117.9	125.4	136.1	8.0

Table 4.2 presents estimates of real EERs for manufactured exports. These are calculated by scaling up the economy's real exchange rate by the total percentage subsidy rate on each sector's exports. The subsidies accrue from tax rebates, subsidized credit, and access to foreign exchange (Milanovic, 1986). As in the earlier period, the most rapid rise in average rates took place in the first year after reform, in 1980. However, comparing the average change in EERs with the actual change in the official rates shows that the average subsidy fell slightly between 1980 and 1981, implying that the real effective rate for manufactured exports rose less than the actual real devaluation. The reverse is the case for the next two years. In 1984, real effective devaluation for exports was close to zero, even though the official rate (in real terms) was devalued by 8.6 percent.

There was considerable variance in the rates of change across sectors. The sectors with the highest increases in real EERs included fabricated metal products, chemicals, leather goods, ceramics and glass goods, and cement. The sectors farthest below average were machinery, nonferrous metals, and transportation equipment.[3]

Import Regime Changes

Although the quota lists were eliminated in 1981, policy reform was more gradual for imports although the government never hid its long-run objective of liberalization in general and elimination of the QR system in particular. Perhaps the main reason for the slow pace in the case of imports was the worry that import liberalization would contribute to balance-of-payments problems and also exacerbate unemployment at a time of macroeconomic stabilization.

This period of gradual change ended at the end of 1983 when the government announced dramatic policy changes, the most significant of which was reform of the remaining elements of the QR system. Previously, commodities not explicitly included on the quota or liberalized lists could not be imported. This system was replaced with three new lists. The first explicitly forbade the import of some 200 commodities, mostly consumer goods. The second required licenses to import some 400 items, accounting for about 45 percent of 1984 imports. The third list covered mainly luxury

---

3 It was not possible to estimate EERs for manufactured imports for the period because data on trade-weighted tariff rates are not available. Unlike the early 1970s, there are no systematic studies of the post-1980 period with estimates of various parameters based on consistent sectoral definitions and aggregations. A proper effort at evaluating nominal effective protection trends at any reasonable level of aggregation would require working up from those six- to eight-digit levels for which tariff information exists and changing the weights yearly, depending on compositional changes in different years. However, since there were only minor changes in tariffs until 1983, it can be inferred that the import EERs changed in approximate proportion to the exchange rate.

goods, which could be freely imported after a special levy had been paid. In contrast with the previous system, the new system allowed all other goods to be freely imported. In addition, licensing procedures were eased. The new system liberalized about 60 percent of 1983 imports. Table 4.3 shows the sectoral composition and percentage of liberalized goods. Almost all consumer goods were liberalized, but they accounted for only US$172 million of total imports in 1983. Intermediate goods were liberalized far more than capital goods. Total liberalized goods accounted for 43 percent of 1984 imports.

Table 4.3 Changes in protection and comparative advantage, 1984 (percent)

	Elimination of QRs[a]	Estimated overall tariff change[b]	Estimated change in nominal protection[c]
Agricultural products	69.3	7.4	Uncertain
Live animals, plants	2.6	1.1	Increase
Fruit and vegetables	93.3	31.9	Probable increase
Meat products	100.0	0.8	Decrease
Sugar, confectionery	100.0	9.9	Uncertain
Beverages and tobacco	14.2	86.7	Increase
Textiles and clothing	95.8	2.8	Uncertain
Textiles	98.0	3.2	Uncertain
Clothing	0.6	−3.6	Decrease
Total consumer goods	93.6	4.5	Uncertain
Metal ores	87.1	0.0	Decrease
Chemicals	81.8	−3.8	Decrease
Rubber and plastics	27.4	0.9	Decrease
Leather and furs	100.0	4.9	Uncertain
Wood and paper	78.5	−18.9	Decrease
Glass and ceramics	19.6	−2.6	Decrease
Iron and steel	0.1	3.2	Decrease
Nonferrous metals	−2.2	−27.4	Decrease
Total intermediate goods	69.2	−4.4	Decrease
Metal products	6.5	−2.7	Decrease
Nonelectrical machinery	11.9	−0.1	Decrease
Electrical machinery	60.2	−14.9	Decrease
Transportation equipment	14.3	3.8	Probable increase
Measuring equipment	45.8	−10.3	Decrease
Electronic equipment	100.0	20.5	Increase
Total capital goods	23.5	−2.1	Decrease
Grand total	60.1	−3.3	Decrease

[a] Percentage of imports (in value terms) in each category that had QRs removed in 1984.
[b] Nominal tariff reduction multiplied by the share of that category's imports which had tariffs reduced.
[c] Combines the previous measures. If QRs and tariffs declined, then so did protection. Other cases may be ambiguous.
Source: World Bank, 1985

Table 4.4 Changes in nominal tariff protection, 1983–1984 (percent)

	1 Average tariff before Dec 1983	2 Average tariff after Jan 1984	Column 2 – column 1
Agricultural products	11.1	20.0	8.9
Live animals, plants	1.0	71.6	70.6
Fruit and vegetables	20.6	93.0	72.4
Meat products	3.9	4.7	0.8
Sugar, confectionery	70.8	80.9	10.1
Beverages and tobacco	128.9	296.6	167.7
Textiles and clothing	26.1	33.3	7.2
Textiles	24.9	32.8	7.9
Clothing	67.6	52.7	– 14.9
Total consumer goods	18.0	26.2	8.2
Metal ores	8.1	2.7	– 5.4
Chemicals	47.0	22.5	– 24.5
Rubber and plastics	43.8	48.1	4.3
Leather and furs	4.0	9.9	5.9
Wood and paper	42.0	18.0	– 24.0
Glass and ceramics	68.0	2.1	– 65.9
Iron and steel	19.7	9.3	– 10.4
Nonferrous metals	41.4	9.4	– 32.0
Total intermediate goods	40.8	18.6	– 22.2
Metal products	31.3	21.2	– 10.1
Nonelectrical machinery	40.3	36.7	– 3.6
Electrical machinery	44.5	21.8	– 22.7
Transportation equipment	42.6	9.9	27.1
Measuring equipment	38.7	94.9	– 28.8
Electronic equipment	72.8		22.1
Total capital goods	44.0	32.0	– 12.0
Total	38.8	2.3	– 36.5

The values are average weighted tariff protection for items whose protection was affected by the changes.

Source: World Bank, 1985a

Concurrent with this reform were significant reductions in tariff structure that brought tariffs for the majority of imports down to about 20 percent of value. Although the first reduction, in December 1983, drew criticism from some affected sectors, the second reduction, in January 1984, was even greater. This can only be interpreted as evidence of the new government's determination to move forward.

Table 4.4 summarizes the sectoral pattern for those goods whose tariffs changed. On average, nominal protection increased for domestically produced goods owing to new levels imposed on consumer goods. Tariffs decreased for other categories, most sharply for intermediate goods, and declined by 16 percent on average. The total reduction in tariff changes was 3.3 percent, as shown in table 4.3.

Not all tariffs were reduced; some were increased. In an obvious attempt to cushion the impact of liberalization of the licensing system, there was to be an inverse correlation between those sectors which were hit hardest by the loss of licensing protection and those which had tariffs reduced. Although consumer imports, for example, were almost completely liberalized, their level of nominal protection was increased, particularly through the use of dollar-denominated levies. The reverse occurred for capital goods, where tariffs were reduced to a greater degree, but most capital goods remained on one list or another. Only intermediates seem to have suffered on both counts. Administrative procedures were centralized in the Treasury and the Foreign Trade Secretariat, permitting more rapid changes in rates and licensing.

This is consistent with the government's announced intention of continuing with a multilevel protection system, with the lowest levels provided for intermediate goods. This suggests that Turkey's traditional emphasis on industrialization has not died completely.

Restrictions on International Capital Movements

Until recently, Turkish citizens were not permitted to hold foreign exchange, and capital transfers abroad were subject to government approval. Foreign investment in Turkey is regulated according to the terms of the Law to Encourage Foreign Investment, which has been in effect since 1954. Under this law, foreign investments in "priority" sectors are accorded preferential treatment. Transfers of dividends and of proceeds from the sale of shares of companies included in the 1954 law are guaranteed by the Ministry of Finance. Partly because of the unattractiveness of the law's terms and partly because of high risk factors, foreign investment in Turkey has been fairly limited.[4]

These policies were unaffected by the 1970 devaluation and its associated policy changes. However, liberalization of capital accounts is a long-run objective of the 1980 reforms. Although initially there were no policy changes in capital accounts, perhaps because of fears that immediately lifting restrictions on them would have a detrimental impact on the balance of payments, significant movement in this area began in 1984 when the government announced that it would make the Turkish lira a convertible currency.

4 For a detailed study of foreign investment issues in Turkey, see Erdilek (1982).

Under the new set of provisions, Turkish citizens are allowed to hold foreign currency and to open foreign exchange deposit accounts. Simultaneously, the role of commercial banks in foreign dealings has been expanded. Banks are allowed to set foreign exchange buying and selling rates within a margin of 6 percent above or below a parity rate determined by the Central Bank. They are also permitted to raise short- and medium-term foreign exchange in international financial markets.

More recently, local governments, after gaining some autonomy in economic decision making following the administrative reforms, have started borrowing in the international markets. However, shortsightedness and the absence of any coordinated foreign borrowing strategy between the central and local governments could make future debt problems worse.

Foreign investment in Turkey has been quite low, but this is due more to neglect and bureaucratic problems than to the investment laws, which are quite liberal. Periodic problems with profit remittances have compounded the problems of attracting foreign investment, which has been a government objective since 1980. The laws were liberalized to broaden the number of sectors in which outside investment is allowed, and repatriation was guaranteed. Red tape has been reduced (at least in principle) and investment encouraged by further relaxing foreign exchange restrictions. However, foreign direct investments have not increased sufficiently to keep pace with Turkey's foreign exchange financing needs.

Macroeconomic Policies

The 1980 reforms included fiscal and monetary stabilization measures to reduce inflation, to help reduce demand for imports, and to stabilize the balance of payments and restore Turkey's international creditworthiness. For the most part, these reforms were orthodox in nature, involving attempts to limit the rate of growth of the money supply and domestic credit, as well as attempts to reduce government expenditures and government borrowing requirements.

Since 1980 there has been some success in moderating Central Bank lending in general, and lending to the public sector in particular. This is especially noticeable with public enterprises, where lending did not come close to keeping pace with inflation. However, Central Bank lending to commercial banks grew very rapidly through 1983. After 1981, commercial bank lending grew much more rapidly than Central Bank lending. Lending for foreign trade and tourism grew by more than 600 percent between 1981 and 1983. Lending to industry declined in 1983 before beginning to rise in the first half of 1984.

Beginning in 1981, there was a steady decline in the nominal growth rate of total money creation (Baysan and Blitzer, 1988, appendix table 4.1). Note, however, that it grew by 85 percent in 1981, although inflation was only 37 percent. Nevertheless, even though the money supply increased by 53 percent in 1982, inflation fell to 27 percent. The rate of money creation fell by almost 40 percent in 1983, but inflation started to increase again. In 1984 the annual rate of increase was 28 percent, while inflation reached 50 percent by mid-year.

The principal objective official policy after 1980 was to reduce public sector borrowing requirements as a share of national income, both through increases in taxes and reductions in the rate of growth of public expenditures, including subsidies to SEEs.

The attempt was partially successful. The government deficit as a proportion of revenues declined from 28 percent in 1980 to 11 percent in 1982 before jumping to 18 percent (before the 1983 elections) and then increasingly sharply to 32 percent in 1984 before declining in 1985 after the imposition of a value-added tax. Real growth of public expenditures was slightly negative in 1981 and then fell by about 25 percent in 1982. In 1983, however, government expenditures rose twice as fast as GDP, with the expenditure-to-GDP ratio increasing by 4 percent. The composition of government expenditures (investment, current, transfers) did not change substantially (Baysan and Blitzer, 1988, appendix table 4.2).

Some progress was also made on tax reform. Direct taxes as a share of total revenue rose by 11 percent in 1980 and then held constant. After 1980, taxes on services increased at the fastest rate. Despite tariff rate changes in 1984, trade taxes have continued to increase, even in real terms. A major reform began in 1985 with the imposition of a value-added tax. In its first year it accounted for 20 percent of government revenue.

The deficit-to-GDP ratio peaked at 5.4 percent in 1980 and then fell rapidly to just under 2 percent in 1982. It subsequently increased substantially, reaching almost 5 percent in 1984. Contractionary policies in 1985 led to a decline in the deficit ratio. In every year, however, the government deficit was less than government investment, implying that investment expenditures were being financed partly by taxation and partly by borrowing. Total public sector borrowing was greater than the government deficit largely as a result of SEE borrowing. When that is included, the ratio of public sector borrowing to GDP was 12.6 percent in 1980, 8.5 percent in 1981, 6.9 percent in 1982, 8.7 percent in 1983, 9.7 percent in 1984, and 7.8 percent in 1985.

Domestic Price Controls

Since 1980 the government has attempted to correct the most pronounced price distortions in the domestic economy. Its strategy has been to rely on market forces, to insure better resource allocation, to rationalize government budget expenditures, and to strengthen the financial position of the SEEs. Exchange rate policies have also played a major role.

Major steps were undertaken by the government in 1980 to control the price of SEE goods. Many prices charged by SEEs were increased, and some consumer subsidies were reduced or eliminated. The immediate effectives were considerable. Price increases ranged from 45 percent for gasoline to 300 percent for paper and paper products, and to 400 percent for fertilizer (World Bank, 1982). Since 1983 the SEEs have had greater freedom to raise their prices without explicit government approval. When the government does establish a fixed price, it is committed to covering any resulting losses. The most important element in the long run will be continued efforts to move relative prices more in line with world prices.

Regarding post-1980 labor policy, four points should be mentioned. First, following the military takeover in 1980, strikes were prohibited along with most other union activity. This gave the government greater leeway to pursue more open trade policies. Second, the government has held down the growth rate of public sector wages. This was done largely for budgetary reasons, but it has led to large declines in the real income of this large class of workers. Third, during the period when union activity was banned, layoffs were effectively prohibited in manufacturing firms. This had the effect of lowering marginal production costs to the affected companies, although increasing fixed costs. Fourth, the macroeconomic stabilization program has lowered real wages.[5]

Economic Performance after Liberalization

Major Prices

Inflation was a major macroeconomic concern at the time of the 1980 liberalization. Table 4.5 indicates that prices increased by some 100 percent in 1980. Domestic monetary policy, the rise in world oil prices, and the real devaluation of 1980 all helped to push prices up.

Between 1981 and 1983, however, inflation fell considerably. The GDP deflator rose at a slower rate in each succeeding year, although inflation accelerated in the second half of 1983.[6] The overall moderation in the inflation rate was due to a combination of forces. First, the government succeeded in reducing public sector borrowing in real terms, and thereby reducing the rate of real money creation. Second, world oil prices began to decline in 1982. Finally, there was moderation in real devaluation.

5 Although layoffs were limited by government decree in the early 1980s, the unemployment rate rose because new jobs were not created and the urban labor force continued to grow.
6 The conventional explanation is that the government attempted to reflate the economy before the fall 1983 elections. Nevertheless, the government (that is, military) party lost the election to Ozal's new party, which promised a return to "sound" economic management and continued liberalization. Not much was said about austerity.

Table 4.5 Major price trends, 1979–1985

	1979	1980	1981	1982	1983	1984	1985
Wholesale price index	35	73	100	125	164	249	348
Consumer price index[a]	37	73	100	133	171	249	361
GDP deflator	35	70	100	128	165	247	354
Real exchange rate[b]	76	106	100	110	115	119	118
Real wage rate[c]	145	108	100	96	101	104	95

[a] Consumer price index for Istanbul.
[b] Average for the year.
[c] As reported by the Social Insurance Institute.
Source: World Bank, 1986

Inflation continued to accelerate through 1984, averaging about 45 percent, and then leveled off. It has not declined substantially since then.

In association with macroeconomic stabilization and devaluation, real wages fell by about 25 percent in 1980. They continued to decline, but at a less rapid rate, in 1981 and 1982 before increasing slightly in 1983 (the election year). In 1983, however, real wages were still only 70 percent of their 1979 level. The decline of the early 1980s would undoubtedly have been extremely difficult to sustain had it not been for the prohibition of both strikes and layoffs. In 1984 and 1985 real wages fell by a total of 6 percent, leaving them about 0.3 percent lower than in 1979.

In 1980 (and earlier), real interest rates were highly negative. Defining the real interest rate as the nominal rate less inflation in the wholesale price index, the rate paid on one-year convertible deposits (CDs) was −74 percent. The real rates charged by commercial banks on credits were approximately the same. However, the banks might have received higher real rates through hidden charges. This is supported by actions of the Central Bank, which rediscounted at even greater subsidization. The negativity was even larger for subsidized credit of agriculture, exports, and favored investment projects.

Nominal interest rates were considerably higher in 1981 than at the beginning of 1980 (Baysan and Blitzer, 1988, appendix table 4.3). Since inflation in 1981 fell 40 percent below the 1980 level, real interest rates rose dramatically. The real rate on one-year CDs was 13 percent, and nominal rates on nonsubsidized credit were approximately equal to the inflation rate. The real rate on Central Bank credit fell from the −80 percent range to the −6 percent range.

Real interest rates continued to increase in 1982, largely because of reduced inflation. However, the Central Bank continued to support a system in which commercial bank lending rates on nonsubsidized credit (averaging a real 11 percent in 1982) remained below the rate paid on

Table 4.6 Merchandise exports by category and destination, 1979–1985 (million current US dollars)

	1979	1980	1981	1982	1983	1984	1985	Average annual growth 1979–85 (%)
Agriculture and livestock	1,343.6	1,671.7	2,219.4	2,141.2	1,880.6	1,749.4	1,719.4	4.2
Cereals and pulses	164.2	181.0	326.1	337.3	376.3	267.1	234.4	6.1
Nuts, fruit, and vegetables	647.7	753.9	795.1	648.6	590.7	646.1	560.6	– 2.4
Hazelnuts	353.0	394.8	301.8	240.7	245.0	304.0	255.4	– 5.3
Raisins	114.8	130.3	130.2	100.3	71.4	62.3	74.9	– 6.9
Others	179.9	228.7	363.1	307.6	274.3	279.0	230.3	4.2
Industrial crops	448.0	605.9	813.4	741.6	531.5	492.5	659.3	6.7
Tobacco	177.0	233.7	395.0	348.3	237.8	216.4	330.1	10.9
Cotton	227.8	322.6	348.3	296.6	196.5	168.1	169.8	– 4.3
Others	43.2	49.6	70.1	96.7	97.2	108.0	159.4	24.3
Forestry products	4.7	8.1	19.7	33.4	14.8	23.7	105.8	68.0
Livestock products	62.0	108.2	258.2	389.7	362.1	323.3	244.2	25.7
Fishery products	21.7	22.7	26.6	24.0	20.3	20.3	21	– 0.5
Mining and quarry products	132.5	191.0	193.4	175.3	188.9	239.8	243.8	10.7

Industrial products	785.1	1,047.4	2,290.1	3,429.4	3,658.3	5,144.5	5,994.8	40.3
Agriculture-based process products	135.0	190.2	411.6	568.2	669.7	808.2	646.6	29.8
Textiles	390.7	439.8	802.8	1,056.3	1,299.1	1,875.4	1,789.5	28.9
Forestry products	4.7	8.1	19.7	33.4	14.8	23.7	105.8	68.0
Hides and leather products	43.6	49.5	82.1	111.4	192.1	400.6	484.4	49.4
Chemicals	27.2	91.9	165.6	208.3	197.2	270.0	373.5	54.7
Petroleum products	0.0	38.5	107.5	343.9	232.4	408.8	372.0	—
Cements	44.9	39.6	198.5	206.6	80.6	56.0	43.7	−0.5
Glass and ceramics	37.1	35.9	102.1	103.7	108.2	146.0	189.6	31.2
Nonferrous metal	14.6	18.3	29.8	44.6	78.9	85.5	115.5	41.2
Iron and steel	31.1	33.9	100.2	362.2	407.2	576.4	968.8	77.4
Metal products and machinery	18.1	29.8	85.0	143.0	122.8	134.5	450.4	70.9
Electrical appliances	4.5	11.5	26.1	75.2	69.0	99.6	118.9	72.6
Motor vehicles	26.6	50.3	117.5	110.2	126.3	135.0	146.6	32.9
Others	7.0	10.1	42.1	62.4	60.3	124.9	189.5	73.3
OECD countries	1,446.4	1,679.7	2,263.7	2,556.0	2,760.1	3,739.7	4,106.2	19.0
Eastern Europe	301.6	490.6	326.9	323.2	245.3	283.7	334.5	1.7
Middle Eastern countries	232.2	494.8	1,893.3	2,540.1	2,438.1	2,759.7	3,238.2	55.0
Other countries	280.0	245.0	219.0	326.7	284.3	350.4	279.3	0.0
Total	2,261.2	2,910.1	4,702.9	5,746.0	5,527.8	7,133.5	7,958.1	23.3

—, not applicable.

Source: World Bank, 1986

one-year deposits (a real 25 percent). In 1983 and early 1984, real interest rates declined as inflation rose. The spread between subsidized and nonsubsidized credit increased to 30–40 percent before the government raised rates in May 1984, although many borrowers (mainly in agriculture and the SEEs) retained access to subsidized credit. Spreads among borrowers have persisted, despite the government's agreement to reduce them as soon as possible.[7] The government argued that raising interest rates at that time would have contributed to inflation. There have been no substantial changes in either real or nominal rates since 1984.

External Transactions

Export performance since 1979 is summarized in table 4.6. The dollar value of exports grew very rapidly, at an average rate of 23 percent between 1981 and 1984. The nominal value of exports did not increase in 1983, although growth resumed in 1984 and early 1985 before leveling off in 1986. Manufactured exports grew even faster (more than 60 percent annually from 1979 to 1982, and 40 percent for the period 1979–85). As a share of total manufacturing output, exports went from 8.5 percent in 1980 to 15.8 percent in 1983. This performance is frequently cited to illustrate the success of the 1980 reforms.

Exports of textiles, leather goods, chemicals, iron and steel products, nonferrous metals, machinery, electrical goods, and transportation equipment grew faster than the average of total imports. In the manufactured categories, only tobacco products and cement lagged behind. Export-to-production ratios increased in all manufacturing sectors, most rapidly in the basic heavy industries. During this period the economy-wide export ratio almost tripled.

The pattern of export destinations changed very rapidly. Although exports to all regions grew substantially, trade with other countries in the region expanded dramatically. In 1979 Middle Eastern countries received about 10 percent of Turkey's exports; by 1981 this had grown to 40 percent. In 1981 exports to these countries tripled, and then rose by an additional 33 percent in 1982. There was little additional growth until 1985, when these exports increased by US$820 million. As a result of oil price reductions, exports to the Middle East declined slightly in 1986.

Table 4.7 provides data on imports since 1979. During this period the average growth was 12 percent per year, with the bulk of the growth concentrated in the first two years and in 1984. Imports fell slightly in 1982, and then rose by 4 percent in 1983, 16 percent in 1984, and 5 percent in 1985. Real imports in 1980 and 1981 grew more slowly than dollar costs, and afterwards grew faster, reflecting the reduction of global inflation and

7 This commitment was one of the conditions of a World Bank structural adjustment loan.

world oil prices. In any case, the growth rate of imports was slower in this period than in the late 1970s. How much was due to devaluation and how much to austerity and recession cannot be determined easily, but recession undoubtedly was a very important factor.

The composition of imports underwent some modest changes. The rapid growth in the mining and quarrying category seen in table 4.7 reflects increased oil costs.[8] Imports of agricultural products and foods increased rapidly, as did nonferrous metal imports. Imports of petroleum products fell, although imports of crude did not. Most other imports did not vary much. Imports of consumer goods have grown extremely rapidly since 1984, although from a very small base.

The figures clearly show a pattern of increasing commerce with the rest of the world. Since the 1980 reforms the total trade ratio (imports plus exports as a share of GDP) has increased by about 50 percent from the earlier 20–30 percent range. After discounting for depreciation of the lira against the dollar when calculating GDP, the trade ratio rose from 13 percent in 1979 to 43 percent in 1984. For manufacturing the trade ratio went from 31 percent in 1980 to 41 percent in 1983.

Table 4.7 Composition of imports by commodity, 1979–1985 (million US dollars)

	1979	1980	1981	1982	1983	1984	1985	Average annual growth 1979–85 (%)
Food and beverages	115	301	229	176	203	432	487	23.0
Textiles	46	80	78	103	97	117	146	23.0
Wood products	1	3	2	6	3	4	8	34.6
Hides and leather	0	0	1	0	2	6	16	n.a.
Chemicals	1,025	1,303	1,439	1,127	1,402	1,696	1,294	3.4
Petroleum products	750	910	621	221	423	264	290	− 12.7
Ceramics and glass	20	35	40	34	57	62	63	12.3
Cement and cement products	0	0	1	0	1	0	1	n.a.
Iron and steel	345	463	605	592	675	859	1,060	17.4
Nonferrous metals	55	87	141	122	195	220	224	22.2
Metal products and machinery	918	866	1,246	1,346	1,462	1,630	1,588	8.1
Electrical appliances	251	270	336	374	398	563	664	14.9
Transport equipment	221	222	358	594	478	468	813	20.5
Agriculture and livestock	36	51	125	176	138	138	375	39.8
Mining and quarrying	1,068	3,095	3,478	3,739	3,441	3,644	3,626	19.1
Industrial products	3,965	4,762	5,330	4,927	5,655	6,695	7,342	9.2
Total	5,069	7,909	8,933	8,842	9,235	10,757	11,344	12.2

n.a., not available.

Source: World Bank, 1986

8 The bulk of these costs are for crude oil and do not show up in the top part of the table, which includes only refined products.

The trade deficit declined by US$2.75 billion, or 60 percent, between 1980 and 1982, but has risen moderately since then. This improvement is associated with the rapid increase in exports compared with imports and with depreciation of the real exchange rate. However, it would be incorrect to find a direct causal link with exchange rates.

The deficit is also associated with foreign borrowing. The reduction in the trade deficit is mainly due to domestic austerity programs and greater discipline in foreign borrowing – policies that were instituted to restore Turkey's creditworthiness. The increase in the deficit since 1983 can be interpreted as a reflection of improved creditworthiness, due in part to better export performance.

Between 1980 and 1983 total foreign disbursed debt remained constant at the US$15.8 billion level before beginning to rise again as current account deficits increased after 1984. An unusually high proportion of this debt is owed or guaranteed by the government. The most striking feature is the rapid growth in debt-servicing costs. While the increased interest payments are not surprising (given that much of the debt was pegged to floating rates), repayments increased almost as rapidly. In fact, total debt-servicing costs have risen even faster than exports since 1979 (about 27 percent annually). The debt service ratios all increased annually, although the ratio to export earnings has been nearly constant since 1980. In 1984 it was about 23 percent. (See Baysan and Blitzer, 1988, appendix tables 4.4 and 4.5.)

Income and Product

Real growth has been sluggish at best. Real GDP growth averaged about 3.8 percent through 1985. There was a fall of about 1 percent in 1980, after which growth resumed in the 4–5 percent range. As a result of a substantial improvement in the trade deficit, domestic spending increased at a slower rate, slightly less than 2 percent annually. What growth there was was due to public sector spending. Public investment and consumption increased annually by 3.4 percent and 1.7 percent respectively. Private consumption grew slowly (by about 2 percent per year), and private investment still has not returned to 1979 levels. Total private spending in real terms was about 5 percent higher in 1985 than in 1979.[9]

The levels of investment expenditure, which fell in 1980 and did not reach 1979 levels until 1983, are particularly worrisome. This lack of investment shows up in the low levels of GDP growth as well as in the sectoral composition of GDP. Construction did not grow at all during this

9 About 35 percent of real aggregate growth has gone abroad in the form of worsened terms of trade and reduced trade deficits. For details, see Baysan and Blitzer (1988, appendix table 4.5).

Table 4.8 Real value of manufacturing production (1981 = 100)

	1981	1982	1983	Growth 1981–3 (%)
Food processing	100	101	109	2.9
Beverages	100	95	101	0.4
Tobacco processing	100	108	113	4.1
Textiles	100	103	112	3.9
Wood products	100	104	111	3.6
Paper and paper products	100	105	111	3.6
Printing	100	103	106	1.9
Hides and leather	100	104	109	3.0
Rubber products	100	115	133	10.1
Plastic products	100	109	120	6.3
Chemicals	100	104	112	3.7
Petroleum products	100	118	117	5.3
Ceramics and glass	100	106	109	3.0
Cement and cement products	100	102	100	0.1
Iron and steel	100	107	130	9.0
Nonferrous metals	100	100	102	0.6
Metal products and machinery	100	104	113	4.3
Electrical machinery	100	103	107	2.3
Transport equipment	100	117	135	10.5
Consumer goods	100	102	110	3.1
Intermediate goods	100	109	115	4.9
Investment goods	100	108	119	6.0
Total	100	106	107	4.2

Source: World Bank, 1986

period. The fastest-growing sector was government services, where value added increased at a 5 percent rate. Most other nontradeables increased faster than average, as did industry as a whole.

Estimated values for real production in selected manufacturing sectors are summarized in table 4.8.[10] Manufacturing has been dominated by consumer and intermediate goods, and capital goods industries have accounted for only an eighth of the total value of production during the 1980s. These shares have not changed appreciably. As real growth in capacity has been very small, this is not surprising.[11] In terms of value of

10 Not all years are covered. The reason is that a consistent data series was not available for all years. These tables should be read with great caution. The values for all years since 1980 have been revised almost annually.
11 The real growth that shows up here is due mainly to increased capacity utilization and completion of projects begun before 1980.

Table 4.9 Labor force, employment, and unemployment (thousands)

	1979	1980	1981	1982	1983	1984	1985	Growth 1979–85 (%)
Total civilian labor force (domestic and abroad)	17,622	17,956	18,248	18,618	18,846	19,099	19,347	1.6
Domestic civilian labor force	16,827	17,063	17,297	17,533	17,773	18,016	18,269	1.4
Total civilian employment	15,239	15,231	15,368	15,467	15,577	15,776	15,955	0.8
Agriculture	9,529	9,520	9,369	9,481	9,451	9,420	9,390	− 0.2
Industry	1,794	1,771	1,822	1,855	1,911	1,984	2,052	2.3
Mining and quarrying	123	124	126	114	109	112	113	− 1.4
Manufacturing	1,572	1,548	1,594	1,628	1,685	1,748	1,804	2.3
Electricity, water, and gas	100	99	102	113	116	124	135	5.1
Construction	578	581	582	584	586	606	623	1.3
Transportation, storage, and communications	492	480	491	498	507	523	541	1.6
Wholesale and retail trade	637	628	656	675	696	730	763	3.1
Banking, insurance, and real estate	208	211	214	216	217	224	229	1.6
Services	1,727	1,767	1,818	1,884	1,935	2,016	2,083	3.2
Unspecified	273	273	273	273	273	273	273	0.0

Urban and rural unemployment excluding agricultural labor surplus	1,588	1,832	1,929	2,066	2,196	2,240	2,314	6.5
Agricultural labor surplus at peak season[a]	700	700	700	665	665	665	665	– 0.9
Domestic labor surplus	2,288	2,532	2,629	2,731	2,861	2,905	2,979	4.5
Domestic labor surplus ratio	13.6	14.8	15.2	15.6	16.1	16.1	16.3	3.1
Labor stock abroad	795	893	951	1,085	1,073	1,083	1,078	5.2
Total labor surplus	3,083	3,425	3,580	3,816	3,934	3,988	4,057	4.7
Total labor surplus ratio	17.5	19.1	19.6	20.5	20.9	20.9	21	3.1

[a] Appears also as part of employment in agriculture.

Source: World Bank, 1986

production the most important sectors are food processing, petroleum products, and textiles, which together account for more than 50 percent.

Real output growth during the first part of the 1980s was fastest in the transportation equipment, rubber products, and iron and steel industries. Production of beverages, printing, cement, and nonferrous metals grew the most slowly. The data also show considerable changes in relative prices during the 1980s. Some sectors where value of production increased much faster than the average actually grew slowly, reflecting rapid increases in prices. These sectors include electrical machinery, ceramics and glass, wood products, and oil refining.

Employment

Tables 4.9 and 4.10 present labor force data for 1979–85 and employment data for 1979–83. Both show that employment increased throughout this period, but at a much slower rate than the labor force. Also, as shown in table 4.5, real wages remained about a third below pre-1980 levels. The level of unemployment (domestic labor surplus) grew by 3.9 percent annually. The unemployment rate (labor suplus ratio) rose from 17.5 percent to 21.0 percent in 1985. In large part, this poor performance reflects austerity measures, low levels of investment, attempts to control the public sector budget deficit, and attempts to improve the efficiency of the SEEs. On this last point, table 4.10 shows that public sector employment fell by 8 percent in 1979–82 (perhaps largely owing to dismissals by material law authorities and retirements), while private sector employment increased by a modest 14 percent.

Employment grew slowly in all major sectors of the economy in the 1980s. It actually declined in agriculture as rural–urban migration continued, and increased more slowly in industry than in services. In industry, the only sector in which employment increased at a faster rate than real production was electrical machinery. Other manufacturing sectors with relatively rapid employment growth included plastics and refining. Employment decreased in tobacco processing, rubber products, basic metals, and transportation equipment. Since production of transportation equipment increased, there was apparent growth in labor productivity in that sector. In general, there is a close correlation between the ranking of sectors in terms of employment growth (see table 4.10) and production growth (see table 4.8).

Capital and Investment

As noted above, 1979–84 was a period of low investment and low excess capacity. Capacity utilization bottomed out in 1980 and has gone up slowly since then. For private sector manufacturing, capital utilization rates

Table 4.10 Employment in manufacturing industry (thousands)

Industry	1979	1980	1981	1982	1983	Growth 1979–83 (%)
Food and beverage	125.0	134.5	134.6	135.7	122.2	− 0.6
Tobacco processing	51.7	52.8	50.4	44.5	47.5	− 2.1
Textiles and clothing	183.5	182.5	189.9	198.1	198.3	2.0
Wood products	16.5	17.8	18.5	17.7	16.0	− 0.8
Paper and paper products	15.8	18.2	18.5	18.9	18.7	4.3
Printing	10.6	10.9	11.6	11.4	9.8	− 1.9
Leather and fur	4.1	4.4	5.3	5.7	4.2	0.6
Rubber products	11.5	10.5	9.8	12.8	10.3	− 2.7
Chemicals	43.5	43.1	43.8	46.5	46.6	1.7
Petroleum I	9.7	10.1	10.1	10.7	10.7	2.5
Nonmetallic minerals	58.4	61.0	64.1	60.5	58.7	0.1
Basic metals	81.1	76.8	76.9	77.1	74.1	− 2.2
Metal products	38.3	40.4	39.9	41.7	37.0	− 0.9
Machinery	47.3	48.1	54.1	53.0	47.6	0.2
Electrical machinery	31.5	29.9	31.4	33.4	32.7	0.9
Transport equipment	53.3	49.9	51.4	49.7	50.2	− 1.5
Plastic products	5.6	5.3	5.9	6.2	6.0	1.7
Other manufacturing	12.4	12.2	13.6	13.6	9.3	− 6.9
Total	799.8	808.6	829.8	837.7	800.0	0.0
Public sector	293.2	289.1	277.6	266.1	280.4	− 1.1
Private sector	506.6	519.5	522.2	571.1	519.6	0.6

Source: World Bank, 1986

rose from the 50 percent range in 1980 to the 70 percent range in recent years (Baysan and Blitzer, 1988, appendix table 4.6). This increase of about 40 percent is associated with real production increases, on average about 20 percent (see table 4.8), which indicates negative real net investment in the sense that real production capacity appears to have been lost.

Table 4.11 shows the sharp and continued decline in real investment across all sectors. Public and private investment have remained lower in the 1980s than before liberalization. Public investment has decreased largely for budgetary reasons associated with stabilization efforts. Private investment, which has declined even more sharply, is almost certainly negative in net terms.

The standard explanations include a lack of effective demand, high inflation and uncertainty about its future course, and high real interest rates for unsubsidized credit. Between September 1980 and December 1983 a caretaker government was in office, and there was no certainty about the economic program that would follow a return to civilian rule.

Table 4.11 Real growth of fixed investment, 1980–1985

Industry	Share in total investment 1981	Percentage change from previous year					
		1980	1981	1982	1983	1984	1985
Private sector							
Agriculture	5.3	10.8	27.5	9.2	7.0	2.1	−11.2
Mining	0.3	−26.5	1.3	8.6	4.4	0.7	26.6
Manufacturing	11.1	−14.1	−2.0	0.6	1.0	5.6	2.8
Utilities	0.3	−18.0	6.7	3.9	5.7	12.7	2.0
Transportation	6.7	34.5	29.0	12.8	9.3	13.8	5.3
Tourism	0.3	4.4	2.2	6.3	5.7	46.2	57.5
Housing	11.9	−17.3	−34.7	4.8	5.0	5.7	17.1
Education	0.1	−36.5	6.7	5.6	2.4	10.0	4.5
Health	0.1	−23.0	6.0	4.3	1.7	6.7	4.2
Other services	2.1	−21.8	4.4	2.2	2.6	11.7	5.7
Total	38.2	−17.3	−8.8	5.5	4.7	7.3	7.0
Public sector							
Agriculture	6.2	−9.7	54.6	8.0	−15.2	−5.5	−13.2
Mining	5.9	−17.6	37.4	−17.4	19.4	−4.5	24.0
Manufacturing	14.9	9.7	−8.5	−15.9	−3.3	−0.7	2.5
Utilities	14.6	−2.4	4.4	11.6	10.5	0.7	11.7
Transportation	10.8	−11.2	6.0	16.7	5.7	5.1	38.4
Tourism	0.3	−37.4	21.2	−11.3	20.6	29.4	−18.8
Housing	1.4	−30.6	34.9	−27.0	0.9	44.6	0.3
Education	2.4	1.3	22.8	22.0	−11.4	−12.9	25.8
Health	1.2	−9.4	36.8	9.7	−28.0	−12.6	0.0
Other services	4.1	−2.0	17.6	16.1	−5.7	10.6	30.5
Total	61.8	−3.7	9.4	2.2	1.9	1.4	17.1

1983–5 figures exclude losses from SEE investments.

Source: data supplied by SPO, 1985

This was probably a very important factor in the weak investment performance in those years. Continuing high inflation and high interest rates have been the primary factors negatively affecting private investment during the past four years, although there may be lingering uncertainty about the course of future policy as well.

The downward trend in investment appears to have affected all major sectors. The only sectors in which real investment increased after 1980 were beverages (where output has declined), printing, refining, fertilizers, and electrical machinery. The data do not indicate any apparent relationship between export performance and investment. This supports the conclusion that export growth was due in large part to weak domestic demand and not to support of new export-oriented industries.

Income Distribution

No data are yet available on changes in income distribution after 1980. The data already discussed show that real wages declined sharply, by about a third, and fell faster than private spending. This supports the conclusion that income distribution has shifted from labor and, by implication, toward capital. The government, largely for budgetary reasons, has not expanded relief programs, and has followed a policy of holding growth in public sector salaries to a rate well below the inflation rate. With the gradual removal of martial law and a return to normal political life (including union activity), it is unclear how much longer these trends will continue.

The pattern of rent-seeking behavior has changed dramatically since 1980. Import liberalization has led to the disappearance of scarcity rents for import licenses, while misuse of the export tax rebate system has led to the emergence of rent-seeking activities on the export side.

Discussion of Issues

The second liberalization episode is far from complete. Although it began in 1980, significant reform of QRs only started in 1984. In a very real sense, therefore, it is too early to know what results these policy changes will bring. The liberalization occurred simultaneously with an austerity program that has led to large reductions in effective demand, and economic growth has not yet been fully restored. Therefore the resource-allocation effects of liberalization have yet to be seen. Moreover, analysis is hampered by a lack of availability of some data, particularly on sectoral production.

Three issues related to this episode are discussed in greater depth: (a) the factors explaining the rapid rise in exports after 1980; (b) how economic expectations have changed during the period of liberalization; (c) overall strategy and conflicts among objectives.

Explanations of Export Performance

The most frequently cited positive result of liberalization has been Turkey's spectacular export performance, particularly in the growth of manufactured exports. The period of export growth, beginning in 1980, coincided with substantial real devaluation and expanded export subsidies. These included tax rebates in excess of indirect taxes paid, subsidized export credits, and access to foreign exchange that could be used to finance duty-free intermediate imports. Depreciation of the real exchange rate and increases in real and nominal EERs for exports work mainly on the supply side for a small trading country such as Turkey, and affect the relative profitability of exporting. There has been a clear correlation between improved incentives for exporters and export growth since 1980. However, correlation is not proof of causality, and other supply and demand factors undoubtedly were very important as well.

In particular, depressed domestic demand and excess capacity have also been significant supply-side factors. It is important to recognize that the growth in manufactured exports did not stem from the establishment of new export industries but from existing capacity in industries that previously had been producing almost entirely for the domestic market (that is, industries which had originally been established for import substitution). The period after 1980 has been one of macroeconomic stabilization, characterized by austerity policies that have depressed domestic incomes and demand. The level of real investment has been low and, arguably, net investment in manufacturing has been negligible. In this environment, exports provided an alternative to falling domestic demand. Diversion of production into exports may have been necessary for many firms to avoid bankruptcy or government bail-out.

In the short run, with capacity fixed and domestic demand slack, a sufficient condition for the profitability of exporting is that marginal revenue (foreign exchange price times the real EER) exceeds marginal costs. Although devaluation raised the costs of many intermediates, the marginal costs that Turkish firms actually faced declined sharply in late 1980 as a result of the prohibition on layoffs which, in effect, made labor costs fixed, leaving only intermediate inputs and their costs truly marginal. Moreover, with excess capacity in almost all sectors throughout the period, it is likely that marginal costs were quite flat.[12] In a period in which export supply functions were relatively flat and shifting to the right because of weakening domestic demand, improved EERs provided the required push on the supply side. At the same time, EERs above the level corresponding to marginal costs would, in the short run, be expected to generate little additional supply response but would improve profits for exporters.

Several factors seem relevant on the demand side. Perhaps most importantly, the government has been very actively involved in this period in arranging bilateral trade deals. For political and economic reasons, Turkey's oil suppliers (Iran, Iraq, Libya, and Saudi Arabia) became more willing to enter into what in effect were barter deals in which crude oil was exchanged for Turkish agricultural and manufactured goods. In 1980, Turkey's imports from these four countries amounted to US$2.9 billion (about 37 per cent of total imports), and exports were just under US$324 million (11 percent of exports). By 1985,

12 In other words, additional devaluations would shift the marginal costs curve (measured in US dollars) outward but not make it steeper.

imports had increased to US$3.2 billion (29 percent of the total), while exports to these countries had jumped to US$2.5 billion (32 percent of total exports). Exports to the entire Middle East grew by a factor of 14 between 1979 and 1984, accounting for 55 percent of total export growth. Turkey's regional trade deficit fell from US$2.6 billion in 1980 to US$0.7 billion in 1985. For the most part, this trade was arranged under governmental auspices.

Since Turkey's share of world exports in all exported manufacturing commodities is small, it is reasonable to say that devaluation did not change the foreign exchange price of its exports. At the same time, it has certainly been the case that Turkey has faced stiff price competition from Asian countries, especially in the European textile markets. For these commodities, increases in real EERs would be expected to lead to some demand responses, although there is no way yet to measure what the strength of these effects has been.

Although export growth to the OECD countries has averaged almost 20 percent annually since 1980, it is likely that such exports would have grown even more rapidly if the macroeconomic situation (especially in Europe) had been more favorable. Slow growth in aggregate demand for imports by these countries meant that QRs for several important Turkish exports were often binding and increasing slowly, implying that the demand curves were kinked at the level of the QRs. The short-run demand functions for newer less traditional exports may also have been severely kinked, but here the dynamic outward shift depends on marketing and on building a reputation for quality and reliability.

Several statistical tests were made to measure the quantitative relationship between the performance of manufactured exports and price incentives. One question was whether those sectors in which exports have grown relatively rapidly since 1980 were also sectors that received the most favorable treatment in terms of subsidy rates. Another important question was whether additional real devaluation after 1980 contributed to aggregate or sectoral export performance.

Data on sectoral exports, total subsidy rates, and real exchange rates for the period 1980–4 showed no statistically significant relationships, however.[13] In other words, neither changes in subsidy rates nor their valuation between sectors nor changes in the real exchange rate seem to explain the sharp differences among sectors in export growth performance. These negative results provide weak support for the hypothesis that, in

13 Two methods were used. In one, rank correlation statistics were calculated for sectors based on their export growth rates and their real EERs. In the other, the ordinary least-squares method was used to estimate regression equations with sectoral export levels, export growth rates, or export shares as dependent variables, using subsidy rates, real exchange rates, and real EERs as independent variables.

general, uniform and somewhat lower export subsidies (or real EERs) would have been sufficient supply-side incentive for export growth.[14] It may be that a more complete trade model might have given stronger results. For instance, it would be useful to break down sectoral exports by destination, to have a consistent time series on sectoral production, and to have a more complete model of both the supply and demand sides of exports.

It must be stressed that the real exchange rate and real EERs are only one set of supply-side factors affecting export performance. While maintaining a realistic exchange rate is a necessary condition for improving export performance, it is not sufficient for achieving sustained strong export growth. While export response to more effective direct export incentives may result in better utilization of existing capacity in the short run, export performance in the long run will depend on permanent changes in resource allocation, new capacity creation, product diversification and differentiation, information gathering, marketing, quality control, and so on. Turkey has only recently started learning the art of exporting as a business, and so far there has been little in the way of creation of new capacity.

Liberalization and Expectations

Presumably, one benefit of maintaining consistent policies in which long-run objectives are clearly stated is that the expectations of firms will begin to reflect these policies and these expectations will be reflected in production and investment decisions. Since trade liberalization has been stated as a long-run policy since early 1980, it might be expected that the importance of trade policy in determining firms' economic expectations would have increased since then.

The State Institute of Statistics (SIS) regularly collects data relevant to this question. It conducts a quarterly survey of manufacturing of 350 commodities at the three- and four-digit levels. The public and private sector firms surveyed account for at least 80–90 percent of the value of production in these industries. The SIS surveys employment levels, quantity of output by tons, and value of output in lira. It also asks questions about capacity utilization, reasons for excess capacity (for example, domestic or imported materials shortages, labor problems, financial problems, lack of domestic or foreign demand), changes in stock, new orders, changes in output and input prices and wages, and investment plans. Firms are also asked about their expectations as to how these variables may change in the future.

14 The only regressions in which the real exchange rate was a significant independent variable were those in which it was the only independent variable and aggregate exports were the dependent variable.

Although the coverage and quality of the survey data are questionable, we have organized the data for the period to shed some light on expected changes in production and investment. Values at the three-digit level for one quarter in each year from 1979 to 1984 are presented in tables 4.12 and 4.13. Throughout the period, a larger proportion of public sector firms expected to increase output in the next period. Except for end-1983, about 63–6 percent of private sector firms expected to increase production. Private sector expectations improved in 1980 and then stayed in the 44–50 percent range (except for 1981). There has been considerable variance in these expectations, particularly in the public sector, but the variance shows no obvious trend.

The depressed levels of investment previously mentioned show up again in table 4.13. On average, the proportion of all firms expecting to undertake new investment in the next period was in the 20–5 percent range. Despite liberalization, which presumably led to changes in relative prices and expectations that future bad investments would not be protected as they had been in the past, the dispersion as measured by variance has not increased. Nor does the table reveal strong trends in particular industries.

To further test the hypothesis that trade liberalization has influenced firms' expectations, we calculated a series of rank correlation coefficients comparing expectations about changes in production with actual changes in value of production, employment levels, and export EERs. Some results for public and private sector firms are presented in table 4.14.

For public sector firms, as expected, the ranking of sectors by expectations about production increases is positively correlated with EERs, value of production changes, and employment growth. In the case of the latter two variables the coefficients are significant. The correlation of rankings of sectors with levels of export EERs is less strongly significant, and there appears to be no significant relation with annual changes in the EERs. That is, sectors in which the EERs increased most rapidly were not those in which a high proportion of firms expected to be increasing production. Curiously, the calculations for private sector firms are worse, in the sense that the ranking of sectors by expectations about future production growth does not appear to be closely correlated with any of the other rankings. Only a few of the coefficients are statistically significant.

Comparing across years, we did not find any significant trends. In particular, there is no evidence that EERs (used here as a proxy for liberalization) played a relatively stronger role in determining expectations. This perhaps is explained by the fact that substitution of exports for domestic sales does not have much effect on capacity utilization.[15]

15 However, it is puzzling why firms that clearly benefit from subsidies (regardless of the quantity impact) would not be relatively more optimistic than other firms. If nothing else, their profits are improved, which should make capacity expansion easier.

Table 4.12 Expectations of increased production levels, public and private manufacturing sector, 1979–1984 (percent expecting increase)

Classification	Quarter III 1979 Public	Private	Quarter IV 1980 Public	Private	Quarter IV 1981 Public	Private	Quarter III 1982 Public	Private	Quarter IV 1983 Public	Private	Quarter III 1984 Public	Private
Food	56	39	28	30	55	33	53	43	55	34	62	44
Animal feed	35	46	36	36	40	54	n.a.	n.a.	17	51	35	70
Beverages	33	35	53	26	29	43	33	59	40	23	65	20
Tobacco	57	19	36	16	41	8	63	28	25	n.a.	38	n.a.
Weaving	62	34	80	45	69	41	77	47	62	38	65	52
Clothing	n.a.	30	n.a.	72	n.a.	36	76	44	n.a.	44	n.a.	59
Leather goods	n.a.	41	n.a.	26	n.a.	26	n.a.	59	n.a.	25	n.a.	46
Shoes	50	67	100	44	100	27	n.a.	63	75	28	n.a.	39
Wood	66	35	60	46	70	30	36	37	50	36	60	45
Furniture	n.a.	17	100	46	n.a.	39	n.a.	33	n.a.	27	100	48
Pulp and boxes	40	25	57	50	50	39	62	38	67	43	38	61
Newspapers	n.a.	52	38	32	56	39	44	37	50	36	78	55
Chemicals and fertilizers	100	50	60	71	45	57	38	51	80	57	58	56
Paint, drugs, and soaps	40	38	80	59	75	59	75	55	83	55	67	60
Refineries	67	n.a.	67	n.a.	100	n.a.	100	n.a.	50	n.a.	67	n.a.
Tar, coke, grease, and gas	n.a.	37	n.a.	33	n.a.	27	67	42	33	35	33	41
Tires and rubber	n.a.	32	n.a.	29	n.a.	17	n.a.	42	n.a.	37	n.a.	40
Plastic	100	24	100	49	100	39	100	49	n.a.	42	n.a.	35
Pottery and china	100	33	50	54	100	67	33	33	33	60	67	30
Glass	n.a.	53	n.a.	50	n.a.	43	n.a.	52	n.a.	50	n.a.	63
Cement, lime, and plaster	47	26	52	24	30	20	29	18	45	21	21	20
Iron and steel	100	23	100	44	60	42	100	36	43	35	100	63
Nonferrous metals	50	30	50	33	40	31	71	47	72	48	71	58
Hardware and furniture	75	36	75	47	33	38	60	48	20	39	50	48
Engines and machines	83	30	67	62	73	45	67	40	61	49	82	46
Electronics	67	36	67	60	60	30	100	58	72	52	71	66
Vehicles	67	41	78	67	57	55	75	53	80	65	78	55
Cameras and watches	n.a.	13	n.a.	50	n.a.	60	n.a.	50	n.a.	80	n.a.	62
Jewelry, music, sports	n.a.	23	100	41	n.a.	36	100	44	100	45	100	58
Three-digit mean	64.8	34.5	66.7	44.4	61.1	38.6	66.3	44.7	55.1	42.8	63.9	49.6
Three-digit variance	471.9	136.5	497.7	207.4	527.4	180.4	551.5	103.8	470.3	178.3	453.9	166.0

n.a., not available.

Source: SIS, Quarterly Survey of Manufacturing Industry, various issues

Table 4.13 Investment expectations of firms in manufacturing subsectors (percent expecting to make an investment next quarter)

Classification	Quarter III, 1979	Quarter IV, 1980	Quarter IV, 1981	Quarter III, 1982	Quarter IV, 1983
Food	13	8	10	9	13
Animal	18	10	10	10	13
Beverages	14	7	16	21	19
Tobacco	10	5	8	11	11
Weaving	9	12	13	16	20
Clothing	9	11	28	22	29
Leather goods	5	19	14	12	25
Shoes	n.a.	11	n.a.	n.a.	7
Wood	14	7	4	7	13
Furniture	7	26	3	9	4
Pulp and boxes	4	28	12	21	21
Newspaper	n.a.	13	2	12	16
Chemicals and fertilizers	25	19	29	41	39
Paint, drugs, and soaps	15	21	19	26	30
Refineries	100	75	100	100	100
Tar, coke, grease, and gas	33	36	39	50	25
Tires and rubber	15	7	13	17	17
Plastic	14	15	13	12	10
Pottery and china	67	44	n.a.	20	45
Glass	38	48	20	39	39
Cement, lime, and plaster	14	15	13	10	13
Iron and steel	17	15	26	12	27
Nonferrous metals	29	17	18	25	36
Hardware and furniture	11	15	9	6	17
Engines and machines	23	23	20	14	20
Electronics	7	29	16	17	32
Vehicles	23	25	19	20	32
Cameras and watches	n.a.	22	40	13	20
Jewelry, music, and sports	5	17	19	10	25
Three-digit mean	20.2	20.8	19.1	22.1	25.2
Three-digit variance	382.1	240.4	299.3	355.0	317.9

n.a., not available.

Source: SIS, Quarterly Survey of Manufacturing Industry, various issues

To summarize, differences in public sector manufacturing firms were weakly correlated with expectations about future production. However, changes in the EERs were not significantly correlated. No clear pattern of correlation emerged in the analysis of private sector firms. The analysis does not seem to support either the conclusion that EERs played an important role in expectations formation, at least through 1984, or that these considerations have become more important as the liberalization program continues.

Table 4.14 Rank correlation coefficients for expected changes in production, actual changes in production and employment, and effective exchange rates

	1980	1981	1982	1983	1984
Public sector firms					
Expected production growth vs actual production growth	0.738	0.392	0.633	0.538	0.548
Expected production growth vs actual employment growth	0.351	0.360	0.717	0.546	0.520
Expected production growth vs EER levels	0.407	0.312	0.079	0.321	0.491
Expected production growth vs change in EER levels	0.096	0.466	0.048	0.124	n.a.
Private sector firms					
Expected production growth vs actual production growth	− 0.193	0.095	0.178	0.305	0.548
Expected production growth vs actual employment growth	− 0.334	− 0.060	0.307	− 0.292	0.520
Expected production growth vs EER levels	0.155	0.154	− 0.139	0.128	0.491

n.a., not available

Conflicts between Liberalization and Other Objectives

The trade liberalization program exists alongside many other economic reforms and reflects only one of a number of important governmental objectives. Not surprisingly, there are conflicts between trade liberalization policies (that is, exchange rate devaluations, export promotion schemes, and import liberalization) and other objectives. These have shown up in the stops and starts in progress toward a more open trading system. Here, we survey some of the most apparent conflicts.

Controlling inflation has been, and remains, a prime macroeconomic objective. The higher costs of imported inputs (intermediate and capital goods) caused by nominal devaluation do feed back through the system and contribute to inflation. This effect has been reinforced by policies that allow the SEEs to determine their own prices in an attempt to reduce pressure on the government budget. Indeed, increases in SEE prices in recent years have been rapid, and greater than average inflation. We have not attempted to measure the degree to which nominal devaluation is responsible for inflation and how much is due to domestic monetary and fiscal policies. However, the linkage is perceived by policymakers to be significant and is one explanation for the ups and downs in the real exchange rate since 1980.

Another goal has been macroeconomic stabilization, in the sense of controlling the public budget. Trade liberalization policy has both conflicted with and supported this objective. The export promotion aspect of liberalization has contributed to creating outlets for domestic production in a period of very weak domestic demand. In contrast, the budgetary costs of export tax rebates and credit subsidies have become significant enough for the government to take steps to limit these expenditures. In the same vein, there has been a conflict between the objective of equalizing interest rates at positive real levels and providing subsidized credit to exporters. However, if the results presented previously are accurate, export growth is not as tightly linked to the subsidies as was previously believed.

It is not clear whether the failure to carry out significant reforms of protection of domestic industries, particularly before 1984, was related to fears that reform would lead to even greater levels of capital creation and unemployment than was already being caused by macroeconomic stabilization. We suspect that these considerations influenced decisions about when to begin trade liberalization.

Conclusion

The liberalization that began in 1980 has been successful in many respects. Export growth – and particularly growth of manufactured exports – has been very impressive. The balance-of-payments position has strengthened to the point where Turkey is now able to enter private international capital markets again. Significant progress has been made in liberalizing imports. The formal quota system has been eliminated, and progress has been made toward reducing protection, although it could be argued that liberalization of imports could have gone further than it has and been undertaken sooner.

However, this is a liberalization episode which is still under way, and a key question is whether it will be sustained in the future or whether Turkey will revert, as it has in the past, to a more restrictive and inward-looking trade regime. The possibility of a major reversal is real. The principal threat is likely to come from macroeconomic problems, specifically inflation, growth, employment, and real wages. The present government was elected largely on the basis of its economic promises, but if it is unable to deliver reduced inflation, increased employment, and higher real income levels, its political support could evaporate quickly.

The previous discussion argued that trade liberalization has not been a significant factor in reduction of real wages, the fall in the aggregate growth rate, or the rise in unemployment. The argument was that macroeconomic situation after 1980 would have been much worse if steps had not been taken to devalue and to promote exports. Neither is there evidence that import liberalization *per se* has been a major cause of inflation, although there is a strong link between inflation and exchange rate policies. However, this is not necessarily the conclusion of the Turkish electorate. There are increasing signs that Turkish citizens associate trade liberalization with macroeconomic problems. It may turn out that trade liberalization will become the unfortunate victim of political reaction if employment, income, and inflation problems are not resolved soon.

5

The Sequencing of Liberalization Policies

Introduction

The purpose of this chapter is to suggest some answers to the following questions. To what degree can the two liberalization episodes discussed in this case study be considered successful? What are the most important characteristics of the Turkish experience? What inferences can be drawn that might be applicable in other countries?

The August 1970 Devaluation Package

The 1970 devaluation was a once-and-for-all attempt to remove the overvaluation of the Turkish lira and thereby to reduce balance-of-payments problems. Subsidiary measures accompanying the devaluation were intended mainly to remove restrictions on imports and to establish uniformity in the exchange rate system. Specifically, the lowering of the stamp duty from 25 to 10 percent and the reduction of import guarantee deposit rates by 50 percent were intended to contain the rise in the landed costs of imports after the devaluation. However, the August 1970 package did not include any major change in the tariff and quota structures. The number of quota categories remained in the same range as in the late 1960s, and the ratio of quota list imports to liberalized list imports fell only slightly. The export regime remained the same except for the introduction of a more simplified export tax rebate system.

Neither the August 1970 devaluation package nor subsequent actions indicated that the government intended to liberalize foreign trade activities permanently. This conclusion is supported by the fact that there were no significant changes in the import quota system or in tariff schedules. Even more convincing evidence is provided by the absence of any notable change in public sector investments. If the government had intended to move toward a more neutral trade regime, there would have been changes in the sectoral distribution of public sector investments and a concomitant reduction in emphasis on import-substituting industries. Throughout the early 1970s, however, more than 86 percent of public sector investment destined for the manufacturing sector went to import-substituting industries. Nor did private sector investment show any major shift, demonstrating the sector's expectation that there would be no significant near-term alteration in the trade regime. In short, there was no permanent shift in resource allocation in the post-devaluation period.

The August 1970 devaluation package was successful in terms of achieving its main objective – that is, improving the balance-of-payments situation. Indeed, substantial increases in remittances and export proceeds not only encouraged a less restrictive import regime, thereby allowing a large expansion of imports, but also contributed to a dramatic short-run improvement in the balance of payments. The current account showed a surplus for the first time in many years, and reserves passed the US$1 billion and then the US$2 billion mark. A more liberal import regime instituted by the EEC, in compliance with the terms of Turkey's associate membership, was also a factor in the improved export performance of this period.

However, the benefits of devaluation subsided within a short time. Export growth slowed down owing to devaluation-related gains in the real exchange rate. Meanwhile, expansionary policies accelerated import growth. These developments led to the reemergence of balance-of-payments difficulties, which were exacerbated by the first oil shock.

Lack of discipline in macroeconomic management appears to have been the main reason that the short-term benefits of the August 1970 program were not turned into a long-term success. To some degree this lack of discipline might have been due to the political instability of the early 1970s. However, whether or not a stronger government could or would have instituted a more prudent macroeconomic policy from the start is also an open question. In any case, Turkey lost an opportunity in the early 1970s by not capitalizing on the short-term benefits of the August 1970 program. When the reserve position was strong and the current account showed a surplus in 1973, some steps could have been taken toward a more neutral trade regime accompanied by appropriate domestic policy changes.

The Liberalization Episode of the 1980s

The liberalization episode that began in January 1980 marks a major turning point in Turkish economic history. For the first time, a Turkish government committed itself to sustained policy reform aimed at making the economy more outward looking and market oriented. This was a fundamental shift.

Turkey entered the late 1970s facing dire economic circumstances. Severe balance-of-payments problems necessitated long and detailed negotiations with its creditors and with its NATO allies to come up with large amounts of increased aid. Inflation was accelerating, unemployment was rising, shortages were common, and labor unrest had reached crisis proportions. Even worse, political violence was spreading.

In the face of these problems, the government announced a broad series of policy reforms in January 1980. Some were implemented immediately. These included a 48.6 percent devaluation of the lira, increases in direct export incentives, and limitations on public spending and credit. These steps were similar to actions taken in similar economic circumstances, such as in 1970. However, the government went much further in 1980, declaring its intention to gradually but fundamentally change the way that the economy was managed. The long-run objectives included increasing the role of the private sector, making SEEs efficient and competitive, dismantling the QR system, opening up the foreign capital account, and so forth. In short, the apparent goal was to liberalize the entire economy.

No specific plans, timetables, or sequential orders of changes were announced. It is unlikely that a comprehensive plan was ever formulated. Nonetheless, subsequent actions revealed the basic elements of a reasonably coherent plan. The immediate problem in 1980 was a lack of foreign exchange. Consequently, the first steps were aimed at increasing foreign exchange earnings. There was an immediate devaluation, followed by regular smaller devaluations. These were attempts to establish and maintain a more reasonable exchange rate, where "reasonable" is measured in purchasing parity terms or in terms of premiums in the then flourishing private (black) markets. A more realistic rate would have the beneficial effects of stimulating greater remittances and of a greater proportion of these flows going through official financial institutions. In addition, it was hoped that devaluation would stimulate greater exports and, if not reducing total imports, at least would limit excess demand for imports.

In the first stage, direct export incentives were used as a major tool to increase exports. The rise in exports coincided with real devaluation, increased rebates, interest subsidies for exporters, and other benefits. Although a great deal of noise was made about import reform, in part to satisfy the World Bank and other sources of nonproject credit, not much was actually done. Some commodities were shifted from the more restrictive to the less restrictive list. In 1981, 17.5 percent of the previous year's licensed imports were liberalized, and at the same time the explicit import quota system was abolished. There were few other shifts until 1984. The system remained dominated by licensing, QRs, and protection for domestic industry.

The second stage began at the end of 1983 with the announcement that the import regime would be liberalized in 1984. About 60 percent of licensed imports were liberalized. Of even greater long-run importance were structural changes in the administrative system for importing. Instead of banning all goods that had not been explicitly included on a list (the old system), now any goods not explicitly prohibited could be imported. The number of prohibited items is very small. In addition, there is a list of imports subject to licensing (mostly domestically produced goods) and a list of goods subject to a special levy (mainly luxury items). A number of tariff changes were also announced at the end of 1983. These affected about 20 percent of imports and, on average, lowered nominal protection on these by about 16 percent.

Of course, considerable protection still remains. About 25 percent of 1984 imports were for goods requiring a license. However, there is no question that significant trade liberalization has occurred. The import system is more liberal now than at any time in the past 30 years or more.

In terms of success or failure, the record of economic policy since 1984 is mixed. There have been some notable successes. The government has succeeded in maintaining a flexible and realistic exchange rate. The devaluation of 1980 has not been eroded, although there have been periodic ups and downs related to domestic inflation and changes in the values of external currencies. Exports shot up beginning in late 1980 and, after a pause in 1983, resumed their rise, although not at the 25 percent annual rate of the early 1980s. Progress has been made on imports as well. Explicit quotas have been eliminated, and almost 75 percent of current imports enter Turkey without a license. The average rate of nominal tariff protection was reduced, although owing to the escalation of tariffs effective rates of protection might be higher for some domestically produced import substitutes. It appears that a wider range of goods (particularly consumer goods) are being imported. The replacement of the former liberalized list system with one allowing the import of any good not specifically prohibited also constitutes significant progress.

The balance-of-payments position is now much better than it was at the beginning of 1980. The trade deficit is lower, whether measured in nominal dollars, real 1980 dollars, or relative to national income. Although the currency is more convertible than before, there are few signs of capital flight. Turkey's creditworthiness has improved.

The domestic fiscal situation has also improved, at least measured in terms of the deficit and public borrowing requirements. The financial situation of the SEEs is much better than before, largely as a result of reforms in their pricing policies. Their management is also more autonomous. Real interest rates have been raised significantly and are positive (with the exception of interest rates charged to the SEEs and agriculture). Deposit rates are also positive.

On the negative side, the most obvious failures (which are not generally related directly to trade policy) have been the inability of Turkey to reduce inflation, promote real economic growth, or maintain real wages and employment. After falling during most of the first stage, inflation accelerated in late 1983 and 1984 and remains in the 40–50 percent range. Public investment has been squeezed by austerity measures and by the desire to reduce the role of the government. Private investment has declined even more sharply and to date shows no signs of recovering. The business community points to high interest rates, high inflation, and lack of effective demand as reasons for low investment. The financial position of many private firms and commercial banks remains weak.

Lessons from the Turkish Experience

Appropriate Speed and Staging of the Liberalization Process

The issue here is how fast liberalization should proceed and whether it should be thought of as a multistage process. The 1970 episode was certainly a one-stage episode but, since it was not aimed at long-run liberalization, that is not relevant. The current episode has been gradual, but since there is no comparable example it is impossible to determine whether a one-stage approach would have been preferable.

However, given that Turkey has followed both statist and import substitution policies for several generations, it probably would have been exceedingly difficult for the government to have eliminated all protection for existing industries overnight. Political circumstances, particularly prior to the military takeover in late 1980, support the contention that a one-stage approach would not have worked.

As noted previously, the present liberalization episode can be divided into two stages. The first lasted from 1980 to 1983, when policy reform concentrated on promoting exports and maintaining a realistic exchange rate. Import liberalization was largely ignored.

It is hard to judge whether the strategy of holding back of import liberalization until the economy improved was a sensible course. However, that policy was essentially abandoned in 1984. At that time the government undertook a substantial import liberalization without waiting for macroeconomic conditions to improve. Thus far, there is no evidence that the macroeconomic situation has weakened or that unemployment has increased as a result of import liberalization. However, as noted above, inflation worsened in this period. While devaluation may be a contributory influence, import liberalization should provide a partial brake on inflationary pressures.

The evidence indicates that little if anything was gained by waiting an additional four years to institute import liberalization. (This is a tentative conclusion which could be buttressed by some general equilibrium analysis.) However, the government may have felt constrained from moving more quickly for fear of worsening both employment and the financial position of existing firms. It can be argued that too rapid liberalization in a period of austerity would have been counterproductive because many firms might not have been able to cover marginal costs and would have been forced into bankruptcy. The key advantage of a gradual approach, if done properly, is that it permits existing firms to remain in business by providing the proper signals so that new investments can respond to changed prices that reflect long-run comparative advantage. The downside to a gradual approach is that signals on long-run prices may not be credible.

More generally, it seems that the implementation of liberalization since 1980 has been too slow. There is no evidence that liberalization contributed to Turkey's economic difficulties, which would be a sign of moving too rapidly. On the contrary, expanded exports permitted firms to maintain higher output levels, contributed to the restoration of creditworthiness, and supported modest real growth. A faster pace of liberalization, particularly on the import side, would have been feasible in a period of strong (military) government, when the unemployment effects would have been minimized because of regulations against layoffs. In our view, import liberalization was probably delayed for too long; little or nothing would have been lost if import liberalization had begun in earnest in 1980 or 1981.

In addition, the evidence on firms' expectations indicates that adjustment in expectations to announcements of intentions to liberalize is both slow and weak. The delay in import liberalization has raised questions about whether the process will continue, especially when the political alternatives to the present government are not philosophically committed to liberalization and are mostly statist in outlook. It also appears that the Turkish business community is uncertain about the speed and direction of the policy, and that it views the policy as having been erratic.

A closely related question is the desirability of a separate stage consisting of the replacement of QRs by tariffs. Post-1980 experience sheds some light on this issue. Beginning in 1981, all explicit quotas were removed. This did not really result in a tariff-based system because licenses were still required for most imports, including virtually all imports that competed with domestic production. A more significant attempt to remove QRs (licensing) came in 1984–5. Imports that had been prohibited implicitly now could be freely imported under the tariff system unless explicitly subjected to licensing or because they were on the banned list. While most import-competing goods are still subject to licensing, a number are now under the tariff system. In switching (mainly consumer) goods from licensing to tariffs, the government replaced the implicit protection that licensing provided with increased nominal and effective protection. This appears to be a sensible approach to import liberalization in Turkey. First, movements to a tariff system give firms an opportunity to focus more on the price system and less on manipulating the bureaucracy. This "training" in how to do business in a freer economy is likely to have long-run benefits. Second, removing all protection could result in too much adjustment if firms whose long-run marginal (including capital) costs were greater than world prices, but whose short-run marginal costs (because of existing capacity) were below world prices, were forced out of business because all protection had been removed. Temporary tariff protection is justifiable on a second-best basis. A final advantage to eliminating QRs (even if real effective protection does not change immediately) is that those groups having a vested interest in maintaining protection are weakened by the elimination of a powerful administrative apparatus. The elimination of a licensing system is one way in which the government can signal the irreversibility of the process and perhaps have a quick effect on the formation of expectations.

A final related issue is the desirability of a separate stage concerned with export promotion. Beginning in 1980, Turkey used a variety of policies to encourage exports. These included export tax rebates, preferential access to foreign exchange for exporters, subsidized export credits, and overall real devaluation. Of particular importance was the government's active participation in arranging bilateral trade agreements. These actions, and other factors related primarily to the macroeconomic policy described previously, were associated with very rapid export growth rates. Substantial progress on import liberalization began only in 1984. Since this is the path that Turkey has followed, there is no direct evidence that this separate stage was necessary or desirable. Therefore the following comments are based largely on intuition.

It can be argued that in the economic circumstances of the early 1980s it would not have been feasible to rapidly liberalize the import regime at the same time that exports were being heavily promoted. Turkey had been following an inward-looking strategy for so long that neither firms nor the bureaucracy could absorb or adjust to numerous changes quickly. Moreover, given parallel stabilization policies, import liberalization might have been resisted strenuously on the grounds that it threatened the viability of already weak firms and would increase unemployment.

Export promotion had the important advantage of supporting domestic production and national income at a time when domestic demand was declining in almost all sectors. Stabilization policies resulted in large reductions in real investment and, in the short run, import demand could have been reduced further only through reduced production. Therefore export growth was the only feasible way to improve the balance-of-payments situation quickly. Debt-servicing requirements were also relatively fixed, and to improve creditworthiness Turkey had to work on the denominator of the debt service ratio. These provided compelling reasons to focus on export promotion in the early 1980s.

However, the available evidence does not indicate that export subsidy policies played a crucial role in export growth, at least in the short run when there was considerable excess productive capacity because of weak domestic demand. It could be argued that it would have been preferable to keep the bureaucracy away from managing export subsidy programs. In contrast, the role of the government in arranging trade deals, especially with neighboring countries, was an indispensable part of the rapid export growth.

While we are neutral about the desirability of a separate stage for export promotion, the Turkish case probably illustrates the proposition that, if there is to be a staged approach, export promotion must come first. Export promotion has already been mentioned as an important way to compensate for weak domestic demand and creditworthiness. In addition, it is very likely, at least in the Turkish case, that strong export growth was essential for the survival of trade liberalization and that it takes longer to mobilize resources to support long-run export growth than it does to support import growth. The reason is that export promotion is a positive activity requiring resource commitment, while import reform in a country like Turkey involves avoiding actions that are uneconomic. For export growth to succeed in the long run, the signals need to be given early, firmly, and credibly.

Note the contrast here between the short run, when exports can increase quickly because of slack domestic demand, and the long run, which requires the establishment of new industries and capacity. In this context it can be pointed out that long-term responses depend very much on long-term resource commitments by private sector firms. This might be forthcoming only when the business community is definitely persuaded about the credibility of policy.

Uniform versus Discriminatory Treatment of Sectors

Since the 1980 liberalization began, discriminatory treatment of sectors has been the rule rather than the exception. While the underlying rationale for varying the amounts of export subsidization to different sectors was that different real EERs were needed to stimulate export sales, it does not appear that any specific analysis was undertaken in selecting the subsidy rate. In fact, the total subsidy rates have varied widely across manufacturing sectors (from a few percent to more than 100 percent). This suggests that more uniform treatment on the export side would have been preferable.

The Turkish case since 1980 does suggest that discriminatory treatment of exports by sector has little effect on short-run export performance. Instead, discriminatory treatment works primarily as an income transfer mechanism to improve firms' balance sheets. It should be emphasized that this applies only in the short run during periods of excess productive capacity.

Since 1984, those sectors in which competing imports are allowed without licensing have been afforded higher levels of nominal protection than previously in order to compensate for the loss of the implicit protection accorded through licensing. Nominal protection for goods whose import is still subject to licensing has generally been reduced, with the largest decrease for intermediate goods. The pattern of tariff changes reflects the government's stated objective of maintaining a system of escalating tariffs on manufactures, especially consumer goods. While it is too early to measure the impact of this nonuniform treatment, we have strong doubts abouts its desirability. The preference for such tariff escalation is little more than a reflection of Turkey's long-held strategy of encouraging industrialization through import substitution. As such, this type of discriminatory treatment undermines one of the fundamental objectives of liberalization, which is improved efficiency of resource use.

Uniform treatment would also have the advantages of both moving firms away from their traditional rent-seeking behavior and minimizing the involvement of government bureaucrats and decision makers in subsectoral issues. In any case, the data required to determine optimal protection strategies do not exist.

Whenever a system allows discriminatory treatment, it has the potential for manipulation. The Turkish example underscores how easy it is to provide inappropriate levels of protection when there is little will or few resources to conduct the type of analysis required to make optimal protection and subsidy decisions. Turkey's experience supports the notion that the costs of abuses of discriminatory treatment outweigh the potential gains.

More generally, our intuition is that discriminatory treatment should be avoided in all but special cases. One exception might be a firm whose long-run costs are greater than world prices but whose marginal costs are less. Proper policy would ensure that such firms could continue to produce but that capital stock not be replaced or expanded. Another special case might be in situations where, because of something intrinsic to the investment, infant industry arguments can be made. Unfortunately, throughout most of this century Turkey has granted protection whenever a domestic production industry began, without setting any high standard of justification for it.

Appropriate Circumstances for Introduction and Sustainability

Turkey's liberalization episodes occurred during periods of severe balance-of-payments difficulties. Although there may be theoretical advantages to introducing liberalization during periods of growth, prosperity, and a strong reserve position – to minimize adjustment costs and to induce structural change through reallocation of investment – as a practical matter this would have been unlikely in a country like Turkey which has had a strong tradition of protection and import substitution. Very likely it is possible to overcome political resistance and move away from prior policies only when the old system is no longer feasible. Liberalization had been periodically considered by governments since the 1950s and regularly urged by outside advisors and creditors, but it was rejected summarily when growth rates were satisfactory. There was no pressure to change the system when conditions were favorable.

There is also an element of luck involved in timing. Even if reforms are made only when the domestic economy itself is in difficulty, favorable external conditions can make the transition period easier. In this regard, Turkey was fortunate that the war between Iran and Iraq created favorable conditions for expanded exports to those countries. Turkey would have been even better off if the world economy had been healthier or if real interest rates on foreign debt had declined.

The credibility of liberalization is linked to the credibility of the government itself. In the Turkish case, the initial policy announcements were made during a period of weak coalition governments when domestic violence was increasing. It is doubtful that the announcement of intentions carried much credibility. However, those weak governments were soon followed by military intervention and the establishment of a strong government that continued to back liberalization and adjustment policies.

The liberalization policies of 1970 were quickly reversed. We have argued that this was not due to a failure of policy but to success in achieving limited objectives. While one effect of devaluation was to reduce price distortions, the main objective was to improve the balance-of-payments situation. Long-run movement toward a more open and market-oriented industrialization strategy was never an objective. Thus erosion of "liberalization" was a natural consequence of restored creditworthiness and import-substitution-led growth. Despite its limited objectives, the 1970 devaluation could have produced more long-term benefits if macroeconomic management had been more prudent and if steps had been taken to adjust the economy after the first oil price shock.

A more interesting issue is the sustainability of the current liberalization episode. Liberalization has continued without significant interruption since 1980. The present government is firmly committed to its continuation.

However, we should not be too optimistic that there will not be a reversal. There is no specific timetable for the next stages of import liberalization. While the government seems determined to continue dismantling the licensing system and reducing direct export subsidies, it is unclear whether this will go much farther in the short run. Further reductions in rebates were planned for 1987–8. Unemployment is high, and further import liberalization may threaten the viability of existing import-competing firms. In addition, replacing direct export subsidies with greater real devaluation may have a negative effect on inflation, control of which is now the government's primary objective.

Liberalization is new to Turkey and is not yet fully accepted by business or labor. Trade unions and some of the press are beginning to criticize the effects of liberalization. The business community has complained that changes are random and difficult to predict, particularly with respect to special levy rates. The opposition parties are generally opposed for nationalistic or political reasons. Long-run sustainability thus hinges on building a national consensus that supports liberalization.

The fact is that trade liberalization has yet to bring benefits at the individual level. Liberalization occurred at the same time that real wages were falling. National per capita spending remains below 1979 levels. The longer real income stagnates and the longer investment remains depressed, the more likely it is that liberalization will be blamed.

There is no evidence that trade liberalization has contributed to overall economic stagnation. Indeed, the opposite could be argued – that, without export growth, the fall in real income would have been even more severe. However, liberalization is highly visible and widely publicized. In a country with a strong nationalistic orientation, it is difficult to persuade the electorate that liberalization will produce long-term benefits unless real growth and real per capita disposable income begin to increase measurably.

In this context, the sustainability of the liberalization effort will depend largely on the success of macroeconomic policy. The attempt to control inflation has led the government to continue tight fiscal and monetary policies, with the result that domestic demand remains weak and real growth low. These policies may work to reduce inflation and then permit a reduction in real interest rates to stimulate investment and aggregate demand. However, it is not clear whether inflation can be controlled by the demand-management policies of the 1980s. The degree to which the sustainability of the liberalization program is held captive by the success or failure of macroeconomic policy cannot be overemphasized.

References

Baysan, Tercan (1974) "Economic implications of Turkey's entry into the Common Market." Ph.D. Dissertation, University of Minnesota.

Baysan, Tercan and Charles Blitzer (1988) "Liberalizing foreign trade: the experience of Turkey, statistical appendices." Available from the Brazil Department, World Bank, Washington, DC.

Central Bank of Turkey, *Annual Report*, various years.

Central Bank of Turkey, *Quarterly Bulletin*, various issues.

Central Bank of Turkey, *Monthly Bulletin*, various issues.

Cohn, E. J. (1970) *Turkish Economic, Social and Political Change*. New York: Praeger.

Corden, W. M. (1966) "The structure of a tariff system and the effective protection rate." *Journal of Political Economy*, 34, June, 221–37.

Corden, W. M. (1974) *Trade Policy and Economic Welfare*. Oxford: Clarendon.

Ebiri, Kutlay, Z. Bozkurt, and A. Culfaz (1977) *Turkiye Imalat Sanayiinde Sermaye ve Isqucu*. Ankara: SPO, Publication no. 1624.

Economic Report of the President (1985). Washington, DC: US Government Printing Office.

Erdilek, Asim (1982) *Direct Investment in Turkish Manufacturing: An Analysis of the Conflicting Objectives and Frustrated Expectations of a Host Country*. Institut für Weltwirtschaft an der Universität Kiel.

Fry, J. Maxwell (1972) *Finance and Development Planning in Turkey*. Leiden: Brill.

Hershlag, Z. Y. (1968) *Turkey: The Challenge of Growth*. Leiden: Brill.

IMF (International Monetary Fund) (1956) *Annual Report*. Washington , DC: IMF.

IMF (1957) *Annual Report*. Washington, DC: IMF.

IMF (1981a) *International Financial Statistics, Supplement on Price Statistics*. Washington, DC: IMF, Supplement Series no. 8.

IMF (1981b) *International Financial Statistics, Supplement on Exchange Rates*. Washington, DC: IMF, Supplement Series no. 1.

IMF (1983) *International Financial Statistics, Supplement on Money*. Washington, DC: IMF, Supplement Series no. 5.

IMF (1984) *International Financial Statistics, Supplement on Output Statistics*. Washington, DC: IMF, Supplement Series no. 8.

IMF, *International Financial Statistics*, various issues.

Kepenek, Yakup (1984) *Turkiye Ekonomisi*, 2nd edn. Ankara: Savas.

Krueger, Anne O. (1974) *Foreign Trade Regimes and Economic Development: Turkey*. New York: Columbia University Press.

Krueger, Anne O. and Baran Tuncer (1980) "Estimating total factor productivity growth in a developing country." Washington, DC: World Bank, Staff Working Paper no. 422.

Krueger, Anne O. and Baran Tuncer (1982) "Growth of factor productivity in Turkish manufacturing industries." *Journal of Development Economics*, 2 (3), December.

Milanovic, Branko (1986) "Export incentives and Turkish manufactured exports, 1980–84." Washington, DC: World Bank Working Paper no. 768.

Mineral Research and Exploration Institute (1981) *Known Ore and Mineral Resources of Turkey*. Ankara: Mineral Research and Exploration Institute, Publication no. 185.

Ministry of Finance (1983) *Annual Economic Report*. Ankara.

Pick Publishing Corporation (1972) *1972 Pick's Currency Yearbook*. New York: Pick Publishing Corporation.

Pick Publishing Corporation (1975–6) *1975–1976 Pick's Currency Yearbook*. New York: Pick Publishing Corporation.

SIS (State Institute of Statistics) (1961) *Census of Population, 1950*. Ankara: 515, Publication no. 410.

SIS (1963) *Census of Population, 1955*. Ankara.

SIS (1965) *Census of Population, 1960*. Ankara.

SIS (1969) *Census of Population, Social and Economic Characteristics, 1965*. Ankara.

SIS (1973) *Turkiye Milli Geliri-Kaynak ve Yontemler: 1948–1972*. Ankara.

SIS (1977) *Census of Population, Social and Economic Characteristics, 1970*. Ankara.

SIS (1978) *Turkiye Milli Geliri: 1962–1977*. Ankara.

SIS (1982) *Census of Population, Social and Economic Characteristics, 1975*. Ankara.

SIS (1984) *Census of Population, Social and Economic Characteristics, 1980*. Ankara: SIS, Publication no. 1072.

SIS, *Foreign Trade Statistics*, various years.

SIS, *Monthly Bulletin of Statistics*, various issues.

SIS, *Quarterly Survey of Manufacturing Industry*, various issues.

SIS, *Statistical Yearbook of Turkey*, various years.

SPO (1962) *First Five Year Plan 1963–1967*. Ankara.

SPO (1969) *Second Five Year Plan 1968–1972*. Ankara.

SPO (1979) *Dorduncu Beş Yillik Kalkinma Plani 1979–83*. Ankara: SPO Publication no. 1664, April.

SPO (1984) *Developments Prior to the Fifth Five-Year Development Plan: 1972–1983* (in Turkish).

SPO, *Annual Program*, various years.

SPO, *Ucuncu Beş Yil Plani 1973–1977*, Ankara: SPO Publication no. 1272.

Ticaret Bakanligi, T. C. (1974) *50 Yilda Turkiyede Ihracat Tesvik Tedbirleri*, 50. Yil, Ankara.

Turkish Republic, *Offical Gazette*, various dates.

World Bank (1951) *The Economy of Turkey*, Washington, DC: World Bank.

World Bank (1980) *Turkey: Policies and Prospects for Growth*. Washington, DC: World Bank.

World Bank (1982) *Turkey: Industrialization and Trade Strategy*. Washington, DC: World Bank.

World Bank (1983) *Turkey: Country Economic Memorandum*. Washington, DC: World Bank.

World Bank (1984, 1985, 1986) *World Development Report*. Washington, DC: World Bank.

World Bank (1985a) *Trade Policy Issues in the Structural Adjustment Process*. Washington, DC: World Bank.

World Bank (1985b) *Turkey: Annual Data Tables*. Washington, DC: World Bank.

World Bank (1985c) *Fifth Five Year Plan Review, Turkey*. Washington, DC: World Bank.

World Bank, *World Debt Tables*, various years.

Yaser, B. S. (1972) "Economic aspects of the devaluation of the Turkish lira of August 10, 1970." Ankara: AID Discussion Paper, no. 5.

Index